Ethical Issues in Family Representation

Ethical Issues in Family Representation

Barbara Glesner Fines

Carolina Academic Press
Durham, North Carolina

Library of Congress Cataloging-in-Publication Data

Fines, Barbara Glesner.
Ethical issues in family representation / Barbara Glesner Fines.
p. cm.
ISBN 978-1-59460-517-8 (alk. paper)
1. Attorney and client--United States. 2. Domestic relations--United States.
I. Title.

KF311.F56 2010
346.7301'5--dc22

2009044111

Carolina Academic Press
700 Kent Street
Durham, North Carolina 27701
Telephone (919) 489-7486
Fax (919) 493-5668
www.cap-press.com

Printed in the United States of America

To David and Dan

Contents

Preface

Ethical issues that arise in family representation are often unique to the field. Many of the core issues are simply not addressed by professional regulation. Thus, we find a growing number of specialized codes of conduct to meet the unique demands of representing family members. One of the major concerns for reform of family law education has been to address the unique professional responsibility demands of the field. This text is designed to help fill that gap.

Each chapter begins with a statement of learning objectives. In any given class, you and your professor may have different or additional learning objectives for the topics covered. Most doctrinal materials are explained in textual discussions. Cases and other primary source materials are selected to illustrate not only the legal principles but the difficulties of applying those principles. Most sections have a series of questions for your reflection and discussion. While citations may sometimes be provided to give you examples of cases or other materials addressing the issue, reading these materials, while helpful, is neither necessary nor sufficient to answer these questions, as the law is still very much evolving.

In addition, the text provides two types of assignments designed to help you personalize your study. First, because regulation of attorney conduct and regulation of family matters are both areas in which standards differ significantly across the states, you will find "research assignments" throughout the text. An appendix identifies sources you might use to research these and other issues of professional conduct. Second, you will find problems entitled "Portfolio Problems." These problems are designed to help you extend the learning from the chapter in practice settings. Careful preparation of these portfolio assignments will give you practical tools to use throughout a career in family representation.

A few words about citation conventions: All jurisdictions in the United States except California base their attorney disciplinary rules on the American Bar Association's Model Rules of Professional Conduct. In this text, these rules will be referred to as "Model Rule X.X." Sometimes the text will summarize the rules of professional conduct or their comments. In practice, of course, attorneys should always refer to the complete disciplinary rules of their own jurisdiction, as reference to the primary sources of regulation is always necessary to insure accuracy and currency of the law, especially as state rules often have significant variations from the ABA models. The Model Rules are on the ABA Web site at www.abanet.org. Where the text refers to "Restatement" the reference is to the Restatement (Third) of the Law Governing Lawyers. Other Restatements will be given their full names.

The appendix contains the full text of model standards. Where the text references these standards, you should read the relevant section.

In editing materials in the text, I have used the following conventions: Modifications of the original materials are indicated by [bracketed phrases]. Where the only modification is deletion of material in the original, I have inserted ellipses, regardless of the length of the deleted material. I have freely deleted citations and footnotes from original materials without indication of the deletion. Original footnotes that have been retained are renumbered to preserve the flow of footnote sequence in the chapter.

This book has benefitted tremendously from so many conversations and correspondences with too many individuals to name. My clients have inspired and challenged me to keep their interests at the center of this book. The students in my Ethics of Family Representation course from 2004 to today have all "test driven" the materials. Most of those students are now practicing law in fields serving families and they, as well as so many members of the bench and bar, have been kind to share their experiences and insights. My colleagues in the family law program have endured countless hours of conversation and read reams of drafts and I am indebted and inspired by them: Professors Mary Kay Kisthardt, Mary Kay O'Malley, Nancy Levit, Mary Weir, Peter Raith, and June Carbone. Dean Ellen Suni has provided substantial assistance for the project, both as Dean in supporting the project and as a professional responsibility colleague. Student research assistants who have contributed to the book include Steven Skinner, Mark Haefner, Orron Hill, Kevin Kelly, Alison Trimble, and Elizabeth Hodges Williams. The errors are my own alone.

I hope this text will help you to become a better learner, lawyer, and agent of justice. If you have comments, questions, or suggestions, I am always interested. My email address is glesnerb@umkc.edu.

Ethical Issues in Family Representation

Chapter One

Forming the Attorney-Client Relationship

Learning Objectives for This Chapter

After you have read this chapter and completed the assignments you should be able to:

- Describe a variety of possible models for delivery of legal services to families.
- Identify the core tasks in forming an attorney-client relationship.
- Identify billing methods attorneys use in family representation and the ethical limitations on those methods.
- Explain the proper scope of delegation of legal tasks to non-lawyer assistants.
- Draft a basic representation agreement, including an agreement for limited scope representation.

A. The Varieties of Family Representation

We begin with the various forms of legal services for family representation. Family lawyers provide legal services for families in crisis or transition—from transactional planning (estate planning, adoptions, prenuptial agreements, or family business formation) to dispute resolution (divorce, custody, paternity, and other intra-family disputes) to the prosecution and defense of state protections (criminal law, juvenile delinquency, or termination of parental rights).

Family lawyers practice in a wide variety of practice settings. A 1997 American Bar Association survey of family lawyers revealed that 41% of family lawyers were solo practitioners and another 24.3% practiced in very small firms of three persons or less. Increasingly, though, medium-sized family law specialty firms can be found in any major city. Some large firms have one or two family law attorneys on staff to accommodate the needs of their clients and to provide pro bono representation. Family law attorneys may act as third-party neutrals in resolving family law disputes. In addition, attorneys may act as mediators, arbitrators, expert evaluators, commissioners, or judges.

Family law attorneys can also be found in a number of governmental positions. Prosecutor and public defender offices regularly deal with family law matters such as domestic violence and sexual assault, child support enforcement, or child abuse and neglect. In larger cities, these offices may have specialized departments for these matters. Juvenile or Family courts also have attorneys who bring actions for child protection, in juvenile delinquency and child abuse and neglect matters. In many of these actions, there is a constitutional right to appointed counsel, which is filled by public attorneys or private attorneys who are appointed by the court. Attorneys may be appointed by the court to act as guardians ad litem or attorneys for children, representing children or their best interests (or both) in a variety of actions. Similarly, attorneys may practice in state agencies dealing with elder abuse and neglect or adult guardianship.

The non-profit public interest sector also employs family law attorneys. Attorneys may work for organizations advocating for legal reform. They may represent individual clients through legal aid offices or upon referral from other non-profit organizations. They may act as corporate counsel to organizations that serve children and families.

The demand for legal services for families is likely to remain strong. Not only do families continue to generate crises, but the complexity of our society and technological advances (such as reproductive technologies) keep the field of family law ever growing. For low and moderate income individuals, however, there is little access to legal representation. This is the single largest area of legal need brought to legal aid offices, though less than half of that need can be met with the resources of these offices.[1] A study conducted by the Utah Bar Association reported that family issues "represent the greatest civil legal need of low-income households." More than half of the family law issues involved violence (domestic abuse, stalking, and child abuse).[2] A study of self-representation in family law cases in Wisconsin found that in 2005 more than

---

1. Legal Services Corporation, *Documenting the Justice Gap in America: The Current Unmet Civil Legal Needs of Low-Income Americans* 12 (2005) *available at* http://www.lsc.gov/press/documents/LSC%20Justice%20Gap_FINAL_1001.pdf.

2. Domestic abuse accounted for 5.7% of all legal problems, divorce and separation 4.2%, stalking 2.4%, child abuse or neglect 2.3%, child support 2.1%, child custody 1.9%, other 0.8%, other child disputes 0.6%, and alimony or property division 0.4%. D. Michael Dale, *The Justice Gap: The Unmet Legal Needs of Low-Income Utahns* 12 (2006), *available at* http://www.uls.state.ut.us/The%20Justice%20Gap%20-%20Needs%20Assessment.pdf.

60% of parties in family cases represented themselves. The most cited reason for self representation was the inability to afford an attorney.[3]

Portfolio Problem: Improving Access to Justice

How can the legal system respond to this unmet need? Think of this as a vast, untapped legal market. To serve this market, you need only devise a system in which you can deliver low-cost legal services to individuals.

Brainstorm as many ideas as you can. Then, choose one idea and prepare a business plan. Specifically identify the legal needs you will be meeting and the clientele you will be serving. Describe how you will finance your representation. If the clients are paying, how can you keep costs low? If you will be providing free or below-cost legal services, how will you generate income? Identify the possible regulatory barriers to your plan. Review the rules of professional conduct for your state, particularly as they relate to fees and advertising. Brainstorm other laws that might impact your idea (e.g., antitrust, consumer protection laws, debt collection regulation, etc.)

To learn more about researching issues in professional responsibility, see Appendix D.

B. Forming the Attorney-Client Relationship

The setting in which you choose to practice will affect many of the subsequent ethical issues you will face. For private attorneys, the most recurrent and important ethical choice is the decision to represent a particular client. Being able to identify the clients you would not want to represent is as important to your practice as identifying the client base you do wish to develop.

How would you screen for the clients you want to avoid? Consider some common examples:

You must always decline a client under circumstances that would cause you to violate a rule of professional conduct. For example, the rules governing competence require that you reject cases that are outside your field of competence unless you can become competent through study or association with another attorney. The rules prohibit representations in which you have a conflict of interest. Thus, you need to have a system for screening clients to determine

3. State Bar of Wisconsin, *Bridging the Justice Gap: Wisconsin's Unmet Legal Needs* 12 (March 2007) *available at* http://www.wisbar.org/am/template.cfm?template=/cm/contentdisplay.cfm&contentid=63639.

the risk of those conflicts. At a minimum such a system requires that you keep records of the names of your current, former, and prospective clients, the names of any parties whose interests are materially adverse to those clients, and a brief description of each engagement or prospective engagement.

Another category of client for whom representation would cause you to violate the rules is the client who is seeking your assistance to commit a crime or fraud. For some clients, this will be obvious, because they wil make their intent clear, often not realizing that their plan is a crime or would constitute fraud. For others, it may be less clear that their intent involves misdeeds, especially when a client is willing to lie to you. How do you assess the honesty and credibility of your clients? What questions could you ask? What information might be available from other sources that you could easily access? In most jurisdictions, you can access court dockets and determine whether your client has a criminal record or has been involved in prior civil litigation. Do you feel comfortable screening your clients in this way?

You may wish to decline other representations even if they do not pose a risk of risk of violating the rules of professional conduct. Some clients are simply not worth the trouble. There are two questions you can ask in the initial interview that will help to identify these potential problem clients. One of those questions is "Have you spoken with others about this matter?" This question will identify those clients who come to you with a range of information and advice (for good or ill) from others. If the client has spoken to other attorneys on the matter, you will want to know why they chose not to work with those attorneys. These clients may be impossible to satisfy or could be a real risk for disciplinary complaint or malpractice suits. Consider asking the client for permission to speak to the attorneys with whom they have previously worked.

A second question is one that is core to your representation: "What do you want?" (Or variations on that theme such as "What do you expect to get from this action?" or "What do you hope I can do for you?") Asking this question early, before you agree to represent a client, can identify clients with unrealistic expectations—who want something the law cannot provide or who expect results to be obtained in an unrealistic manner, timeframe or cost. Exploring objectives can also reveal client motivations that you would prefer to avoid (such as the client whose primary goal is angry revenge). Finally, this question can identify those "expert" clients who not only know exactly what they want but believe they know exactly how you should be accomplishing those objectives.

The client who will not pay for your representation is one to avoid as well, unless you intend to provide pro bono representation. As we will explore further in this chapter, a discussion with your clients at the very beginning of the representation regarding their ability to pay for your services, along with the prudent use of advances, is your best protection against acquiring an unintentional pro bono case.

There are likely other types of representations you may wish to avoid. The rules of professional conduct provide attorneys a broad discretion in selecting clients. Indeed, you will rarely be at risk for discipline or liability for rejecting a client. Conceivably, an attorney, particularly a public sector attorney, might face liability for invidious discrimination in the selection of clients. Many states have a provision in their rules of professional conduct prohibiting discrimination against a range of traditionally protected classes. However, few extend the rule expressly to client selection.

You do have a responsibility to provide some pro bono assistance in order to insure access to legal services for those with limited financial means. In most states this obligation is an aspirational standard rather than a legal duty. The same is not true when a court appoints you to represent a client. No longer do you have nearly unlimited discretion in choosing a client. Every state's disciplinary code except that of North Carolina provides that an attorney may not seek to avoid an appointment without good cause. This obligation is generally enforced by the appointing court rather than the disciplinary system. Attorneys may seek to avoid these appointments on the grounds that they are incompetent in this specialized field, but if the court rejects that argument, an attorney may then be held in contempt for any further refusal to undertake the representation.[4] Because of the overwhelming need for attorneys in juvenile court matters, appointment of attorneys and guardians ad litem are especially common in this field of practice.[5]

If you do decline to represent an individual, make sure you do so clearly and firmly. If a client has a reasonable expectation that you are or will be representing them, you may have duties of competence, confidentiality, and loyalty to that individual, regardless of your subjective intent. Follow up all initial client interviews with a letter clarifying the status of the relationship. If you are willing to represent the client, but the client has not yet agreed to your representation, send a letter explaining that you do not represent the client and will take no action on their behalf until they instruct you to do so (usually by signing and returning an engagement letter). If you will not be representing the client, send a "non-engagement letter" explaining that you do not and will not represent the client.

4. *State ex rel. Picerno v. Mauer*, 920 S.W.2d 904 (Mo. App. 1996).

5. For an analysis of the issues regarding appointment of attorneys in juvenile court matters, see Barbara Glesner Fines, *Almost Pro Bono: Appointed Attorney Representation in Family Court*, 72 UMKC L. Rev. 337 (2003).

For those clients you do choose to represent, the initial task of forming the relationship of trust and confidence with the client is essential. You should not expect that your clients will immediately trust you—they are likely to be quite anxious about revealing the personal details of their lives. Acknowledging that discomfort can help to build rapport. You might explain to a client, "The attorney-client relationship is an unusual one: I need to learn all the private details of you and your family life and you won't be learning any details about my private life." Explaining your duty of confidentiality and the protections of the attorney-client privilege can facilitate client trust as well.

The most effective way to build a relationship, however, is to be patient and work to truly understand the client. That understanding starts with discovering the client's goals, expectations, and emotional state. Your fundamental ethical duty, found most specifically in Model Rules 1.2 and 1.4, is to help the client clarify the lawful and prudent objectives of representation and then honor those objectives. Clients sometimes come to attorneys with unrealistic expectations of what the legal system can accomplish for them. Unfortunately, attorneys sometimes feed those unrealistic expectations out of a desire to reassure a client, to "sell" the representation, or simply to create an illusion of certainty in situations of uncertainty. However, failing to manage client expectations early on in the representation will almost inevitably interfere with your ability to effectively represent your client later. Some of the most important and difficult conversations you will have with a client are those in which you tell the client that they cannot achieve a certain goal or that their behavior is unwise, unethical, or ineffective.

In assessing the client's goals and expectations, the client's emotional state is an important factor to consider. Family representation may often involve situations of profound loss: from death, divorce, or the termination of parental rights. A client's perspective on the situation and her goals from representation will shift over time as she moves through the grieving process. An attorney in these circumstances must be keenly aware of this process and have patience and resources for client referral. The client, who today comes to you feeling ambivalent or guilty and ready to surrender important rights or make important concessions, may feel very differently at a later stage. Clients may not want to consider that they may feel differently about a decision in the future, but effective legal counseling requires you to provide this perspective to a client and to manage the process so that clients are in the best position to make informed decisions.

Finally, you will want to make sure that your client understands the roles and responsibilities each of you have in the relationship. A client needs to understand your policies regarding communications—how do they reach you? With whom can they speak in your office? How often can they expect to hear from you? With whom should they avoid speaking? Clients need to understand their own responsibilities—what information will you require? What behaviors should they avoid? They need to be educated about the process they are facing—attorneys may provide a list of helpful books or videos about divorce, adoption, medical decisions, or other relevant topics. Some of this information will be included in the representation agreement but consider carefully this decision, as representations made in the engagement letter or agreement can become contractual duties. Some information is better provided in the form of informational letters, brochures, checklists, and referrals.

Reflecting Journaling Assignment: Turning Down a Client

With a partner, practice declining a client an initial client interview. Take turns acting as a client presenting representations that an attorney should decline (e.g., a case too complex, too rushed, or too frivolous; a client too impecunious, too rude, or too devious). After you have each had a turn at declining a representation, write a short reflection on your experience in both roles. As a client, did you understand that the representation was being declined? How did you feel when the attorney declined to represent you? As an attorney, how difficult was it to decline the representation? How did you explain your declination to the potential client? If you were able to give the potential client advice or referrals, without taking on further representation, what was it? Is there any risk the client might misunderstand and believe that advice means that you agreed to the representation? If you would be willing to represent the client under different circumstances in the future, did you say so? Do you think the client would be likely to hire you in the future?

C. Charging for Legal Services

Many people do not hire attorneys because they believe they cannot afford the representation. Concerns about the cost of legal services drive much of the public's distrust of attorneys. Access to justice is affected by the standards relating to the reasonableness of fees, the rights and duties regarding communication with clients about fees, and the availability of contingent fees or other fee agreements. The integrity and independence of the profession is critically influenced by the standards regarding an attorney's ability to recover fees, division of fees with others, and contingent fee limitations. As a practical matter, individual attorneys must recognize the importance of careful planning and communication in this area as in all others. In family representation especially, attorneys must give very careful attention to the way in which they set fees, communicate fees to their clients, and collect those fees.

The American Academy of Matrimonial Lawyers, in its Bounds of Advocacy, notes that more disputes between attorneys and clients arise from family law cases than any other category. The Bounds explain some of the challenges for family law practitioners in setting and collecting fees:

> It is not unusual for a party to a divorce to lack sufficient funds to pay an attorney. This lack of resources, various strictures against contingent fee contracts, the unwillingness of some courts to redress the economic imbalance between the parties with fee awards, and the tendency of overwrought clients to misunderstand the fee agreement or to blame their attorneys for undesirable results, can make payment extremely difficult.[6]

How you set your fees can affect your ability to perform work competently and without conflict of interest, as well as your satisfaction with your work/life balance. The Rules of Professional Conduct in each state provide a baseline for determining how to set fees. The American Bar Association's Model Rule 1.5(a) specifies, "A lawyer's fee shall be reasonable." It goes on to specify the factors to be considered in determining a fee's reasonableness. For most attorneys, the hourly rate and the time spent on the representation constitute the two most important factors in determining their fees. In general, a fee is more likely to be considered reasonable if it is similar to fees customarily charged in the community, if it is not disproportionate to the value of the case as a whole, and if the client freely agreed to the fee. Fees are more likely to be considered unreasonable if they appear duplicative, do not represent work performed, or if the attorney has engaged in any misrepresentation or overreaching.[7] While courts do not easily find that a fee is unreasonable, where they do, they do not hesitate to impose sanctions.[8]

---

6. American Academy of Matrimonial Lawyers, Bounds of Advocacy, Standard 4 (2000) (*infra* appendix A).

7. Douglas Richmond, *For A Few Dollars More: The Perplexing Problems Of Unethical Billing Practices By Lawyers*, 60 S.C. L. Rev. 63 (2008)(discussing reasons attorneys engage in unethical billing practices and making suggestions for firm policies to discourage overbilling).

8. *See, e.g., In re* Dorothy, 605 N.W.2d 493 (S.D. 2000) (in which an attorney was reprimanded for charging a client $60,000 in a child custody action which did not present any especially novel facts or law and in which the other attorneys in the case had charged less than $20,000).

1. Communicating about Fees

Since an attorney's fee is not displayed on a menu at the front door, attorneys have a fundamental duty to communicate with their clients about fees. Model Rule 1.5(b) requires communicating your fee and the client's responsibilities for expenses "before or within a reasonable time after commencing the representation."

At the beginning of each representation, you should speak with the client about the costs of legal representation, the timing and methods of payment of those costs, and the client's ability to pay. For many new attorneys, these are not easy conversations. Family law clients are often reluctant and fearful to discuss fees. New attorneys may have no basis for estimating the time and expense involved in even routine representations. Often, your most honest answer to "How much is this going to cost?" must be "I don't know." Nonetheless, it is your responsibility to raise the issue and speak with the client early on. Of course, the fee discussion need not be the first words out of your mouth, but clients should not be the ones to have to raise the issue, nor should you waste your client's time in collecting extensive case information or explaining other aspects of your representation if the client ultimately cannot afford your services.

Though not necessarily required by the rules of conduct (check your state for its approach), you should think twice before ever undertaking a representation without a written agreement. See AAML Standard 4.1 and the comments in Appendix A. Not only does a written agreement provide documentation of the client's understanding of your fees, it also can be an important tool for communicating other aspects of the representation, such as the scope and limits of representation and allocation of responsibility.

Communication about fees does not end with the agreement—you should bill clients regularly. Regular billing is an important tool in communicating with the client regarding the progress of the representation and the ongoing costs. It is also one of the best methods to insure that you will be paid. See AAML Standard 4.2 in Appendix A. Billing statements should communicate what work has been done, who has completed that work, the time spent and the total charged. Billing statements can include reminders of your payment policy and prompts for clients to contact you if they have concerns.

Portfolio Problem: Counseling a Client about Fees

Difficult conversations about fees, whether in the initial retainer conference or when subsequent problems arise, are easier if you have a "script" or certain "stock phrases" you can call upon. That is not to say that these pre-rehearsed statements should replace genuine communication, but they do reduce awkwardness in the beginning.

Practice your default "script" for difficult fee conversations. Be prepared to answer the following questions:

- What is this interview costing me?
- Do you charge by the hour? How much?
- Do you charge by the hour for your staff time as well?
- Do you charge for telephone calls?
- How will you bill me?
- How often?
- When do you expect payment? What happens if I'm late in a payment?
- Do you take credit cards?
- Do you require payment in advance?
- How likely is it that the advance payment will not be enough? When will I know that?
- How much will this cost?
- How long will it take?
- How likely am I to succeed?

2. Contingent Fee Agreements

Some fee arrangements that are common in other fields are largely unavailable in family representation. For example, while the ABA Model Rules of Professional Conduct generally allow contingent fees, Rule 1.5(d) prohibits a lawyer from charging or collecting "any fee in a domestic relations matter, the payment or amount of which is contingent upon the securing of a divorce or upon the amount of alimony or support, or property settlement in lieu thereof." Why? The traditional justification is that contingent fees in these cases discourage reconciliation.[9] More modern justifications look to the potential conflicts of interest that contingent fee agreements might create. For example, a client's primary interest may be in resolving a divorce and custody matter in as peaceful a manner as possible, willing to sacrifice property value for quick resolution and a better chance of securing strong custody rights. If an attorney is representing that client on a contingent fee basis, however, the attorney's self interest would be to maximize the dollar value and recovery in property division.[10] Finally, because family law judges have the authority to order one

9. Jordan v. Westerman, 28 N.W. 826 (Mich. 1886).

10. *In re* Cooper, 344 S.E.2d 27, 33–34 (N.C. App. 1986).

spouse to pay the other spouse's attorney's fees as part of the division of property and debts, contingent fee payments are not as critical for access to attorneys as in other cases in which fee shifting is not ordinarily the rule.

The ban on contingent fees does not apply to every family representation. For example, a comment to Model Rule 1.5 indicates that "This provision does not preclude a contract for a contingent fee for legal representation in connection with the recovery of post-judgment balances due under support, alimony or other financial orders because such contracts do not implicate the same policy concerns." [11] The line here is not always clear however. Consider the Kansas Supreme Court's decision in *In re Jarvis*, 254 Kan. 829, 869 P.2d 671 (1994), in which a divorce attorney had agreed to investigate, after a divorce trial had concluded, whether the opposing party had understated income. The fee agreement provided that he would recover half of any increase in alimony he obtained for his client as a result of that investigation. The court found this to be an unethical contingent fee in a domestic relations matter, subjecting the attorney to public censure. Likewise, the New York Supreme Court, Appellate Division, held that an attorney may not charge a contingent fee in a case that combines divorce claims with other non-matrimonial claims (such as tort, constructive trust, or partnership), because the contrary rule would "create an incentive for attorneys to characterize most, if not all, of the proceeds of a settlement as deriving from the nonmatrimonial claims in order to maximize the value of, and therefore the contingency fee derived from, those claims." *Ross v. DeLorenzo*, 813 N.Y.S.2d 756, 759 (N.Y. App. Div. 2006).

Cases that are not technically "domestic relations" matters, such as paternity cases or tort suits, are less likely to fall within the prohibition. However, you should always check the rules and decisions in your own state regarding the line between prohibited and permissible contingent fees. Even where a contingent fee is permissible, best practice dictates giving your client an hourly option for the representation and giving the client time to seek the advice of another attorney regarding the contingent fee.

Some attorneys negotiate fee agreements with their clients in which the final fee for services will include a "bonus" for "results obtained." These attorneys argue that this is not a contingent fee because it is not based strictly on winning or losing but merely on the amount of the final financial recovery.[12] Some courts have

11. *See, e.g.*, Fletcher v. Fletcher, 591 N.E.2d 91, 95 (Ill. App. Ct. 1992)(holding that contingent fee agreement to recover past due child support was permissible because the obligation to pay support was preexisting, and the amount of support owed was predetermined).

12. Louis Parley, The Ethical Family Lawyer 45–6 (American Bar Association 1995).

approved this approach while others have flatly rejected it.[13] For example, the Supreme Court of Oklahoma held that "any fee arrangement in which the attorney will receive an enhanced fee if his efforts produce a more favorable property division or alimony award to his client involves a personal interest because the greater amount he obtains for his client, the greater he can charge as a fee." *Okla. Bar Ass'n v. Fagin*, 848 P.2d 11, 14 (Okla. 1992). Notably, the attorney in that case had learned to negotiate this "results obtained" fee agreement at a state bar association CLE program, a fact the concurring judge found especially troubling.

For our study, the lesson to be learned is to tread carefully in adopting novel fee agreement approaches and, even if a fee approach is one that other attorneys use, conduct your own examination of the ethical implications of any agreement you make.

3. Advances and Retainers

One of the best ways to insure that you will not encounter collection difficulties with a client is to collect your fees in advance. Perhaps the most important rule to keep in mind with advances is that you must never commingle client funds with your own. Until you have actually earned a portion of the advance, keep the advance in the client trust account. As you earn the fees, you must notify the client and then withdraw the portion that you have earned. Any unearned fees at the end of representation need to be refunded. Simple enough, but neglecting this accounting task provides the basis for the most serious of discipline.

Some attorneys charge clients retainer fees. A true retainer is not the same as an advance—it is a nonrefundable sum paid simply to engage an attorney's services. State courts vary in the evaluation of the ethics of these nonrefundable fees. Attorneys defend these fees by arguing that every time an attorney agrees to represent a client, the attorney has taken on the potential for conflicts of interest and the commitment of time and resources that may preclude other employment. Thus there is a "lost opportunity" cost to the attorney in simply agreeing to represent a client. Additionally attorneys will argue that there is value to a client in being able to say that they have hired an attorney—especially if the attorney has a widespread and quality reputation. Nonetheless, many state courts have rejected these arguments and have held that non-

13. *Compare In re* Marriage of Malec, 562 N.E.2d 1010 (Ill. App. 1990)(allowing results obtained fee); Eckell v. Wilson, 597 A.2d 696 (Pa. Super. 1991) (allowed); *with* King v. Young, Berkman, Berman & Karpf, 709 So. 2d 572 (Fla. App. Ct. 1998)(results obtained fee unenforceable); Salerno v. Salerno, 575 A.2d 523 (N.J. Super. Ch. Div. 1990) ("results accomplished" fee too vague to give client notice).

refundable retainers violate public policy and are unethical unless there is some specific, identifiable employment that would be precluded by the client's engagement of the attorney.[14]

Problem for Discussion

Clarissa Client hired Lawrence Lawyer to represent her in a divorce action. Client signed a retainer agreement stating that she would pay Lawyer "a MINIMUM FEE OF $4,000.00" and that Lawyer's hourly rate was $195. The retainer agreement also provided that the client "understands that NO portion of the MINIMUM FEE referred to above is REFUNDABLE, to the client, under any circumstances." After Lawyer invested approximately 6.4 hours in the case, Client terminated the attorney-client relationship, saying that she and her husband had reconciled. Client requested a refund of the unused portion of the $4,000 minimum fee. Lawyer concluded that he was not obligated to refund any portion of the fee, but nevertheless decided to return half of the remaining balance, or $1,385.75, to Client. Client objected to the partial reimbursement, and complained to the Attorney Grievance Commission, which then served Lawyer with a request for investigation and filed a formal complaint against him. The complaint alleged that Lawyer charged and collected an illegal or clearly excessive fee, and failed to refund the unearned portion of fees paid by Client, in violation of Rules 1.5(a) (reasonable fees), 1.15(b)(client trust accounting), 1.16(d)(obligations upon withdrawal), and 8.4(a)–(c)(misconduct).

Assume you have been asked to submit an amicus brief on behalf of your state family law association. What position would you take on this issue? Compare your analysis to that of the court in *Grievance Administrator v. Cooper, Michigan*, No. 135053, (December 12, 2008). The opinion, briefs, and amicus briefs by the Majority of the Michigan Bar Association, the American Academy of Matrimonial Lawyers, and by the law firm of Varnum, Riddering, Schmidt & Howlett LLP are available at http://courts.michigan.gov/supremecourt/Clerk/ 11-08/135053/135053-Index.htm.

4. Fee Shifting

In domestic relations matters, unlike most other civil litigation, there is a possibility that one might be able to shift the responsibility for fees to the op-

14. Columbus Bar Ass'n v. Halliburton-Cohen, 832 N.E.2d 42 (Ohio 2005); *In re* Kendall, 804 N.E.2d 1152 (Ind. 2004).

posing party. Generally, courts have wide discretion to grant an award of attorney's fees. In the eight states that have adopted the Uniform Marriage and Divorce Act, §313,[15] a court may order that one of the parties pays the other party's reasonable costs. In the states that have not adopted the UMDA, most also give their courts the discretion to award attorney's fees.[16]

A court may award attorney's fees to a party even if that party did not prevail at trial. The purpose for allowing the court to award attorney's fees to either party "is to equalize the parties' positions by providing a financially disadvantaged party with the financial means to prosecute or defend a divorce action.[17]

To determine whether or not the parties' positions require an attorney's fee award, the courts consider both the financial need of the party requesting fees and the other party's ability to pay the fees. First, a court will consider the ability of the requesting party to pay. For instance, in *H.P.A. v. S.C.A.*, 704 P.2d 205, 212 (Alaska 1985), wife appealed the trial court's requirement that she pay attorney's fees on the grounds that the husband had far greater financial resources and earning power. The court affirmed the trial court decision because the wife had the ability to pay attorney's fees. Second, a court considers whether the non-requesting party has the ability to pay fees. Even if the requesting party has sufficient financial need, a court will not require the other party to pay attorney's fees if that party cannot pay.[18]

Finally, for a court to award attorney's fees, those fees must be reasonable. The amount of attorney's fees awarded should be "fair compensation for only those services which were reasonable and necessary to the action."[19] In determining a reasonable fee, most jurisdictions use standards of reasonableness that are based on Model Rule 1.5. For example, Illinois's formulation of the standard says that the factors include "the skill and expertise of the attorneys employed, the nature of the controversy, the novelty or difficulty of the questions raised, the degree of responsibility involved, the time and labor required, the usual and customary charge in the community, and the benefit or result pro-

---

15. Arizona, Colorado, Illinois, Kentucky, Minnesota, Missouri, Montana, and Washington.

16. *See* W. Va. Code §48-5-504(a) (2008); Waldon v. Waldon, 806 S.W.2d 387, 389 (Ark. Ct. App. 1991).

17. D. E. v. S. M. E., No. CN02-07783, 2003 Del. Fam. Ct. LEXIS 211, *2 (Del. Fam. Ct. Dec. 19, 2003).

18. Price v. Price, 951 So. 2d 55, 59 (Fla. Dist. Ct. App. 5th Dist. 2007) (court did not require husband to pay wife's court costs because the husband would have had to take out loans to do so).

19. *In re* Marriage of Pitulla, 559 N.E.2d 819, 827 (Ill. App. Ct. 1st Dist. 1990).

vided."[20] New Jersey requires parties requesting attorney's fees to submit an affidavit that includes a listing of the services and disbursements that make up the fee. N. J. Court R. 4:42-9(b). That court rule explicitly refers to the standards of fee reasonableness present in Rule 1.5 of New Jersey's Rules of Professional Conduct.

You may request fees during the preliminary stage of the action in most jurisdictions, or you might wait until the end of the proceeding and include fees in the final distribution of property and debts. Fee shifting is, of course, a discretionary decision, and so is difficult to predict. If you decide to represent a client on the chance that you will be able to collect from the other party, both you and your client need to understand and agree that your client cannot count on that outcome and that he or she may still end up with liability for your fees.

5. Collecting Fees

What if, despite your best efforts, a client does not pay? You may not simply curtail services (or threaten to do so) or otherwise prejudice your client's case as a way to coerce payment. You may, however, have the option to withdraw. If you do have the withdrawal option, the choice is to either withdraw or to represent—there is no middle ground of "temporary withdrawal" or "suspended services." Remember also that once you have entered an appearance on behalf of a client, you may not withdraw without permission of the court.

You should let the client know from the very beginning the circumstances upon which you will request to withdraw for failure to pay. The AAML suggests that you include this information in the fee agreement itself. See AAML Standard 4.6 in Appendix A.

While it is important to let your client know that you may request to withdraw if they do not pay your fees, trying to secure a client's advance consent to a withdrawal for nonpayment is neither effective nor ethical. Under Model Rule 1.16 and its state counterparts, an attorney may withdraw from representation if a client has failed to fulfill a substantial obligation and has been given a warning that the attorney may seek withdrawal. To the extent a fee agreement purports to give an attorney the right to withdraw for any nonpayment of fees and without any further notice to the client, the agreement misrepresents the attorney's discretion. Moreover, even with a client's consent, a court may not approve an attorney's withdrawal. Finally, even if withdrawal may be premised on a client's consent, advance consent is unlikely to be suf-

20. *Id.*

ficiently informed to be considered reasonable. Accordingly, you may inform a client that the rules permit attorneys to seek withdrawal for non-payment of fees, but that is a different statement than asking the client to agree to your withdrawal based on circumstances that have not yet arisen.

When disputes regarding fees arise, attorneys may use a variety of approaches to resolution. Increasingly, state fee dispute resolution services offer mediation or arbitration of fee disputes. You may wish to include a provision in your fee agreement requiring the use of these dispute resolution methods should a fee dispute arise. See AAML Standard 4.7 in Appendix A. As a last resort, you may choose to sue your client for your fee; however, beware. Fee collection claims have a way of generating malpractice counter-claims.

The best approach, of course, is to avoid trouble in the first instance by carefully screening your clients, communicating with them regarding fees at the outset and regularly thereafter, and documenting these communications with written fee agreements and detailed billing statements.

Portfolio Problem: Assessing the Market

Interview an attorney who represents families in an area of practice of interest to you. What is a fairly routine representation they provide? How much does it usually cost and how long does it usually take? What does the attorney think is a standard hourly rate for new attorneys? Ask if the attorney has other advice about charging and collecting fees. If the attorney works for a public or not-for-profit agency, ask about how they secure and allocate resources for representations.

For more information about the economics of practice in your area of interest, contact your local or state bar associations for names of attorneys and for any surveys or publications they might have on economics of practice. Networking is an important skill for attorneys and this assignment can give you some practice.

D. The Scope of Representation

In addition to specifying terms about fees, you should always state the scope of representation in your agreement. In most cases, the scope of representation will involve handling a client's transaction or dispute from beginning to end. Limited scope representation is permissible however, and represents an important development in delivering legal services to persons of limited means.

Clear definitions of the scope of representation are important for several reasons. The scope of representation that you describe in an agreement with your client will prevent subsequent client misunderstandings and disappointment (and the malpractice actions they might generate). If a client sues you, your duties will be defined by your agreement with the client. If you are assessing the degree to which your current representation presents a conflict of interest, your representation agreement will provide important evidence. An open-ended or vaguely defined scope of representation may leave open the question of whether your representation has ended—making any conflicts analysis subject to the more stringent requirements for avoiding conflicts with current clients. Even if the representation has obviously ended, the scope of that representation will determine whether your former client's matter is the "same or substantially related" to your current client's matter. Accordingly, best practice requires you to carefully draft and clearly communicate the scope of your representation in your agreement with your client.

One of the most important aspects of the scope of representation is the allocation of authority between you and your client. Generally, the attorney has the discretion to determine the means by which the representation is to be carried out, while the client determines the objectives. The Restatement's description of this allocation of authority is especially helpful:

> A lawyer has authority to take any lawful measure within the scope of representation ... that is reasonably calculated to advance a client's objectives as defined by the client..., unless there is a contrary agreement or instruction and unless a decision is reserved to the client.... A lawyer, for example, may decide whether to move to dismiss a complaint and what discovery to pursue or resist. Absent a contrary agreement, instruction, or legal obligation..., a lawyer thus remains free to exercise restraint, to accommodate reasonable requests of opposing counsel, and generally to conduct the representation in the same manner that the lawyer would recommend to other professional colleagues.

Restatement (Third) of the Law Governing Lawyers § 21, comment 3 (2000).

Describing the scope of your authority with your client in the retainer agreement can provide important clarity and protect you from subsequent liability. So, for example, you may wish to have the client agree that you have the authority to determine scheduling, lest an angry client view your agreement to a continuance as an act of disloyalty.[21] As a matter of agency law, if a client instructs an attorney not to pursue a particular strategy or investigation, the attorney may not simply ignore the client's objection, even if the action would otherwise be legal or even necessary to the representation. For example, in

21. Purtle v. Comm. on Professional Conduct, 878 S.W.2d 714 (Ark. 1994).

McInnis v. Hyatt Legal Clinics, 461 N.E.2d 1295 (Ohio 1984), an attorney was held liable for violating an agreement with his client to keep the client's divorce out of the newspaper, even though service of process required some form of publication. If you believe you can represent the client competently and diligently without pursuing the objectionable means, you may continue the representation. Otherwise, you must withdraw from the representation.

In defining the relative scope of authority with your client, you can also include responsibilities for the client. This can lower the cost of the representation and help empower the client to feel better about the case. At a minimum, you will want to ask your client to gather relevant documents. Depending on the type of representation, you may ask clients to collect correspondence, financial statements, inventories and appraisals, or health or education records. You may also ask a client to prepare new documents, such as safety plans or journals/chronologies of past and ongoing events in the matter. Whenever you do engage clients in information gathering, be sure you counsel them regarding the legal limits (e.g., wiretapping or trespass laws) and prudent practices (when, where, and with whom they should or should not speak), lest your client complicate a situation.

1. Drafting Representation Agreements

Whether letters or agreements, how do you go about drafting these important documents? You might simply look around for a good sample and use it, right? Forms and samples are useful tools in drafting, but only if used correctly. Simply adopting someone else's form poses a multitude of risks. No matter what the source, there is no guarantee that the form is free from error or ethical difficulty. Without knowing who drafted the form, why, and with what preparation, you may simply be republishing someone else's errors.

As you consider how to draft any given representation agreement, remember that contracts are designed to memorialize an agreement—they are not the agreement itself. A term that you do not understand, have not spoken to the client about, or do not know is in the contract is worse than useless. If your representation agreement is called into question, you bear the burden of proving that the terms of the agreement were fair, the negotiation of the agreement was fair, and that the client understood the terms. If you cannot explain why a provision is in the agreement or what it meant to the client, you will have a difficult time meeting that burden.

In addition, take care regarding the promises you make in a representation agreement. Clients will want you to predict the end results of their case and identifying the range of possible outcomes is an important part of counseling the client. However, you should take care that you do not turn those evaluations into guarantees. You may even consider drafting a "no guarantees" clause in your retainer agreement to reinforce to the client that you cannot make certain an inherently uncertain process.[22] Even a seemingly innocuous provision promising to provide "the highest quality legal services in a responsive, efficient manner" can impact later liability. A malpractice suit may be based on contract principles, enforcing an attorney's representations regarding the quality of their legal services, rather than the more common tort theory of malpractice. The significance of this shift in legal theory is that, if a client is basing a malpractice claim on a breach of your contractual duty, damages will not be an element of the prima facie case as it would be in a negligence-based malpractice action. Moreover, depending on the nature of the representation, the law may impose a higher standard of care on attorneys making these quality representations than would be imposed by ordinary negligence standards.[23]

So what should you do to prepare effective representation agreements? Use a three-step process to draft a representation agreement: prepare, compare and repair.[24]

First, prepare. Generate a checklist of the issues you want to address in the agreement. You can get checklists from form books, CLE materials, or colleagues, but you should also brainstorm the unique demands and risks your particular practice poses. An example of a basic checklist can be found in the New York court rules governing domestic relations matters. Those rules require that all attorneys who charge for their representation must have a written retainer agreement. The rules go on to provide 13 specific areas that the agreement must address:

1. Names and addresses of the parties entering into the agreement;
2. Nature of the services to be rendered;
3. Amount of the advance retainer, if any, and what it is intended to cover;
4. Circumstances under which any portion of the advance retainer may be refunded. Should the attorney withdraw from the case or be discharged

22. For an example of such a disclaimer, *see* Louis Parley, The Ethical Family Lawyer 36 (1995).

23. Abramson v. Wildman, 964 A.2d 703 (Md. App. 2009)(Holding that statement in attorney's engagement letter that, "You may expect our firm to be both sensitive and professionally responsive to your situation" created a contractual duty enforceable through malpractice action).

24. I was taught this method by Mary Barnard Ray at the University of Wisconsin in 1982 and it is a very effective method for approaching any drafting task. You can access her excellent instruction in Mary Barnard Ray & Barbara J. Cox, Beyond the Basics: A Text For Advanced Legal Writing (1991).

prior to the depletion of the advance retainer, the written retainer agreement shall provide how the attorney's fees and expenses are to be determined, and the remainder of the advance retainer shall be refunded to the client;

5. Client's right to cancel the agreement at any time; how the attorney's fee will be determined and paid should the client discharge the attorney at any time during the course of the representation;
6. How the attorney will be paid through the conclusion of the case after the retainer is depleted; whether the client may be asked to pay another lump sum;
7. Hourly rate of each person whose time may be charged to the client; any out-of-pocket disbursements for which the client will be required to reimburse the attorney. Any changes in such rates or fees shall be incorporated into a written agreement constituting an amendment to the original agreement, which must be signed by the client before it may take effect;
8. Any clause providing for a fee in addition to the agreed-upon rate, such as a reasonable minimum fee clause, must be defined in plain language and set forth the circumstances under which such fee may be incurred and how it will be calculated;
9. Frequency of itemized billing, which shall be at least every 60 days; the client may not be charged for time spent in discussion of the bills received;
10. Client's right to be provided with copies of correspondence and documents relating to the case, and to be kept apprised of the status of the case;
11. Whether and under what circumstances the attorney might seek a security interest from the client, which can be obtained only upon court approval and on notice to the adversary;
12. Under what circumstances the attorney might seek to withdraw from the case for nonpayment of fees, and the attorney's right to seek a charging lien from the court;
13. Should a dispute arise concerning the attorney's fee, the client may seek arbitration, which is binding upon both attorney and client; the attorney shall provide information concerning fee arbitration in the event of such dispute or upon the client's request.

New York Rules of Court: Procedure for Attorneys in Domestic Relations Matters § 1400.3

Many attorneys include in their retainer agreements provisions regarding communication, tactics (especially regarding children), responsibility for aspects of the investigation, and other terms.

Second, compare. Compare the terms of the agreement you have discussed with your client with the terms you find in the forms and checklists you have gathered and prepared. Compare the language of the draft forms you have with the law governing those issues in your state. Choose or draft those contract terms that best fit the needs of your representation.

Third, repair. Repair your draft by editing your collage of provisions into a final representation agreement. Check that you have covered all the terms important to this representation; edit the language so that it is clear, simple and precise. Make sure that terms are consistent with both the law and each other. Finally proofread the agreement carefully.

The more you go through this process, the more efficient you will become at drafting representation agreements. But never assume that the day will come that you need not think about your representation agreement. Even after you have a highly polished and tested "standard" representation agreement and the client presents a "standard" case, you will still need to prepare by assessing the client's goals and expectations and compare your "standard" agreement to the needs of this particular representation. Never sign something you have not read, even if it contains familiar terms.

The representation agreement should certainly not be the last written communication you have with your client. Throughout the representation, you should be communicating with your client in writing. Your billing statement is one type of regular communication that is extremely important. Even if you have taken an advance on fees, you must regularly report to the client when you are withdrawing earned fees from the trust account. Use these billing reports to keep the client informed on where they are in the process of the representation—not only what has been done but what the next steps are. Even if nothing is happening in terms of a particular representation—as when you are waiting for the court or other parties to take actions—you will want to regularly report to your client on the status of their case. Additionally, there are a number of important points at which you will want to write letters to your client to reinforce the seriousness of a particular decision and protect yourself against future exposure to discipline or malpractice. If, for example, your client wishes to limit discovery, waive a particular right or protection, or accept settlement terms or take other action that is against your advice, you will want to memorialize your advice and the client's decision to reject that advice in a letter. These defensive letters are best sent in a manner that requires your client to acknowledge their receipt of the letter. Finally, you must send a closing letter when the representation has ended, returning all documents and papers, and making it clear that you no longer represent the client.

2. Limited Representation Agreements

Some clients may request that you provide only a limited service—reading a pleading and explaining it to them for example. May you limit your representation in this way? About twenty states have amended their rules to expressly provide for limited scope representation. In the rest of the states, a majority have adopted a version of Model Rule 1.2, which allows some limited representation if the limitation is reasonable under the circumstances and the client gives informed consent. The comments to that rule give as an example of a permitted limited scope representation an attorney providing a brief telephone conversation to provide general information about the law where that is sufficient to give the client advice upon which they can reasonably rely.

Limited scope representation may provide a method for reaching clients who would not otherwise hire an attorney. For reasons of financial ability or distrust of the legal system, some clients might prefer this approach to hiring an attorney. Many of these limited scope representations may evolve into a traditional full representation as clients realize the complexity of the legal system and learn to trust and appreciate the services you can provide to them.

One of the most difficult issues presented by limited task representation is determining when such a limited representation is "reasonable." States vary on the extent to which certain tasks are permitted to be carved out for discrete representations. Suppose a client has asked you to draft an answer to a divorce petition that he could sign and file, and then carry on the case with no further representation on your part. May you provide this limited representation? The practice of "ghostwriting" has been condemned by a number of federal courts for "a possibly unethical exploitation of pro se leniency, violations of Rule 11, violations of local court rules regarding attorney withdrawal, and violations of ethics rules prohibiting misrepresentation to the court."[25]

State ethics opinions and some state court rules have been more accepting of attorney's preparing pleadings for pro se litigants, though some do require that the pleading or other document indicate if attorney assistance was provided. For example, Florida's Family Law Rules of Procedure place responsibility on the pro se party who files a pleading or other document of record with the assistance of a lawyer to certify that assistance was received.[26] In California, a lawyer

---

25. John C. Rothermich, Note, *Ethical And Procedural Implications Of "Ghostwriting" For Pro Se Litigants: Toward Increased Access To Civil Justice*, 67 Fordham L. Rev. 2687, 2689 (1999).

26. Fla. R. Fam. Law R. Proc 12.040(d) (2009).

in a family law proceeding is not required to disclose involvement in preparing court documents as long as the lawyer does not make an appearance in the case.[27]

Another issue attorneys must regularly address with limited task representation is the degree of investigation required. Generally, attorneys must investigate a client's facts any time the information supplied by a client is "inconsistent, suspect, or materially incomplete."[28] However, the comment to Model Rule 1.1 explains that "the required attention and preparation are determined in part by what is at stake; major litigation and complex transactions ordinarily require more elaborate treatment than matters of lesser consequence." Does a lesser standard for factual investigation apply in limited task representation? May you draft a settlement of a divorce without having conducted any discovery as to marital assets? May you draft a simple will without examining the client's financial situation?

Ultimately, the baseline for information gathering may be found in the requirement that a client give "informed consent" to discrete task representation. In *Lerner v. Laufer*, 819 A.2d 471 (N.J. Chancery App. Div. 2003), a client sued the lawyer whom she had employed to review an agreement arrived at through mediation. The attorney told the client that he would be unable to give her much advice without factual investigation into the husband's assets and would only be able to read the agreement for clarity and consistency of terms. He sent the client a letter, reproduced in full in the opinion, explaining all of the matters on which he could not advise her without discovery. The wife later argued that, regardless of their agreement, the lawyer had a larger advocacy obligation than the contract reflected. New Jersey's Rules of Professional Conduct expressly permit lawyers, with consent of the client after consultation, to limit the scope of representation. The court upheld the limited scope representation agreement, stating that "the law has never foreclosed the right of competent informed citizens to resolve their own disputes in whatever way may suit them."

Limited representation may include the duty to counsel the client on the possibility of remedies or solutions not within the scope of the representation. For example, suppose your client has agreed to care for her cousin, whose parents tragically died in an auto accident. She has asked you to prepare a petition for adoption. You realize that your client could achieve her objectives as readily through a guardianship as she could adoption. Must you advise the client regarding this alternative? Comment 5 to Model Rule 2.1 provides that "a lawyer is not expected to give advice until asked by the client" but goes on

27. Cal Rules of Court, Rule 5.70 (2009).

28. ABA Comm. on Ethics and Professional Responsibility, Formal Op. 335 (1974).

to suggest that the duty of communication may require an attorney to provide unsolicited advice where to do otherwise would result in "substantial adverse legal consequences."

Some courts have held that counseling on other options or remedies is required even in limited representation. For example, in *Nichols v. Keller*, 19 Cal. Rptr. 2d 601, 608 (Cal. Ct. App. 1993), the court held that limited representation of a client in a workers compensation action required the attorney to counsel the client on other available remedies. Likewise the court in *Keef v. Widuch*, 747 N.E.2d 992 (Ill. App. Ct. 2001), stated that, "Although a representation agreement may limit the scope of representation to a particular legal course of action, the client must be made to understand that the course of action is not the sole potential remedy and that there exist other courses of action that are not being pursued." These cases should warn us that we can not eliminate the risks of claims for liability for failing to disclose specific risks or options merely by providing a boilerplate caution such as "there are risks to a limited representation and you may have other rights and remedies outside the scope of this representation."

The bottom line here is that limited scope representation is not for every client. You must keep in mind that limited representation does not come with limited liability exposure and you must choose and counsel your clients wisely.

At the core of the limited representation is the client's informed consent to that limitation. Before agreeing to undertake a limited scope representation, consider whether your client is able to understand the legal issues and their relationship to the client's goals. For the client's consent to be "informed" you must explain the limitations, and potential risks, of limited service. Thus, you must have sufficient information to decide the appropriate range of services for this particular client so you can provide alternatives to the limited representation. Consider the following suggestions from the Colorado Bar Association:

> A lawyer who limits the scope of the representation must consult with the client about the limited representation and obtain the client's consent to the limitation. Colo. RPC 1.2(c). As noted in the Terminology section of the Colorado Rules of Professional Conduct, "consult or consultation denotes communication of information reasonably sufficient to permit the client to appreciate the significance of the matter in question." A lawyer engaged in unbundled legal services must clearly explain the limitations of the representation, including the types of services which are not being provided and the probable effect of limited representation on the client's rights and interests. Where it is "foreseeable that more extensive services probably will be required" the

> lawyer may not accept the engagement unless "the situation is adequately explained to the client." Comment, Colo. RPC 1.5.[29]

Part of educating clients is warning that matters may become much more complicated than they expect and that, especially in a hearing or trial, there will not later be an opportunity to get help. You should explain to the client, for example, that rules of evidence and procedure can be complicated and raise unexpected legal issues and that rulings or decisions might be made that the client might not understand.

After you have studied your own state's position on limited scope representation and have screened your client for the advisability of limited scope representation, you will want to be sure to have a clear and complete limited representation agreement. The agreement should detail the counseling you have given the client on the risks and benefits of limited scope representation and should make clear that it is the client's choice to proceed with this form of representation. The agreement must make absolutely clear what legal issues and services will and will not be included in the representation. The agreement should indicate the source or sources of information upon which you will be relying in the representation and advise the client on the need for additional legal advice regarding other matters.

What if your client later wants you to provide additional drafting, advice or representation? It is easier to move from limited to full representation than the other way around. What appears to cause some attorneys difficulty is in acting as though they are still providing unbundled representation, when the client is in fact relying on them for all aspects of the legal matter. When renegotiating a limited scope representation agreement or agreeing to provide additional services to a client for whom you have previously provided limited representation, counseling the client regarding the scope of representation and drafting a clear agreement is just as important as in the initial representation.

Portfolio Problem: Drafting a Representation Agreement

Harold Husband has come to you in the midst of his self-represented divorce. Harold is 33 years old and has been married for 12 years. He has a master's degree in accounting and works for a large accounting firm. His wife is a grade school teacher. They have no children. Harold is seeking a divorce because he has fallen in love with another woman he met at work and she is expecting his child. Thus far, Harold has prepared and filed his divorce action. His wife Winifred is represented by a local family law attorney.

---

29. Colorado Bar Ethics Opinion 101 (2002).

Harold has responded to all discovery and he and his wife's attorney have worked out agreements on property and debt division. This past week, he received a copy of his wife's amended answer, indicating that she is asking for maintenance. He has done some legal research and is confused about his legal rights. How narrow a representation would you be comfortable providing him?

Would you agree to:

- Answer a couple of specific questions about the maintenance statute?
- Provide, for a set fee, an opinion on whether and how much he would likely be liable for maintenance under the law of your state?
- Review a letter he has written to counsel responding to the request for maintenance and proposing a different property settlement in lieu of maintenance?
- Draft a motion and memorandum in support of the motion asking the court to strike the amended answer as untimely?
- Prepare a negotiation strategy and coach him on negotiation over this issue?
- Assist in preparing for trial on the issue of maintenance, including reviewing lists of questions, exhibits, and arguments?

What special provisions would you want in your client engagement agreement for any of these limited services? Choose one of these limited scope representations and draft the agreement you will offer to the client, along with the format you will use to document your client's consent. See examples of fee and scope provisions in the comments to AAML Standard 4.1 in Appendix A.

Research Assignment

Research your own state's approach to an issue raised in this chapter. For example, what types of fee dispute resolution services are offered in your state? How does your state treat the issues of "ghostwriting" pleadings or other limited task representation? For questions such as this, you may find that the internet is an excellent place to start, particularly the resources you can find through the American Bar Association website or your local bar association. Always be careful when using the internet for research to verify the qualifications of the source (is this an official government website or a website advertising a service or advancing a particular public policy agenda?) Consider the date of the source—some web pages providing information regarding the currency of the materials provided while others give no clues at all. See Appendix D for more guidance on how to research professional responsibility issues.

To Learn More

Jay G. Foonberg, How to Start & Build a Law Practice, 5th Edition (ABA 2004).

A classic text on how to start a law practice.

Mark A. Chinn, How to Build and Manage a Family Law Practice (ABA 2006).

This book and CD provides advice, forms and checklists for attorneys starting a family law practice. The book explores how to gain practical experience in the area, how to address the business aspects of a family law practice, and how to manage staff, cases, and finances.

Michael Millemann, Reporter, ABA Handbook on Limited Scope Legal Assistance (2003). http://www.abanet.org/litigation/taskforces/modest/report.pdf.

This handbook is the official report of the Modest Means Taskforce of the ABA Section on Litigation. The Handbook provides a thorough guide to limited-scope representation, including sample forms, pleadings, and proposed court rules.

Center for Computer Assisted Legal Instruction. http://www.cali.org

For additional instruction on the regulation of attorneys fees, students at CALI mmber schools may access the lesson on Fees (catalogue number PR 13).

Chapter Two

Competency in Family Representation

Learning Objectives for This Chapter

After you have read this chapter and completed the assignments you should be able to:

- Identify the unique demands of family representation.
- Articulate the elements of malpractice and ineffective assistance of counsel claims.
- Critique the effectiveness of competency standards in regulating attorneys who represent elders, children, and parents.
- Explain steps you will take to reduce your risk of incompetence.
- Be able to identify the interdisciplinary sources you will use to educate yourself and help your client.

A. Why Representing Families Is Different

Representation of children and families presents challenges that are unlike many other areas of legal practice.

First, the law is by no means "easy." While some attorneys may think that "anyone can do family law" they soon find that the legal and practice demands in the field are far more complicated and demanding than they expected. Most matters relating to family relationships are heard by specialized courts (juvenile court, family court, and probate court) with their own rules of practice and procedure. Because family status impacts so many rights and responsibilities in society (e.g., taxation, bankruptcy, tort liability), the attorney representing families must be well versed in a broad range of law. Even then, the substantive law doctrines of contracts, property, and torts often have unique applications when families are involved, so one must never assume that general legal knowledge translates perfectly in the family arena.

In addition, despite an increasing federalization of many aspects of the law affecting families, much of the law regulating divorce, custody, and probate still varies dramatically from state to state and even among court systems within any given state. In many areas of family representation, controlling standards are highly discretionary. This is especially so when it comes to representation regarding children. Consider one court's explanation of the standard of review in child custody cases:

> Because a chancellor charged with deciding a question of child custody must utilize to the fullest extent all of his powers of perception in evaluating the witnesses, their testimony, and the child's best interest, there are no cases in which the superior position, ability, and opportunity of the chancellor to observe the parties carry as much weight as in those involving child custody. Our deference to the chancellor is correspondingly greater in such cases.[1]

In addition, the client problems are complex and unique:

> The problems the clients bring to family law attorneys are relationship problems. They are not about "transactions or occurrences," but people. "Few human problems are as emotional, complicated or seem so important as those problems people bring to matrimonial lawyers."[2] As a consequence, a client's emotions and attitudes are central to problem solving and planning. (Not to say that emotions and attitudes are irrelevant in other areas of law, but they are not typically a central consideration.) Professor Robert Mnookin points out, for example, that most legal rules require determination of the facts relating to some event and are thus "act- oriented." By contrast, child custody determinations are "person-oriented," making relevant "the attitudes, dispositions, capacities, and shortcomings of each parent."[3] Similar observations could be made about the many other legal issues facing families.
> Clients are unlikely to be equipped to easily address those emotions. In disputes, the interests and positions of the parties are likely to be

1. Word v. Remick, 58 S.W.3d 422, 424–25 (Ark. Ct. App. 2001).

2. American Academy of Matrimonial Lawyers, The Bounds of Advocacy, Preface (1992).

3. Robert H. Mnookin, *Child-Custody Adjudication: Judicial Functions in the Face of Indeterminacy*, 39 Law & Contemp. Probs. 225 (1975).

> unstable and difficult to determine. The "stakes" in family disputes may be economic, but the economics are imbued with fundamental psychological layers (whether the action is a challenge to an estate plan or the dissolution of a marriage or a family business). Even planning transactions for families is unlike most transactional planning. A prenuptial agreement is not planned to facilitate a successful marriage, but to plan for the failure of the marriage. An estate plan is a plan for death. The "collateral" issues raised when one is anticipating the "mortality" of marriage or self can become central factors influencing client decisions. Moreover, many clients in these cases may have broader limitations on their own decision-making capacity (children, frail elders, victims of abuse, etc.). Yet, nowhere is the need for personal empowerment greater....
>
> Finally, as relationship problems, these disputes are never truly over. While most law follows a "dispute resolution" model that views problems as one-shot, finite issues, in most family law disputes, the reality is that law is merely setting a framework for on-going adjusted relationships. For attorneys representing families, the "standard philosophical map[4] will not suffice for competent representation. Family attorneys must be interdisciplinary. They must understand the psychological, social, and cultural influences on their clients' decisions and decision-making. They must understand how their own biases and personal familial histories affect their worldviews of families in general and clients in particular. Family law attorneys must have well-developed skills in social work. Because the law can provide so few real solutions for many family law problems, attorneys must be able to identify and access a range of other professional services for their clients to provide effective representation.[5]

How are attorneys doing in rising to the challenge of practice in the unique world of representing families? There are a number of signs that we are not doing very well. Complaints to disciplinary agencies, malpractice rates, and a public increasingly looking to other professionals to assist them in adjusting family relationships are all signs of a profession that could do a better job serving its clients. In the remainder of this chapter, we will examine some of these competency problems in more detail and look for solutions.

4. Leonard L. Riskin, *Mediation and Lawyers*, 43 Ohio St. L.J. 29 (1982).

5. Barbara Glesner Fines and Cathy Madsen, *Caring Too Little, Caring Too Much: Competence and the Family Law Attorney*, 75 UMKC L. Rev. 968–69 (2007).

B. Standards of Competence in Family Representation

While rules of professional conduct regulate competency, in most areas of legal practice, it is the law of malpractice that more often provides the most direct regulation.

1. Malpractice Standards

Let's begin by considering the tort liability system's standards for competence in family law representation.

London v. Weitzman

884 S.W.2d 674 (Mo. App. Ct. 1994)

In this action seeking damages for legal malpractice, the jury assessed plaintiff's damages at $500,000 and assessed fault at 60 percent against defendant and 40 percent against plaintiff. Both plaintiff and defendant filed motions for judgment notwithstanding the verdict (JNOV). The trial court denied plaintiff's motion but granted that of defendant. Plaintiff appeals. We reverse....

The thirty-two year marriage of plaintiff Ina Carole London, and Norman London was dissolved by decree of the Circuit Court of Cole County on June 29, 1984. During the early years of the marriage, plaintiff was a homemaker and raised two children while Mr. London developed a successful practice in the field of criminal law. When the children were older, plaintiff worked as a travel agent and for several years operated her own travel agency which was financed by her husband. This agency was sold in 1978 and the proceeds of the sale were retained by plaintiff's husband. Thereafter, plaintiff had two brief periods of employment in the field of hotel management during 1979 and 1981. During the time plaintiff operated her travel agency, she engaged in one incident of marital infidelity while on a trip to Europe. Although aware of the incident, her husband did not want to end the marriage until plaintiff insisted upon a divorce in 1984. On the other hand, plaintiff testified that her husband's persistent heavy drinking and violent displays of temper contributed to the breakup of the marriage.

By late 1983, after several attempts to resolve their problems by consultation with marriage counselors, plaintiff was living almost full-time at the home they had built in Scottsdale, Arizona, while her husband was continuing his full-time law practice in St. Louis and sporadically visiting his wife. She wrote her husband a letter in which she stated "our marriage is over." Although he neither wanted nor asked for a divorce, he called her and said she should file for divorce.

Plaintiff testified that throughout the marriage she had, without objection on her part, been "kept in the dark" about finances. She had no idea of what her husband's income was nor did she have any information concerning investments. Her husband gave her $3,000 or $4,000 per month to operate the household, and she was content not to make any inquiry about financial matters.

On the advice of a friend's husband, a stockbroker, she prepared a list of her yearly expenses which totaled $47,143.70. This figure was low because of some expenses, such as property taxes, insurance, and medical expenses, which her husband always paid. The broker provided her with two alternatives which he stated would supply her with an income of $40,000 to $42,000 per year: 1) a property settlement of $500,000 to be paid over a period of two or three years, or 2) a lump sum cash payment of $250,000, the house in Arizona, maintenance of $30,000 for 10 1/2 years, and maintenance thereafter of $10,000 per year.

By telephone plaintiff retained Mr. Gerald Rimmel, a St. Louis attorney, to represent her in the dissolution proceeding. She sent him her expense list and the two proposals outlined by the stockbroker and asked him to obtain information concerning marital assets and her husband's income. Plaintiff then called her husband and told him she had retained a lawyer. He flew to Arizona and persuaded her to fire Mr. Rimmel. He told plaintiff that if a hostile attorney forced a public revelation of his financial condition, serious consequences could result. Her husband dictated a letter discharging Mr. Rimmel which she typed and mailed. Her husband then recommended that she retain defendant, Bernard Weitzman, who was an old friend. Defendant had been the best man for her husband at their wedding. Her husband contacted defendant and made arrangements for her to be represented.

Plaintiff talked to defendant concerning the divorce on two occasions. Somehow defendant had obtained the information she had mailed to Mr. Rimmel. In their first conversation, defendant told plaintiff that the $500,000 proposal was "way too much based on what Norman had" and the second alternative was much more reasonable. Defendant told plaintiff that she could never get more than that because the law passed in 1974, due to "woman's lib", actually hurt a wife's ability to obtain alimony. He told plaintiff the second alternative was very generous. In their second conversation, defendant told plaintiff her husband had agreed to the second proposition. He assured her that it was more than fair. At no time did defendant tell plaintiff that he would not represent her if there was any dispute with her husband. She never received a list of her husband's assets. She signed and returned the petition for dissolution and a separation agreement which defendant mailed to her.

She acceded to her husband's wish to have the court proceeding in Jefferson City in order to avoid publicity. She flew to St. Louis on June 28, 1984, and plaintiff, her husband, and defendant drove together to Jefferson City the next day. Her husband told her the judge would ask her some questions and she should answer "yes" to whatever he asked. She did so. She signed a number of papers but did not read them. Defendant did not explain any of the papers to her.

If plaintiff had been told that her husband's income in 1984 was $505,000, over $300,000 the year before that and over $600,000 before that, she would not have agreed to settle for $30,000 per year for ten years. If she had been advised that the marital assets totaled $1,840,000 plus the $250,000 paid to her as her share of the marital property, she would never have agreed to settle for what she did.

Defendant admitted he never gave plaintiff any advice regarding her rights under the laws of Missouri. He knew from plaintiff's letter to Mr. Rimmel that she had been kept in the dark about financial matters and had requested that Mr. Rimmel obtain tax returns and other financial information from her husband. He did not tell the dissolution judge that he considered himself a mere scrivener and he had not given plaintiff any advice. He never obtained any information concerning plaintiff's husband's income and, although required by local court rule, he did not file a statement of income and expenses for either party.

As mentioned above, this evidence was sharply disputed by defendant. However the jury resolved this dispute by finding in favor of plaintiff and assessing her damages at $500,000. The jury assessed forty percent fault against plaintiff, and the court entered judgment of $300,000. Defendant filed a motion for judgment notwithstanding the verdict. Plaintiff filed a similar motion, asking the trial court to set aside the submission and finding of comparative fault and to enter judgment for the full amount of the verdict. She also moved for pre-judgment interest. Neither party filed a motion for new trial. The trial court sustained defendant's motion for JNOV and denied plaintiff's motions.

I. Submissibility

It is well-established in Missouri that a plaintiff seeking to recover damages for legal malpractice must prove: (1) that the defendant lawyer was negligent by showing that he or she failed to exercise that degree of skill and diligence ordinarily used under the same or similar circumstances by members of the legal profession; (2) that plaintiff sustained some loss or injury; and (3) a causal connection between the negligence and the loss. To prove damages and causation, the plaintiff must establish that "but for" the attorney's negligence the result of the underlying proceeding would have been different.

In a written memorandum of law filed with his order sustaining defendant's JNOV motion, the trial judge acknowledged that plaintiff had produced evidence sufficient to establish all three elements of legal malpractice. The motion was sustained solely on the ground that the plaintiff failed to prove a specific amount of damages with reasonable certainty. In so ruling, the court misconstrued the rule against speculative damages which relates not to the difficulty in calculating the amount of damages but to the more basic question of whether there are specifically identifiable damages. The rule is well-stated by R.E. Mallen and J.M. Smith, Legal Malpractice, Volume I, § 16.3 (3d Ed.1989):

> In a legal malpractice action, a court may be tempted to characterize the plaintiff's damage claim as speculative because of the difficulty in liquidating the claim. This is because legal malpractice litigation often involves hypothetical questions which have real consequences. For example, how much did the client lose when the lawsuit was not prosecuted? Or, how much better off would the client have been had the suit been defended or been defended more competently?
>
> No one can say precisely what the plaintiff lost or should have lost in such situations, but difficulty or imprecision in calculating damages does not exculpate the attorney. Even though damages cannot be calculated precisely, they can be estimated. Otherwise, attorneys could avoid liability merely because damages are difficult to measure. The beneficiaries would tend to be those attorneys whose errors were the greatest and whose conduct succeeded in complicating the issue of calculating the extent of the client's injury. Thus, damages are speculative only if the uncertainty concerns the fact of whether there are any damages rather than the amount.

Plaintiff's expert witness, Allen Russell, an attorney experienced in the field of family law, testified that the process by which a dissolution court divides marital property begins at the point of a 50/50 split. The division may be affected by marital misconduct which has led to the breakup of the marriage or has imposed an undue burden upon the relationship. However, where the injured party wants to continue the marriage even after the misconduct of the other party, such misconduct would not normally be considered. Mr. Russell further testified that in advising plaintiff to accept a settlement of twenty percent of the marital assets defendant failed to exercise the appropriate standard of care that an attorney must meet. This evidence was sufficient to permit the jury to find the existence of identifiable damages caused by defendant's professional negligence and to make an informed estimate of the amount of plaintiff's damages. The trial court erred in refusing to allow plaintiff's expert to express an opinion based upon his years of experience regarding what a fair and equitable distribution of marital property would be under all of the facts and circumstances shown in evidence. Moreover, the trial court erred in ruling on the motion for JNOV that such testimony was an essential element of plaintiff's case. The order granting defendant's motion for JNOV is reversed.

II. Comparative Fault

Plaintiff's second point on appeal charges trial court error in overruling her motion requesting the court to enter judgment in the full amount of the jury's assessment of damages without reduction for comparative fault. She alleges the court erred in submitting an issue of comparative fault on the theories advanced by defendant.

It is important to bear in mind that in addressing this issue we are concerned only with the question of submissibility of the issue of comparative fault. Much of plaintiff's argument on the point is directed toward challenging the three disjunctive theories submitted to the jury in defendant's comparative fault instruction patterned after MAI 32.01(2), which reads as follows:

In your verdict you must assess a percentage of fault to plaintiff, if you believe:

First,

- plaintiff failed to inform defendant she did not know her marital rights, or
- plaintiff fired Gerald Rimmel as her lawyer at her husband's request and hired defendant knowing a settlement had not been reached, or
- plaintiff agreed to the terms of the separation agreement without knowing her marital assets or her husband's income, and

Second, plaintiff was thereby negligent, and

Third, such negligence of plaintiff directly caused or directly contributed to cause any damage plaintiff may be (sic) sustained.

The term "negligent" or "negligence" as used in this instruction means the failure to use that degree of care that an ordinary careful and prudent person would use under the same or similar circumstances.

We agree with plaintiff's contention that the instruction is erroneous. Plaintiff's failure to inform defendant she did not know her marital rights, assuming she had some duty to do so, could not have been a proximate cause of her damages. It is undisputed that defendant possessed a copy of plaintiff's letter to Mr. Rimmel advising him that she had been kept in the dark regarding financial affairs and requesting that he find out about her husband's income and the marital property. Her failure to advise defendant of what he already knew is not negligence contributing to her loss. Furthermore, firing Mr. Rimmel was antecedent to, not contributory with, the negligence of defendant as a causative factor.

However, neither in the trial court nor before this court has plaintiff requested a new trial because of the erroneous instruction. Rather, she seeks only to have the judgment assessing a percentage of fault against her set aside. For this purpose our concern focuses on the submissibility of the issue of comparative fault and whether any one of defendant's theories was supported by the evidence and was sufficient in law to warrant the assessment of a percentage of fault against plaintiff.

By her own admission, plaintiff agreed to the terms of the separation agreement without knowing about the marital assets or her husband's income. She was under no compulsion to do so until defendant obtained and furnished her with the information which she now claims it was his duty to provide. The jury could have found that by willingly bringing the dissolution proceeding to a conclusion without sufficient knowledge or information with which to determine the fairness of the settlement agreement plaintiff failed to exercise that degree of care that an ordinarily careful and prudent person would have exercised under the same or similar circumstances. The verdict of the jury finding plaintiff was forty percent at fault is supported by the law and the evidence. Point denied....

The judgment of the trial court is reversed, and the cause is remanded with directions to reinstate the judgment in favor of plaintiff in the amount $300,000 plus costs. Costs on appeal assessed against defendant.

Questions

1. Why do you think attorney Weitzman took on this representation? Was his agreement to represent Mrs. London itself a violation of ethics rules? In what other situations might attorneys be tempted to represent clients in family law matters despite the risk of discipline or malpractice?
2. The clearest cases for application of comparative fault are instances in which a client chooses to ignore an attorney's advice or actively interferes with the attorney's management of the case. What do you think of the use of comparative negligence in this case? If this case had been appealed to the Supreme Court of Missouri, what arguments might you expect regarding the use of comparative negligence in legal malpractice cases in general and in family law cases in particular? Compare *Tarleton v. Arnstein & Lehr*, 719 So. 2d 325, 330–31 (Fla. Dist. Ct. App. 1998)(attorney who gave inaccurate advice about a release clause in a divorce settlement could not maintain that the client was at fault for failing to understand the language of the release because clients are entitled to rely on their attorney's expertise).
3. The failure to adequately investigate, discover or secure assets is one of the most common bases for legal malpractice in domestic relations cases. *See, e.g.*, *Grayson v. Wofsey*, 646 A.2d 195 (Conn. 1994); *Baldridge v.*

Lacks, 883 S.W.2d 947 (Mo. Ct. App. 1994); *Callahan v. Clark*, 901 S.W.2d 842 (Ark. 1995). Suppose your client has instructed you that you may not take steps you believe necessary to adequately discover or value property in the marital estate, such as hiring an expert or a private investigator or pushing discovery sanctions for failure to provide requested information?

What steps might you take to protect yourself from the risk of malpractice in these circumstances? Keep in mind that under Model Rule 1.8(h) and its state counterparts, attorneys may not simply ask a client to waive malpractice. The Model Rule prohibits attorneys from making agreements "prospectively limiting the lawyer's liability to a client for malpractice unless the client is independently represented in making the agreement."

Do the client's reasons for her instructions matter? What if she fears her husband's retaliation? What if she "knows" the property and numbers you have are "close enough." What if she simply cannot afford more extensive discovery? For an excellent discussion of these issues, see Andrew S. Grossman, *Avoiding Legal Malpractice in Family Law Cases: The Dangers of Not Engaging in Financial Discovery*, 33 Fam. L.Q. 361 (1999).

4. What is the responsibility of the court in a case such as this? This settlement would have been reviewed and approved by the court before incorporating into the judgment. Was the court as negligent in this case as anyone? Does allowing malpractice actions provide divorce litigants an unjustified "second bite at the apple" when they later become dissatisfied with a settlement? Consider the rule adopted by the court in *Muhammad v. Strassburger, McKenna, Messer, Shilobod & Gutnick*, 587 A.2d 1346 (Pa. 1991), cert. denied, 502 U.S. 867 (1991) which barred a dissatisfied client from commencing a malpractice action following a marital settlement agreement that she had agreed to, unless she could establish that she was fraudulently induced to enter into the settlement agreement. (Subsequent Pennsylvania decisions have limited the *Muhammad* case to its facts, that is, cases in which the attorney's negligence concerns the "exercise of judgment regarding an amount to be accepted or paid in settlement of a claim." *McMahon v. Shea*, 688 A.2d 1179 (Pa. 1997).)
5. Attorneys who provide family law representation as a small part of a diverse practice will run a much higher risk of error than those who specialize in this area. Consider the Michigan attorney who was sued for malpractice based on his drafting of a prenuptial agreement. The attorney had provided his client (Wife) with the agreement and instructed her to attach a list of assets to the agreement. She did so, but without including values of the assets on the list. When, in her subsequent divorce, the antenup-

tial was set aside for failure to disclose financial assets, Wife sued the attorney for malpractice. The majority of the court of appeals upheld the trial court's summary judgment on the basis that the failure to disclose values in the asset list was only one factor in the court's decision to set aside the prenuptial, so that Wife could not prove that the attorney's negligence was the proximate cause of the court's action. A scathing dissent in the case castigated the attorney for his sloppy approach to family law representation in general and drafting in particular:

Defendant devoted a relatively small portion of his practice to family law, so it is not too surprising to discover that he left the tailoring of a boilerplate antenuptial to his client and his secretary.... Attorneys are legal professionals who are hired to forge binding agreements and are best equipped to detect any fatal flaws. Just as a doctor may not provide a patient with plaster and gauze and expect the patient to set and encase her own broken leg, an attorney may not leave the most legally sensitive portion of a contract to a client's drafting skill and expect that it will survive judicial scrutiny. If a contract fails because of a flaw related to the attorney's abandonment of the drafting process, we should hold the attorney responsible.

Winkler v. Carey, 2005 Mich. App. LEXIS 2989 (December 1, 2005)(unpublished opinion).

6. The court pointed out that the attorney in this case told his female client that she could not get a larger maintenance award than that offered by her husband because of "woman's lib." The court's inclusion of that detail might have signaled a suggestion that the attorney had some degree of gender bias in his representation. One of the most significant challenges in representing families is providing advice and representation that is sensitive to the client's needs, interests and values, untainted by personal bias. See AAML Standard 2.7 in Appendix A. Developing effective cross-cultural counseling skills is an essential aspect of family law practice. As Professor Jean Koh Peters explains, in her text on representing child clients:

All lawyering is cross-cultural because the law and its practice are itself a culture with strong professional norms that give meaning to and reinforce behavior. The law has its own jargon, its own language, its own customs, and its own traditions. It has its own etiquette, and own rules of behavior. To some lawyers, and some clients, the culture of the law is different, while it reflects many values with which they have grown up. For others, the law is a completely foreign culture with values and assumptions that do not match lay life. Therefore, even when a lawyer and client share common cultural attributes in other ways, lay clients and lawyers will experience the lawyer-client relationship as a cross-cultural experience.

> For our child clients, the culture of the law is a deeply adult intellectual culture in which they have no toeholds for understanding. In general, many similarities and differences deeply affect the lawyer-client relationship, arising from other, more traditionally understood components of culture: race, class, nationality, language, ethnicity, age, region, accent, gender, and sexual preference, to name only a few.
>
> The key point of this principle is that cross-cultural lawyering is not relegated to a small subset of one's cases that happen to involve clients who look visibly different from us. Lawyers should assume from the start that culture is an important component of every case, and an essential component to the assumption that the lawyer brings to the situation. Thus, the habits of cross-cultural lawyering should pervade the lawyer's daily life and should instinctively become part of the arsenal of legal skills that the lawyer brings to the case.
>
> Jean Koh Peters, Representing Children in Child Protective Proceedings: Ethical and Practical Dimensions 257 (2nd Ed. 2001).

2. Competence and Public Attorneys

In many critical areas of family representation, indigent clients have a right to appointed counsel. The Sixth Amendment to the United States Constitution provides a right to counsel in criminal cases. Indeed, in any proceeding in which an individual may be subject to a loss of liberty — whether detention in a juvenile home (*In re Gault*, 387 U.S. 1, 34–42 (1965)) or commitment to a mental institution (*Vitek v. Jones*, 445 U.S. 480 (1980))—the subject of the proceeding has the right to representation.

Outside this context, however, the right of individuals to be represented in legal proceedings is less clear. Federal courts have repeatedly rejected a generalized constitutional right to counsel in civil cases.[6] However, advocates have had some limited success in establishing a fourteenth amendment right to counsel for children and their parents in civil actions based on abuse and neglect. In *Lassiter v. Department of Social Services*, 452 U.S. 18 (1981), the United States Supreme Court addressed the question of whether an indigent parent facing a possible termination of her parental rights had a right to appointed counsel. The Court held that there was no absolute right to counsel in these types

6. Hon. Robert W. Sweet, *Civil Gideon and Confidence in a Just Society*, 17 Yale L. & Pol'y Rev. 503, 503 (1998) (right to counsel in civil cases is necessary to help "courts maintain the confidence of the society and to perform the task of insuring that we are a just society operating under a rule of law.")

of cases. Rather, the Court concluded that due process might, in an individual case, require appointed counsel and that the decision must be made on a case-by-case basis. The right to counsel is determined by applying the three-part due process calculus of *Mathews v. Eldridge*, 424 U.S. 319, 335 (1976), in which the court weighs the state's interest against the private interest implicated and the risk of erroneous decision. While indigent parents and children in the federal courts must establish their right to counsel on a case-by-case basis, most states have provided broader protection for these litigants. Most states provide the right to counsel in termination of parental rights cases, for example, by statute or court rule, others through an application of the Mathews balancing test.[7]

To meet the requirement of providing assistance in these cases, most states use staffs of government attorneys or panels of contract attorneys. These public attorneys often carry astonishingly high caseloads and are often placed in the unfortunate position of being unable to provide the level of quality representation their devotion to the field might otherwise command. Other states rely on pro bono and appointed counsel, but these systems are frequently criticized as requiring unconstitutionally conscripted malpractice by unwilling and incapable attorneys.

In either case, the question of competence is of continual concern. Yet a variety of legal standards create a lower degree of accountability for attorneys representing these clients. Malpractice liability does not ordinarily operate to regulate the competence of these attorneys. In a number of areas of practice, public attorneys are deemed to be representing the state rather than the individuals on whose behalf they appear. For example, as we will examine more closely in Chapter Seven, most states provide either qualified or absolute immunity for attorneys representing a child's best interests or acting as a guardian ad litem for the court and performing quasi-judicial duties such as preparing reports and making recommendations. Similarly, attorneys representing clients through child support enforcement agencies are deemed, by judicial interpretation and state legislation, to expressly disclaim any duty to the parent on whose behalf these attorneys are collecting child support. *Blessing v. Freestone*, 520 U.S. 329 (1997)(holding that parent recipients of child support enforcement services do not have a right to "substantial compliance" with the child support enforcement

---

7. *See, e.g.,* In the Matter of Ward v. Jones, 757 N.Y.S.2d 127,129 (2003)(no right to counsel for parents seeking visitation); *but see* Adoption of Holly, 738 N.E.2d 1115, 1121 (Mass 2000)(finding state constitutional right to court-appointed counsel for parents in termination of parental rights cases); Danforth v. State Dep't of Health and Welfare, 303 A.2d 794, 800 (Me. 1973) (holding that due process requires appointment of counsel to indigent parents in case in child neglect case).

legislation). These attorneys owe no duties of competence or conflict-free representation to the recipients of their legal representation other than the protections that flow from their agency's regulation. Thus, these attorneys too are given the cloak of immunity and the state is relieved of its burden to fund a system that can provide true individualized representation.

In termination of parental rights or juvenile court appointments, where attorneys represent only the clients on whose behalf they are appointed, standards for competence are nonetheless blunted. The standard for reviewing the effectiveness of counsel in these cases is, in most states, borrowed from the criminal defense field: the two-pronged standard of *Strickland v. Washington*, 466 U.S. 668 (1984), which requires proof of both incompetent representation, clearly shown on the record, and proof of actual prejudice to the client. The prejudice prong of this test means that even objectively poor performance may not result in a finding of ineffective assistance of counsel and the requirement that ineffectiveness be shown on the record may practically place much conduct out of judicial oversight. The standard leaves courts facing the unenviable task of deciding just how bad representation can be.

Brice v. Denton

135 S.W.3d 139 (Tex. Ct. App. 2004)

The issue in this case is whether an indigent parent who was proceeding pro se is denied effective assistance of counsel when an attorney ad litem is a) appointed on the day of a final hearing on the petition to terminate his parental rights, b) does not request a continuance, c) does not communicate with her client, and d) proceeds to trial. We hold that he was denied effective assistance of counsel.

Background

Lisa Denton filed suit to terminate the parental rights of Gene Brice, the biological father of their two children. Brice is currently an inmate of the Texas Department of Criminal Justice, Institutional Division. Brice filed a pro se answer opposing termination, along with a "Declaration of inability to pay costs." Eight days before the scheduled hearing, Denton sent Brice a letter informing him of the setting of a "final hearing" on the case. Brice, in prison, received this notice five days before the hearing and could not attend the hearing. The trial court appointed an attorney ad litem for Brice on the day of the final hearing.

Without consulting with Brice, the appointed attorney allowed the hearing to proceed. After hearing no evidence from Brice during the hearing except a perfunctory cross-examination of Denton by Brice's appointed attorney, the trial court found by clear and convincing evidence that Brice engaged in criminal conduct that resulted in his being "convicted or placed on community supervision" for violating section 22.021 of the Texas Penal Code. Further, the trial court found that termination of Brice's parental rights was in the best interest of the children. The court signed an order terminating Brice's parental rights. We granted an extension of time to file a notice of appeal, which Brice did.

On appeal, Brice… contends that the attorney appointed to represent him provided ineffective assistance of counsel during the hearing.… We will reverse the trial court's order and remand the cause for further proceedings.

Termination Cases—The Legal Standard

The termination of parental rights involves fundamental constitutional rights. Given this significance, involuntary-termination statutes must be strictly construed in favor of the parent.…

The Texas Supreme Court has held that "the statutory right to counsel in parental-rights termination cases embodies the right to effective counsel." Thus, when the trial court decided to appoint counsel to represent Brice, counsel's obligation to provide effective assistance arose.

In analyzing the effectiveness of counsel in the context of a termination of parental rights, we follow a two-pronged test that was set forth by the United States Supreme Court in *Strickland v. Washington*, to determine whether an attorney's representation was so inadequate as to be in violation of the Sixth Amendment right to effective assistance of counsel. *Strickland v. Washington,* 466 U.S. 668 (1984)). In order to show ineffectiveness of counsel in a termination-of-parental-rights case, the appellant must show that counsel's assistance fell below an objective standard of reasonableness and that counsel's deficient assistance, if any, prejudiced the defendant. We acknowledge that there is a "strong presumption that counsel's conduct falls within the wide range of reasonable professional assistance."

Ineffective Assistance of Counsel

Brice's fourth issue contends that the attorney appointed to represent him provided ineffective assistance of counsel during the termination hearing. The trial court appointed Brice's attorney ad litem on the day of the final hearing. Nothing in the record suggests that Brice's appointed counsel requested a continuance from the trial court. The appointed attorney had no opportunity to meet with or consult her client, who was in prison, and she apparently requested none. The record further shows that counsel's preparation for this hearing was to review Brice's "criminal history." Her presentation of evidence filled one and a half pages of the reporter's record of the final hearing and consisted of a cross-examination of Denton. During this cross-examination Brice's appointed counsel adduced evidence that Brice had been "arrested for numerous things including harassment and stalking and several indecency [sic] with a child and indecent exposure, DWI." Applying the first prong of the effectiveness-of-counsel test, we conclude that counsel's assistance in this case fell below an objective standard of reasonableness.

Next we must consider the question of whether counsel's deficient assistance in this case prejudiced Brice. For guidance we look again to Strickland, where the United States Supreme Court made it clear that although the burden upon the appellant is high, a criminal defendant "need not show that counsel's deficient conduct more likely than not altered the outcome in the case." *Strickland*, 455 U.S. at 693. In fact, "in every case the court should be concerned with whether, despite the strong presumption of reliability [of the trial's outcome], the result of the particular proceeding is unreliable because of a breakdown in the adversarial process that our system counts on to produce just results." *Id.* at 696, at 2069. In this case there was just such a breakdown in the adversarial process. Counsel took no opportunity to interview Brice, to request a writ of habeas corpus ad testificandum, to find and interview potential witnesses, to investigate the conviction that was the basis for termination, to request a jury, or to challenge the pleadings or the statute. Applying the second prong of the test, we believe that Brice was prejudiced by his counsel's deficient assistance. Accordingly, we hold that Brice was denied effective assistance of counsel. We therefore reverse the judgment and remand the cause for further proceedings.

dissent

Dissenting Opinion

Tom Gray, Chief Justice.

... I respectfully but strenuously dissent.

III. Effective Assistance of Counsel

Lastly, the majority clearly errs in holding that Brice establishes that his appointed attorney at litem did not render effective assistance of counsel at trial. The overriding obstacle to establishing ineffective assistance of counsel is the strong presumption that counsel rendered effective assistance, which can be overcome only by a record affirmatively demonstrating the contrary. The record certainly does not show that Brice's attorney ad litem did not render reasonably effective assistance. If the record showed, as the majority concludes, that Brice's attorney failed even to contact him, not to mention other alleged failings, then the circumstances in which we would not find that the attorney rendered deficient performance would be very few. But the record does not affirmatively establish counsel's actions or inaction, much less the reasons therefor. Moreover, the majority fails to undertake any significant prejudice analysis, a necessary part of the ineffective-assistance analysis.

III. A. Legal Background

The Texas Supreme Court has held that Texas's statutory right to an appointed attorney ad litem in suits for the termination of the parent-child relationship "embodies the right to effective counsel." That Court adopted as the standard for evaluating effective assistance in termination suits the standard established by the United States Supreme Court for criminal cases in *Strickland v. Washington,* 466 U.S. 668 (1984)....

The Strickland standard has two prongs: performance and prejudice.... Procedurally, the ineffective-assistance analysis rests on two principles: deference to trial counsel and respect for the record. First, "[j]udicial scrutiny of counsel's performance must be highly deferential." "[I]t is all too easy for a court, examining counsel's defense after it has proved unsuccessful, to conclude that a particular act or omission of counsel was unreasonable." For this reason,

> [a] fair assessment of attorney performance requires that every effort be made to eliminate the distorting effects of hindsight, to reconstruct the circumstances of counsel's challenged conduct, and to evaluate the conduct from counsel's perspective at the time. Because of the difficulties inherent in making the evaluation, a court must indulge a strong presumption that counsel's conduct falls within the wide range of reasonable professional assistance....

Strickland at 689. Otherwise, representation will be reduced to jumping through specific hoops to avoid being found ineffective, rather than effectively advocating the client's case. *Strickland* at 689–90.

The other procedural principle of the analysis is that the presumption of effective assistance can only be overcome by an affirmative record. The United States Supreme Court has recently reiterated the importance of an adequate record in ineffective-assistance cases. See *Massaro v. United States*, 538 U.S. 500 (2003). In order for ineffective-assistance claims to be evaluated fairly, the record must show what counsel's performance comprised, and the reasons for it. Otherwise,

> [i]f the alleged error is one of commission, the record may reflect the action taken by counsel but not the reasons for it. The appellate court may have no way of knowing whether a seemingly unusual or misguided action by counsel had a sound strategic motive or was taken because the counsel's alternatives were even worse. The trial record may contain no evidence of alleged errors of omission, much less the reasons underlying them.... Without additional factual development, moreover, an appellate court may not be able to ascertain whether the alleged error was prejudicial.

Id., 538 U.S. at— (internal citations omitted). Since the evidence offered at trial pertains to the issues of the cause of action on trial, and not to the assistance of counsel, "the resulting record in many cases will not disclose the facts necessary to decide either prong of the Strickland analysis." *Id.*

III. B. Application

The majority's analysis largely ignores the record requirement, and effectively ignores the prejudice prong entirely....

1. Performance

The very language of the majority opinion [regarding the performance prong of Strickland] demonstrates that the record does not support it. Phrases such as "[n]othing in the record suggests" and "[a]pparently" indicate that the majority has not observed the requirement that the allegations of ineffective assistance be firmly founded in the record. Rather, not finding support in the record for its findings, the majority speculates. But we cannot draw conclusions from a silent record or from the absence of a record....

The majority also states that "Brice's appointed counsel adduced evidence that Brice had been 'arrested for numerous things including harassment and stalking and several indecency [sic] with a child and indecent exposure, DWI.'" —S.W.3d at——, (slip op. at 5) (alteration in original). This is unequivocally false. Brice himself phrases his argument in these terms: that his attorney asked "questions that would be asked by [Denton's] counsel not by an attorney ad litem defending" Brice's case. In cross-examining Denton, Brice's attorney did thus summarize the evidence of Brice's course of criminal conduct that had come out on direct examination. Brice's attorney went on to elicit testimony that Brice's incarceration had caused his limited visitation with the children and his inability to support them, and that the children had not been the victims of some of Brice's criminal offenses. While this evidence only weakly supports Brice's case, such may have been the best that his attorney could do given the material with which she had to work. "Merely because counsel's trial strategy ultimately 'backfired,' does not render his performance deficient." *Graves v. State*, 994 S.W.2d 238, 249 (Tex. App. 1999).

The majority also notes that Brice's attorney's "presentation of evidence filled one and a half pages of the reporter's record of the final hearing and consisted of a cross-examination of Denton." —S.W.3d at——, (slip op. at 5). The majority concludes from this that counsel's representation was necessarily deficient. This fails to take into account the cursory nature of the trial, of which Brice does not complain. The Strickland analysis must take into account "all of the circumstances surrounding the case," including "the totality of the representation and the particular circumstances of each case,". In hearings on the termination of parental rights, the National Council of Juvenile and Family Court Judges recommends only that courts allocate sixty minutes. Nat'l Council Of Juv. & Family Court Judges, Resource Guidelines, Improving Court Practice in Child Abuse & Neglect Cases 98. In this case, Denton, who bore the burden of proof, completed her case in less than two and a half pages of the record. The attorney ad litem for the children presented her case in only four lines, without examining any witnesses at all. Under these circumstances, Brice does not show deficient performance.

Accordingly, Brice does not establish that his attorney ad litem rendered deficient performance.

2. Prejudice

Next, the majority does not undertake even a cursory analysis of the prejudice prong of the analysis....

It is well-established that the prejudice analysis is distinct and independent from the performance analysis, and that an ineffective-assistance holding requires findings of both deficient performance and prejudice resulting from that performance. "[I]neffectiveness claims alleging deficiency in attorney performance are subject to a general requirement that the defendant affirmatively prove prejudice." "An error by counsel, even if professionally unreasonable, does not warrant setting aside the judgment of a ... proceeding if the error had no effect on the judgment." *Strickland* at 691. The cases in which a party need not show prejudice from counsel's deficient performance are very few, and the conduct of Brice's counsel does not fall within them. Thus, the prejudice analysis cannot, as the majority does, merely state allegedly deficient performance, then add, "we believe that Brice was prejudiced by his counsel's deficient assistance." See —S.W.3d at——, (slip op. at 5). A court's mere belief, unsupported by law, precedent, or rationale, is worthless....

The majority does not suggest how, even if supported by the record, which they are not, these allegations would undermine confidence in the outcome of this trial. In light of the unchallenged evidence, this termination cause of action comes at least very close to being established as a matter of law. Brice argues only that his attorney might have prevented a judgment of termination by avoiding a finding that termination was in the best interest of the children. Brice does not argue that counsel could have defeated findings on Brice's convictions and imprisonment, the predicate acts alleged as grounds for termination. Indeed, Brice's convictions and imprisonment themselves are strongly probative that termination would be in the best interest of the children. Of course, an incarcerated parent is "unable to care for the child from prison." Evidence of a parent's criminal history may be probative of a parent's "pattern of conduct that is inimical to the very idea of child-rearing." It is probative on the emotional and physical danger to the child. It is also probative on the acts or omissions of the parent which may indicate that the parent-child relationship is improper. A parent's criminal conduct is most probative on the best interest of the child when it can be inferred from the conduct that the parent has directly endangered the safety of the child and when the conduct results in the parent's long imprisonment.

It is almost inconceivable that a rational finder of fact would not find that it was in the best interest of the children to terminate Brice's parental rights. The evidence introduced at trial was that Brice had been convicted of "molesting" his children and sentenced to thirty years' imprisonment, of which he had served about four years at the time of trial. Brice does not suggest that this is false. A defendant imprisoned on a thirty-year sentence for aggravated sexual assault of a child will not become eligible for parole for at least fifteen calendar years. Even after such a defendant becomes eligible for parole, it is doubtful that the parole board would recommend parole for a child abuser. The children were nearly ten years old at the time of the termination trial in 2001. It is, therefore, very unlikely that the children would ever even see Brice during the remainder of their childhood.

Under these circumstances, Brice's allegations of deficient performance by his attorney ad litem do not undermine confidence in the outcome of the trial. Accordingly, Brice does not show prejudice.

III. C. Conclusion

The record before us, in showing neither that Brice's attorney ad litem rendered deficient performance nor that Brice suffered prejudice from her performance, does not rebut the presumption that the attorney rendered effective assistance of counsel. Thus, I respectfully dissent from the sustaining of Brice's ineffective-assistance issue.

Questions

1. If the majority accurately characterizes the representation, did the attorney in this case violate the competency standards of the rules of professional conduct? If so, what more must she have done? How would you have approached this representation? Note that, while prevailing in this action in this case, Mr. Brice was less successful in a subsequent malpractice action against his attorneys, in which the court granted summary judgment in favor of the attorneys. *Brice v. Wilson*, No. 09-05-527 CV, 2006 Tex. App. LEXIS 9717 (2006).

2. The majority finds a deficient performance and appears to presume that the defendant was necessarily prejudiced by such limited representation. The dissent seems to suggest that, even if it agreed that there was proof of deficient performance, Brice could not prove prejudice because he almost certainly would have lost his defense in the termination case even with additional evidence, testimony, or legal argument. Which approach to the relationship between performance and prejudice is better? If a client has a seemingly hopeless case, does the quality of representation really matter? What other values are at stake besides insuring correct outcomes?
3. In a footnote to his dissent, Chief Justice Gray suggested that a right to effective assistance of counsel may not even exist in these cases. He noted that the Texas Court of Criminal Appeals distinguished a requirement of "competent counsel" from "counsel who provide competent representation" and held that the state's habeas statute required only the former. *Ex parte Graves*, 70 S.W.3d 103, 114 (Tex. Crim. App. 2002). ("The reference to "competent counsel' in [the statute] concerns habeas counsel's qualifications, experience, and abilities at the time of his appointment. All of these provisions concern the initial appointment of counsel and continuity of representation rather than the final product of representation.") What do you think of this approach to defining competency?
4. Suppose you had been appointed to represent Mr. Brice in the termination proceeding and had provided superior representation. Nonetheless, Mr. Brice lost and his parental rights were terminated. Now your client has asked that you file an appeal on his behalf. You sincerely believe that there is almost no possibility of his succeeding on appeal and would be hard pressed to discover any issues that you could even argue with a straight face on appeal. What should be your course of action?

   Note that, in the criminal context, attorneys are required to follow their clients' directions to file a notice of appeal even if the attorney believes the appeal is unlikely to be successful. *Roe v. Flores-Ortega*, 528 U.S. 470 (2000). Moreover, if the criminal defense attorney cannot find a basis for that appeal, the attorney is nonetheless required to review the record and file a brief discussing any issue that "might arguably support the appeal." *Anders v. California*, 386 U.S. 738, 744 (1967). Should such a procedure be required of attorneys appointed to represent parents in termination proceedings?

C. Communication — The Core Competency

Advising and representing individuals in planning and adjusting their family relationships requires excellent interpersonal communication skills. Often the most important and effective problem solving is not necessarily based on legal procedures and remedies, but on sound counseling and effective negotiation. The ethical duty to communicate with your client is a core duty, expressed in the Model Rules as the duty to "keep a client reasonably informed about the status of a matter" and "explain a matter to the extent reasonably necessary to permit the client to make informed decisions regarding the representation."[8]

We can learn from studies of doctor-patient communication how important this communication can be to client satisfaction and the risk of malpractice actions or disciplinary complaint.

> Lawsuits against primary care physicians were more likely when the physicians were less skilled in educating patients, when they did not encourage or facilitate patients' expressions of concerns or opinions, and when humor or laughter was minimal in physician-patient interactions. Visit length was 20 percent longer in the no-claims group. Nonverbal expressions of affect held the strongest predictive value of any variable ... [9]

What do we know about how lawyers counsel clients in family law cases? Empirical studies of client counseling sessions are limited, undoubtedly due to the ethical barriers to conducting such research with actual clients. Surveys of clients by bar associations provide other insights into how well attorneys are serving their clients' counseling needs. The available evidence leads to troubling conclusions. One of the leading researchers in this area has concluded that "interpersonally the lawyer-client relationship is deeply troubled. All too often lawyers are thought to be inattentive, unresponsive, insensitive, nonempathetic, uncooperative, and arrogant." [10]

What kinds of attorney practices help to improve this picture? One survey of divorced parents found three types of assistance most commonly reported as helpful:

---

8. Model Rules of Prof'l Conduct R. 1.4 (2009).

9. Kathleen A Zoppi & Ronald M. Epstein, *Interviewing in Medical Settings*, in Handbook of Interview Research: Context and Method 355, 372 (Jaber F. Gubrium & James A Holstein, eds., 2001).

10. W.L.F. Felstiner, *Professional Inattention: Origins and Consequences*, in The Human Face of Law 121, 124 (Keith Hawkins ed., 1997).

> First, they needed information and guidelines about what to expect from the legal process, and wanted their attorneys to serve as "interpreters" of the system's unfamiliar language and procedures. Second, parents appreciated when their attorneys were stabilizing factors in the divorce, helping them to maintain focus and a balanced perspective. Specifically, helpful attorneys encouraged parents to stay "realistic," "rational," "see various sides," and "minimize conflict." Third, clients indicated that attorneys provided emotional sustenance in the forms of calming and listening to them, and encouraging them to feel less helpless.[11]

In sum, communication skills involve the ability to listen to your clients, educate them about the legal process and their role in it, counsel them on available alternatives and likely outcomes, and provide emotional support.

1. Developing Listening Skills

When you picture a lawyer communicating, what do you see? For most people, the picture tends to be of a speaker—the incisive questions in cross examination, the compelling speech in closing argument, the careful statement of position in a negotiation, or the sage advice to a client. This picture is perhaps understandable, given the orientation toward speaking in our society. Even the ethics rules on communication tend to focus on the importance of providing the client information needed for decision making. Yet an even more critical and underdeveloped skill is that of listening. Before you can know what question to ask, what argument to advance, what advice to give, you must have information about the person to whom you are speaking. You must listen.

All listening requires a set of discrete skills: whether you are listening to clients, colleagues, adversaries, or decision-makers. Like any skill, however, you will learn only through sincere practice. Luckily, the legal community gives you plenty of opportunities to practice—there's always someone talking! Listening goes far beyond mere hearing. Hearing is a physical process; audition is a process of perception; but listening is a process of communication.

The first essential skill in listening is empathy. In order to listen effectively, you must want to truly know and understand what the speaker is saying; not what you think they should be saying. You must not be listening for your own

11. Marsha Kline Pruett, Tamara D. Jackson, *Legal Ethics: Some Current Issues in the Practice of Family Law, The Lawyer's Role During the Divorce Process: Perceptions of Parents, Their Young Children, & Their Attorneys*, 33 Fam. Law Q. 283, 294–95 (1999).

purposes—to refute, to persuade, or to critique. Rather, your purpose must be to understand the other person—their feelings and ideas from their own unique experience. This means you must set aside your own presuppositions about what the other person might or should be feeling and thinking (or what you personally would think or feel in the same circumstances).

This listening attitude can be a challenge in any circumstance. Some common circumstances make listening even more difficult. Suppose your speaker is someone who holds a belief or position with which you differ strongly. Likewise, imagine listening to someone whose life experiences are very different from your own. Sometimes, reaching across those barriers of ideology and culture can require an extraordinary mental and emotional effort. Yet, even when the speaker is someone with whom we believe we share culture and opinion, we must monitor our attitude. The more we share in common with our speakers, the more likely we are to assume that we know what they are saying or feeling. Yet these assumptions undermine our motivation to discover the ideas and emotions being expressed.

For an experienced attorney, one of the most significant barriers to effective listening is stereotyping of clients. It does not take long when practicing in a highly specialized field for your clients to all begin to sound the same. Assumptions about facts close off questions and inhibit effective listening.

Your motivation to adopt an empathetic, listening attitude can vary considerably depending on the context. Imagaine, for example, that you are listening to a colleague who is angry with you about your not having completed your part of a joint project. While listening is often one of the most effective ways to diffuse anger, the natural defensiveness of most people makes listening in these circumstances very, very difficult. There are a number of circumstances in which the speaker's frame of mind can interfere with one's ability to listen. Whether the speaker is a nervous lecturer or a person in position of authority providing critique, one must push past the barriers of distraction and defensiveness to reach for the underlying message.

Or suppose that the speaker is a guest lecturer in a class or CLE program, speaking about a dry and complicated case for which you have not read the background materials and about which you have no clear need to master the material. Sometimes the subject matter itself can provide a barrier to effective listening. If you find the subject to be complex, foreign, boring, or irrelevant, you are unlikely to desire full understanding.

Environmental conditions can be another barrier to listening. Suppose you are listening to someone who is in another office speaking to you through a speaker phone on a conference call with several other persons. (You are on a phone in your office). No matter how much you want to listen in these circumstances, that desire can be sapped by poor sound quality, lack of non-verbal content, and myriad distractions. (How often do you doodle or play computer games while you are on the phone?)

In contrast, consider the degree to which you are likely to maintain a listening attitude when you have gotten lost in a strange city, are late for an important appointment, and the speaker is a gas station attendant giving you directions to your destination. No matter what the barriers to communication in these circumstances—no matter how poorly the speaker communicates, how distracting the surroundings, how difficult the directions are to understand—your motivation in these circumstances is to understand. Think of how you will listen.

You will certainly listen physically and mentally. Your body will be turned toward the speaker, your eyes focused on him or on where he is pointing. You may repeat his gestures. You will have a strong desire to know, not only what this speaker is saying (how to get there) but what his perspective and attitudes are as well. (Does he really know where this place is? Is he likely to be giving me bad directions just to play games?) You will set aside your fear and frustration over getting lost so that you can get the directions you need.

You will listen actively. You won't be content to simply listen to the directions without checking. You won't interrupt unless necessary. You will encourage him to fill out his directions. You will ask questions if you don't understand and repeat the directions you were given to insure you have understood. You will use a tone and language that will insure you are communicating clearly and accurately.

So, you already know how to listen well. Effective listening requires a combination of physical circumstances (the ability to hear and understand the message, a clear source of communication, and silence) and listening attitudes (empathy, motivation to receive the message, respect, genuineness, and trust). The key is applying these same skills that you call out in an emergency listening situation to every important listening situation.

Sometimes passive listening alone is sufficient. You may be able to build rapport and gain information and perspectives simply by listening without any feedback. Many times, however, your listening must also communicate. You must restate, summarize, reflect, and interpret what you have heard in order to facilitate communication, diffuse emotions, translate content, or insure accuracy. These are the skills of active listening.

There are many components to effective active listening. Some are non-verbal and physical. The expression on your face, your degree of eye contact, your body posture, all either reinforce or undermine the message of "I'm listening and want to understand." You must provide your speaker your focused attention, accept the speaker's thoughts and feelings without judgment, and provide time to develop a full understanding of his experience and perspective. This is the response that will most encourage others to continue to speak.

Interrupting a speaker to change the subject violates all of these principles. Even some well-meaning minimal interruptions can interfere with listening. Responses that may help establish empathy, such as "I would have felt the same" or "I understand," while helpful in some contexts, nonetheless have the effect of shifting attention away from the speaker. In particular, judgmental responses—even positive judgments—may place the speaker in a defensive position. This doesn't mean you may never disagree with a client. Attorneys play critical roles in providing a "reality check" to clients with bad ideas — but reserving judgment is necessary to first hear out the idea.

Another common shift in attention occurs when a listener's first response is to give advice. Many listeners — especially lawyers—assume that a speaker, in relating a problem or situation, is asking that the speaker solve the problem or give advice. That assumption, however, may not be correct at all. The speaker may have already worked out a resolution or may not want to try to resolve the problem until his own understanding of the situation is clearer. In other words, they may simply want you to listen. Listening requires time—advice giving shortens listening time by moving to closure.

One of the best ways to encourage speakers and facilitate listening is to ask questions. In most circumstances, open-ended questions or prompts ("What happened?" "Tell me more") will best facilitate speaking. However, many new attorneys (and some experienced ones) find themselves conducting a "checklist" interview in which the only questions they ask are narrow questions to elicit very specific information. While this narrowing and gathering of specifics is vitally important to complete fact gathering, it is a very poor method of developing a complete picture, understanding the client's viewpoint, or building rapport.

The most difficult aspect of active listening may be providing the feedback loop. At least two messages are being sent when someone speaks: the factual content and the emotional message. To provide a complete feedback loop, the listener should paraphrase factual content and check perceived emotions.

To check your understanding of the ideas, information, or suggestions of others, state the speaker's idea in your own words or give an example that shows what you think the speaker is talking about. You need not agree with a client's view or perception, but you do need to let the client know that you understand what he or she is saying. You can sometimes clarify content by asking, "What do you mean?" A paraphrase improves communication by showing your present understanding and thus enables the person to clarify any misunderstandings.

To check your perception of the feelings of someone else, state what you perceive that person to be feeling. Effective active responses not only correctly identify the speaker's emotion, but also correctly identify the intensity of that emotion. If the speaker is "uncomfortable" that is a different feeling than "nervous"; an event may have troubled one person, but shocked another (similar feeling, but different intensity). Learn to develop a vocabulary of emotions to draw upon in reflecting a client's feelings. Gauging the intensity of those emotions requires listening to what is said and also considering the client's nonverbal messages (vocal tone, facial expression, body posture, etc.). Not every expressed emotion need be reflected; remember that the emotions that inform facts, perceptions, and decisions relevant to the current dispute are the ones you especially want to get right.

How one phrases a perception check can be particularly critical to maintaining rapport. When reflecting feelings, you should phrase your response in a form that reflects sincere listening. Your goal is to simply recognize and accept the emotion. Mere parroting of the client's exact language or trite phrases like "what I hear you saying is ..." often will sound phony and break down communication.

Likewise, reassurances that the client will "feel better" do little to recognize the immediate emotional state of the speaker. It is certainly a natural reaction to emotional statements to move to reassurance. Parents will rock a crying child and murmur "Shh, shh, shh" or "It'll be okay." However, consider that reassurance in a client interview can close off communication of emotion. Clients need to have an opportunity to express their emotions without being closed off by assurances that they will feel better or different at a later time. Be sure that your reassurances are not simply your own effort to close off an uncomfortable (for you) emotion. Reassurances have their place of course—reassuring the client that you will do your best to help or that a solution is possible—can be an important part of the closure in counseling a client. But do note that reassurances provide just that: closure. The best form for active listening responses simply reflects. ("You were frightened.") Even a clumsy but sincere attempt at recognizing a client's emotions is better than no attempt at all.

In summary, active listening requires a listening attitude and feedback loops to check content and emotion. How can you improve your own listening skills? Only through practice. Unfortunately, our society fills us with so much sound to "tune out," we must consciously work to "tune in" in order to improve our listening.

Practice Assignment

Try working with a friend. Tell them you want to practice your listening skills and ask them to talk to you about a particular subject. Practice the skills of: keeping silent, using open ended questions, focusing on the speaker, paraphrasing content, and reflecting emotion. Don't be surprised if these skills seem awkward at first. Remember the key to this skill starts with your attitude. If you maintain a sincere desire to understand the other person, that sincerity will overcome a host of errors of "technique." If you are simply trying to learn a "skill" in order to "win" or "persuade", you have missed the entire point.

2. Communication and the Role of Emotions

Clients must decide what they want from a representation and, to some extent, how to accomplish those objectives. The ethical obligation of attorneys is not only to respect the client's lawful choices, but also to insure that the client has been adequately informed in arriving at these decisions. So important is communication as an aspect of competence that the Model Rules set out the duty to communicate as a separate rule. Model Rule 4.1 emphasizes that "A lawyer shall explain a matter to the extent reasonably necessary to permit the client to make informed decisions regarding the representation." Even as to means by which you pursue your client's objectives, you have the duty to consult with the client. The AAML Bounds of Advocacy emphasize this duty of communication and, in particular note that when counseling clients on divorce, the attorney should discuss the emotional and economic impact of divorce and the possibility of reconciliation. Read AAML Standard 1.2 and AAML Standards 2.1 through 2.4 and their comments in Appendix A.

Surveys of family law clients indicate that attorneys are failing in this duty of consultation and communication more than any other. Clients feel that they are neither informed nor empowered by their attorneys. Some simple office procedures and habits of practice can go a long way toward improving communication. Have a policy to return phone calls within twenty-four hours and honor that policy. If you cannot return calls yourself, have an assistant return the calls and explain when you will be available. Copy your client on all correspondence and pleadings. Document all phone calls and meetings so the content of communications does not get lost or confused.

While practice management can reduce some complaints about communications, even attorneys who have a diligent communications policy may still find their clients unhappy with the attorney's communication.

Emotions make communication difficult. Clients in many situations of family representation are dealing with difficult emotions and are under significant stress. Many attorneys may consider these emotions irrelevant to the "legal issues" and discourage the client from expressing emotion or ignore those emotions when expressed. In their landmark research into client counseling in family law offices, Professors Austin Sarat and William Felstiner offer the following description of typical attorney reactions to client emotions:

> Because they regard the client's emotional agenda as volatile and dangerous, lawyers often avoid responding to clients' characterizations of their spouse or of some event during the marriage; they try to discourage the expression of emotion in or through the divorce and make a professional practice of being emotionally unresponsive to what are for many of their clients the central issues in the divorce. In this sense, "clients largely talk past their lawyers.' Lawyers seek to define or redefine the divorce dispute by focusing on the financial rather than emotional aspects of the dispute and by trying to get their clients to think about the future rather than the past.
>
> Consider, for instance, the following excerpt from a conference in Massachusetts between a woman and her male lawyer. The lawyer and client were talking about her future educational needs. The client responded by focusing not on the future but on the past, on her sense that her husband had discouraged her from pursuing her education and had emphasized her duties as a wife.
>
> CLIENT: There was harassment and verbal degradation. No interest at all in furthering my education. None whatsoever ... If there was ever any time when I did not need or want sex, I was subject to, you know, these long verbal whiplashings. Then the Bible would be put on the counter with passages underlined as to what a poor wife I was ...
>
> LAWYER: Mmm uh.
>
> CLIENT: There was ... what I was remembering the other day, and I had forgotten. When he undertook to lecturing me and I'd say, "I don't want to hear this. I don't have time right now." I could lock myself in the bathroom and he would break in. And I was just to listen, whether I wanted to or not. And he would lecture me for hours ... There was no escaping him, short of getting in the car and driving away. But then he would stand outside in the driveway and yell, anyhow. The man was not well.
>
> LAWYER: Okay. Now how about any courses you took.
>
> The lawyer simply ignores the client's characterization of her husband. Although his "okay" may seem out of place in response to what he has just been told, it is part of his determined effort to get the conversation back on track. His response is typical of the way lawyers respond

to clients' efforts to talk about the reasons for the divorce or at least to enlist a sympathetic response from their lawyers.[12]

What's the problem here? Aren't attorneys doing exactly what they are supposed to do if they help their client focus on the legally relevant information? Isn't that what is "reasonably necessary to permit the client to make informed decisions regarding the representation"? No it is not. Feelings are facts that are relevant to the client's informed decision-making.[13] To ignore fear, anger, anxiety, sadness, denial, or any other psychological states is to leave the client in a state that makes rational informed decision-making difficult if not impossible.

Extreme stress interferes with the client's ability to receive information. Simply put, if you are so distracted by the fear ringing in your ears, you literally cannot hear much of what someone is saying to you and are unlikely to remember accurately that which you did hear.

Stress and fear also interfere with the client's ability to make decisions. Consider the attorney who, in providing estate planning representation, raises the issue of the need for an advanced health care directive. Anticipating death is difficult emotionally for most clients, but for many it is even more difficult to anticipate incapacity. "The client can dismiss the suggestion of any need to discuss the area in question as being unnecessary, premature, or not applicable, at least not at the time. By touching such deep anxiety, the attorney's mere suggestion could provoke resistance, hostility, anger, and quick rejection."[14] You could try to ignore the underlying emotional and psychological state and simply leave a client's clear legal need unmet or you could simply bully one's way through the issue without addressing the client's anxiety directly. In either case, you have not helped your client to make an informed decision.

Rather, you must be sure that early on you specifically ask about and address your client's key concerns — even if those concerns aren't "legally relevant." You must learn how clients view their situation, how they feel about it, and what their values and goals are in going forward. The process of listening to the client's story, providing attention to and acceptance of the client's emotions, and helping the client sort out goals is a powerful service — sometimes it is all the client needs to empower them to address a situation. Often, it is the

12. Austin Sarat, *Lawyers and Clients: Putting Professional Service on the Agenda of Legal Education*, 41 J. Legal Educ. 43, 47 (1991).

13. Thomas L. Shaffer & James R. Elkins, Legal Interviewing and Counseling in a Nutshell 9 (2d ed. 1987).

14. Bruce J. Winick, *Legal Counseling About Advance Directive Instruments: Client Denial and Resistance in the Advance Directive Context: Reflections On How Attorneys Can Identify and Deal With a Psycholegal Soft Spot*, 4 Psych. Pub. Pol. and L. 901, 903 (Sept. 1998).

service that clients most desire. Moreover, sound counseling skills are not "extras" — they are fundamental skills that keep an attorney from becoming a discipline/malpractice statistic.

"But," you may object, "I'm not qualified to be a counselor. I might do more harm than good!" Indeed, you should know your limits and not attempt psychological therapy. Referral to or collaboration with a mental health professional may be in order for some clients. In some cases, attorneys may be professionally negligent if they fail to suggest counseling. For example, in *Boyd v. Garvert*, 9 P.3d 1161 (Colo. Ct. App. 2000), the Colorado Court of Appeals affirmed a verdict for professional negligence against an attorney who had represented a couple in relinquishing their child for adoption to a couple in Kansas. The couple claimed emotional distress damages based on the attorney's failure to advise them of counseling. The court noted that the attorney's duty arose both from the Colorado statutes that required relinquishment counseling and from a common law duty established by expert testimony that the reasonable and prudent attorney would advise counseling regardless of the statutory requirement.

While referral or collaboration may be necessary or useful, it does not relieve you of the independent obligation to communicate effectively — including the responsibility to address the client's issues from the client's perspective. Note this comment to Model Rule 2.1, the only rule of professional conduct addressing the role of attorney as counselor:

> Matters that go beyond strictly legal questions may also be in the domain of another profession. Family matters can involve problems within the professional competence of psychiatry, clinical psychology or social work; business matters can involve problems within the competence of the accounting profession or of financial specialists. Where consultation with a professional in another field is itself something a competent lawyer would recommend, the lawyer should make such a recommendation. At the same time, a lawyer's advice at its best often consists of recommending a course of action in the face of conflicting recommendations of experts.[15]

For family law attorneys who understand the need to address the client's emotion, there can be a danger in the other direction. Family law clients often rely on their attorneys for more than legal advice. They may look to their attorneys to be counselor, friend, or parent. Attorneys need to be aware of this dy-

---

15. ABA Model Rule 2.1, Comment 4 (2002).

namic, understand it, and learn to protect their own psychological and emotional health.

The duty to maintain your own emotional health is an implicit part of the basic notion of fitness to practice law. Indeed, Model Rule 1.16(a)(3) and its state counterparts provide that if a lawyer's "physical or mental condition materially impairs the lawyer's ability to represent the client;" he or she must withdraw from representation. Recognizing the prevalence of stress-related problems in the profession, every state sponsors a lawyer's assistance program to help attorneys suffering from substance abuse and other addictions as well as general stress management.

Burnout and compassion fatigue are very real risks for the family law practitioner. What can you do to protect yourself against the fallout of too much emotional connection with your clients?

Balance is one of the most critical skills for being able to maintain emotional competence in family practice. Balance your caseload: make sure that you have "happy outcome" cases as well as those involving tragic trauma. Work in collaborative settings when possible so that you can have peer support.

A critical protection for attorneys is setting appropriate boundaries; that is, maintaining appropriate professional relationships and keeping one's own personal interest separate from the client. Ethical guidance on this point is sparse. Conflicts of interest rules refer generally to situations in which an attorney's own personal interests may materially limit his or her ability to competently and diligently represent the client (Model Rule 1.7) and insist that an attorney maintain independent professional judgment (Model Rule 2.1). There are few explicit rules of professional conduct that address boundary failures. Extremes addressed by rules such as prohibitions on initiating a sexual relationship with a client (Model Rule 1.8(j)) or lending money to a litigation client (Model Rule 1.8(e)) address clear examples of becoming too personally involved in a client's life. But since the rules of professional conduct are primarily for the purposes of regulating that ethical misbehavior that threatens clients, the courts, or the public, there is little consideration given to crafting guidelines for attorneys to help protect their own psychological and emotional health.

Every attorney must establish clear boundaries with their clients, though where the lines are drawn may differ from attorney to attorney. These include structural boundaries of space and time (for example, not giving out home phone numbers or limiting locations where one will meet clients). Even more important, and more difficult to establish, are the permeable boundaries of the balance of emotional distance and connection. Even the clearest emotional boundaries may not protect you from emotional overload. The best practice to protect yourself emotionally is knowing yourself and having opportunities to reflect on how your practice is affecting you.

> One very important aspect of boundary setting is knowing how your own experience of family or personal history of trauma might impact your ability to represent certain clients. If an attorney finds connections between his own experiences and those of his clients, this may positively help him empathize and connect with the client. Yet these very commonalities may also present risks as the attorney may begin to see the client's situation too much through the lens of his own experience, overlooking or discounting aspects of the client's situation that differ from that of the attorney's. Further, if the attorney has a personal history of trauma, such commonalities also risk raising sensitive and unresolved issues on the part of the attorney that may interfere with competent client representation.
>
> Finally, attorneys must learn to take care of themselves. Certainly this is much easier said than done, and in the end is a very individualized process. Nonetheless, general parameters of self-care include finding a balance between work and life, finding creative outlets or spiritual practices that replenish the helping professional, and systematically monitoring one's own emotional and mental health. These are all critical aspects of the family law practitioner's program of competence. Attorneys have an increasing number of resources available to help address self-care issues. State lawyers' assistance programs, once accessed primarily by attorneys with alcohol and other substance abuse issues, are increasingly being asked to present programs and provide resources for all attorneys to maintain their fitness to practice. Within law schools, courses and programs to teach students how to maintain balance in the practice are gaining momentum. Clearly, the profession generally is recognizing that self-care is an important component of competent lawyering. In no other segment of the legal profession is that realization more critical to the health of the profession than in family law practice.[16]

---

16. Barbara Glesner Fines and Cathy Madsen, *Caring Too Little, Caring Too Much: Competence and the Family Law Attorney*, 75 UMKC L. Rev. 965, 997 (2007).

Reflective Journaling: Emotional Aspects of Legal Representation

Reflection is an important tool for improving your awareness of your client's emotions and your own. Practice reflection by writing down some thoughts in response to the following questions:

Who is your family? How is your experience of family likely to affect your representation of others?

How do you manage emotion? Are there some emotions that you find more threatening than others?

How do you manage stress? What are some of the best coping mechanisms you have found for balancing stress? What other mechanisms would you like to try?

Portfolio Problem: Policy Proposals

Given the materials you have studied, prepare one proposal that would improve the competence of family law attorneys. Be creative. For example, your proposal might:

- be addressed to state lawmakers, such as courts or legislatures, and recommend changes in the law;
- be addressed to professional organizations for programs or certifications;
- be addressed to law schools to recommend curriculum reforms; or
- be a business proposal for a service to be developed and marketed.

Please prepare only one proposal with some detail (in other words, a list of random ideas is not a proposal). At a minimum, your proposal should identify precisely the challenge to competency that your proposal is designed to address, describe the proposal in some detail, explain what would be necessary to implement the proposal, and project the impact of the proposal on the quality of representation of families.

To Learn More

Professional organizations dedicated to aspects of family representation provide excellent resources for improving competence in family representation. Some of these organizations include:

- American Bar Association Family Law Section *http://www.abanet.org/family/*
- American Bar Association Center on Children and the Law *http://www.abanet.org/child/*

- American Bar Association Children's Rights Litigation Committee *http://www.abanet.org/litigation/committees/childrights/*
- American Academy of Matrimonial Lawyers *http://www.aaml.org*
- Association of Family and Conciliation Courts *http://www.afccnet.org*
- National Council of Juvenile and Family Court Judges *http://www.ncjfcj.org/*
- National Association of Counsel for Children *http://www.nacchildlaw.org/*
- *American Academy of Adoption Attorneys* http://www.adoptionattorneys.org/
- *National Academy of Elder Law Attorneys* http://www.naela.org/
- National CASA (Court appointed Special Advocates) *http://www.nationalcasa.org/*

Chapter Three

Working with Other Professionals

Learning Objectives for This Chapter

After you have read this chapter and completed the assignments you should be able to:

- Explain the attorney's duty of supervision of non-lawyer professionals.
- Develop clear guidelines for the proper role of paralegals.
- Understand some of the ethical and philosophical differences in world-view of attorneys and mental health professionals.

A. Using Non-Lawyer Professionals

One way to lower the cost of family representation is to shift much of the legal representation to lower-cost technicians. For purposes of this discussion, this section will refer to these technicians as "paralegals" but the principles discussed apply to a wide range of non-lawyer assistants such as secretaries, document managers, investigators, or bookkeepers. If you structure your practice to include extensive use of these non-lawyer assistants, there are three basic guidelines you must follow: always remember that you, as the attorney, are ultimately responsible; make sure you delegate responsibility clearly and with adequate training to avoid violating ethical rules; and have policies in place to insure that everyone is aware of the limits of a non-lawyer's authority and responsibility.

1. Attorney Supervisory Responsibilities

Under the Model Rules, if a paralegal engages in conduct that, if performed by a lawyer would constitute a violation of the Rules of Professional Conduct, then the lawyer is responsible if the lawyer orders or ratifies the conduct. The lawyer also may be responsible for the paralegal's actions if the lawyer has "direct supervisory authority," knows of the conduct in time to remedy it, and fails to do so. If an attorney fail to exercise appropriate supervision, the attorney, rather than the paralegal, will suffer the legal repercussions, which can include procedural sanctions, suspensions, and even disbarment.[1]

A non-lawyer professional can create disciplinary and liability risks for an attorney in a wide array of circumstances. Paralegals can create an attorney-client relationship when a prospective client reasonably believes the paralegal has the authority to engage the attorney. Paralegals can violate rules governing solicitation of clients or fact investigation. Paralegals can breach duties of confidentiality, conflicts, competence and communication for which their attorneys will be held responsible. For example, a recent Virginia State Bar ethics opinion concluded that a lawyer has a duty of confidentiality that could raise conflict of interest issues when a prospective client calls the lawyer's office and speaks with a secretary even if the lawyer never talks with that person. Virginia State Bar Standing Comm. on Legal Ethics, Op. 1832 (May 10, 2007). Thus, attorneys must train support staff to avoid any actions or statement that would imply that they are able to commit the attorney to a representation. They should be trained to minimize confidential information obtained from prospective clients before a conflicts check is complete.[2]

It does little good for the attorney to say, "But I didn't know!" Even when you delegate tasks to non-lawyer assistants precisely because they are better at those tasks than you are, you have a duty to supervise their work. For example, consider *In re Williams*, 711 S.W.2d 518 (Mo. 1986). In that case, an attorney was disbarred for failing to make timely, accurate, and adequate accounting of funds to a client. The attorney sent his client a check for his award in a workmen's compensation claim. The bank dishonored the check several times and the client did not receive payment until after he filed a complaint with the bar committee. The attorney admitted the facts but claimed that the violation was unintentional. He explained that an employee was re-

---

1. *See, e.g.*, Spencer v. Steinman, 179 F.R.D. 484, 489 (E.D. Pa. 1998) (where paralegal issued subpoena duces tecum on non-parties without prior notice to defendant in violation of Fed. R. Civ. P. 45, the lawyer was sanctioned under Rule 11 for not "assuring himself that [the paralegal] had adequate training" and for his failure to "adequately supervise her once he assigned her the task of issuing subpoenas"); Matter of Disciplinary Action Against Nassif, 547 N.W.2d 541 (N.D. 1996) (disbarment for failure to properly supervise which resulted in the unauthorized practice of law by office paralegals).

2. A helpful resource for training paralegals is the Model Code of Professional Responsibility for Paralegals offered by The National Federation of Paralegals Associations (NFPA) http://www.paralegals.org/displaycommon.cfm?an=1&subarticlenbr=133.

sponsible for writing checks and balancing the trust account and he did not know that the account had insufficient funds. The court held that, while the attorney may not have known of the specific problems with the client's payment, he was well aware of prior problems with the account and knowingly and intentionally failed to correct the ongoing problems or supervise the account. Similarly, in *Attorney Grievance Commission of Maryland v. Hallmon*, 681 A.2d 510 (Md. 1996), the attorney's license was suspended for 90 days when, among other problems, the lawyer gave over all the responsibility for a case to a paralegal without supervising or reviewing the paralegal's work.

Interestingly, in both these cases, the attorney's paralegal was also his wife. That tells us something about the importance of not letting personal relationships interfere with professional duties to supervise. If you are partners or best friends with a non-lawyer assistant out of the office, you simply cannot carry that equal relationship into the office. While the paralegal/attorney relationship is a personal one in which the two must be able to communicate frankly and easily with one another and trust one another, it is not one of equality. It is often a good idea to have an "independent audit" of your relationship for just the kinds of lax supervision that can sometimes occur in long-term paralegal/attorney relationships.

2. Appropriate Delegation and Policies

Lawyer regulation permits attorneys to delegate administrative and secretarial tasks to non-lawyer assistants. However you may also want to delegate tasks that are legal in nature. Here you must be careful not to cross the line into assisting others in engaging in the unauthorized practice of law. Unfortunately, the line is less than clear. While the rules of professional conduct prohibit assisting in the unauthorized practice of law, one must look to case law and statutes to determine whether an activity is unauthorized legal practice.

The practice of law varies significantly among the states, with most defining the practice of law as essentially whatever lawyers do. While most states have statutes defining legal practice,[3] in most of these same states, it is the courts that have the ultimate authority to define the practice of law. Many of these courts simply define legal practice on a case-by-case basis, noting that "it is impossible to lay down an exhaustive definition of 'the practice of law.'"[4] Various states have regularly allowed non-attorneys to perform services that

3. The ABA Task Force on the Model Definition of the Practice of Law has collected these statutes at http://www.abanet.org/cpr/model-def/model_def_statutes.pdf.

4. State Bar v. Arizona Land Title & Trust Co., 366 P.2d 1, 8–9 (Ariz. 1961).

might be interpreted as falling within the field of legal practice, such as completing approved form real estate documents or selling generalized legal publications and "kits."[5] However, these exceptions arise primarily when the legal work is limited, provides little discretion or advice giving, and is ancillary to the non-lawyer's ordinary business.

The key factor most courts look for in identifying the practice of law is a situation in which the individual is exercising legal judgment and skill in advising individuals on their particular legal needs. Thus, representing clients in court, preparing legal documents, and advising individuals regarding legal matters are generally agreed to constitute the practice of law. What part, if any, of these tasks may be shared with a paralegal?

Some tasks are simply not delegable. The clearest and easiest is advocacy before a tribunal (unless a statute expressly authorizes lay representation). While a paralegal can assist in court or at a deposition by maintaining documents and exhibits and taking notes, a paralegal may not advocate or question.

More difficult issues arise when paralegals are dealing with clients and others. Paralegals may communicate administrative information (scheduling, for example) and may act as a conduit for clearly defined information and even advice from the attorney. Paralegals may not, however, give legal advice of their own or negotiate on a client's behalf. The problem is that, when a paralegal conveys a message containing legal advice from the attorney to the client, the client's perception may be that the advice is coming directly from the paralegal and may request more.

Your responsibility in this regard is two-fold: first, educating the client and second, training and supervising the paralegal.

First, you must help clients understand the paralegal's role in their case. Attorneys in family law practice often delegate the day-to-day communication with clients to paralegals. Sometimes clients simply want to have someone listen to their fears, frustrations, and hopes. An attorney is wise to encourage clients to engage professional counselors to assist them in crisis, but some clients still insist on "on call" counseling from their attorneys. Much of this "emotions management" work can be delegated to non-lawyer assistants. If you will be delegating communications duties to a paralegal, you should make clear to your clients, however, what the paralegal can and cannot do for them.

Second, as to the paralegal, no matter how much training is provided, you may not simply turn over cases to paralegals. For example, the Michigan court in *In re Pinkins*, 213 B.R. 818 (E.D. Mich. 1997), held that although lawyers

5. In Re Mid-America Living Trust Associates, Inc., 927 S.W.2d 855, 859 (Mo. 1996).

may delegate certain activities to non-lawyers, lawyers must have direct client contact; lack of direct contact "precludes proper delegation." Likewise, paralegals may never give legal advice, plan strategy, negotiate settlements, appear in a representative capacity in court, or make legal decisions. For example, the attorney in *In re Discipline of Laub*, No. 86322, 2002 Nev. LEXIS 113 (2002), was suspended from practice for six months for allowing a paralegal to conduct initial interviews with potential clients, to evaluate whether potential clients had a meritorious claim, to advise potential clients about the possibility of recovery, and to execute contingency fee agreements on behalf of the firm all without the attorney's involvement.

Among the tasks that you may delegate to properly trained paralegals are:

- researching legal matters;
- developing a form or system for a routine action, procedure, technique, service, or application;
- preparing and interpreting legal documents for your review;
- selecting, compiling, and using technical information;
- assisting the lawyer in court;
- handling administrative matters with the tribunal (e.g., scheduling matters); and
- handling will attestations and real estate closings.

Even with these tasks, remember that you must supervise the tasks. It may seem a waste of time to read every single document prepared by a paralegal before signing it, when that paralegal has prepared that same document dozens of times previously and is a highly competent and reliable paralegal, but supervision demands taking this simple, often neglected step in supervising the non-lawyer assistant.

Along with training on where the paralegal's role begins and ends, you must develop policies to insure that paralegals understand and comply with your key ethical duties to your clients. Make sure paralegals are adequately trained and delegation of tasks is appropriate to their ability and education. Provide standards and protocols for routine tasks such as research, case management, and document preparation. Insure that paralegals disclose their status as a paralegal in all communication (written or oral) with any other persons. Develop standards and protocols for communication with clients and others in the legal system. Limit non-lawyer receipt of and access to confidential information, especially in initial interviews or contacts. Insure that paralegals understand the attorney's ethical duties of confidentiality and, in terms of disclosure, develop a policy of "when in doubt, ask." Include paralegals in conflict checking and have appropriate screening mechanisms in place to protect against conflicts.

Having these policies and asking paralegals to read them is insufficient training. Regular reinforcement is necessary to maintain competence. This training should be grounded in the discrete problems that arise in your office. A medical model of "grand rounds" would be an effective training mechanism for insuring that policies are understood and kept current.

Portfolio Problem: Memo to the File

Assume that, as a new attorney, you have begun working in a family law office with two other attorneys and three paralegals. Stephanie, the paralegal with whom you will be working most closely, is the most senior of the paralegals. She had worked for the firm's founding attorney, who recently retired. She is highly trained and has much greater experience in the day-to-day operation of divorce practice in your jurisdiction than you do. Stephanie is gracious and helpful to you and takes direction from you without any indication that she resents being supervised by such an inexperienced attorney.

Recently, you agreed to represent a woman pro bono in a divorce and custody action against her husband. The woman was referred to you by the local domestic violence shelter, where she and her children are living after a horrific attack by her husband. After you had your initial conference and had obtained a restraining order on behalf of the client, you learn that your client is an immigrant and that her visa will soon be expiring. She is desperate to be able to remain in the United States, fearing she will lose custody of her children if she is deported. She is considering returning to her abusive partner so that she can petition for permanent resident alien status as the wife of a citizen.

You know nothing about immigration law but Stephanie assures you that she has completed "dozens" of immigration self-petitions on behalf of the firm's clients. She reassures you that she can prepare the necessary documentation and guide you through the process. You really would like to help this client but are unsure whether you can do so ethically.

Can you accept Stephanie's offer of assistance? Prepare a memorandum to the file in which you analyze your options and justify the course of action you decide to take.

B. Working with Mental Health Professionals

In many settings of family representation, the legal system must undertake tasks for which it is ill-suited: making predictions of how people will function in the future in a complex web of human relationships. Thus, lawyers and judges must collaborate with mental health professionals, whose strengths lie in viewing human problems from a systemic perspective with an eye to long-term and ongoing problem solving. Increasingly courts are incorporating interdisciplinary perspectives in their dispute resolution. These may include expert witnesses, child custody evaluators, non-lawyer mediators, parent educators, parenting coordinators, or mandatory counseling programs.

As a family law attorney — particularly in divorce and custody litigation — you should be aware of the enormous influence these other professionals can have on the process and outcome of cases and at least a rudimentary knowledge of the theories and viewpoints from which they proceed. The starting point is self-education. Divorce attorneys should know about the psychology of divorce and family systems and the developmental needs of children; attorneys serving children should understand basic principles of child psychology; attorneys helping elders and the infirm should be familiar with the basic literature on aging and death and dying.

In this section, we explore two significant hurdles in working with other professionals. First we will explore the structure of interdisciplinary cooperation and the ethical constraints on those structures. Second, we will examine some of fundamental differences in perspective that make interdisciplinary cooperation difficult.

1. Structures for Collaboration

A seemingly effective answer to improving collaboration and competence in family representation would be for attorneys to go beyond merely learning about other professionals and actually joining together with mental health professionals (and other allied professionals such as financial planners) in practice. However, the rules of professional conduct of most states prohibit sharing legal fees with non lawyers,[6] entering into law practice partnerships with non lawyers,[7] and practicing law in a firm in which a non lawyer owns a financial interest.[8] These rules are under pressure, however, as more attorneys seek to work in collaborative settings. A California State Bar report has outlined a number of structures for interdisciplinary practice that attorneys might use. Within the context of family representation, what ethical issues are raised by each of these models?

---

6. Model Rules of Prof'l Conduct R 5.4(a) (2009).
7. Model Rules of Prof'l Conduct R. 5.4(b) (2009).
8. Model Rules of Prof'l Conduct R. 5.4(d) (2009).

The Cooperative Model: This model involves the rendition of legal services on a "stand alone" basis in "cooperation" with other nonlawyer service providers ... Lawyers ... employ nonlawyer professionals under the lawyer's control to assist in providing legal services to clients. Lawyers are also free to work with nonlawyer professionals employed directly by clients. But the lawyers' services ultimately "stand alone" from all other services.

The Ancillary Business Model: This model permits a law firm to own and operate an ancillary business entity that renders nonlegal services to clients of the law firm and to others. The entities, however, operate on a non-integrated basis. Legal services are provided on a "stand alone" basis. ABA Model Rule 5.7 on ancillary services requires that recipients of the ancillary services understand that the ancillary business exists as an entity separate and distinct from the law firm....

The Contract (Strategic Alliance) Model: This model contemplates an express agreement between a law firm and a professional service firm setting forth various mutually beneficial terms. For example, the agreement might state that: (1) the law firm agrees to note its affiliation with the professional service firm on its law firm letterhead, business card, and other materials; (2) the law firm and the professional service firm will engage in mutual client referrals on a nonexclusive basis; or (3) the law firm agrees to purchase goods and services from the professional service firm such as equipment, communications technology, and staff management. This model, also called a "strategic alliance," like the above models, operates without fee-splitting and common equity interests. The legal services are provided on a "stand alone" basis....

The Command and Control Model: This model reflects the situation that currently exists in Washington, D.C., under its variation of ABA Model Rule 5.4. Lawyers are permitted to share law firm fees and equity interests with nonlawyers subject to specific limitations, including requirements that: (1) the activities of the firm be limited to the provision of legal services; (2) the involved nonlawyers agree to comply with the lawyers' rules of professional conduct; and (3) the lawyers, who are principals or who have management authority, take responsibility for the acts of the nonlawyers. Although fees and equity interests are shared with nonlawyers, all services are controlled by lawyers and relate directly to the rendition of legal services....

The Fully Integrated Model: This model is a single fully integrated professional services firm. The single firm has organizational components that provide legal services, consulting services, accounting services, and/or other professional services. It is marketed as a one-stop shopping center for clients interested in legal services and other professional services. The various services may be provided to a single client on a single matter or on multiple related or unrelated matters. Legal services may be provided independently of other services, and vice-versa, and may involve the lawyers seeking professional services for the client from the other professionals and vice-versa.... [Note that the Model Rules of Professional Conduct currently prohibit this form].[9]

2. Differences in Perspective

Not only do ethical rules provide constraints on collaboration with other professionals, differences in world view between other professionals and attorneys can create collaborative challenges. Consider the differences in training and perspective between mental health professionals and attorneys working in abuse and neglect matters summarized in this article:

Mary Kay Kisthardt
Working in the Best Interest of Children: Facilitating the Collaboration of Lawyers and Social Workers in Abuse and Neglect Cases

30 Rutgers Law Record (Spring 2006)[10]

A. Linguistic Differences

Lawyers and social workers not only view the world in different ways but also speak of it differently. One of the most significant barriers to effective collaboration between lawyers and social workers is this difference in language.

One example of the differing orientations of the professions is evidenced in the language related to services. Social workers use a "helping" language, while lawyers' language is one of "rights." The language of social work stresses interdependence and relationship; whereas the language of lawyers is focused on individualism and the vindication of individual positions.

The second and related problem is one of understanding what constitutes "evidence." Attorneys say, "Give me the facts." Social workers respond by pro-

9. State Bar Of California, Report and Findings on Multidisciplinary Practice (2001), *available at* http://calbar.ca.gov/calbar/pdfs/reports/2001_MDP-Report.pdf.

10. Reprinted with permission from Volume 30 Rutgers L. Rec. 1 2006.

viding information that includes inferences based on their past experiences. They are hurt and offended when attorneys discount these inferences because they consider it a discounting of their expertise. They believe that the judge should value their opinions when they state, "I just know that child is not safe, the parent has hurt him before, and I am sure he is doing so now."

....

A fourth complication arises concerning the idea of "protection" and the meaning of "risk of harm." The law requires that a child should remain in the home unless he cannot be protected there. Although all would agree that harm is difficult to predict, the acceptable risk of harm clearly differs among the lawyers as well as between social workers and lawyers. The most likely source of this difference in perception is a philosophical one based on a difference of opinion regarding the effect of alternative care. The idealists set the bar fairly low; if the parent has acted in a way that has harmed the child in the past and there is an indication that past behavior is re-occurring, the child should be removed. The focus is on avoiding any harm at the hands of a parent. At the other end of the spectrum are those who, while agreeing that the home may not be ideal ask the question "as compared to what?" They focus on what else is available to offer a child—safe foster homes or other types of alternative care? Even beyond that they ask, what are the emotional ramifications of taking a child from an environment that he has become accustomed to and may not perceive as dangerous?

Second, is the question of who will be to blame if a child remains in the home and suffers injury. In terms of exposure, it is far more likely that a judge's actions will be subject to scrutiny if he is does not remove a child who is subsequently injured than if the child is harmed by a separation from a parent. For this reason, judges are more likely to err on the side of safety. Judges are risk adverse; they are more likely to take risks if they will not know the outcome, and taking a child from a family is safer, with an outcome unknown rather than leave the child who then may be killed and the judge blamed. Social workers, on the other hand, are more likely to appreciate the risk of an improper removal. While these questions go beyond simple language barriers, the words that are used—"risk of harm," imminent danger"—are important for shaping the debate.

Finally, mental health professionals and attorneys view time differently as well. Lawyers are likely to view the situation presented as a "case" for which there needs to be a resolution. What attorneys know is a procedure whereby disputes are resolved by the application of objective criteria to a set of facts. From the attorney's point of view, the child abuse and neglect case is a time-limited representation of an individual client resulting in a judicial resolution.

For social workers the "case" is more about process than resolution. The social worker recognizes that the judicial resolution in these cases is just one piece of the process of working with these families. It is neither the beginning nor the end. Because social workers tend to view these cases as long term, they are more likely to focus on long term versus short term goals. The attorney, on the other hand, is more likely to focus on vindicating the client's rights, which usually results in a focus on short term as opposed to long-term goals....

Another reflection of the differences between the professions is the ethical codes that govern their actions. Social workers are sometimes frustrated because they misunderstand the ethical constraints of attorneys.

One of these constraints is in the identification of and loyalty to the client. For example, the attorneys who represent the child protection agency see themselves as corporate counsel. Their allegiance is to the agency, not to individual workers. Consequently, when there is a conflict between what would be good for the agency from a policy perspective and the actions of individual workers, the attorneys must promote the agency. This leaves individual workers feeling further abandoned by their own attorneys and often results in their turning elsewhere (to the court's attorneys and sometimes the guardians ad litem) for legal advice. This is likely to occur when policies are changed and individual workers disagree or when the agency makes treatment availability decisions based on fiscal policy and the worker nevertheless believes that the judge will order the service to be provided.

Perhaps the most fundamental difference between social workers and attorneys is in how they view the "client" child or family. While attorneys may have some difficulty in defining their role in the system, they are usually pretty clear about the identity of their client. The attorneys for the court represent the interests of the state in promoting the protection of children; the guardians ad litem are officers of the court whose job it is to identify and advocate for the best interests of the child; attorneys for a state agency represent that agency's interest and attorneys for parents represent the parents. All of these roles present the potential for a conflict of interest (the state fiscal interest versus an individual child's need for expensive care; the guardian's recommendation versus what the child wants; the state agency versus an individual worker; mom's interest versus dads). But lawyers are trained to look for the conflicts and resolve them in ways that most often lead to the advancement of a single client's interest.

Social workers, on the other hand will often identify the "client" as the "family," an entity that may include individuals with clearly conflicting legal positions. This is intensified by the law's mandate that whenever possible, children should be with their families. This orientation suggests that the family is to be protected as a unit and that individuals within the system should advance this goal.

The difference between social workers' and lawyers' orientations ultimately stems from drastically different ethical perspectives. Systems thinking underlie contemporary social work; holism, interactionism and interdependence characterize the philosophy of social work. Social workers view a child abuse and neglect case from a systems perspective. They understand that the problem is not with an identified "client" but with the family as a system. The law's emphasis on individual rights and responsibilities is inherently inconsistent with the social worker's family system's worldview. The law's devotion to single-minded and zealous advocacy for the client stands in stark contrast to the social worker's holistic view of acting in the best interests of the client broadly defined....

Another significant difference in ethical perspectives is the treatment of confidentiality. Attorneys are confounded and restrained by ethical rules that require the protection of confidentiality in a context where the judge needs information to ascertain the best interest of the child. The rules of evidence require a kind of strategizing and information hiding that would appear nonsensical outside of the adversarial context. A social worker's ethical duty is to gather and share the broadest range of facts to promote a stable, healthy family....

Lawyers and social workers also see their responsibility to their clients in different ways. Lawyers have an obligation to advance their client's interest. As long as those interests are within the limits of the law, the potential negative effect of those actions on the greater goals of society do not preclude the representation. On the other hand, the social workers Code of Ethics provides that while their primary responsibility is to promote the well being of the client, a social worker's responsibility to the larger society may supersede the loyalty owed to clients.

More particularly in terms of frames of reference, social workers and lawyers view conflict differently. Social workers most often engage in counseling, not conflict. "Counseling" has different connotations in law and social work. Although social workers recognize that conflict may be inevitable, they use strategies to avoid conflict. Adversarial actions are reserved for extreme situations. Lawyers on the other hand are much more comfortable with conflict, and are less likely to see it as a negative. Some commentators have suggested that those drawn to the law are left-brained, where as those drawn to social work possess a right-brained tendency....

The juvenile court systems around the country continue to struggle for a coherent paradigm by which to guide their system. The struggle between a rehabilitative, systems perspective from social work and a right's based, adversarial perspective from law continues. No matter how the courts continue to try to strike the right balance between rehabilitation and rights, and experiment with new options for resolving child abuse and neglect actions, the problems brought before these courts simply cannot be solved without the cooperation of both attorneys and social workers....

Ultimately, of course, the collaborative challenge cannot be met with laws, programs, or procedures, as it requires the willingness of each set of professionals to be open to the other's language, ethical perspectives and worldviews. While training is important, it will not get at the heart of the difficulty, which is misunderstandings and misperceptions resulting from a different world view. The key to success lies beyond one-time training programs to on-going conversation. Attorneys and social workers must talk and more importantly, listen to each other.

Portfolio Problem: Working with Other Professionals

Traditionally, law schools do a poor job of preparing attorneys to collaborate with other professionals. Where can you go to educate yourself about the basic psychological dynamics involved in the areas of family law in which you intend to practice? Research resources you might use in educating yourself on the fundamental content of other disciplines that you will need in practicing family law. Identify at least one allied professional in your community (psychologist, social worker, etc.) to whom you can turn for referral, collaboration, or education. Contact that individual and ask them about working with attorneys. What works well? What frustrates them? What would be the one thing they wish attorneys would understand?

To Learn More

In addition to the articles and web resources cited in this chapter, you may wish to consult the following web resources:

For more information on ethical use of paralegals in your practice, see The American Bar Association Model Guidelines for the Utilization of Paralegal Services, available at http://www.abanet.org/legalservices/paralegals/downloads/modelguidelines.pdf.

For ongoing education on developments in other professions that affect your legal practice, become involved with an interdisciplinary organization that addresses issues in your field of practice. For example, the Association of Family and Conciliation Courts provides resources and networking for attorneys, judges, and mental health professionals working with clients in family and juvenile court matters. See more at http://www.afccnet.org.

Chapter Four

Clients and Conflicts

Learning Objectives for This Chapter

After you have read this chapter and completed the assignments you should be able to:

- Identify situations in which there is a high risk of misunderstanding client identity and implement methods to reduce that risk.
- Apply the standards for current and former client conflicts of interest to common family representation situations.
- Identify the ambiguities inherent in representing an entity client.
- Identify the tensions in representing parents and determine your resolution of the more common dilemmas presented when your parent-client's interests conflict with those of their children.

A. Conflict of Interest Risks and Family Representation

Conflict of interest issues arise frequently in family representation. In her book, *Tangled Loyalties: Conflict of Interest in Legal Practice,* sociologist Susan P. Shapiro studied how attorneys in practice deal with conflicts of interest. She notes some of the reasons that conflicts in family representation are so common:

> Families pose conflicts of interest for their lawyers in at least three ways. First, ... family representations tend to snowball—they lurch from one legal problem to the next, rarely waiting for one to reach closure before another begins, respecting few boundaries, amassing new confidentialities, and frequently collecting different constellations or additional members of family networks with each revolution....
> This impetus for legal business to snowball through families comes from many sources. Clients develop trust in their lawyers. They have

entrusted their lawyers with their financial wherewithal, their dreams, vulnerabilities, or most embarrassing secrets and have not been betrayed, maybe even feel well served. Their lawyers know them, their histories, their business operations, and their values and preferences. Clients have paid to bring their attorneys up to speed and now hope to bank on this investment in future legal skirmishes or opportunities. Clients happily reuse these rare resources and willingly share them with members of their social networks in need (Curran 1977). And even if none of this is true, some legal problems are dire emergencies; when the call from the police awakens the CEO at two in the morning, there may be only one lawyer he knows to call.

Law firms nurture this networking phenomenon as well. Some eschew advertising or explicit marketing of their services and rely on referrals from current or former clients to stay in business. Large firms increasingly diversify to offer expertise in the areas to which corporate client snowballs typically roll, frequently establishing estate planning or matrimonial departments, for example, to meet the personal needs of many of the corporate officials with whom they work.

Second, these snowballs often produce confounding unit-of-analysis questions, in which some engagements pertain to a single family member, some to spouses, some to households, some to family businesses, some to children or siblings or cousins, some to heirs, and some crossing several generations. And the shoots of even relatively simple engagements for a single natural person—a grandfather's will whose tentacles reach across nuclear families and generations, for example—can grow, eventually becoming hopelessly entwined throughout the family tree.

Finally, law is especially invoked at times of or in planning for family transition—birth (e.g., adoption or estate planning), marriage (e.g., prenuptial agreements), divorce, remarriage, financial crisis (i.e., bankruptcy), retirement, incapacity, and death—the very points at which fault lines emerge and chasms develop as the interests and alliances of family members shift, clash, and reconfigure. But because of popular stereotypes of families as safe, loving, harmonious, nurturant havens, the festering disputes and grievances and the structurally irreconcilable interests are less likely to be recognized or acknowledged than in other organizational settings.[1]

---

1. Susan P. Shapiro, Tangled Loyalties: Conflict of Interest in Legal Practice 82–83 (2002).

As you can see, the nature of family practice presents significant risks of confusion and conflicts among our clients. In this chapter we will examine a number of examples of these problems. We begin with the unintentional conflicts that can arise from confusions regarding client identity. We will then look at some frequent situations of conflict of interest in various settings.

B. Identifying the Client

The classic model of the attorney-client relationship is one in which the attorney represents an individual client. Even when attorneys are representing a collective entity, such as a corporation, rules of professional conduct treat that client as though it has a single voice and interest to be served. Yet, what if the entity's sole purpose is to provide legal services to individuals? What if the individuals seeking your representation view themselves as an entity (e.g., "a family") and seek representation as such? What if you are representing an individual who needs or wants to communicate with you about the representation through a third person?

Sometimes, the family matters brought to attorneys are such that it is difficult to decide which interest, of the many individual interests in the family, the attorney actually represents. However, the failure to properly identify that interest can have distressing results. For example, estate planning attorneys have known for some time that, while the client is the individual planning a transfer of assets, if the attorney is negligent in the representation, she may be liable to the beneficiaries of that plan.[2] Similarly, in representing married individuals, courts have sometimes found that representation of one spouse necessitates some consideration of the interests of the other spouse. For example, the California appellate court held that when a husband and wife consult an attorney about a personal injury, the attorney who undertakes representation of the injured party also has a duty to inform that party's spouse of the potential cause of action for loss of consortium. The court dismissed arguments that this extension of the law would create an undue burden on the profession. "To the contrary, it will vindicate the reasonable expectation of persons who seek legal advice about their

2. Lucas v. Hamm, 364 P.2d 685 (Cal. 1961), *cert. denied,* 368 U.S. 987 (1962); Espinosa v. Sparber, Shevin, Rosen & Heilbronner, 612 So. 2d 1378, 1380 (Fla. 1993); Donahue v. Shughart, Thompson & Kilroy, P.C., 900 S.W.2d. 624 (Mo. 1995).

rights, the providing of which is the unique office of an attorney."[3] Case law such as this that extends your responsibility beyond your client is relatively unusual, but you must be alert to the unique situations in which this extended duty arises.

The more common risk for attorneys is found, not in ignoring interests other than their clients, but in extending the representation or disclosing information to individuals who are not clients. Attorneys who allow family members to sit in on conferences with their clients may jeopardize the attorney-client privilege. Attorneys may unintentionally create an attorney-client relationship with more than one member of the family and then find themselves in an irreconcilable conflict.

How do you know if someone is or is not your client? The answer to the question depends in part on why you are asking the question. Standards for determining the existence of an attorney-client relationship are found most clearly stated in malpractice case law. You have an attorney-client relationship if you expressly agree to represent someone (orally or in writing), or if the court appoints you to represent someone. However, an attorney can also acquire a client by actions alone. Under a contract theory of malpractice, an individual may be your client if she asks you for advice in your capacity as an attorney and you provide that advice and she reasonably relies on your advice. Under a tort theory of malpractice, an attorney-client relationship can be based on an attorney's advice given in circumstances in which the attorney could reasonably foresee harm to the client if the advice is negligently given.[4] As you saw in the previous chapter, an attorney-client relationship can be based on statements of an attorney's support staff as well. [5]

Note that it is advice, as opposed to general information about the law, that creates the relationship. A lawyer may answer a "general question about the law, for instance in a purely social setting, without a client-lawyer relationship arising."[6] Under both the tort and contract approaches to implied attorney-client relationships, the key element is reasonableness—without reasonably foreseeable harm or reasonable reliance, no attorney-client relationship will be implied for purposes of malpractice.

---

3. Meighan v. Shore, 40 Cal. Rptr. 2d 744 (Cal. Ct. App. 1995). *See also*, Jordan v. Lipsig, Sullivan, Mollen & Liapakis, P.C., 689 F. Supp. 192 (S.D.N.Y. 1988).

4. Togstad v. Vesely, Otto, Miller & Keefe, 291 N.W.2d 686 (Minn. 1986).

5. DeVaux v. American Home Assurance Co., 444 N.E.2d 355 (Mass. 1983) (an attorney's secretary's instructions to a prospective client may have been sufficient to justify the client's reliance upon the attorney to attend to the client's legal matter).

6. Restatement (Third) of the Law Governing Lawyers § 14 cmt. c (2000).

If the question is whether you must keep a secret, however, an even larger group of individuals might be considered your client. An attorney may indeed have a fiduciary duty to a "client" to preserve confidentiality even if the individual would not necessarily be considered a client for other purposes. "A fiduciary relationship may result because of the nature of the work performed and the circumstances under which confidential information is divulged."[7]

Moreover, the duty of confidentiality can impact conflicts analysis. Whenever you have confidential information and your duty to keep that information confidential would materially limit your ability to represent your new clients, you have a conflict of interest. For example, long before the adoption of Model Rule 1.18 regarding prospective clients, courts recognized that attorneys owed some duty of confidentiality to would-be clients.[*]

How do you limit the risk of an unintentional representation? Whenever you communicate with third parties and potential clients, be clear that you do not represent them. Let them know, in writing if there is a significant risk that they may not understand, that they are not your client, that you will not represent their interests, that you will not protect their confidences, that you will not avoid acting in ways contrary to their interests, and that they should seek the advice of an attorney. Of course, disclaimers are of little value if you subsequently act in a manner inconsistent with your statements.

Some representations present special problems of ambiguity in identifying the client. For example, if a fiduciary for an estate comes to you for representation, how do you know if you are representing the fiduciary individually or the estate? The answer will be found in the interest you are being asked to represent. If you are asked to advise the fiduciary about matters affecting the estate, you represent the fiduciary in his or her representative role. You represent the fiduciary individually when you are asked to advise the fiduciary regarding his or her own personal interests, such as compensation or personal liability, rather than those of the estate or beneficiaries.[8] In either case, you must make it clear to the fiduciary which interests you are representing and which interests you are not representing.

---

7. Westinghouse Elec. Corp. v. Kerr-McGee Corp., 580 F.2d 1311, 1320 (7th Cir. 1978).

* ABA Comm. on Ethics and Prof'l Responsibility, Formal Opinion 90-358 (1990) (Model Rule 1.6 covers information given to a lawyer by a potential client seeking legal representation even if the lawyer performs no legal work for the client and declines the representation).

8. American College of Trusts and Estates Counsel, Commentaries on the Model Rules of Professional Conduct, Commentary on MRPC 1.2 (1999) *available at* http://www.actec.org/pubInfoArk/comm/toc.html.

Likewise, when one person seeks representation for another client, an attorney may be confused about the identity and authority of the client. A family corporation may ask for representation of one of the family members in a matter arising out of the business. A romantic partner may seek out an attorney for his paramour's divorce. Increasingly, children will be seeking legal representation for their elder parents. How do you know whether you are jointly representing these individuals or whether one is simply financing the other's representation?

The question of client identity is one you need to resolve at the earliest possible time, not only so that you understand whose interests you are representing and to whom you owe duties, but also so that you can determine what authority the client may wish to delegate to you or others. [9] Suppose Father, who is your current client, asks you to prepare an irrevocable trust for Father's daughter, who will soon attain her majority. Daughter will be entitled to receive money from a custodianship that was established for her under the Uniform Transfers to Minors Act. Father would like you to establish an irrevocable trust for her into which to place these funds. Father has indicated that he would pay the cost of your services in connection with the preparation of the trust. Who is your client in this transaction?

The daughter is the client, as you are setting up the trust on her behalf. However, since Father is your current client in other matters, you should be sure you can represent both Father and Daughter without a conflict of interest. Moreover, you must follow the guidelines of Model Rule 1.8(f), which directs that an attorney may accept payment from third parties for representation but only if the client consents, the third parties understand that they have no right to receive information or to direct the representation, and the attorney's independent professional judgment is not compromised. Finally, you should not prepare the trust at the request of Father without meeting with Daughter personally.[10]

As you can see, in these and other situations in which third parties seek to involve themselves in the representation, the duty of communication is critical. Problems regarding influence of third parties in the representation are so common in family law representation that the American Academy of Matrimonial

9. Professionalism and Ethics Committee of the National Academy of Elder Law Attorneys, Aspirational Standards for The Practice of Elder Law With Commentaries 7 (2006), *available at* http://www.naela.org/pdffiles/AspirationalStandards.pdf.

10. This problem is based on example 1.8-1 of the American College of Trusts & Estates Counsel, Commentaries on the Model Rules of Professional Conduct: Third Edition (1999), *available at* http://www.actec.org/pubInfoArk/comm/toc.html.

Attorneys in its Bounds of Advocacy provides specific guidance on this issue. Read AAML Standard 2.6 and comments in Appendix A.

Questions for Discussion

1. You are an attorney in one of three domestic relations firms in your small town of Remote. Six months ago, you spoke on the phone with Justin Justshop, who was thinking of divorcing his wife. Justin indicated that he had not yet made up his mind about filing for divorce and that at this point he was just looking for an attorney. You told him you would be happy to set up an appointment to discuss the matter. Justin, however, insisted he be able to ask a couple of questions first.

   You ended up speaking with him for about 20 minutes, during which time he asked you a number of questions about your experience in divorce litigation. He told you he needed a really good lawyer because he had a large amount of property he held as part of his real estate business. His wife was unaware of his holdings, and he was concerned about whether it would be at risk in a divorce. You said, "Well, it certainly could be. You would be required to disclose your assets in the first set of interrogatories." Justin got very angry and began to raise his voice, saying: "Well, I won't do that. It's none of her business. I'll just make sure no one knows about it." You instruct the client that, under the circumstances, you will not represent him, thank him for his time, and hang up.

   Suppose Justin filed for divorce and his wife is represented by one of your close friends Amanda Attorney. You and Amanda are having lunch together one day and she is discussing the difficulties she is having in discovery in the Justshop divorce. She expresses some surprise at the limited assets Justin has disclosed in his answers to interrogatories but, since Mrs. Justshop agrees that this is an accurate inventory, she has decided not to investigate further.

   "Justin lies to his wife," you tell her.

   "How do you know?" she asks.

   "Just trust me," you answer, "dig deeper and you'll find more."

   Have you violated any ethical duties?

2. In divorce actions, it is not unheard of for clients to talk to several divorce attorneys simply to set up conflicts of interests so that their spouse will have limited options for representation. See AAML Standard 2.8 in Appendix A. If you know that a client has interviewed you solely for this reason, you have no duty of loyalty. The Restatement §15 cmt. c (2000) notes that "In

deciding whether to exercise discretion to require disqualification, a tribunal may consider whether the prospective client disclosed confidential information to the lawyer for the purpose of preventing the lawyer or the lawyer's firm from representing an adverse party rather than in a good-faith endeavor to determine whether to retain the lawyer." *See also*, *In re American Airlines, Inc.*, 972 F.2d 605, 613 (5th Cir. 1992); Va. Op. 1794 (June 30, 2004). The difficulty in relying on these rules is that of proving the client's intent to "set up" a conflict. How might you screen for this problem?

Portfolio Problem: Letters Clarifying the Relationship

In any case in which a third party might be confused about your relationship with them, Model Rule 4.3 requires that you clarify your role. Good practice dictates that you document that clarification. In some cases, a blunt and simple disclaimer is all that is required. For example, consider this letter, written by an attorney for the personal representative of an estate to one of the potential beneficiaries of the estate:

> Due to my role as the attorney for the personal representative of your mother's estate, I think any advice or information that I give you regarding your mother's estate would not be believed by you and would be a waste of your time and mine. I strongly suggest that you hire an attorney to represent your interest in this case.

Heutel v. Stumpf, 783 S.W.2d 421, 423 (Mo. App. 1989). The court in this case found this letter sufficient to insulate the attorney from duties toward the unrepresented daughter.

In other cases, you will need to provide much more detail and warning in order to properly document your relationship (or lack thereof) with an individual who might believe that you represent his or her interests. Try your hand at writing a letter clarifying your relationship in the following case:

You represent Harry Husband in a divorce. Harry is a partner in a formal partnership that conducts farming operations. His partner in the operation is his brother Bart, who handles most of the finances of the operation. Harry's wife Wendy has filed for divorce and appears to be trying to get as big a financial settlement out of the divorce as possible.

You have met with Harry and Bart to discuss the financing of the partnership. The farming partnership consists of 1,000 acres and substantial equipment. The brothers are in a 50/50 partnership. Supposing that the partnership assets are all marital, so that Wendy, based upon a normal equitable split, will stand to take 25% of the land and assets. This could be a substantial monetary figure in a buyout situation that could lead to the failure of the farming partnership or otherwise disrupt operations with a transfer of title of a significant portion of the land. Harry is upset and indecisive at this point but Bart goes out of his way to let you know what he thinks you should do. He wants as little of the partnership assets to be considered by the court as being marital assets or at least he wants as much of the property division as goes to Wendy to come first out of other marital assets. Bart appears to presume that, since the outcome of the divorce affects the partnership assets, you must certainly work for him. How will you handle this distraction? Write a letter to Harry and another to Bert that explains your perspective on the role each has in this divorce.

C. Conflicts of Interest Analysis

To understand conflicts of interests, you must recognize the various policies underlying these doctrines. In general, courts will be concerned about protecting your clients' reasonable expectation that you will devote yourself to their cases and provide undivided loyalty to their interests. Underlying the concern for loyalty is your fiduciary relationship with your clients. You have power over your client and that gives you the responsibility to safeguard the client's information, not use that information either to harm the client or to benefit yourself, and not dilute your motivation to act competently or diligently in pursuing your client's interests.

All of these policies make courts more likely to find conflicts of interest in family representation than, for example, in the representation of corporate clients. The clients in family representation tend to be less sophisticated, so consents may not be as reasonable in these representations. In some instances, clients may not even have the capacity to consent to a conflict. The information an attorney gains in representing family members ranges widely and often involves highly personal and sensitive matters. Thus, the concern for confidentiality that drives much of conflicts analysis is likely to apply even more strongly in family representation. For example, if a lawyer represents one spouse in a business transaction and thereby learns a lot of information about her assets, the lawyer may not thereafter represent the other spouse in a divorce proceeding, because the lawyer will have learned material confidential client information during the first representation.

There are countervailing policies that may cause courts to be less likely to disqualify attorneys for conflicts. One of the most significant is the price of applying conflicts rules broadly. In any given case, disqualification of an attorney for conflicts will likely cause a delay and impose additional costs on the client whose attorney is disqualified. Because of these consequences, courts are sensitive to the risk of abuse of disqualification motions. In areas of law in which access to justice remains an ongoing struggle, courts may be especially reluctant to disqualify attorneys for conflicts when there are few attorneys available to take their place.

To screen for conflicts of interest, begin by identifying the interests of a potential client. Then look for commonalities with current and past representations. Where you find an overlap, ask yourself whether the interests of the potential client are adverse to the interests of the current or past client. Adversity might be direct in the sense that serving the potential client's goals will defeat the goals for which you were retained by the other client. More often, conflicts arise a little less directly: representing one client may require you to jeopardize your confidentiality obligation to another client, or your sense of loyalty to one client may cause you to represent another client with less diligence or competence than you would otherwise. Sometimes a conflict doesn't currently exist, but you anticipate that one might arise depending on how the representations develop. You may not simply ignore these probable future conflicts, but must assess the likelihood they will develop and whether there are steps you can take to eliminate or reduce the probability. You will need to balance the probability of a future conflict arising and the seriousness of consequences should the conflict arise. Any future conflict that presents a substantial risk of adversity should be considered a current conflict.

Concluding that a conflict exists does not end your analysis of course. You may be able to obtain your clients' informed consent to proceed with the representation if you reasonably believe that the conflict will not interfere with your ability to represent the interests of both clients and the rules do not otherwise make the conflict non-consentable. Of course consent means "informed consent" and there may be situations in which, because of confidentiality duties or because of your client's ability to understand the nature of the conflict, you simply cannot provide enough information to secure informed consent. In some instances, you may want to propose a more limited scope of representation or other steps to reduce the risk of conflict as an additional reassurance to your client. Any consents to conflicts of interest should be in writing and should lay out the nature of the conflict and the risks and benefits of proceeding in the face of that conflict.

Even if your screening process does not identify a conflict, or your clients have consented to proceed in the face of a conflict, you should continually monitor your representations for changes that may create new conflicts.

Every attorney should have a system to identify conflicts of interest. A conflicts system begins with a database that describes the who, what, and when of every representation. The "who" list should include all clients, adverse parties, family members and additional parties and any critical witnesses (including mental health professionals) involved in any representation. Names of the client's employer or any businesses closely owned by the client should also be included. Each name should be cross referenced to an entry that describes the representation: the nature of the legal and factual issues involved and the time the representation began and ended. A conflicts system can be built on a billing system, but simply relying on billing records alone can allow some critical conflicts to slip through the cracks, especially where the person being billed and the person being represented are not the same. In a firm setting, attorneys must have a system for sharing this conflict identification system. Larger firms often have a partner or committee whose responsibility is managing conflicts identification.

As with any system, the key is to use the system. At the first contact by a potential client, and before obtaining any confidential information about the matter, you should obtain the same "who" information from the potential client that you have in your conflicts database. You may wish to explain to the potential client that a list of all the persons who might be involved in the matter allows you to check for disqualifying conflicts of interest before the client invests their time, money, and private information. These names can then be checked against the conflicts database. If that check reveals a conflict, you then can consider whether the conflict is one for which consent may be obtained or whether the conflict precludes representation. If you must decline the representation because of a conflict, you should send the client a non-acceptance letter. Since the fact that a conflict exists might itself require revealing confidential information, a non-acceptance letter need not say that the reason you are declining the representation is a conflict of interest. Instead, you may simply indicate that, while you would ordinarily be pleased to take on the representation, you are simply not in a position to do so at this time.

1. Conflicts and Prospective Clients

Even if you decline a representation, if you have gained enough confidential information, you may have placed yourself in a position in which you can be subsequently disqualified. Even brief consultations can be sufficient to create a conflict of interest if you do not take steps to limit your receipt of confidential information and document the scope of the information you have obtained. Model Rule 1.18(b) provides that you must keep confidential a prospective client's information that you received as a consequence of a consultation in the same way as if he or she were a former client. Moreover, Model Rule 1.18(c) applies conflict of interest analysis to these clients as well, prohibiting representation of a client "with interests materially adverse to those of a prospective client in the same or a substantially related matter if the lawyer received information from the prospective client that could be significantly harmful to that person in the matter." The rule does, however, allow another attorney in the firm to represent such a client if both the current client and the prospective client have provided written informed consent and the disqualified attorney has limited his exposure to disqualifying information and is screened from participation in the subsequent representation. Not all states have adopted Model Rule 1.18 and some have adopted the rule with variations, such as eliminating the provision for screening, so it is important to know your state's approach to this issue.

The importance of limiting the information you receive and documenting the extent of each potential client interview is illustrated by *In the Interest of Z.N.H.*, 280 S.W.3d 481 (Tex. Ct. App. 2009). In that case, Father and his second wife met with an attorney for an initial consultation in which they said that they discussed personal information regarding Father's ex-wife's desire to relocate with their child and then they decided not to retain the attorney's services. Six months later, the same attorney entered an appearance on behalf of the ex-wife in her motion to relocate. Father moved to disqualify the attorney based on his prior consultation. The attorney indicated that he did have a record that he had met with Father but did not recall any details of the meeting. Based on the attorney's reputation for ethical conduct and his assurance that he did not remember receiving any information from his meeting with Father, the trial court denied the disqualification. After a four-day trial, Father appealed and the case was reversed and remanded for a new trial based on the conflict of interest.[11]

If you are declining the representation because of insufficient expertise or resources, for example, you may want to document that reason. If you are declining because you do not believe the client has a strong case, explaining that conclusion in a disengagement letter is really providing a client with an opinion letter and you ordinarily would not want to do that, lest the client later

11. This same fact situation arises with alarming regularity. *See, e.g.*, Foulke v. Knuck, 784 P.2d 723 (Ariz. Ct. App. 1989)(attorney interviews husband as prospective client and then later represents wife in divorce); King v. King, 369 N.E.2d 1358 (Ill. Ct. App. 1977)(attorney disqualified from representing wife in a divorce proceeding based on her husband's thirty minute consultation with the attorney two years earlier regarding a divorce); Okla. Bar Assoc. v. Berry, 959 P.2d 975 (Okla. 1998)(attorney represented wife in first divorce; the couple then reconciled and remarried; attorney then represented husband in second divorce); Ky. Bar Assoc. v. Newcomer, 977 S.W.2d. 20 (Ky. 1998)(attorney interviewed wife as potential client but she was not able to afford his services; attorney then represented husband in the divorce and used wife's confidential information against her).

claim that they gave up a meritorious claim based on your advice. Likewise, explaining that you must decline the representation because of a conflict of interest may itself reveal another client's confidential information. Your letter should, however, direct that, if they continue to desire representation, they should seek out another attorney promptly as time limits might apply to their matter.

Practice Portfolio: Letters Clarifying the Relationship

Edit the following non-engagement letter. Explain the reasons for your changes.

January 3, 20XX
Mr. Norman Negative
100 South
City, State
RE: Non-Engagement Letter
Dear Mr. Negative:

Thank you for the opportunity to consult with you regarding your desire to relocate with your children and your concerns regarding the effect this would have on custody and child support. As we discussed, I will not be able to represent you on this matter because I have concluded that you will be unable to afford the difficult and extensive litigation that will likely result given your ex-spouse's current position on your desire to relocate. Moreover, given our prior representation of your ex-spouse regarding your child, we have a conflict of interest that requires our declining the representation.

We are returning the documents you provided to assist us in evaluating your matter, including the copy of your divorce judgment and parenting plan, the certified letter you had sent to your spouse notifying him of your desire to relocate, and his reply. I am sorry we are unable to assist you in this matter. Do feel free to contact other attorneys.

As we discussed, the $50.00 you provided our office covers the entire cost of our initial consultation. Thank you again for the opportunity to speak with you.
Sincerely,
FIRM NAME
Attorney Name

2. Conflicts and Concurrent Representation

Attorneys who represent family members often are faced with a request to represent more than one member of the family at the same time. Model Rule 1.7 provides that an attorney may not represent clients whose interests are "directly adverse" or where another's interest will "materially limit" the attorney's ability to provide competent and diligent representation to the client.

The rule specifically prohibits attorneys from representations in which one client is asserting a claim against another client. This type of conflict is not subject to a client's consent. This express prohibition is especially relevant to family law attorneys as married couples not often will ask one lawyer to represent both of them in "their" divorce. Joint representation is appealing to a couple in a relatively amiable divorce, as it substantially reduces the costs and may reduce the animosity that might otherwise develop in an adversarial setting. However, Model Rule 1.7(b)(3) prohibits representation involving "the assertion of a claim by one client against another client represented by the lawyer in the same litigation or other proceeding before a tribunal." This rule would appear to prohibit joint representation of spouses in a divorce, because no matter how amicable or settled the issues are, the divorce is still an adversary proceeding.[12] The AAML also suggests that this dual representation is never appropriate. See AAML Standard 3.1 and comments in Appendix A. An attorney who represents husband and wife in a situation of conflict may not only be subject to discipline but may face subsequent liability to one of the clients as well.[13]

In a few states, an attorney may represent husband and wife in uncontested divorces where there is no disagreement regarding the terms of the divorce. California case law, for example, permits attorneys to act as "scriveners" — drafting divorce settlements but giving no advice and resolving no disputes between the parties.[14] However, even in these states, attorney's choosing to

12. *See, e.g.*, Holmes v. Holmes, 248 N.E.2d 564, 570–71 (Ind. App. 1969)(joint representation of husband and wife impermissible in both negotiating agreements and in representing parties before the court); Lawyer Disciplinary Bd. v. Frame, 479 S.E. 2d 676 (W. Va. 1996)(attorney reprimanded for representing husband in divorce and also preparing answer for unrepresented wife to sign). *See generally*, Utah State Bar Ethics Advisory Op. Comm., Op. 05-03 (2005)(concluding that public policy dictates prohibition on dual representation even in uncontested divorces).

13. In Vinson v. Vinson, 588 S.E.2d 392 (Va. Ct. App. 2003), the trial court found that an attorney's retainer agreement in which the attorney identified both husband and wife as his client in a divorce "on its face" was a "gross conflict of interest." The appellate court affirmed the court's finding of liability in the husband's suit against the attorney.

14. Klemm v. Superior Court, 142 Cal. Rptr. 509 (Cal. Ct. App. 1979)(attorney represented the husband and wife in a uncontested dissolution proceeding after they agreed to waive support; court held that the same counsel may represent both husband and wife in an uncontested dissolution proceeding if the conflict of interest is potential, not actual, and the parties give an informed, intelligent consent in writing after full disclosure.) *See also*, *In re* Eltzroth, 679 P.2d 1369 (Or. Ct. App.1984) (lawyer may represent both parties in amicable divorce, but when property settlement they reach is obviously inequitable and based

represent both husband and wife are presenting themselves and their clients with considerable risk.[15] In terms of a any settlement reached, "the validity of any agreement negotiated without independent representation of each of the parties is vulnerable to easy attack as having been procured by misrepresentation, fraud, and overreaching."[16]

Other multiple representations in family law litigation are equally problematic. For example, representing both parties to a prenuptial agreement would be unwise because one of the factors for determining whether a prenuptial agreement is valid is whether each of the parties were represented by counsel. Thus, while joint representation is not a *per se* conflict, "[i]ndependent counsel for each party to a prenuptial agreement is strongly recommended because the interests of the parties to a prenuptial agreement are frequently adverse." *In re Marriage of Leathers*, P.2d 263, 266 (Ore. 1990). Likewise, the AAML suggests that it is never appropriate to represent a client in a divorce and, at the same time, represent an individual with whom that client is sexually involved. See AAML Standard 3.3 and comments in Appendix A.

Ordinarily one would not want to represent both parents in an abuse and neglect or termination of parental rights proceedings, though some courts have held that this multiple representation is not a *per se* conflict. For example, in *Arteaga v. Texas Department of Protective and Regulatory Services*, 924 S.W.2d 756 (Tex. Ct. App. 1996), the court held that the interests of a father in a parental-termination proceeding were not adverse to the mother's interests, where both parents contested the termination of their parental rights and there was no current custody dispute between them.[17] Nonetheless, as one commentator notes, these representations are very risky:

> Attorneys should rarely accept dual representation of mothers and fathers in child dependency proceedings in which only one of the parents is alleged to have abused their children because of the high potential for conflicts of interest. It is very common for the nonabusing parent

---

on inaccurate information, lawyer must withdraw from representing either of them and advise clients to retain separate lawyers). " *Id.*, at p. 901.

15. *See, e.g.*, *In re* Gamino, 753 N.W.2d 521 (Wisc. 2008)(Attorney suspended for dual representation of husband and wife in acting as "scrivener" for divorce and property settlement without informed consent and then appearing in court on behalf of husband only).

16. *Klemm*, at 514.

17. *See also*, Baker v. Marion County Office of Family & Children, 810 N.E.2d 1035 (Ind. 2004)(no conflict of interest in representing both parents in termination of parental rights proceeding).

> to appear supportive of the abusive parent at an initial client interview based on 1) a true belief that the abuse allegation is untrue 2) a sense of duty to one's spouse or lover even if the abuse has occurred 3) fear derived from threats by the abusive spouse; or 4) a fear that cooperation with the Department might lead to loss of the abusive spouse during a period of incarceration in the criminal case which might reduce the economic vitality of the family.[18]

Even if the parents consent to your representation of both of them in these cases, the likelihood of a conflict arising at a later time is significant if, for example, the state brings failure to protect charges against the non-abusive parent or that parent is forced to choose between losing a partner or a child.

In non-adversarial settings, such as estates or business planning, are there situations in which it would be preferable to undertake simultaneous representation of more than one client? What if a couple asks you to draft wills for them? The American College of Trusts and Estate Counsel Commentaries argues that: "In some instances the clients may actually be better served by such a representation, which can result in more economical and better coordinated estate plans prepared by counsel who has a better overall understanding of all of the relevant family and property considerations." [19] However these economies can be at the cost of significant conflicts if those risks are not addressed early in the representation.

If you do decide to represent more than one family member at the same time, you must make sure the clients understand whether this will be a separate or a joint representation. In a separate representation, even though you are representing the family members at the same time, each representation is separate, and neither client will have a right to receive information about the other client's matter. In a joint or common representation, you are representing the family members on the same matter. In joint representations, the clients waive the attorney-client privilege among themselves. They should understand this and consent to freely share information among themselves.

Thus, in representing husband and wife in drafting their wills, you may determine that a joint representation is more appropriate; whereas if you are drafting estate plans for two adult clients who happen to be parent and child

18. William Wesley Patton, Legal Ethics in Child Custody and Dependency Proceedings 16 (2006).

19. American College of Trusts and Estate Counsel, Commentaries on the Model Rules of Professional Conduct, Third Edition: Commentary to Rule 1.7 (1999).

and do not have shared assets or businesses, separate representation may be appropriate. As the National Academy of Elder Law Attorneys emphasizes, "The attorney should take reasonable steps to ensure that all the clients understand how different types of representation impose different duties on the attorney and different consequences for the clients. The more complex the situation, the more important a well-drafted engagement agreement becomes."[20] That engagement agreement should explain the benefits and risks of the multiple representation, the effects on confidentiality duties and privilege, and the risks that, should conflicts arise among the clients, you will be required to withdraw from the representation.

Are there other types of multiple representation that you should presume create conflicts of interest? Would it ever be appropriate to represent both the birth parents and adoptive parents in an adoption proceeding? Consider the following case:

In the Matter of the Adoption of Baby Boy Irons

235 Kan. 540, 684 P.2d 332 (Kan. 1984)

[In this appeal from an order of adoption, the baby's unwed, eighteen-year-old mother, Anjanette Irons, argued that her consent to the adoption was a product of undue influence. Her doctor, Dr. Alvin Silvers, had urged her to give up the baby for adoption and had recommended that she speak with his daughter Lori Klarfeld who was an attorney. The attorney met with the mother and explained the adoption process, but also said that she was not representing the mother. The mother signed a consent presented to her by the attorney in the hospital the morning of the child's birth.

When mother challenged the adoption a week later, the trial court found there was no evidence of undue influence by either Dr. Silvers or Attorney Klarfeld. Further, it found that the mother had failed to meet her burden of proof to show her consent to the adoption was not freely and voluntarily given.

On appeal, mother argued that the burden of proof regarding the voluntary nature of her consent should have shifted to the adoptive parents because of the presumption of undue influence raised by the doctor and lawyer's relationship with her. The majority and dissent both agreed that the trial court erred in placing the burden of proof on the mother, but disagreed regarding whether that error was sufficient to merit reversal.]

20. Professionalism and Ethics Committee of the National Academy of Elder Law Attorneys, Aspirational Standards for The Practice of Elder Law With Commentaries 11 (2006), *available at* http://www.naela.org/pdffiles/AspirationalStandards.pdf.

This court has held a presumption of undue influence is not raised and the burden of proof is not shifted by the mere fact that an individual occupies a confidential or fiduciary relation with another. Such a presumption is raised and the burden of proof shifted, however, when, in addition to the confidential relation, there exist suspicious circumstances.

The question then is whether there was sufficient proof, not only of the existence of a confidential relationship but also whether there was sufficient proof of suspicious circumstances surrounding ... Lori Klarfeld's position as an attorney in this situation ... to shift the burden of proof....

The relationship of Lori Klarfeld and Anjanette Irons is more complicated and requires careful scrutiny. It has been stated:

> The authority of an attorney begins with his retainer; but the relation of attorney and client is not dependent on the payment of a fee, nor is a formal contract necessary to create this relationship. The contract may be implied from conduct of the parties. The employment is sufficiently established when it is shown that the advice and assistance of the attorney are sought and received in matters pertinent to his profession.

7 Am. Jur. 2d, Attorneys at Law § 118, pp. 187–88....

As previously indicated, Ms. Klarfeld was contacted by Anjanette Irons at the suggestion of Dr. Silvers for the specific purpose of discussing the legal aspects of adoption. They met in Dr. Silvers' office on March 10, 1982. Anjanette was merely eighteen years of age and was not represented by other counsel. At the meeting, attorney Klarfeld advised Ms. Irons about adoption. She also told Ms. Irons she was not her attorney but was attorney for the adoptive parents. As it turned out, Klarfeld did not have a client. A couple had previously discussed adoption with her, but when she contacted them about adopting Ms. Irons' baby they advised Ms. Klarfeld they had already adopted a child. Anjanette Irons and Lori Klarfeld subsequently had a telephone conversation and one additional meeting about the adoption. The second meeting was in the hospital, a few hours after the birth of the baby on April 22. Ms. Klarfeld had been notified by her father that Ms. Irons had given birth. Ms. Klarfeld prepared a consent to adoption and a waiver of notice and brought them to the hospital for Anjanette's signature. At this time, Anjanette was still not represented by other counsel. In the meantime, Ms. Klarfeld had been employed by the adoptive parents, Bruce and Susan Lieberman. Ms. Klarfeld explained the content of the consent and waiver to Ms. Irons. Ms. Irons then signed the documents.

Taking into consideration all the circumstances of this case—Anjanette's age, her lack of experience and her contacts with Ms. Klarfeld—we find an attorney-client relationship existed between them. The only reason Anjanette contacted Ms. Klarfeld was to seek legal advice. In adoption cases, such as this, the attorney can represent both the natural and adoptive parents. The attorney owes both sets of parents a duty to provide good faith advice concerning the legal consequences of their acts. This multiple representation can continue so long as no conflict develops between the parties. However, if a conflict occurs, the attorney must choose which conflicting interest he or she will represent. The best way to apprise the parties of the choice is by use of a frank discussion before representation commences, as was done by Ms. Klarfeld. Since Lori Klarfeld's relationship with Anjanette Irons was confidential, she owed Anjanette the duty of complete legal advice concerning the nature and consequences of adoption.

As previously noted, in order to shift the burden of proof away from the appellant, it is not enough that the confidential relationship alone is proven. Suspicious circumstances must also be shown to exist. In this case, the mere existence of the family relationship between appellant's doctor and attorney was suspicious enough to require the burden of proof to shift. The trial court, therefore, erred in ruling the burden of proof was upon appellant, Anjanette Irons. The separate question is whether this error warrants reversal. We have often held if the judgment of the trial court is correct it is to be upheld even though the court may have relied upon a wrong ground or assigned an erroneous reason for its decision....

[The court then analyzes whether the outcome would have been different had appellant not had the burden of proof and concludes:]

Even though we have the utmost sympathy for the anguish of Anjanette Irons, we have no hesitation in holding appellees sustained their burden of proof. This was a trial to the court. The parties introduced all the evidence they had. The order of events did not affect the result since the court had available to it all the evidence, virtually all of which was uncontested. Thus, the resolution of this controversy was primarily that of weighing the evidence. We think the answer is clear and accordingly hold that Anjanette Irons freely, knowingly and voluntarily gave her consent to the adoption of Baby Boy Irons.

The judgment of the trial court is affirmed.

Schroeder, C.J., dissenting:

In my opinion, due to the involvement of Lori Silvers Klarfeld and Dr. Alvin Silvers, the appellees failed to sustain the burden of proof cast upon them to show the consent of Anjanette Irons, the appellant, was freely and voluntarily given.

[The trial court's] conclusions of law ... establish the appellant was a person subject to influence. Clearly she relied on the advice of her doctor and attorney. The appellant was seventeen years old when she began going to Dr. Silvers for prenatal care and had been eighteen for only two months when the child was born. She did not live at home with her mother, but instead lived with a girlfriend until about a month before the birth. She did not discuss the options available to her or receive independent advice from her mother, close friends, social workers or counselors. At the time of the birth she no longer had a job and had no means of support other than welfare. Such circumstances would present a very difficult, stressful situation for any unwed mother, but particularly for a teenager with no support, emotional or financial, from her family or other sources. Unquestionably the appellant was susceptible to the suggestion and advice of her doctor and attorney....

Dr. Silvers' personal interest in influencing the appellant was established by his own testimony at trial. He testified he has an interest in furthering his daughter's career and assumes if he can supply her with a baby for adoption she will profit from it. Although Dr. Silvers professed concern at trial for the welfare of his patients and their unborn children, it becomes evident when viewing all the evidence presented that his primary concern was not for Anjanette's personal happiness or to ensure that adoption was truly her choice, but to impose his personal beliefs concerning the welfare of unwed mothers and their children upon his patients and to assist in furthering his daughter's career, if possible, by supplying her with babies for adoption.

A conclusion of undue influence is inescapable when one views the circumstances surrounding Anjanette's signing of the consent form in the hospital. It is undisputed that Dr. Silvers instructed the hospital staff not to let anyone see the baby until Anjanette had seen "the lawyer." Dr. Silvers testified he knows a mother is more likely to sign a consent to adopt if she hasn't seen the baby. Without consulting Anjanette or being asked by her to do so, Dr. Silvers telephoned his daughter shortly after the baby was born and advised her of the birth. Uninvited by the appellant, Lori Klarfeld appeared in Anjanette's hospital room, with the consent documents in hand, less than six hours after Anjanette, an unwed eighteen-year-old, had delivered her first child. Anjanette had not yet had an opportunity to visit with any member of her family. She had been informed she could not see the baby because it was a ward of the court. She testified she believed that by signing the consent form she would be allowed to see her baby. Although she knew she was signing a consent for her baby to be adopted, she did not understand it was irreversible. The following testimony of Lori Klarfeld reflects the manner in which the legal ramifications and irrevocable nature of the consent document were explained to Anjanette:

Q. Did you tell her that when she signed that consent that she had irrevocably and irretrievably given up the right to her child?

A. I'm not sure I expressed it that way. That she would be signing a consent and that was —
Q. You told her she was signing a consent to adopt, right?
A. Yes.
Q. Did you explain to her that the statute of this state requires that in the event she should change her mind for any reason whatsoever that the only way she could upset that signed consent was to be able to establish that the consent was not freely and voluntarily given, did you explain that to her?
A. I doubt that I used those terms, no. But I'm sure that I told her her consent was irrevocable. I doubt I used that particular term.
Q. You didn't explain to her what the statute would require her to do in case she wanted to change this consent?
A. No, because there was no suggestion that she wanted to change her consent.
Q. So you didn't feel it was necessary to explain to her what the statute was because you weren't representing her?
A. I explained to her she was signing a consent to an adoption and it was a final proceeding or that her signature was final. I did not say the statute says this or that it was irrevocable, in those terms, no....
Q. And you assumed she understood this was an irrevocable act?
A. Yes.
Q. And you assumed that she understood what the law was in that regard?
A. We didn't talk about the law per se.
Q. Don't you feel that when you talk to her as you did, under the circumstances you did, being referred to her by your father, meeting with her in your father's office, that you owed an obligation to explain the full extent and purport of the law?
A. I explained to Anjanette that I represented the adopting couple and if she had any problem about working with me she could get another lawyer....
Q. Well, you didn't explain what the law said about what it took to set aside a consent, you didn't explain that to her?
A. There wasn't any question about her setting aside a consent.
Q. Okay. But you didn't explain it to her, did you?
A. No.

These facts, taken together, constitute nothing less than coercion and duress on the part of Dr. Silvers and Lori Silvers Klarfeld when the appellant was in a position where she was extremely vulnerable, both emotionally and physically. This type of behavior on the part of a patient's doctor and lawyer should not be approved merely because the patient succumbs to their influence....

From the totality of the attendant circumstances involved in this case it can only be concluded that Anjanette Irons' consent to adopt was not freely and voluntarily given, but was obtained as the direct result of undue influence exerted over her, by Dr. Silvers and his daughter, Lori Klarfeld, prior to and after the delivery....

Concerning the interest of Lori Klarfeld in this case, who stood to benefit most from this transaction, the record discloses these additional facts. Ms. Klarfeld testified her fee for an adoption (to be paid by the adoptive parents) is $1,000 for approximately the first sixteen hours of work she does on the case, and an hourly wage for each additional hour of work required. Ms. Klarfeld has continued to represent the prospective parents throughout this litigation and on appeal even though she was a principal witness in the litigation on the issue of undue influence. Although John C. Amorosa entered his appearance as attorney for the appellees five days after the appellant's defenses to the adoption were filed, Lori Klarfeld has continued to sign her name as attorney for the appellees on various documents found in the court file, entered her appearance as their attorney along with Mr. Amorosa at trial, and has signed motions as attorney for the appellees concerning this appeal filed with the Clerk of the Appellate Courts. Ms. Klarfeld testified Mr. Amorosa is not her law partner but they share the same law office and some legal work. Their practice is referred to as "the law offices of Amorosa and Klarfeld" on the depositions of the witnesses included in the record on appeal. Ms. Klarfeld's conduct in this case is in direct violation of DR 5-102(A) which requires an attorney to withdraw from the case when it becomes obvious he or she or a lawyer in his or her firm will be called to testify concerning contested matters.... It became obvious in this case that Klarfeld would be called as a witness as soon as the appellant's defenses were filed. Klarfeld's failure to withdraw and her continued active participation in the case only serve to emphasize her financial interest in the case, as well as her lack of objectivity or concern for Anjanette Irons. It is also questionable whether it was proper for Mr. Amorosa to accept employment on behalf of the appellees in view of his close legal association with Lori Klarfeld.

It is respectfully submitted the judgment of the trial court should be reversed and the child returned to the appellant, his natural mother.

Questions

1. The majority opinion here states that an attorney may represent both adoptive and birth parents but must withdraw if a conflict develops. Subsequent cases from the same court reiterated the position that there is no per se conflict in representing multiple parties in adoption proceedings. *In re Adoption of Baby Girl H.*, 739 P.2d 1, 3 (Kan. Ct. App. 1987)

(birth mother attempted to revoke consent, alleging that conflict of interest existed when her attorney represented her, her doctor, and potential adoptive couple. Court held that the mere fact of express dual representation was insufficient to void consent.) Do you agree with this position?

Consider the position of the American Bar Association's Informal Ethics Opinion on simultaneous representation of adoptive and biological parents in private adoption proceeding. That opinion stated that the biological parent's right to revoke consent places these parents in conflict with the adoptive parents and that these "inherent conflicts cannot be reconciled." ABA Comm. on Ethics and Prof'l Responsibility, Informal Op. 87-1523 (1987). How would you feel about representing both the biological parent and his or her spouse in a step-parent adoption proceeding?

2. The court found that attorney Lori Klarfeld had an attorney-client relationship with Anjanette Irons. Yet the attorney had told Ms. Irons that she did not represent her and told her to secure her own representation. What more could the attorney have done to prevent the inference of an attorney-client relationship?
3. How important is the fact that Ms. Irons was young, vulnerable, and unable to afford independent counsel? If she had been a sophisticated adult who could have, but chose not to, secure independent counsel, do you think the court would have implied an attorney-client relationship as readily? One lesson you might take away from this case is that, as much as possible, you should avoid communicating with birth parents when you are representing adoptive parents and certainly never provide the birth parent with any information other than the recommendation to get an attorney. But where does that leave birth parents like Ms. Irons?

   Consider Alabama's Rules of Professional Conduct, Rule 1.8(k) (2008):

   > In no event shall a lawyer represent both parties in a divorce or domestic relations proceeding, or in matters involving custody of children, alimony or child support, whether or not contested. In an uncontested proceeding of this nature a lawyer may have contact with the non-represented party and shall be deemed to have compiled with this prohibition if the non-represented party knowingly executes a document that is filed in such proceeding acknowledging:
   >
   > (1) that the lawyer does not and cannot appear or serve as the lawyer for the non-represented party;

> (2) that the lawyer represents only the client and will use the lawyer's best efforts to protect the client's best interests;
> (3) that the non-represented party has the right to employ counsel of the party's own choosing and has been advised that it may be in the party's best interest to do so; and
> (4) that having been advised of the foregoing, the non-represented party has requested the lawyer to prepare an answer and waiver under which the cause may be submitted without notice and such other pleadings and agreements as may be appropriate.

Whose interest is this rule protecting?

4. How important is the fact that the doctor was the attorney's parent? If Ms. Klarfeld had simply been an adoption attorney without any personal relationship or financial ties to Ms. Iron's doctor, would her subsequent actions have been less problematic? What lessons can you draw from this case about the risks of setting up referral networks with other professionals?
5. In addition to the conflict that arises from trying to counsel the birth parent on whether to consent while also representing the adoptive parents, the dissent noted the additional conflict that arises when that consent comes into question. In this case, as might be true in many cases in which only one attorney is involved, Ms. Klarfeld was the principal witness on the question of undue influence. The dissent commented that, because of this, the attorney should have withdrawn under the rules of professional conduct. However, the current Model Rule 3.7 does not strictly require withdrawal but provides only that "A lawyer shall not act as advocate at a trial in which the lawyer is likely to be a necessary witness ..." That rule is designed to prevent confusion that would come from an attorney acting as both witness and advocate in a trial. Does this rule carry as much weight in cases like adoptions given that, like many family law matters, these actions are commonly heard by the court without a jury? Note that, even if the court does not disqualify an attorney or prohibit his or her testimony, the attorney may nonetheless be subject to discipline. *See, e.g., State ex rel. Neb. State Bar Association v. Neumeister*, 449 N.W.2d 17 (Neb. 1989)(lawyer suspended for representing long-time friend in action to have guardian and conservator appointed when it was obvious that the lawyer would be called upon to testify at trial).
6. Attorneys may choose to act as mediators to assist parties in resolving disputes such as divorce or contested adoptions. As Chapter Nine explores, the role of mediator is quite distinct from the role of attorney. As a general rule, an attorney who acts as a mediator may not thereafter

draft an agreement for the parties or represent the parties in court.[21] However, what prevents an attorney-mediator from memorializing the agreement arrived-at in mediation for the parties to use in securing a divorce? Notice that Standard VI(e) of the standards of Practice for Lawyer Mediators in Family Disputes (Appendix C) approves a mediator providing a written summary of the parties' agreement, but also suggest that the mediator should advise the parties to obtain legal advice regarding that agreement. The Illinois Bar has suggested that an attorney-mediator may never draft agreements and divorce papers for the parties to file as pro se litigants as this crosses the line from mediation into joint representation. Illinois State Bar Ass'n Comm. on Professional Ethics, Op. 04-03 (April 2005). Utah State Bar Ethics Advisory Op. Comm., Op. 05-03 (5/6/05), agrees that a mediator may not act as a scrivener for both parties but, in a divided opinion, the majority went on to suggest that under limited circumstances a lawyer-mediator may represent one of the spouses in securing the divorce following mediation. What are the risks these authorities are weighing when considering the mediator-scrivener role?

Portfolio Problem: Agreements Concerning Joint Representation

Failure to clarify the respective roles and obligations in a multiple representation can place you in a no-win ethical situation. For example, in *A v. B*, 726 A.2d 924 (N.J. 1999), a law firm had drafted wills for Husband and Wife, each leaving their entire estate to the other. Soon thereafter, the firm was retained by a woman to bring a paternity action against Husband for the child he had fathered while married to Wife. Because of a clerical error in entering Husband's name in the firm's records, the firm did not recognize the conflict. When they did, they withdrew from the paternity action and told Husband that he should reveal the existence of this child to Wife, as the child could inherit her property if she predeceased her husband. However the Husband refused.

Consider the position the firm was in at this point. On the one hand, what they had learned about the child was confidential information that may not be disclosed. On the other hand, without this information, Wife's estate plan

---

21. David N. Hofstein, *Ethical Guidelines for Attorney-Mediators: Are Attorneys Bound by Ethical Codes for Lawyers When Acting as Mediators?*, 14 J. Am. Acad. Matrimonial Law. 267, 319–320 (1997).

was based on information that was incomplete at best and fraudulent at worst. The law firm's retainer letter had explained that information provided by one spouse could become available to the other, but did not contain an express waiver of confidentiality. Withdrawal couldn't cure the dilemma as the wills had already been drafted. How would you resolve this dilemma?

In this case, the firm told Husband that if he did not tell Wife about the child, they would. Husband obtained an injunction to prevent the firm from revealing the information. On appeal, the New Jersey Supreme Court concluded that the husband had "used the law firm's services to defraud his wife in the preparation of her estate" and permitted the disclosure. New Jersey's Rules of Professional Conduct allows attorneys to reveal information relating to the representation to rectify a fraud resulting in substantial financial harm to another where the lawyer's services were used to perpetrate that fraud. Not all states have such an exception, however.

Draft provisions of a retainer agreement that, had it been used in this case, would have more readily defeated the Husband's initial request for an injunction.

3. Conflicts and Former Clients

In family representation, an attorney may be asked to represent one family member at one time and another family member at a later time. Conflicts of interest based on former client representation are judged by a more lenient standard than that of current client conflicts. Model Rule 1.9 provides that a conflict of interest exists if the current client and former client are directly adverse and the two representations involve the "same or substantially related matter." Once a substantial relationship is shown to exist between the initial matter and the subsequent matter, an irrebuttable presumption arises that confidential information was disclosed.

The purpose behind the former client rule is to protect clients from an attorney's later use of their confidences against them. Thus, in family representations, even apparently unrelated legal representations may be found to be the same or substantially related matters because of the broad scope of private information attorneys often necessarily obtain from clients in family representation. For example, suppose an attorney had represented wife in a divorce action. Wife has now filed for bankruptcy and wants to discharge some of the debts that were allocated to her in the divorce. An attorney who had worked on her divorce action now is in a firm that seeks to represent the husband in contesting the discharge in the bankruptcy action. May attorneys in the firm represent the husband in the bankruptcy action? Here is how one federal trial court analyzed this issue:

> Under the relevant considerations, the issue here is whether the bankruptcy case is substantially related to the dissolution of marriage case. It is a close call. If [Husband] were seeking to modify the terms of the divorce decree, then it seems clear that the matters are substantially related and that a potential conflict exists. However, the issues in the bankruptcy court, concerning [Husband's] allegations of erroneous information in the schedules and the non-dischargeability of the debt, appear to be premised on the four corners of the decree and therefore less likely to be subject to the threat that confidential information obtained by [Wife's former attorney] in the course of the divorce proceedings would be used against the debtor now.
>
> Nevertheless, the decision of whether to disqualify rests in the sound discretion of the court and is subject to particularly strict judicial scrutiny. Doubts should be resolved in favor of disqualification. While [Husband] asserts that matters arising in the bankruptcy case are not the same or substantially related to the dissolution of marriage case, I disagree. The only reason [Husband] is involved in the bankruptcy case is because of the obligations placed upon [Wife] by the decree of dissolution of marriage. Part of the basis for the motion to dismiss is that [Wife] has erroneously listed the monthly amount of certain obligations arising from the dissolution of marriage decree. The only reason [Husband] has filed an adversary proceeding in this bankruptcy case is so that he can litigate the dischargeability of certain obligations arising from the dissolution of marriage decree.
>
> In other words, everything about [Husband's] interest in this bankruptcy case concerns the dissolution of marriage case. The litigation in the bankruptcy court concerns matters arising from the dissolution of marriage decree. The standards governing attorney conduct require disqualification of [attorney] and his firm from representing [Husband] in the bankruptcy case.[22]

Notice that the court here disqualified the attorney even though it concluded that there was little risk of confidential information being disclosed. There is, perhaps, a higher concern for loyalty in family representations than might influence conflicts decisions than in other representational settings. When the conflict is based on the current representation of children and prior represen-

---

22. *In re* Kennedy, 2008 Bankr. LEXIS 1108 (D. Neb. 2008).

tation of other family members, however, "courts appear reluctant to draw the conclusion that the interests of the new and old clients are adverse."[23]

Questions

Consider how the policies regarding former client conflicts would apply in the following cases:

1. Ten years ago, you met with Husband and Wife to discuss the preparation of their wills. Both sought advice as to how they wanted their property to be distributed in the event of their death. Thereafter, the parties returned to your office and eventually they signed wills you prepared in compliance with their instructions. Now Husband would like you to represent him in a divorce action against Wife. May you? What additional facts would you like to have to make this decision? *Gray v. Gray*, No. E2001-02470-COA-R3-CV, 2002 Tenn. App. LEXIS 675 (Tenn. Ct. App. 2002).
2. Husband and Wife hire you to work as mediator to help them resolve the child custody/co-parenting, child support and property issues involved in obtaining a divorce. Working with a team of experts, you assist Husband and Wife in reaching an agreement satisfactory to all parties. The agreement sets forth that Husband and Wife will have joint custody/co-parenting privileges as to their children. At the final hearing to obtain approval of the divorce and agreement, Husband and Wife appeared pro se. The Court refused to approve the stipulation giving sole custody to Wife. Husband would now like to retain your services to appeal this decision. May you? *Barbour v. Barbour*, 505 A.2d 1217 (Vt. 1986).
3. Suppose you represented Father in a termination of parental rights proceeding in which he consented to the termination of his rights. The state has now proceeded against Mother to terminate her parental rights to these same children. May you represent Mother? What facts would you want to have to make this decision? *Arteaga v. Texas Department of Protective & Regulatory Services*, 924 S.W.2d 756 (Tex. Ct. App. 1996).

---

23. *Look for Seven Guidelines Through Law Governing Former-Client Conflicts*, 18 Law. Man. Prof. Conduct 490 (August 14, 2002). *See, e.g.*, Fiddelman v. Redmon, 623 A.2d 1064 (Conn. App. Ct. 1993) (representation of children in dissolution proceedings was not adverse to prior representation of officer assigned to conduct custody study; both officer and lawyer were assigned to protect children's best interests); Adoption of Erica, 686 N.E.2d 967 (Mass. 1997) (interests of child's maternal grandfather in proceeding to dispense with need for mother's consent to adoption of child were not necessarily adverse to interests of child).

4. Ten years ago, you drafted a will and an antenuptial agreement for Husband, in which Wife waived her statutory elective share to Husband's estate. Husband recently passed away and you have been hired by the estate to probate the will and defend against Wife's challenge to the will. See *In re Van Zandt*, 117 A.D.2d 812, 499 N.Y.S.2d 434 (N.Y. App. Div. 1986); *Casler v. Casler*, 2007 Ohio 5862 (Ohio App. 2007).

Portfolio Problem: Consent to Conflicts

Many conflicts can be resolved by obtaining a client's informed consent to the conflict. States vary in terms of their requirements for written consent, but good practice dictates that both the disclosures of the risks and benefits of consenting to the conflict and the consent itself should be in writing. However, never assume that a writing alone is sufficient. You also should be sure to have a conversation with the client or former client who is consenting to a conflict to be sure they understand the decision they are making.

Practice writing a conflict waiver letter in a situation in which husband and wife have come to you to represent them in a stepparent adoption. You will be given an opportunity to role play the initial consultation with the couple. You will play the role of Husband, Wife, or Attorney. After your initial consultation, write a letter that:

- identifies the nature of the conflict (or risk of conflict)
- identifies the harms that could result from the conflict and the steps you have taken to reduce those risks
- identifies the reasons the client wants to waive the conflict (the benefits of the representation)
- advises the client that they can seek other representation
- expressly waives the conflict
- identifies any circumstances in which you would seek to withdraw even given the client's consent
- addresses any confidentiality waivers that might be a part of this consent to conflict

For examples of letters consenting to conflicts, see Frievogal on Conflicts at http://www.freivogelonconflicts.com/ (click on consents/waivers).

3. Conflicts When Practicing in Agencies

Many family law attorneys practice in organizational settings — as attorneys for a government agency or a private organization. When is the attorney representing the family members served by these organizations and when is the attorney representing the organization? If the attorney is representing family members, what is the proper role and relationship with the entity that is making that representation possible?

In most government agencies, attorneys represent the agency, not the individuals whom the agency may serve. This is clearest in criminal enforcement, where most people understand that a prosecutor does not represent a crime victim as his or her client, but rather is serving the public as a whole, with the victim only a witness. So, for example, in *Whitmer v. Sullivent*, 373 Ark. 327 (2008), the Arkansas Supreme Court held that an attorney who is also prosecutor need not be disqualified from representing a father in custody modification at the same time that the prosecutor's offices is bringing criminal charges against the mother's current spouse. The court there reasoned:

> This is also not a case of dual representation requiring disqualification. [In prior decisions] this court explained that an attorney may not sue and defend the same client at the same time.... [However, here the attorney] was acting as [Father's] attorney when the custody suit was filed against [Mother]. Then, when the criminal charges were brought against [Mother's new husband], [the attorney] was acting as a representative of the people of the district. Therefore, [the attorney] was not "defending" [Mother's] interests while he was also "suing" her ... [24]

In other government settings, the public's understanding of the government attorney's role may not be as clear. Consider attorneys employed by the state to assist parents in establishing, enforcing or modifying child support orders. The parent seeking assistance in these cases is very likely to view the child support enforcement attorney as his own attorney. Although the attorney is being paid by the agency, the attorney is bringing an action on the parent's behalf, in the parent's name, and is receiving confidential information from the parent to further that representation. The arrangement is analogous to the relationship between attorneys for insurers and the insured they represent. In that setting, all courts hold that there exists an attorney-client relationship between the recipient of the legal services (the insured) and the attorney providing those services. Moreover, attorneys in child support actions speak on behalf of parents to some extent. Because attorneys ordinarily may not speak on behalf of persons they do not represent, it seems only logical that the recipient parent should be considered a client.

---

24. *Whitmer*, 373 Ark. 327 at 332.

The problems posed by the conclusion that parents are the clients of the child support agency attorneys are the same as those faced by attorneys employed by any third party who significantly controls the terms of the representation. In the past, this confusion regarding client identity led to myriad problems for child support enforcement agencies. Like many government funded legal services, resources were often inadequate to provide consistently competent and diligent representation. Parents did not have the right to control the objectives of representation or even to simply terminate the action. Attorneys in the same office might find themselves representing a custodial parent seeking past due support, the state seeking that same support as reimbursement for government assistance extended to the parent, and the non-custodial parent seeking an adjustment of support. Former client conflicts would be especially common, as custody changed between parents or as one parent would seek support and the other modification.

States have taken a legislative path out of this ethical thicket. Nearly all state statutes expressly disclaim an attorney-client relationship with parents or children or define the relationship as one in which the enforcement attorney represents the state or enforcement agency alone. The majority of states avoid the conflicts of interests in representation of parents by including negative language that precludes any attorney-client privilege between the agency attorney and the parents.

Identification of the state or agency as the attorney's client has practical as well as ethical implications. For example, the child support enforcement attorney cannot give advice to the custodial parent on custody matters. If the individual parent is not a client, there is no conflict of interest when the former support obligor subsequently becomes the custodian/recipient and applies for the same services previously furnished to the other parent. There are no privileged communications with the parent, including conversations involving welfare fraud. The state agency attorney should not accept service of process on behalf of the custodial parent, nor should the attorney attempt to bind the custodial parent in settlement negotiations without the custodial parent's consent and approval.[25]

Even though the state is the client, this does not mean that the child support enforcement attorney has no duty to the parents they are assisting. Recall that Model Rule 4.3 requires an attorney dealing with an unrepresented person to clarify their role. Consider that, before a custodial parent speaks with the attorney, she may have worked with a child support enforcement caseworker for some time. The client may, then, already have a firm understanding of her relationship with the agency and the attorney. If a client discloses

25. United States Office of Child Support Enforcement, Essentials for Attorneys in Child Support Enforcement, Chapter 4 (1999).

confidential information to an attorney under the mistaken assumption that the attorney is representing her, the attorney may have a fiduciary duty to that individual, regardless of what the state statute says.

Regardless of whether agency attorneys are considered to have represented the individuals they serve, once those attorneys leave public employment, they face a very stringent standard for conflicts of interest regarding their former employment. Under Model Rule 1.10 former government attorneys are prohibited from representing clients in matters in which the attorney had participated "personally and substantially" in the previous position. That rule allows a firm to avoid the imputation of conflicts of interest if the former government attorney is screened from participation in the related matters.

In a dramatic example of the application of this rule, the Iowa Supreme Court held that the Youth Law Center (YLC), an organization that represented children in delinquency and dependency actions, was properly disqualified from hundreds of cases because its new executive director had previously worked as an intake officer in the county attorney's office. The executive director Martha Johnson had worked as an intake attorney in child dependency cases for one year before leaving, during which time over 1,000 petitions were filed. Ms. Johnson prepared applications to remove children from their homes, drafted and signed petitions, and sometimes represented the state at removal hearings. In late 2002, Johnson resigned and became executive director of YLC. The YLC did not set up a screen to isolate Johnson from cases on which she had worked for the county.

To address the growing number of disqualification motions, the chief judge of the district court issued an administrative order disqualifying the YLC from handling any cases in which Johnson had provided legal advice to the county, prosecutors, or other state agents, authored any correspondence or reports, signed pleadings, or appeared before the court.

Johnson immediately resigned as executive director of the YLC but the chief judge refused to rescind the administrative order. On appeal, the Supreme Court held that the administrative order was proper as the categories of disqualification were "paradigmatic examples of conflicts of interest."

> We have not previously defined "substantial responsibility" under the I.C.P.R. According to the ABA, however, "'substantial responsibility'... contemplates a responsibility requiring the official to become personally involved to an important, material degree, in the investigative or deliberative processes regarding the transactions or facts in question." ABA Comm. on Ethics and Professional Responsibility, Formal Op. 342 (1975), reprinted in 62 A.B.A.J. 517, 520 (1976) [hereinafter ABA Opinion].

> Upon an examination of the record, we hold the district court did not abuse its discretion in ruling the four categories of cases described by Judge Gamble offend DR 9-101(B) [predecessor to Model Rule 1.10]. Advising a client, authoring correspondence or reports, signing a pleading, and appearing at a hearing each involve substantial responsibility.... In each of the four circumstances, the lawyer becomes "personally involved to an important, material degree, in the investigative or deliberative processes regarding the transactions or facts in question...." ABA Opinion at 520. Indeed, if an attorney signing even a boilerplate complaint fails to investigate or deliberate upon the legal issues therein, she violates both the mandatory rules and aspirational norms of our code of ethics.... .The district court did not abuse its discretion in ordering the performance of these actions should result in disqualification. All four categories constitute "substantial responsibility" under DR 9-101(B).
>
> Plaintiffs argue "the critical inquiry" of DR 9-101(B) is the protection of confidential information, and since Johnson did not have any confidential information to disclose, the YLC was illegally disqualified. There is evidence Johnson had access to confidential information; Johnson, it appears, was sometimes privy to the identification of the complainant in a CINA action, which is confidential. The problem with plaintiffs' argument, however, lies in the fact it fails to recognize there are several policy considerations underlying DR 9-101(B), only one of which is the protection of confidential information. To accept employment in a case for which the lawyer had substantial responsibility while a government lawyer "would be akin to switching sides, might jeopardize confidential government information, and gives the appearance of professional impropriety in that accepting subsequent employment regarding that same matter creates a suspicion that the lawyer conducted his governmental work in a way to facilitate his own future employment in that matter." ABA Opinion at 520.... [26]

The Supreme Court later issued a reprimand against Johnson for violation of the rules of professional responsibility in representing clients under circumstances of conflict of interest.[27]

As you can see from this case, one of the most vexing problems in applying conflicts of interest analysis to agencies is that which results from application of the imputed disqualification rule. Model Rule 1.10 provides that if one attorney

26. Sorci v. Iowa Dist. Court, 671 N.W.2d 482, 492 (Iowa 2003).

27. Iowa Supreme Court Atty. Disciplinary Bd. v. Johnson, 728 N.W.2d 199 (Iowa 2007).

in a firm is disqualified due to conflict of interest, all attorneys associated in that firm are also disqualified. Since agencies serve a relatively discrete population of clients, they will regularly find themselves in a position of representing clients in situations that would otherwise present a former client conflict. If the entire agency is disqualified, the costs of providing representation increase substantially (as independent attorneys must be individually engaged to fill in the gaps).

Increasingly states are being urged to allow firms to use screening to prevent the imputation of conflicts when attorneys bring conflicts into firms. In screening, the disqualified attorney is prohibited from sharing or receiving information about cases from which the attorney is disqualified or from sharing in the fee from these cases. Model Rule 1.11 and its state variations allow screening of former government attorneys to prevent conflicts from being imputed to the firm. In February 2009, the ABA amended Model Rule 1.10 to allow firms to screen attorneys they have hired from other private firms in order to prevent imputation of conflicts.

The ABA has not, however, approved screening to prevent imputation of conflicts arising within a firm or agency, as opposed to those conflicts brought into a firm by a new attorney. Nonetheless, in some cases, courts have been willing to consider separate "branches" or "teams" of government agencies as separate firms for conflicts purposes in order to reduce the need for disqualification. For example, in *In re Charlisse C.*, 194 P.3d 330 (Cal. 2008), the California Supreme Court suggested that one attorney's conflict might not impute to others within the same agency if sufficient safeguards were in place to protect confidential information. That case involved the Children's Law Center of Los Angeles, a publicly funded nonprofit law office that represents parties in the Los Angeles County Juvenile Dependency Court. The Center has three units: a core unit (Unit 1), and two conflict units (Units 2 and 3). In this case, Unit 1 had represented a girl when she was a foster child. Later, Unit 3 represented that same girl's infant who the county social services agency alleged was at risk of abuse or neglect because of her 19-year-old mother's "emotional/mental health condition." The parties conceded that the two representations were substantially related so that the same attorney could not take on both representations. The question was whether the conflict from Unit 1 would vicariously disqualify Unit 3 from the case. The court suggested that there were several policy reasons for a more relaxed vicarious disqualification standard when public agencies were involved:

> Unlike their private sector counterparts, public sector lawyers do not have a financial interest in the matters on which they work. As a result, they may have less, if any, incentive to breach client confidences. Public sector lawyers also do not recruit clients or accept fees. As a re-

> sult, they have no financial incentive to favor one client over another.... [V]icarious disqualification in the public sector context imposes different burdens on the affected public entities, lawyers and clients. Most frequently cited is the difficulty public law offices would have in recruiting competent lawyers. Private sector law firms may hesitate to hire a lawyer from a public law office, to avoid being disqualified in future matters involving that office. Individual lawyers may hesitate to accept public sector jobs, to avoid limiting their future opportunities in the private sector. Clients whose interests are adverse to a public entity could be deprived of their chosen counsel, or find it difficult to retain counsel at all, particularly in highly specialized areas of the law. Public entities may face the same difficulty and be forced to avoid hiring lawyers with relevant private sector experience. Disqualification increases costs for public entities just as it does for private sector litigants. When a public entity is involved, these higher costs raise the possibility that litigation decisions will be driven by financial considerations rather than by the public interest....
>
> Moreover, public law offices often have a special area of expertise not generally shared by the litigation bar. In light of these considerations, courts have more readily accepted the use of screening procedures or ethical walls as an alternative to vicarious disqualification in cases involving public law offices.... [I]n the public sector, in light of the somewhat lessened potential for conflicts of interest and the high public price paid for disqualifying whole offices of government-funded attorneys, use of internal screening procedures or 'ethical walls' to avoid conflicts within government offices ... have been permitted.[28]

Portfolio Problem: Considering Conflicts

Suppose you are an attorney in a family law practice. A local battered women's shelter has proposed the following arrangement: The shelter has obtained a grant that will allow them to hire you (at a salary of $70,000 annually) as an employee of the shelter. In return, you will represent all women and children in the shelter in obtaining protective orders, divorces, or any other needed domestic relations matters. If a judge orders attorneys fees to be paid by the husband of one of your clients (a fairly common remedy), you will re-

28. *In re* Charlisse C., 194 P.3d 330, 341 (Cal. 2008)(citations and internal quotations omitted).

imburse the shelter those fees up to $70,000 annually. You would very much like to agree to this proposal, as it would significantly improve access to justice for this client group. You are excited by the prospects of being able to work with a team of other professionals in serving the range of needs these clients bring to a shelter.

What kinds of ethical issues does this proposal raise? How can you structure this arrangement to reduce or eliminate those ethical problems? Write a memorandum to the file analyzing these issues and suggesting modifications to the proposal as you see fit under your state's ethics rules. See Missouri Supreme Court Advisory Comm., Formal Op. 121 (April 5, 2006).

To Learn More

In addition to the articles and web resources cited in this chapter, the following web resources are helpful to addressing issues of conflicts of interests:

William Freivogal publishes *Freivogel on Conflicts*, an online publication dedicated to conflicts of interest. It contains approximately 250 pages of material and is regularly updated. http://www.freivogelonconflicts.com/.

Ontario's Lawyers' Professional Indemnity Company (LAWPRO) has a practice website with checklists for conflicts and guidelines for conflict-checking systems. While based on Canadian rules, the principles and checklists would provide an excellent starting point for creating your own checklists based on your state's laws. http://www.practicepro.ca/practice/conflict/ident.asp.

Center for Computer Assisted Legal Instruction, http://www.cali.org.

Lesson number PR14, *Client or Not?*

Chapter Five

Clients, Danger, and Confidentiality

Learning Objectives for This Chapter

After you have read this chapter and completed the assignments you should be able to:

- Describe the scope of the attorney's duty of confidentiality and the attorney-client privilege.
- Identify the exceptions to confidentiality that allow an attorney to disclose confidential information in order to protect a client with diminished capacity.
- Identify the exceptions to confidentiality that give attorneys the discretion to disclose confidential information in order to protect third parties from a client's wrongdoing.
- Identify the situations in which an attorney representing families may have a legal duty to disclose confidential information.

A. Confidentiality

The lawyer's duty of confidentiality is one of the defining features of the attorney-client relationship. The duty is protected by rules of professional conduct, the law of evidence (through the attorney-client privilege), the law of agency (the agent's fiduciary duty to preserve the principal's secrets and not to injure the principal), as well as through various statutes and court rules. As you have seen, confidentiality is also one of the core concerns in conflicts analysis.

In order to understand your duty of confidentiality, you first must be clear regarding the scope of that duty. Under Model Rule 1.6 and its state counterparts, the duty of confidentiality extends to any information relating to the representation. It does not matter when you received the information (it could be before the representation had begun or after it was over). It does not matter from whom you received the information (the client, a witness, even a public document). It does not matter in what form you received the information (conversations, documents, observations). It does not even matter who else knows the information. What matters is that it is information relating to the representation.

Sometimes attorneys confuse the duty of confidentiality with the attorney-client evidentiary privilege. In part that is because the scope of confidentiality under the 1968 Code of Professional Responsibility was much narrower and closer to the attorney-client privilege. The Code required attorneys to keep confidential only "confidences and secrets" rather than the broader scope of today's rule.

Knowing the difference between confidentiality and privilege is important because, unlike the duty of confidentiality, the scope of the attorney-client privilege is very narrow. The scope of the attorney-client privilege extends only to communications between an attorney and client for the purposes of seeking legal advice. The privilege, as an evidentiary rule, applies only in the limited circumstance in which a governmental body can use the twin powers of subpoena and contempt to compel someone to reveal attorney-client communications. The ethical duty, on the other hand, applies anywhere else, prohibiting disclosure and use of confidential information at any time (unless an exception applies).

The evidentiary privilege belongs to the client, who can consent to disclosure or expressly waive the privilege. Also, a client can impliedly waive the evidentiary privilege. Implied waiver can occur in a number of ways, such as when the client, the client's lawyer, or another authorized agent of the client voluntarily discloses the communication in a non-privileged communication; when the client or attorney places the confidential communication at issue in trial; or even when the client's attorney simply fails to object to the efforts to obtain privileged communications. Even an inadvertent disclosure may waive the evidentiary privilege, at least in some jurisdictions.

The presence of third parties when conferring with a client can be sufficient to waive the privilege. This becomes a difficult issue in many family representations, where your client may wish to have another family member be involved in the discussions. If the family member is necessary to facilitate communication or provide necessary support for a client with limited capacity to communicate or make decisions, that family member will be considered a "privileged person."[1] Thus, if you are speaking with a child client, the pres-

1. Restatement (Third) of the Law Governing Lawyers, §70 (2000). *See, e.g.*, Stroh v. General Motors Corp., 623 N.Y.S.2d 873, 874 (N.Y. App. Div. 1995)(Privilege not waived by presence of client's adult daughter where the representation involved "an aged woman re-

ence of the child's parent does not waive the privilege where the parents are assisting the child in decision-making and do not have an independent interest in the representation.[2] If your client's spouse is present during your consultations, the communication is generally protected by the marital communications privilege.[3] However, if the non-client spouse should later decide to waive the marital communication, the underlying attorney-client privilege may be difficult to maintain unless the spouse's presence was otherwise necessary to help with the communication.[4]

In contrast to the waiver of privilege, which can occur inadvertently, the attorney's ethical duty to keep confidential the client's information is not so easily lost. The rule allows attorney disclosure when the client gives informed consent to disclosure and in a very narrow range of other circumstances. Attorneys should take care to insure that a client's consent to disclose confidential information is completely voluntary and well-informed. Model Rule 1.6 also permits attorneys to disclose confidential information that is "impliedly authorized in order to carry out representation." For example, an attorney is impliedly authorized to disclose client information to other attorneys in the firm unless the client instructs that particular information be confined to specific lawyers.

---

quired to recall, and perhaps relive, what was probably the most traumatic experience of her life. Her daughter selected the law firm to represent her, transported her to the law office, and put her sufficiently at ease to communicate effectively with counsel").

2. *See, e.g.*, State v. Sucharew, 66 P.3d 59 (Ariz. Ct. App. 2003)(holding that presence of parent in communications with his criminal defense counsel did not waive the privilege because "they were taking an understandable parental interest and advisory role in their minor son's legal affairs. The presence of a parent in such a capacity at a meeting between child and counsel does not defeat the attorney-client privilege").

3. The marital communications privilege permits a testifying spouse to refuse to disclose communications between the spouses made in confidence during a valid marriage and intended to be confidential. United States v. Parker, 834 F.2d 408, 411 (4th Cir. 1987).

4. State v. Gordon, 504 A.2d 1020, 1025–26 (Conn. 1985) (presence of wife of client accused of crime at meetings with lawyer concerning trial strategy waived attorney-client privilege because wife's presence was not necessary to the communication); *In re* Guardianship of Walling, 727 P.2d 586, 592 (Okla.1986) (privilege waived by including client's grandmother in attorney-client communication, when her presence was not reasonably necessary for the transmission of communication).

B. Clients in Danger and the Client with Diminished Capacity

Attorneys representing families in crisis must be prepared to deal with dangerous situations, most commonly situations of impaired decision-making that put a client in harm's way or situations involving family violence. As a matter of competent family representation, you should know how to assess risks of harm in these situations. The attorney who insists that a victim of domestic violence "just get a protective order and leave" may have unwittingly placed that client in a lethal situation.[5]

One of the difficult and sometimes frustrating aspects of representing victims of domestic violence is that they may have difficulty leaving their abusive relationships. While we know that abusive relationships present risks, we also know that the highest risk for lethality arises when a victim is leaving or has just left her abuser. Thus, the decision to leave is a balancing of risks that only the client can make. Your role requires helping the client to assess and minimize the risks of any course of action.

> Attorneys are advised to institute safety measures when representing the victim. An attorney can easily focus on legal proceedings and neglect to consider the unintended consequences of their representation. For example, the victim-client may agree to the filing of a petition for a civil protective order. The attorney drafts and files the necessary papers with the court but does not consider what will happen after service of process or what could happen to the victim before trial. Another example is a case involving name calling and stale allegations of low-level physical abuse that would not appear to warrant ex parte relief. In such a case, the victim could wait a period of time for the trial to be scheduled. If counsel fails to tell the client that papers will be served on the perpetrator prior to trial—a fact the victim may likely be unaware of—the outcome could be deadly. The victim could be home one evening with her abuser when the sheriff knocks on the door to serve a petition containing allegations of abuse, as well as requests for

5. For a general overview of the malpractice issues inherent in the representation of victims of abuse, *see generally* Margaret Drew, *Lawyer Malpractice and Domestic Violence: Are We Revictimizing Our Clients?*, 39 Fam. L.Q. 7 (2005) (urging family law attorneys who lack specialized training in representing victims of domestic violence to retain experts or seek outside assistance for complex issues of domestic violence).

> relief such as a no contact order, custody of the children, possession of the home, support, and other ancillary relief. After the door is closed and the abuser has an opportunity to review the documents, retaliation could be swift and fatal.
>
> In the alternative, service of process could cause the abuser to coerce the victim to drop the matter. If the client decides not to pursue a civil protective order, counsel should confirm that the victim was not encouraged by the abuser to drop the matter. Again, proper action requires accurate information. Communicating with the client to ensure she is safe and that her decision not to proceed is her choice is a legally sound action. Concluding that the client has been coerced without sufficient information or to substitute the lawyer's judgment for that of the client because counsel believes that the only appropriate course of action for the client is to obtain a protection order is, however, another matter altogether.[6]

Respecting a client's choices regarding responses to danger is sometimes extremely challenging. When a client is in danger, you may wish to disclose confidential information in order to protect the client. Ordinarily you would first counsel the client to permit you to make the necessary disclosures. But what if the client is unable or unwilling to consent? May you disclose information in order to protect a client in danger even if the client would prefer you not make that disclosure?

The starting point in answering this question is to make sure that you have sufficient facts and knowledge to accurately assess the threat. Consider, for example, the tragic but all too common situation of a family law client who declares his intent to commit suicide. Could you call the police, hospital, or a family member to get your client help? Under Model Rule 1.6 and many states' versions of this rule, an attorney would have the discretion to disclose information if the attorney reasonably believes that the disclosure would prevent reasonably certain death. However, given the possible consequences to your client of your disclosing his intent to commit suicide, you will want to take care that you do indeed have sufficient information to reasonably believe that he will follow through on his threat. It is often difficult to know with any certainty what a client's true intent may be. The Restatement suggests that, in these circumstances, "Before making disclosure where such facts are ambigu-

6. Dana Harrington Conner, *To Protect or To Serve: Confidentiality, Client Protection, and Domestic Violence*, 79 Temp. L. Rev. 877, 976 (2006).

ous, the lawyer must make a reasonable effort to determine the relevant facts, taking into account the risks inherent in either action or inaction by the lawyer."[7]

Just how much more you would need to know would depend on the circumstances of your relationship with your client and the nature of his suicide threat. The Restatement suggests that, among other factors, an attorney should assess

- the degree to which it appears likely that the threatened death or serious bodily harm will actually result,
- the irreversibility of its consequences once the act has taken place, the time available,
- whether victims might be unaware of the threat or might rely on the lawyer to protect them,
- the lawyer's prior course of dealings with the client, and
- the extent of adverse effect on the client that may result from disclosure contemplated by the lawyer.[8]

Suppose that your client has outlined exactly when, where, and how he intends to commit suicide. Suppose further that you are aware that your client is currently drinking heavily and is extremely depressed. That may be sufficient information for you to act, but you may also wish to seek assistance in assessing the threat. Without revealing any of your client's information, you ask a mental health professional how to assess suicide risk and are told:

> The risk of suicide should be considered imminent if the patient reports the intention to die, has a suicidal plan, and has lethal means available. Expressions of despair and hopelessness also suggest an imminent risk. Comorbid depression and alcoholism may indicate the short-term risk of suicide, even in the absence of suicidal behavior. It is important to note that except for patients that actually admit to having suicide plans, it is extremely difficult to predict which patients in the high-risk population will actually kill themselves.[9]

Given this standard, you have more than enough information to reasonably believe your client will attempt suicide and thereby invoke the exception under Model Rule 1.6(b). Notice how important it is to base this decision not only on the facts you have but also on the collaboration or instruction of other professionals, who can inform your judgment.

---

7. Restatement (Third) of the Law Governing Lawyers §66, cmt. f (2000).
8. *Id.*
9. Leo Sher, *Preventing Suicide*, 97:10 QJM: Int'l J. of Med. 677 (2004).

Some states, however, do not have an exception to confidentiality to prevent death or bodily injury. Under the older Model Code of Professional Responsibility (DR 4-101), which still provides the basis for some states' rules of professional conduct, there is no separate exception to prevent death or bodily injury. Instead, an attorney may disclose information to prevent a client's intent to commit a crime or fraud (any crime or fraud). Under the pre-2002 version of the Model Rules 1.6(b)(1) attorneys had discretion to disclose information "to the extent the lawyer reasonably believes necessary ... to prevent the client from committing a criminal act that the lawyer believes is likely to result in imminent death or substantial bodily harm." Because suicide is not a crime in most states, in states that have retained one of these versions of the confidentiality rules, you may not be able to disclose any information no matter how sure you are that your client will commit suicide.

Some state ethics opinions, uncomfortable with this outcome, have suggested that disclosure might be authorized under the terms of their version of Model Rule 1.14, Client with Diminished Capacity.[10] Model Rule 1.14(b) provides that "when the lawyer reasonably believes that the client cannot adequately act in the client's own best interest" the lawyer either may seek the appointment of a guardian or "take other protective action." The Restatement also suggests this exception.[11] See also AAML Standard 2.5 and comments in Appendix A.

You may feel justified under this rule in overriding a client's choice to commit suicide. However, would you feel equally justified in overruling a client's choice to return to an abusive spouse, for example, by revealing the client's intent to other family members or, for example, to child protective services in order to deter the client from making that choice? At what point does client autonomy demand that you simply allow clients to face dangers as they choose?

Understanding your discretion under Model Rule 1.14 is important because attorneys in family representation may regularly find themselves representing clients whose decision-making ability is diminished, whether by age, disability, mental health issues, substance abuse, or the emotional turmoil of family conflict. Often third persons will seek to intervene to "assist" in the representation. However, those third persons may be no more capable of assisting in the decision-making than are you. Moreover, there are distinct risks to allowing third-parties to interfere with your client's decision making. Those third par-

10. See, for example, Ala. B. Ethics Op. 2005-1 (2005)(http://www.alaskabar.org/ethops/05-1.htm#G); Mass.B. Ass'n, Ethics Op. 01-2 (2001)(http://www.massbar.org/for-attorneys/publications/ethics-opinions/2000-2009/2001/opinion-no-01-2).

11. Restatement (Third) of the Law Governing Lawyers §66 (Comment c)(2000).

ties may not be operating to protect the client's interest. Even where they are, unless third persons are necessary to facilitate communication, allowing these persons to be privy to your conversations with a client can waive the attorney-client privilege and may violate the attorney's duty of confidentiality. See generally AAML Standard 2.6 and comments in Appendix A.

For example, suppose that you represent an elderly woman in estate planning and health care issues. She has asked that her son be permitted to sit in on all discussions. Son appears to be concerned with your client's ability to understand her decisions without his help. You represent the elder, but how do you determine what role, if any, the son should play in this representation? How can you obtain consent from the elder client to allow the son to participate in the representation if you have concerns about her capacity to consent?

Whenever you are concerned about the capacity of a client, you should insist on meeting privately with the client face-to-face. You can explain to both the parent and the son the importance of this separate meeting as a preliminary step. A separate private meeting will allow you to assess the seriousness of a competency issue and to educate the parent regarding her role and her son's role in the representation. If you conclude that your client is able to direct the representation, you can then proceed as you would any other representation, taking direction solely from the client and limiting son's involvement to that which is prudent and helpful to the client.

But what if you believe the client is unable or unwilling to direct the representation without assistance? Suppose the son has come to you with concerns regarding the health care treatment of his mother and the mother is suffering from dementia. How do you assess whether the mother has the capacity to direct the representation? This assessment requires an investment of time and understanding. Understand that capacity is not an all-or-nothing proposition. Capacity can vary according to time and the decisions being made. A client may have capacity to make certain decisions, need assistance in making other decisions, and lack the capacity to make still others.

Assessing capacity may require the assistance of a health professional, but you need to make an initial determination of capacity even to make this choice. In addition to meeting with the client separately, make sure you are patient and do not rush to conclusions about capacity based on limited information. You will need to meet with a client more than once to acquire a truer sense of the client's decision-making capacity. As the client gets to know you and gains confidence and trust in your representation, the client's ability to function optimally will increase. To both increase efficiency and the client's ability to function well, schedule shorter sessions at times when the client tends to be most alert. Multiple meetings over time also allow you to see temporal variations in functioning.[12]

If the client insists on having family members present for meetings, be aware of the interactions among the family members. You may wish to "note any indication of discomfort by the client or influence by the younger family member... the content and tenor of comments, how supportive or dominating the family member may be, and how consistent or inconsistent the client's stated objectives are with prior wishes evidenced by estate planning documents or other expressions of intent."[13] If you believe some family members are interfering with your client's decision-making, you should take steps to limit that interference.

Just as in any family representation, there is no substitute for getting to know your client well: their history, interests and values. "A great danger in capacity assessment is that eccentricities, aberrant character traits, or risk-taking decisions will be confused with incapacity. A capacity assessment first asks what kind of person is being assessed and what sorts of things that person has generally held to be important."[14] Comment 6 to Model Rule 1.14 provides additional guidance for making an assessment of competency:

> In determining the extent of the client's diminished capacity, the lawyer should consider and balance such factors as: the client's ability to articulate reason leading to a decision, variability of state of mind and ability to appreciate consequences of a decision; the substantive fairness of a decision; and the consistency of a decision with the known long-term commitments and values of the client. In appropriate circumstances, the lawyer may seek guidance from an appropriate diagnostician.

If you believe that the client's capacity to act in his or her own best interest is diminished and the client is at risk of harm, you may, under Model Rule 1.14, take "reasonably necessary protective action." This can include revealing confidential information in order to consult with others or even, in the most extreme cases, seeing appointment of a guardian or conservator. While Model Rule 1.14 itself does not expressly provide for an exception to the duty of con-

12. Charles P. Sabatino, *Representing a Client with Diminished Capacity: How Do You Know It And What Do You Do About It?* 16 J. Am. Acad. Matrimonial Law. 481, 488 (2000).

13. Professionalism and Ethics Committee of the National Academy of Elder Law Attorneys, Aspirational Standards for The Practice of Elder Law With Commentaries 9 (2006), *available at* http://www.naela.org/pdffiles/AspirationalStandards.pdf.

14. *Id.* at 486.

fidentiality in these circumstances, these disclosures would fall under the general exception in Model Rule 1.6 for disclosures that are impliedly authorized.[15]

These rules leave you a great deal of discretion. The key to navigating the rule is to remember that your fundamental duty is to maintain a normal attorney-client relationship as much as you reasonably can. This means you will consider and respect the client's autonomy, dignity, and privacy when exercising your discretion to take steps to assist the client.

Portfolio Problem: Assessing and Responding to a Client in Danger

Suppose that you have been representing a particular elderly client for years. Over the years you have gotten to know the client well and he has confided in you that he is afraid of his adult son who lives with him. Your client has mentioned that he is concerned about his safety because the son is an alcoholic and can be verbally abusive. He has kept secret the fact that you have been representing him.

Your client has repeatedly stated that he wanted his other children to have the general power of attorney for his decision-making in case of incapacity and he had you prepare a will leaving a substantial portion of his estate to his other children, in part because he has provided so much financial assistance to the son. Your client has told you that his son thinks that he is incompetent, but you don't think that the client is incompetent. In the past you have discussed with the client whether or not to seek a restraining order or to try to evict his son, but the client never took any action.

You just met with your client again last week and this time he brought his son to the meeting. (You tried to keep the son out of the meeting, but your client insisted it was okay—that he and his son had "worked things out.") So now it's clear that the son has discovered that you have been acting as his father's attorney. Today you received a fax letter from your client discharging you and instructing you to turn over all your files to a new attorney. You tried calling but no one is answering the phone.

What can you do? What should you do?

Consider that under Model Rule 1.16 an attorney shall not represent a client or, where representation has commenced, shall withdraw from the represen-

---

15. ABA Comm. on Ethics and Prof'l Responsibility, Informal Op. 89-1530 (1989)([T]he Committee concludes that the disclosure by the lawyer of information relating to the representation to the extent necessary to serve the best interests of the client reasonably believed to be disabled is impliedly authorized within the meaning of Model Rule 1.6. Thus, the inquirer may consult a physician concerning the suspected disability.)

tation of a client if the lawyer is discharged. Moreover, recall that under that same rule you have a duty upon termination to take steps to the extent reasonably practicable to protect a client's interests.

Recall that most states have an exception to confidentiality for disclosures that are required by law or court order. What if your state is one of the many that has in place a law mandating reports of suspected elder abuse?[16] For example, Texas Human Resources Code §48.051 (2007) provides:

> (a) Except as prescribed by Subsection (b), a person having cause to believe that an elderly or disabled person is in the state of abuse, neglect, or exploitation shall report the information required by Subsection (d) immediately to the department....
> (c) The duty imposed by Subsections (a) and (b) applies without exception to a person whose knowledge concerning possible abuse, neglect, or exploitation is obtained during the scope of the person's employment or whose professional communications are generally confidential, including an attorney, clergy member, medical practitioner, social worker, and mental health professional.

Under this statute, would you be required to report your client's situation to state authorities?

Prepare a memo to your file outlining and justifying your proposed course of action regarding your client.

C. Dangerous Clients

In contrast to clients in danger are those situations in which it is your client who is the source of danger. No matter how carefully you screen your clients for these dangerous individuals, you will eventually find yourself representing a client who you believe may threaten harm to another person or even yourself. What are the rules of confidentiality regarding disclosure of a client's intent to harm another? How do those rules interact with the attorney-client evidentiary privilege?

Let's begin with perhaps the most frightening scenario—a client's threat against you. A 1997 survey of domestic relations attorneys reported that 64% said that they had been threatened with or had actually been the victim of violence by their own clients or by the opposing client.[17] Put yourself in the shoes

---

16. Carolyn L. Dessin, *Elder Law: Should Attorneys Have a Duty to Report Financial Abuse of the Elderly?*, 38 Akron L. Rev. 707, 709 nn. 10–12, (2005).

17. Mark Hansen, *Lawyers in Harm's Way*, 84 ABA J. 93 (March 1998).

of attorney Friedman, for example, who was representing Mr. Kleinfeld, who had been accused of murdering his wife and her attorney during a bitter divorce action. Friedman represented the suspect Kleinfeld in both the divorce and in the criminal case. At one point, Kleinfeld telephoned Friedman, unhappy with his representations, and said "They know I did Eric. I've got nothing to lose by doing you and then turning the gun on myself."[18]

If you were Friedman, you most certainly would want to withdraw from that dangerous representation and report your client's threat in order to protect yourself. The rules of professional conduct in all states would allow you to disclose this information, either because it is a client's intent to commit a crime or because it could prevent a death. But what if you were later subpoenaed to testify regarding that statement in your client's trial for the murder of his wife? Would your conversation with your client be protected by the attorney-client privilege?

In Friedman's case, the Florida court held that the attorney's testimony against his former client could not be compelled because the crime-fraud exception to privilege applied only when a client seeks legal advice to further a future crime. Here, the client's statement was about a past crime and a threat to commit a future crime that was never carried out. While the confidentiality rules permitted an exception here, the court noted that the evidentiary rule is "a different concept than the one contained in the rules governing the ethical conduct of a lawyer."[19]

Threats to kill another person fall within the exception to confidentiality in nearly every state. In some instances, a threat to kill may be so clear that you may even have an obligation to disclose that information. In eleven states, the disciplinary rules require an attorney to disclose information that they reasonably believe necessary to prevent their client's crime that would result in death or substantial bodily harm.[20]

In addition, there may be a duty to warn under tort law. The duty to warn in tort law, established by *Tarasoff v. Regents of University of California*, 551 P.2d 334 (Cal. 1976), established for psychologists a very limited duty to warn when they have special knowledge of a patient's clear threat to kill a foresee-

---

18. Kleinfeld v. State, 568 So. 2d 937, 939 (Fla. Dist. Ct. App. 1990).

19. *Id.* The case is discussed in Mitchell Simon, *Discreet Disclosures: Should Lawyers Who Disclose Confidential Information to Protect Third Parties Be Compelled to Testify Against Their Clients?*, 49 So. Tex. L. Rev. 307, 318 (2007).

20. Ariz. S. Ct. Rule 42 R.P.C. 1.6(b); Conn. R.P.C. 1.6(b); Fla. St. Bar Rule 4-1.6(b); Ill. St. S. Ct. R.P.C. 1.6; Nev. St. S. Ct. R.P.C. 156(2); N.J. R. R.P.C. 1.6(b)(1); N.M. R. R.P.C. 16-106(B); N.D. R. R.P.C. 1.6(a); Tex. St. R.P.C. 1.05; Va. R. S. Ct. Pt. 6 2, C.P.R. DR. 4-101; Wis. St. R.P.C. S.C.R. 20:1.6.

able victim. Tarasoff's application to attorneys is unclear. The court in *Hawkins v. King County*, 602 P.2d 361 (Wash. App. 1979), held that an attorney did not have a duty to warn his client's mother of his client's signs of mental illness when she was as aware of those signs as was the attorney. In contrast, the court in *Washington v. Hansen*, 862 P.2d 117, 122 (Wash. 1993), held that an attorney who was aware of a threat against a judge had a duty to disclose that threat: "attorneys, as officers of the court, have a duty to warn of true threats to harm a judge made by a client or a third party when the attorney has a reasonable belief that such threats are real." The court distinguished *Hawkins* on the grounds that the mother knew about the threat her son might pose whereas the judge in this case was unaware of the threat.

Given that both disciplinary rules and tort law allow, and may require, disclosing a client's fatal threats, why would an attorney hesitate? Think about what happens if you are in a situation in which your client has made a threat to kill a third person. Just as with the client's threat to commit suicide, the first problem you face is in determining the probability that the client will actually carry out the threat. Individuals under the stress of family crisis may make some fairly outrageous threats that serve only to express the depth of their emotions. How can you separate the bluff from the true threat? If you reveal your client's threat to the person threatened, you may be protecting that person or you may simply be escalating the emotional stakes and making the crisis worse rather than better. If you reveal your client's threat to the police or the judge, you have substantially prejudiced your client and will be required to withdraw from the representation. Because revealing a client's threat requires such difficult judgments, most state disciplinary rules leave that decision to the discretion of the attorney.

What about other less fatal wrongdoing? What are your obligations to a client who threatens a wrong that may be criminal but does not necessarily threaten physical harm? For example, suppose you represented a client who is a citizen of another country and is separated from her spouse, a United States citizen, and wishes a divorce. They have two sons, ages 12 and 15. Right now, the children stay with your client during the week and live with her husband on the weekends. This is not pursuant to any formal agreement however and the couple has not agreed on how they will deal with summer vacation.

Next week is the last week of school for the boys. Your client has asked if she can take the boys with her to her home country and file for a divorce there over the summer, without giving notice to her husband beforehand. Your client believes that in her home country, the law would automatically give her sole physical and legal custody of the children.

Your first task is to counsel your client regarding her plan. Model Rule 1.2(d) provides that an attorney "shall not counsel or assist in criminal or fraudulent conduct but may discuss the legal consequences of proposed conduct and may counsel or assist in making a good faith determination of validity, scope, meaning or application." Accordingly, you would explain to your client that her removal of the children to another country would likely be a criminal offense under your state's law,[21] and under federal criminal law.[22] You would also explain that, under the Hague convention,[23] the children could be returned and she would be subject to criminal and civil liability and would worsen her position in a subsequent custody dispute.

Suppose your client then begins to ask questions indicating that she has not been deterred from her plan. She may ask, for example, about how much it would cost and what would be required for her husband to get the children returned under the Hague convention. She might ask whether there are countries that are not signatories to the Hague convention. At the point at which you believe that you are helping the client to plan her criminal activity rather than assess in good faith the legality of her actions, you have moved into prohibited territory. Of course that is a fuzzy line, involving your assessment of the client's intentions and good faith. If you do not stay clear of the line, however, you are running the risk of being charged with assisting your client in abducting her children.[24]

---

21. Catherine F. Klein, Leslye E. Orloff & Hema Sarangapani, *Border Crossings: Understanding the Civil, Criminal and Immigration Implications for Battered Women Fleeing Across State Lines with Their Children*, 39 Fam. L.Q. 109, 110–11 (2005)("statutory provisions concerning the definitions of lawful custodian, the availability of statutory exceptions or defenses, and the severity of the criminal penalty for conviction vary greatly between states."). For a chart comparing state statutes, see the website of the National Center for Missing and Exploited Children (NCMEC) http://www.missingkids.com under the tab for resources for attorneys.

22. 18 U.S.C. §1204 (2008).

23. The Hague Convention on the Civil Aspects of International Child Abduction (Convention). The Convention came into force in the United States in 1988 upon enactment of federal implementing legislation, the International Child Abduction Remedies Act, 42 U.S.C. 11601–11610.

24. Consider the attorney's actions in People v. Chappell, 927 P.2d 829, 830 (Colo. 1996) in which the attorney represented a mother who had been ordered not to leave the state with her children pending a custody determination. Upon learning that a custody evaluation would be adverse to the mother, the attorney "advised her as her attorney to stay, but as a mother to run" and then proceeded to assist the client in assisted her in taking the steps necessary to flee the state with the children and hide her whereabouts. The attorney was disbarred. *See also*, Penn v. State, 44 S.W.3d 746 (Ark. Ct. App. 2001)(attorney found guilty of criminal contempt for assisting in custodial interference cannot also be charged with the crime itself as this would violate protections against double jeopardy).

If you believe that, despite your best efforts, you have not succeeded in dissuading your client from taking the children, you may withdraw (or seek court permission to withdraw if you have entered an appearance on behalf of the client). Model Rule 1.16 allows attorneys to withdraw, even if the withdrawal would adversely affect a client, if the client "persists in a course of action involving the lawyer's services that the lawyer reasonably believes is criminal or fraudulent" or "insists upon taking action that the lawyer considers repugnant or with which the lawyer has a fundamental disagreement."

May you also reveal the client's intent to abduct the children to her husband or to the court? The answer will depend in part on your state's disciplinary rules. In states that have retained the standards from the 1983 ABA Model Code of Professional Responsibility, DR 4-101(C)(3), an attorney may reveal the client's intention to commit any crime and the information necessary to prevent it. In those states, the critical questions are: would the client's activity constitute a crime? (Here, almost certainly.) Would disclosure prevent that crime? (Very likely so.) This very broad exception to confidentiality applies regardless of the consequences of the criminal action, so that you could report your client's intent to abduct the children even if you did not believe the abduction would cause the children harm.

Other states have adopted the more narrow exceptions under a version of the Model Rules. Until recently, Model Rule 1.6(b)(1) permitted disclosure only "to the extent reasonably believes necessary to prevent the client from committing a criminal act likely to result in imminent death or substantial bodily harm." The Ethics 2000 revisions to the Model Rules broadened this very narrow position to allow disclosure simply "to prevent reasonably certain death or substantial bodily harm"—the threat need not be from a client crime and need not be imminent. Similarly, AAML Standard 6.5 provides that "An attorney should disclose information relating to a client or former client to the extent the lawyer reasonably believes necessary to prevent substantial physical or sexual abuse of a child."

Applying these standards, the question of whether you have the discretion to disclose your client's intent to abduct the children would turn on the impact on the children of the abduction. Ordinarily, you should be extremely reluctant to conclude that children who are kidnapped by a parent are unharmed by that event. At a minimum, these children are likely to suffer emotional trauma from the disruption and stress of the resulting secrecy they may have to observe.[25] Because of the harmful effects on children, parental kidnapping can be characterized as a form of child abuse.

---

25. For extensive case studies on the impact of parental kidnapping on both parents and children, see Geoffrey L. Greif and Rebecca Hegar, When Parents Kidnap (1993).

If the parent is fleeing with the children in order to escape domestic violence, you may have an entirely different analysis. First, many state statutes provide a defense to custodial interference for parents fleeing violence. Second, even if your client's actions would still constitute a crime, you may conclude that the harm to the client from disclosure may be greater than the harm caused by her fleeing with the children, particularly if you believe the legal system would not adequately protect her interests.[26]

There may be states in which you have no discretion regarding the decision to disclose your client's action that could harm a child. When it comes to disclosure of information in order to prevent serious bodily harm or death, disclosures are mandatory in some states. Moreover, some jurisdictions have statutes making attorneys mandatory reporters of abuse. The rules of professional conduct in all states provide an exception to confidentiality in order to comply with law or court orders. Thus, if a statute requires or a court orders you to disclose a client's information, the "may" of the rules becomes a "must." Once ordered or compelled by law to disclose, the ethical standards would probably not provide a defense to contempt or criminal charges of obstruction of justice.

What if your client takes the children and you are subpoenaed to testify in an action seeking their return. When a court seeks to compel an attorney to disclose attorney-client communications, the applicable rule is the attorney-client privilege. In most jurisdictions, the privilege is subject to an exception for situations in which a client seeks your advice (or uses your advice) to further a future crime or fraud. Consider the application of the privilege in the following case:

Bersani v. Bersani

565 A.2d 1368 (Super. Ct. Conn. 1989)

Opinion by Freedman, J:

On October 3, 1988, the plaintiff wife instituted an action against the defendant husband for dissolution of marriage. On November 11, 1988, the court awarded custody *pendente lite* of the parties' two minor children to the plaintiff and specific visitation rights *pendente lite* to the defendant.

On March 7, 1989, under an agreement of the parties, approved by the court, the plaintiff was required to give the defendant thirty days written notice of her intent to leave the country. After a hearing on May 9, 1989, the

26. Leigh Goodmark, *Going Underground: The Ethics Of Advising A Battered Woman Fleeing An Abusive Relationship*, 75 UMKC L. Rev. 999 (2007).

court denied a motion filed by the plaintiff in which she sought a court order permitting her to return to Spain with the children pending the final hearing in the dissolution action.

In early June, the defendant learned that the plaintiff had moved out of the house that she was occupying with the children. The defendant sought information concerning the whereabouts of the plaintiff and the children from the plaintiff's attorney. While the plaintiff's attorney acknowledges that she possesses the requested information, she has declined to disclose it on the ground that to do so would violate her obligation to maintain confidential information imparted to her by a client.

By motion dated June 7, 1989, the defendant seeks an order to compel the plaintiff's attorney to reveal the information claiming that the attorney-client privilege must yield to assure that a judicial determination is made and enforced respecting the best interests of the children.

On June 8, 1989, the court found the plaintiff in willful contempt, ordered her to return to Connecticut and awarded temporary custody of the two children to the defendant.

On July 14, 1989, after a hearing that the plaintiff did not attend but at which she was represented by counsel, the marriage was dissolved and the court ordered, inter alia, that custody of the minor children was to be with the defendant....

The common-law rule of privileged communications has been stated as follows: 'Where legal advice of any kind is sought from a professional legal adviser in his capacity as such, the communications relating to that purpose, made in confidence by the client, are at his instance permanently protected from disclosure by himself or by the legal adviser, except the protection be waived.' 8 Wigmore, Evidence §2292, p. 554 (McNaughton Rev. 1961)...." *Rienzo v. Santangelo,* 160 Conn. 391, 395, 279 A.2d 565 (1971). Connecticut has not altered the rule by statute, as have some states. *Id.* "The privilege is designed to remove client apprehension as to compelled disclosure by the attorney, and thereby encourage freedom of full disclosure by the client of all the facts relating to the subject matter of inquiry or litigation." C. Tait & J. LaPlante, Connecticut Evidence (1976) §12.5.

Subsection (c)(2) of Rule 1.6 of the Rules of Professional Conduct provides that a lawyer may reveal information relating to the representation of a client to the extent that the lawyer believes that it is necessary to "[r]ectify the consequence of a client's criminal or fraudulent act in the commission of which the lawyer's services had been used." Rule 3.3 (a)(2) of the Rules of Professional Conduct states that "[a] lawyer shall not knowingly ... fail to disclose a material fact to a tribunal when disclosure is necessary to avoid assisting a criminal or fraudulent act by the client...."

It is the opinion of this court that the plaintiff's willful contempt in leaving the country in violation of the court's order constitutes a fraud on the court, a fraudulent act under Rule 1.6 (c) (2). While it is clear to this court that the plaintiff's attorney did not assist or advise the plaintiff to violate the court's order, the attorney's present refusal to disclose her client's whereabouts does serve to assist the plaintiff in her ongoing violation of the court's order.

The New Jersey Supreme Court in *Fellerman v. Bradley*, 99 N.J. 493, 503, 493 A.2d 1239 (1985), stated that in the context of the "crime or fraud" exception to the attorney-client privilege found at N.J. Stat. Ann. §2A:84A-20 (2)(a), "our courts have generally given the term 'fraud' an expansive reading." Fed. R. Evid. 26 (2)(a). In *Fellerman,* the failure of the defendant's attorney to disclose the whereabouts of his client prevented the court from enforcing a provision of the final judgment in a dissolution action, to which the defendant had previously agreed, requiring the defendant to pay an expert's fee. The court stated that "the client, through his attorney, attempted to perpetrate a fraud on the court—to 'mock' justice—by consenting to and subsequently flouting a judgment that obligated him to bear the costs of an accountant." *Id.* at 505.

The situation in the present case presents more compelling facts than those in *Fellerman* to justify the expansion of the meaning of fraud in Rule 1.6 (c)(2) beyond traditional tort or criminal law definitions to include those which constitute "a fraud on the court." The court in *Fellerman* concluded that the defendant's attempt to escape payment of a court ordered expense constituted a fraud on the court. The plaintiff's deliberate violation of the court's order in the present case has extended ramifications because it impedes the court's ability to implement its subsequent orders regarding custody, orders made in the best interests of the two minor children, not in the interests of either the plaintiff or the defendant....

In *Jafarian-Kerman v. Jafarian-Kerman,* 424 S.W.2d 333 (Mo. App. 1967), a case with facts similar to those of the present case, a Missouri Appellate Court required the defendant's attorney to disclose to the court the information he possessed regarding the precise whereabouts of the defendant and the minor child, whose custody had been temporarily granted to the plaintiff. The court noted that the child had become a ward of the court, and was subject to the court's final decree in the dissolution proceedings instituted by the plaintiff. *Id.* at 339. Noting further that the defendant had gained possession of the child under his visitation privilege and had surreptitiously taken the child to Germany at some address unknown to the plaintiff and the court, the court concluded that "[s]uch conduct of the defendant was a malicious and wanton infraction of the court's orders and brazen obstruction of the administration of justice." *Id.*

In the context of an appeal from a Superior Court order adjudging an attorney to be in contempt for refusing to disclose the whereabouts of his client, who had forcibly removed her child from the custodial home, the Supreme Court of Washington, in *Dike v. Dike,* 75 Wash. 2d 1, 448 P.2d 490 (1968), held that the address of the attorney's client was not privileged information. The court noted that although there was no support for a finding that the client's actions were performed with the attorney's knowledge, that did not alter the fact that the client's wrongful act was continuing and that the attorney became aware of her client's misdeed during its continuance. Concluding that the address of the attorney's client was not privileged information, the court stated: "[W]e will not allow the shield of silence constructed by the privilege to aid the client in continuing his wrongdoing at the expense of other members of society. The information sought by the court did not relate to a completed wrong, nor was the primary purpose of disclosure to punish the client for her misdeeds in the past; rather, the information relates to a continuing wrong which [has been] aided by the silence of the client's attorney. The primary purpose of disclosure is to protect a minor child's welfare which is, at least potentially, being harmed by the client's continuing wrongful actions." *Id.* at 14.

This court, mindful of the importance of the attorney-client privilege and the function it serves in our adversary system, must nevertheless weigh the benefits of that privilege against the state's vital interest as *parens patriae* in determining the best interests of the minor children. While the plaintiff would have this court hold that the issue before it does not involve custody, the issue of custody here is inextricably intertwined with the issue of attorney-client privilege. The facts reveal: (1) that the plaintiff has left the country with the children in direct violation of a court order; (2) that the plaintiff's attorney knows the precise whereabouts of her client and declines to disclose that information; (3) that the failure to disclose that information assists the plaintiff in her ongoing contempt of the court's order; and (4) that the court's ability to effectuate subsequent orders issued in the best interests of the children has been thwarted.

It is this court's opinion, that, under the circumstances, the attorney-client privilege does not apply to information imparted to an attorney by a client in the course of perpetrating a fraud on the court. Moreover, any claim of privilege must yield in these circumstances to the best interests of the children. Accordingly, the defendant's motion to compel counsel to reveal the whereabouts of the plaintiff and the children is granted.

Questions

1. In a number of these cases, attorneys have asserted the attorney-client privilege and, when their objections have been overruled, the attorneys

have nonetheless refused to testify and have been held in contempt. Are you required to go to jail in order to protect a client's confidences? Surely not. But what is the best course of action for an attorney faced with what he or she considers an erroneous, although binding, order to disclose client confidences or produce protected documents?

Recently, the United States Supreme Court in *Industries Inc. v. Carpenter*, No. 08-678, addressed the question of whether the final judgment rule precludes a party's immediate appeal of a judge's finding that it has waived the attorney-client privilege. The Eleventh Circuit Court of Appeals held that the collateral order doctrine, which allows immediate appeals of certain interlocutory orders, did not apply to discovery orders implicating privilege issues. *Carpenter v. Mohawk Indus., Inc.*, 541 F.3d 1048, 1050 (11th Cir. 2008).

> Ordinarily, a litigant seeking to overturn a discovery order has (only) two choices. Either he can comply with the order and challenge it at the conclusion of the case or he can refuse to comply with the order and contest its validity if subsequently cited for contempt for his refusal to obey."

Carpenter, Inc., 541 F.3d at 1053 (quoting *Rouse Constr. Int'l, Inc. v. Rouse Constr. Corp.*, 680 F.2d 743, 745 (11th Cir. 1982)). The Eleventh circuit's position represented the majority position on the issue, with three circuit courts of appeal having held that the collateral order doctrine does apply. As of the time this book was published, the Supreme Court had not yet decided which of these approaches is would adopt. If the Court agrees with the 11th Circuit position, do you agree that the attorney has only two options in responding to the order to disclose what may be privileged communications?

2. What if the client in this case had come to the attorney after having fled with the children and had disclosed their whereabouts to the attorney? Would the crime-fraud exception to privilege apply? In similar circumstances, the court in *Mendel v. Felbert*, 897 P.2d 68 (Alaska 1995) noted:

> The privilege only ceases to exist for ongoing and future wrongdoing, not past wrongdoing. The privilege is designed to encourage those who may have committed a prior wrong to seek protection of their rights, which is why this court distinguishes between past and ongoing or future wrongdoing. In essence, the attorney-client privilege is not designed to encourage those planning to commit a wrong to obtain legal assistance in their endeavor. Significantly,

> although the fraud or crime must have been contemplated by the client at the time of the communication, it is irrelevant whether the attorney was aware of the client's purpose.

Id. at 74 (internal quotations and citations omitted).

3. The court in *Mendel* distinguished *Bernali* and similar cases in this way:

> Although each of these cases also involves a parental or guardian kidnapping, each is distinguishable from the instant case. In each case, the attorney was compelled against his/her will to divulge the address of the client. In the instant case, Mendel has acknowledged that she would have to divulge [Mother's] location if she knew where [Mother] was or the name of anyone she knew who knew [Mother's] location. Mendel stated, "I don't know those things, and I have never wanted to know those things. And I've been very clear with everyone that if they tell me I will tell."

Id., at 74, note 12.

What do you think about attorney Mendel's approach? Should you warn your clients that there are some things you simply don't want to know?

4. The court here states that the attorney-client privilege does not apply because the client's conduct constituted a fraud on the court. In what sense is violating the court's order not to remove the children a fraud? Would violation of any court order constitute fraud? This is an example of the ways in which some courts have adopted a very broad definition of "fraud" under the crime-fraud exception. *See, e.g., In re Sealed Case*, 676 F.2d 793, 812 (D.C.Cir. 1982)("crime, fraud, or other type of misconduct fundamentally inconsistent with the basic premises of the adversary system.").
5. The court also suggests that the best interest of the child is a general principle that can support overruling the evidentiary privilege. This was also the approach taken by the Ohio Supreme Court in a case in which attorneys were required to disclose the name and whereabouts of their clients. The attorneys had attempted to facilitate an adoption for their clients, even though the adoption was illegal as the mother was only seventeen-year-old when she turned over the baby. When mother sought return of the infant, the attorneys refused to assist her. In affirming the trial court's decision to overrule the claim of privilege and require the attorneys to testify, the Ohio Supreme Court held:

> The Supreme Court's overriding concern with the welfare of the infant as a ward of the court overbalances any interest of tech-

> nical claim on the appellant's part with respect to the confidential relationship between him and his clients....
> The disclosure of the client's identity is required where, as at bar, injury would result to the proper administration of justice 'immeasurably greater than the benefit that would enure to the relation of attorney and client.'

Lemley v. Kaiser, 452 N.E.2d 1304, 1312 (Ohio 1983).

What do you think of this approach to privilege? To the extent the attorney-client privilege is designed to encourage clients to communicate freely with their attorneys, does a "best interests of the child" exception sweep too broadly?

Portfolio Problem: Legislative Advocacy

Suppose that your state legislature has been holding hearings on the negative effects of children growing up in homes where violence is present. Even if children are not themselves the direct victims of abuse, the legislature is concerned by the growing evidence that merely witnessing the abuse of a parent can be psychologically damaging to these children and that children who grow up in homes where a parent is the victim of abuse are substantially more likely to perpetrate or become victims of domestic abuse as adults. A group of legislators has proposed a bill that would require all attorneys representing individuals seeking divorce to screen their clients for the presence of domestic violence and report their findings to the court. Attorneys who do not ask the screening questions or do not report information creating reasonable suspicions of abuse are subject to criminal penalties.

Assume that under Rule 1.6 of your state's Rules of Professional Conduct, attorneys could not ordinarily disclose this confidential client information, absent client consent, unless disclosure would be to prevent death or substantial bodily harm. The proposed legislation does not limit the required disclosure to these situations. Assume as well that your state is one in which the supreme court of the state has stated that courts have the sole and exclusive authority to regulate the practice of law. You have been asked by your state bar committee to prepare a legislative briefing regarding the wisdom and enforceability of this legislation. To read the views of others on the subject, see Robert P. Mosteller, *Child Abuse Reporting Laws And Attorney-Client Confidences: The Reality And The Specter Of Lawyer As Informant*, 42 Duke L.J. 203 (1992); Adrienne Jennings Lockie, *Salt in the Wounds: Why Attorneys Should Not Be Mandated Reporters of Child Abuse*, 36 N.M. L. Rev. 125 (2006). For discussion of this issue as related to mediators, see Art Hinshaw, *Mediators as Mandatory Reporters of Child Abuse: Preserving Mediation's Core Values*, 34 Fla. St. U.L. Rev. 211 (2007).

To Learn More

In addition to the articles and web resources cited in this chapter, the following articles are helpful to learning more:

About assessing capacity of older adults

ABA Committee on Law and Aging & American Psychological Association, Assessment of Older Adults with Diminished Capacity: A Handbook for Lawyers (2005).

> The handbook offers a conceptual framework and practice tips for addressing problems of client capacity in the day-to-day practice of law and working with mental health professionals.

About assessing danger in domestic violence

The National Center on Domestic and Sexual Violence has a variety of excellent publications on screening for domestic violence and assessing lethality, most of which are available on-line from their website http://www.ncdsv.org.

About attorney-client privilege

Edna S. Epstein, The Attorney-Client Privilege and the Work-Product Doctrine, Fifth Edition (ABA 2007).

> This comprehensive two-volume set provides law and examples of all aspects of these doctrines in a variety of practice settings, along with practical advice.

Center for Computer Assisted Legal Instruction, http://www.cali.org.

> Lesson number PR16, *The Attorney's Duty of Confidentiality & the Attorney-Client Privilege*, and Lesson number PR17 *Exceptions to the Ethical Duty of Confidentiality Designed to Protect Third Persons from Harm.*

Chapter Six

Candor to Third Parties and the Court

Learning Objectives for This Chapter

After you have read this chapter and completed the assignments you should be able to:

- Identify the attorney's duty to correct misunderstandings or errors in negotiations.
- Apply the standards for meritorious claims in counseling a client seeking to pursue a claim.
- Identify the attorney's duty to provide factual evidence and legal authority to a tribunal.
- Identify the attorney's duty to prevent introduction of false evidence to a tribunal and to correct evidence discovered to be false.

Lies and misrepresentations may constitute some of the most common categories of confidential information that you will wish you had never learned. Whether out of a sense of embarrassment or a desire to deceive, your clients may not tell "the whole truth" to you or to others. Even more often, clients simply do not know the whole truth or seek to assert claims that the law simply does not support. What do you do when you discover that your client's case is built on misrepresentations or mistakes? The answer depends in part on the person to whom the lie is directed. Responsibilities of candor in negotiations differ from the responsibility of candor to the court. In this chapter we will examine the duties and tensions that arise in each of these contexts.

A. Candor in Negotiations

Suppose, for example, you have assisted your client in negotiating a separation agreement with her husband. The couple has not yet filed for divorce or legal separation and are simply operating under the terms of that agreement. What if you discover that your client lied about key financial information in making that agreement? The rules of professional conduct provide that attorneys may not knowingly make a false statement of material fact or law to a third person (Model Rule 4.1). If the client has lied to a third person, the rule provides that attorneys must disclose a material fact "when disclosure is necessary to avoid assisting a criminal or fraudulent act by a client." However, this duty is modified by the duty to keep information confidential under Model Rule 1.6.

Under the Model Rules, until recently, there were no exceptions to confidentiality for crimes or fraud that caused financial injury and attorneys were often left in a situation in which they were aware of a client's fraudulent act and the only recourse was to withdraw and, perhaps, to give notice of the fact of withdrawal and disclaim any documents.[1] In August 2003, the ABA amended Model Rule 1.6 to allow disclosures in situations of client crimes or fraud that result in financial injury. The new exceptions to the rule provide that a lawyer may reveal confidential information if all of the following are true:

- the client intends to commit a crime or fraud or has committed a crime or fraud
- that wrong is reasonably certain to cause or has caused substantial injury to financial or property interests
- the wrong is or was furthered by the lawyer's services
- the lawyer reasonably believes that revealing the information is necessary to prevent the crime or fraud or to prevent, mitigate or rectify the injury flowing from the wrong.

This new rule is consistent with the position already adopted in many states. Under this rule, you would have the discretion to disclose your client's misrepresentation if you had relied on that misrepresentation in preparing the separation agreement and if it would cause substantial financial injury to her husband.

Suppose, however, that you discover that the financial information underlying the agreement is wrong, but not due to your client's misrepresentation. Assume, rather, that the separation agreement was prepared by the other side and contains an error that favors your client. If your client expressly directs you not to disclose that error, does the duty of confidentiality require that you keep quiet? Certainly this would be considered "information relating to the representation" and so would be confidential. Under which exceptions to con-

1. Model Rule 1.2, cmt. 10 (2002).

fidentiality might you have the discretion to disclose this error without your client's consent?

If the error was entirely that of the other side, it would be unlikely to be considered your client's fraud. This would be especially so if the error were one of law or tactics, rather than one of fact. For example, in *In re Marriage of Turner*, 803 S.W.2d 655 (Mo. Ct. App. 1991), the court held that the failure of the husband's attorney to advise the wife's attorney that the pension was marital property subject to distribution was not fraudulent misrepresentation. It seems that, unless the attorney or client had a duty to disclose the error because they had induced it, the attorney would be bound to remain silent if his client directed him to do so.

Yet, there are risks in proceeding in the face of that silence. Even if conduct does not rise to the level of actionable fraud, the court may find an attorney subject to discipline for violation of 8.4(c) or (d) (dishonesty or conduct prejudicial to the administration of justice).[2] Additionally, there is your own personal reputation to consider. Most errors are discovered sooner or later. Your reputation for fair dealing with other attorneys and the court will be severely injured when that happens.

Moreover, there is simply the issue of fairness. Model Rule 4.4 Respect for the Rights of Third Persons provides minimal guidance, prohibiting only the use of means that "have no substantial purpose other than to embarrass, delay, or burden a third person." In 1986, the ABA issued an informal opinion on the ethical duty of a lawyer who has discovered that an agreed clause unfavorable to his or her client has been inadvertently omitted from the final signed version of the agreement. The opinion concluded that the lawyer should contact the other party's lawyer to correct the error and need not contact his or her client about the error.[3] However, that opinion did not reach the issue of what you do if the client wishes to exploit the error. In this circumstance, your duty to notify the opposing counsel of the error may be outweighed by the duty of confidentiality and the principles of agency law. Thus, you may only disclose the error if you can convince your client to consent to doing so.

If the client insists that you capitalize on an opponent's factual error, your only safe option is withdrawal. Model Rule 1.16(b)(2) allows an attorney to withdraw

---

2. *See, e.g.*, Cincinnati Bar Ass'n v. Wallace, 700 N.E.2d 1238 (Ohio 1998) (attorney who assisted client in fashioning real estate transfer to his current spouse in order to avoid child support and in then answering "none" in response to interrogatory regarding real estate ownership was reprimanded for acting in an unprofessional manner).

3. ABA Comm. on Ethics and Prof'l Responsibility, Informal Op. 86-1518 n.1 (1986) (notice to opposing counsel of inadvertent omission of contract provision).

if "the client persists in a course of action involving the lawyer's services that the lawyer reasonably believes is criminal or fraudulent" and (b)(4) allows withdrawal when "the client insists upon taking action that the lawyer considers repugnant or with which the lawyer has a fundamental disagreement." Moreover, Model Rule 1.2, comment 10, provides that "In some cases, withdrawal alone might be insufficient. It may be necessary for the lawyer to give notice of the fact of withdrawal and to disaffirm any opinion, document, affirmation or the like."

Model Rule 1.2 suggests that you may counsel a client as to the legal consequences of their choices and Model Rule 2.1 allows you to counsel the client as to the non-legal ramifications of their choices as well. The consequences of misrepresentation are often much more serious than a client may realize[4] and the chances that an error will be discovered are great. In the end, the most effective message you can send a client in these circumstances is the futility of trying to capitalize on an opponent's error, as demonstrated by the following case:

Stare v. Tate

21 Cal. App. 3d 432; 98 Cal. Rptr. 264 (Cal. App. 1971)

Plaintiff appeals from an adverse judgment in an action to reform a property settlement agreement with her former husband, the defendant, and to enforce the agreement as reformed.

Facts

The agreement in question was signed by both parties on February 21, 1968. It was the culmination of protracted negotiations which had been going on for several years. Both sides were represented by counsel at all times. In the negotiations both sides apparently agreed that the community property was to be evenly divided. They did not agree, however, on the value of certain items and on the community property status of certain stocks which stood in the husband's name alone.

These disagreements centered principally on items which, it was understood, were to be retained by the husband.

In particular the wife, Joan, had an *idée fixe* that certain real property (the Holt property) which she and the husband, Tim, owned as tenants in common with his brother, was worth $550,000. The husband's valuation was some-

4. The client may be in some instances be subject to a civil action for fraud, which can include punitive damages. Burris v. Burris, 904 S.W.2d 564 (Mo. Ct. App. 1995). An action for restitution may also be readily available when the client knew they were receiving benefits mistakenly conferred and did nothing to point out the error. See Restatement (Second) of Contracts § 86, comment c (1981).

where between $425,000 and $450,000. Joan had very little evidence on which to base her contention: First, there was a statement by Tim's parents when they had owned the property that it was worth about $550,000; second, a former attorney of Tim's had, in 1966, written a letter to Joan's attorney which contained a settlement offer based upon a value of $550,000.[5]

The second important area of disagreement centered on the ownership of stock in a family corporation and the proper basis for its valuation. In all Tim owned 25,500 shares. Of these he had owned 5,000 shares long before he married Joan. Joan realized that any claim that these 5,000 shares were community property was tenuous, at best. Similarly, on his part, Tim conceded that a block of 7,500 shares was community property. Another block of 5,000 shares was, according to Joan, given to her and Tim as a wedding present by his parents. Yet another block of 8,000 shares was, again according to Joan, given to both her and Tim as a present during their marriage. The shares were, however, in Tim's name alone and he denied that the community had any interest in them.

The book value of the shares was a little less than $7.00 per share. Joan claimed that the fair market value was, however, $1.50 per share over the book value and that Tim should "buy" her community interest in the shares at that value.

To sum up: If Joan was correct with respect to the value of the Holt property, her community property interest in it was about $25,000 higher than Tim conceded; if she were to succeed on her contentions with respect to the stock, Tim would have had to pay her roughly $40,000 more than he was willing.

In January 1968, Joan's attorney prepared a document entitled "Second Proposal For A Basis of Settlement—Tate v. Tate" which, among other things, arrived at a suggested figure of $70,081.85 for the value of Joan's share in the Holt property. This value was arrived at by a computation set forth in the proposal.

888 East Holt Avenue, Pomona
(Note: value as per previous offer)

Total value	$550,000.00	
Less encumbrance	–308,362.99	
Net value	$141,637.01	
One-half community		$70,081.85

5. Based on the $550,000 figure, taking into account several encumbrances and the fact that the community only owned a 50 percent interest in the property, the attorney arrived at an equity of $60,000. As will be seen, about 15 months later the equity based on the $550,000 figure was worth, roughly, $120,000. The record does not indicate why there was such a big change in such a relatively short time. Presumably, at least part of it is due to payments on the encumbrances.

It is obvious that Joan's attorney arrived at the figure of $70,081.85 for the community equity in the property only by making two substantial errors. First, the net value after deducting the encumbrances from the asserted gross value of $550,000 is $241,637.01, not $141,637.01; second, one-half of $241,637.01 is substantially more than $70,081.85. The correct figure for the equity should have been $120,818.50 or, roughly $50,000 more.

The mistake did not escape Tim's accountant who discovered it while helping Tim's attorney in preparing a counteroffer. He brought it to the attention of the attorney who, in his own words, reacted as follows:

> "I told him that I had been arguing with [the wife's attorney] to use the value that was on the—on the real property tax statement, but I knew that that was low and [he] would never go for it, that his appraisal had been $425,000.00 when the building had been purchased by said owners, and I thought that until we got it, that we would use something like a $450,000.00 value, and he said, 'Fine.' It is my recollection that I said to him, 'You know, you might as well use the figure that Walker has there because his mistake is a hundred thousand dollars and we value it at a hundred thousand dollars less, so it is basically the same thing, so give it a $70,000.00 equity,' and that is what he did and that is how it came about."

A counteroffer was then submitted to Joan and her lawyer. It lists all of the community assets, with the property in question being valued at $70,082.00, rounding up the erroneous figure in Joan's offer to the nearest dollar. There can be no reasonable doubt that the counteroffer was prepared in a way designed to minimize the danger that Joan or her attorney would discover the mistake. While all other encumbered properties are listed at an agreed gross value, with encumbrances shown as a deduction therefrom, the only figure that appears next to the Holt property is the equity!

The counteroffer said nothing about attorneys' fees. One of its terms was that Joan would assume a note of not quite $11,000. It was based on only 7,500 shares of the family corporation's stock being community property and a valuation at book. In other words, it represented a demand for total surrender by Joan on the two major items in dispute.

Based on the figures in the counteroffer Tim would have received substantially more in assets than Joan. This difference was to be made up by a cash payment of $46,534.

On February 16, 1968, the parties and their attorneys had a settlement conference. The counteroffer was the basis for the discussion. There was no mention that the figure of $70,082 for the equity in the Holt property was based on an agreed value of $550,000 or any other figure. In the discussion it was agreed that the husband was to assume the liability on the $11,000 note and was to pay Joan's attorney $7,500, a figure somewhat smaller than counsel's time charges up till then. The result of all this give and take was that the cash payment from Tim to Joan was to be reduced to $40,000.

A few days later a formal agreement was signed. It simply recites who was to get what, without ascribing any value to any of the properties. It also provides for the $40,000 cash payment. Sometime in March 1968, Joan obtained a divorce.

The mistake might never have come to light had not Tim desired to have that exquisite last word. A few days after Joan had obtained the divorce he mailed her a copy of the offer which contained the errant computation. On top of the page he wrote with evident satisfaction: "PLEASE NOTE $100,000.00 MISTAKE IN YOUR FIGURES...." The present action was filed exactly one month later.

Tim testified that he did not learn of the arithmetical error until after the property settlement agreement was signed. The record contains no evidence to the contrary.

Discussion

There is really no substantial conflict in the evidence and it is hard to understand how the trial court could do anything but grant Joan's prayer for relief.

Section 3399 of the Civil Code provides: "When, through fraud or a mutual mistake of the parties, or a mistake of one party, which the other at the time knew or suspected, a written contract does not truly express the intention of the parties, it may be revised on the application of a party aggrieved, so as to express that intention, so far as it can be done without prejudice to rights acquired by third persons, in good faith and for value."

Clearly there was a mistake, Joan and her attorney thinking that a $550,000 value resulted in a community equity of about $70,000. The mistake was known to Tim's former attorney who swept it under the rug in the counteroffer by setting forth just the equity, instead of the value minus encumbrances, as he did with respect to other properties. True, he apparently justified this to himself morally by the fact that the value which Tim had been claiming all along resulted in a $70,000 equity, but he never drew the other side's attention to the fact that the counteroffer was based on Tim's previous position on the value of the Holt property. Joan and her attorney were, of course, quite satisfied in believing that Tim had surrendered his point on Holt since she was to abandon her position with respect to the ownership of 13,000 shares and the method of valuing of the entire block of 20,500 shares. Inasmuch as the error was discovered by Tim's attorney, it is, of course, no defense that it was negligently made by Joan's attorney.

Nor was the defense based on any such theory. Rather what the defense proceeded to do was to isolate the problem of the correct valuation of the Holt property from all others that were on the table during the final settlement negotiations, by offering proof that it was worth no more than an amount which would result in the $70,000 equity. The trial court clearly went along with this approach, permitted Tim to prove the value of the Holt property by expert testimony and other means, found that the property was worth no more than $425,000, that Joan had received an equitable division of the community property "and that no reformation is required for said reason."

Joan's counsel at all times resisted this compartmentalization of the issues that divided the parties before the property settlement agreement was signed. He was, of course, quite correct. If it is the law that reformation in this case can only be had if the trial court felt that the division of community property was fair, how could it possibly make such a finding based only on the value of the Holt property? As noted, Joan's extremely tenable position with respect to the stock would, if sustained, have been worth about $40,000, while the fight over the Holt property meant only $25,000. How did the trial court take into account the fact that Joan waived alimony? What the court did, in effect, was to retry just one of the many issues that could have arisen in a litigated divorce, to find that she would not have prevailed on that issue and to conclude from that that the entire property settlement agreement was fair.

This approach was wholly wrong. It ignores that the parties had settled their claims, thereby giving up any right to have a court determine them. That goes for Tim, as well as for Joan. The only legitimate question which was before the trial court was whether the settlement agreement should be reformed to express Joan's intent which was known to Tim who also knew, through his attorney, that the instrument did not express it.

Counsel for Tim argues, as defendants in these cases usually do, that Tim never intended to enter into a settlement based on the $550,000 figure and that a court of equity cannot make a new contract for the parties, whether a mistake is unilateral or bilateral. The law is, however, more subtle, in that it estops the party who knows of the plaintiff's mistake from claiming that his intent differs from what he leads the other to believe it is. In *Eagle Indem. Co. v. Industrial Acc. Com.*, 206 P.2d 877 (Cal. Appl. 1949), an insurer knew that a certain policy did not provide for certain coverage, and that the insured thought it did. It was held that the policy was subject to reformation according to the insured's intent. "Petitioner argues that the commission by ordering reformation of the policy created a new contract for the parties. Of course, reformation cannot be ordered so as to create a new and different contract for the parties but where, as here, the case falls within the language of Civil Code, section

3399, [when], through … a mistake of one party, which the other … knew or suspected, a written contract does not truly express the intention of the parties …" the contract which was intended by the party acting under unilateral mistake known or suspected by the other, is, as a matter of law, the contract of the parties…." *Eagle Indem. Co. v. Industrial Acc. Com.*, 206 P.2d at 879. Indeed, in view of the express wording of section 3399 of the Civil Code any other rule would thwart the legislative intent.

The rule that the party who misleads another is estopped from claiming that the contract is anything but what the other is led to believe, appears to be quite generally accepted. Citing many cases from other jurisdictions and noting no contrary authority Corbin says: "Reformation may be a proper remedy even though the mistake is not mutual. If one of the parties mistakenly believes that the writing is a correct integration of that to which he had expressed his assent and the other party knows that it is not, reformation may be decreed. The conduct of the other party in permitting the first to execute the erroneous writing and later attempting to enforce it may be regarded as fraudulent; but it is enough to justify reformation that he knows the terms proposed by the first party and the meaning thereof and leads that party reasonably to believe that he too assents to those terms. This makes a contract; and the writing may be reformed to accord with it. The fact that the first party was negligent in failing to observe that the writing does not express what he has assented to does not deprive him of this remedy. The ground for estoppel is against the other and non-mistaken party, not against the mistaken party even though he is negligent." (3 Corbin on Contracts, §614, pp. 730–732.) The rule is also in accord with the Restatement of Contracts.

Therefore the fact, stressed over and over again by defendant, that he never affirmatively assented to a $550,000 valuation, is quite immaterial….

The court found four different times that plaintiff knew that the counteroffer was not based on the $550,000 value. There just is nothing in the record to support that finding. Even if we attach no sinister significance to the fact that the counteroffer did not set forth the value on which the $70,000 equity depended and on the fact that no value was mentioned during the negotiations of February 16, 1968, we are still left with a plaintiff who mistakenly believed that her valuation had been accepted and a defendant who knew of that belief.

The court found that Joan would have entered into the property settlement agreement if she had not obtained the acceptance of the $550,000 valuation. This, of course, is a far cry from finding that she would have settled if she had known that the settlement was based on $450,000. In any event there is nothing whatever in the record to support the finding. Tim argues that the finding is justified by Joan's knowledge he would not accept her $550,000 figure. As we have shown that finding is not supported in the evidence. The finding is thus based solely on conjecture. Settlement negotiations of the kind that were had between the parties are usually nothing but a high stake game of poker. Since it appears that each was holding the cards close to the vest, it does not appear possible to determine judicially who was bluffing. Finally we have found no case which indicates that it matters what Joan would have done had Tim been more frank. By permitting her to enter into the contract in the belief that he had accepted her $550,000 value, he simply took the risk that if she discovered the mistake and sought judicial redress, the contract would be enforced on the terms which she mistakenly thought she had already received.

The court found that Tim did not conceal any item of community property and that he disclosed the "nature, description and value" of all the items. What Tim concealed, however, was his discovery of the error or errors, which concealment, or to put it more charitably, which lack of disclosure is the nub of this litigation.

The case was fully tried and, as we said at the outset of our discussion, the record supports nothing but a judgment for the plaintiff as prayed.

The judgment is reversed with directions to make findings and conclusions and to enter a judgment in conformity with this opinion.

Questions

1. How could Joan's attorney have avoided placing his client in this position?
2. How would you characterize the reasoning of Tim's attorney in justifying his preparation of the counteroffer based on the mistaken numbers?
3. What if the settlement agreement had been drafted by Joan's attorney with the mathematical error in that agreement and there had been no counteroffer. Would the agreement have been subject to reformation if Tim had simply signed the agreement with no further negotiations?
4. If you were Tim's attorney, how would you convince Tim that you could not capitalize on the other side's error, given that this case had been going on for years?

B. Candor to the Court

Unlike the duty of candor in negotiations, the duty of candor to a tribunal trumps the duty of confidentiality. Under Model Rule 3.3, if an attorney knows that a client has lied to the court, the attorney must take remedial measures, including disclosure, even if the information is otherwise confidential. The duty only applies if the attorney or the attorney's client has offered false evidence. If an attorney is aware that others have offered false evidence, the attorney has no general duty to rectify that error but may not further the fraud by using that false evidence in any way. Moreover, the duty to rectify false evidence under the rules only applies until the close of the proceedings.

Taking the unfortunately common issue of a client who lies about financial information in a divorce, if you become aware that a client's misinformation has been submitted to the court, whether through testimony or through filing documents with the court, you are obligated to correct that error. In most instances, this will require disclosing the error to the court.

Closely related to the problem of misrepresentation of financial information is the problem of dissipation of marital assets. In many states, the filing of a divorce operates to trigger an injunction against transferring or conveying property.[6] In the remainder of the states, courts have authority to grant these injunctions when appropriate. Model Rule 3.3(a)(2) provides that a lawyer shall not knowingly fail to disclose a material fact to a tribunal when disclosure is necessary to avoid assisting a criminal or fraudulent act by the client. Applying that rule to a client's violation of a court order prohibiting dissipation of marital assets, an attorney would ordinarily be required to disclose that violation if prior statements made to the court would be fraudulent in light of the dissipation. Even if the client is in the process of dissipating assets, the attorney's continued representation may constitute assisting in a fraud on the court where the client has a continuing duty to report changes in financial information. Read AAML Standard 5.1 and the comments in Appendix A for additional perspectives on this issue.

Not all client violations of court orders would require an attorney to take remedial measures.

> There are numerous circumstances in which a lawyer may be aware that her client is in violation of a court order—even one issued in the context of the matter in which the lawyer is representing the client—but has no reason to anticipate that the violation materially will affect the resolution of the litigation. For example, a court may order that a defendant in a criminal case comply with certain requirements as a condition of release; a domestic relations court may issue a "stay-away" order in a divorce case; or any court may issue a protective order providing for the confidentiality of information obtained in discovery. A

6. Colo. Rev. Stat. 14-10-107(4)(b)(2008); 13 Del. C. 1509 (2009); 750 ILCS 5/501.1 (2009); Or. Rev. Stat. 107.105(1)(f) (2009).

> lawyer's failure to report a violation of such an order by her client would not appear to constitute assistance to the client in committing a criminal or fraudulent act so as to require the lawyer under Rule 3.3 to either withdraw from representation of the client or disclose the client's violation to the court.[7]

Needless to say, while you may not always be required to disclose a client's violation of a court order, your duty always requires you to attempt to dissuade the client from taking that course of action.

One of your first obligations when representing a client in litigation is to insure that you have a good faith basis for the claims or defenses you will be bringing on behalf of that client. That obligation is created by both ethical and legal rules. Model Rule 3.1 provides that attorneys may not bring frivolous claims or defenses, as do state and federal rules of civil and criminal procedure, such as Federal Rule of Civil Procedure 11.

These rules do not require attorneys to bring only those claims that they believe have a good chance of succeeding. Attorneys may, for example, bring a claim based on a good faith argument for the extension, modification or reversal of existing law even though these arguments generally are not successful. Nonetheless, there must be at least some objectively realistic possibility of success in order to have the requisite good faith required by these rules.

These same rules equally prohibit a claim or defense brought with improper motivation. So, for example, ABA Model Rule 4.4 provides that an attorney should not engage in practices "that have no substantial purpose other than to embarrass, delay, or burden a third person." Likewise, Rule 11 requires that pleadings not be "presented for any improper purpose, such as to harass or to cause unnecessary delay or needless increase in the cost of litigation." Generally speaking, if an assertion is not objectively frivolous, it is difficult to show that the purpose in pursuing that assertion has no substantial purpose. Nonetheless, at least some courts have stated that if one can show that a claim is brought in subjective bad faith, there is a violation of the rules of professional conduct, "even if the claim would otherwise meet the objective test of a non-frivolous claim." *In re Levine*, 847 P.2d 1093, 1100 (Ariz. 1993).

The history of family law is one in which manufactured claims and evidence were, at one time, the norm. One of the oft-cited reasons for no-fault divorce reform was the prevalence of collusion and fraud on the court in states with fault-based systems. While collusion or fraud may be less common today in securing a divorce, pressures for fraudulent claims still exist. The law does not

7. ABA Comm. on Ethics and Prof'l Responsibility, Formal Op. 98-412 (1998).

allow or enforce purely private resolution of most family law matters. Parties cannot, without court supervision and regulation, agree to divorce or agree to assume or reject the status of parent, or even agree to alter the law's imposition of financial responsibility toward one another. Yet family members may feel that this degree of government intrusion on their relationships is illegitimate, that they should be able to structure their relationships as they see fit, so long as no harm is done. This attitude may create pressures for attorneys to engage in "creative lawyering" to achieve their client's objectives. But when does that creativity cross the line into unethical conduct?

Certainly, an attorney will not choose to represent a client who is manufacturing false claims with vindictive motives. But how do you know whether your client's claims are true? Particularly in the highly subjective and emotional context of family law disputes, how can you ascertain whether a claim is "well grounded in fact"? What is your duty to investigate your client's statements? Moreover, at what point can you determine that a client's claim, no matter how factually substantiated, is one being pursued solely for an improper purpose? Consider the view of the attorneys and the judges in the following case raising these issues:

In re Mirabile, 975 S.W.2d 936

(Mo. banc 1998)

Opinion

The Chief Disciplinary Counsel charged that respondents James P. Moroney and Salvatore J. Mirabile filed a fraudulent petition for legal separation, and a sham stipulation, in order to avoid a child support obligation. Each information charged respondents with violating Rules of Professional Conduct 4-3.1, 4-3.3, 4-8.4(b) and (c). The informations request that both respondents be disbarred. Because this Court cannot find by a preponderance of the evidence that these respondents committed professional misconduct, the informations are dismissed.

I.

.... This Court finds the following facts. In 1992, Joseph Leahy retained his close friend, respondent Moroney, to represent him in a child support modification action brought by his ex-wife in Jackson county circuit court. At that time, Leahy, a self-employed voice artist, was the president and sole shareholder of Jovial, Inc., a corporation that had as its sole business the sale of Leahy's voice. At trial, Leahy submitted a Form 14 presumed child support worksheet, signed by Moroney, listing his monthly income as $7,000.

On June 16, 1992, the Jackson county circuit judge (since deceased) met with respondent Moroney and opposing counsel in chambers. The Jackson county judge advised that he was imputing income of $16,250 per month to Leahy and intended to raise Leahy's child support obligation from $500 per month to $2,080 per month. Moroney immediately stated that his client would appeal. He angrily stated to the judge that his client would be better off if he and his present wife, Joyce Leahy, were divorced, and that if he had created the corporation, Joyce Leahy would have owned all the stock.

Moroney left the judge's chambers and immediately met with Joyce Leahy in the hall nearby; Joseph Leahy was not in Missouri that day. Upon hearing that the judge planned to increase the child support for the child of Joseph's first marriage, she also became angry. She asked Moroney to recommend an attorney to represent her in filing for divorce. Moroney recommended his friend, respondent Mirabile, among other attorneys. That day Joyce Leahy called Mirabile and asked him to represent her.

That night, Moroney and Joseph Leahy met with Mirabile at Mirabile's family's restaurant in Kansas City. Mirabile was serving as maitre d' and, throughout a three-hour period, stopped at the Moroney-Leahy table to discuss the legal separation, child support, maintenance, and control of assets. Joyce Leahy was not present. By the next day, Moroney and Mirabile had prepared a petition for legal separation, a joint stipulation, and a joint motion for temporary order. Joyce Leahy, who had not yet met in person with her attorney Mirabile, appeared with opposing counsel Moroney in Ray county circuit court to file the petition.

Joyce Leahy later testified by deposition, but not in person, before the Master. She stated that her purpose for filing the petition was to protect herself and her five children's financial interests. She testified she wanted a legal separation, and was angry with her husband for not having resolved the problems with his ex-wife.

Joyce Leahy verified the petition for legal separation, which alleged that the parties had separated the previous day. The joint stipulation provided that Joyce Leahy would receive $5,000 per month maintenance and that their five children would receive $2,000 per month child support, for a total of $7,000—exactly the amount of the monthly income claimed on the Form 14 filed in the Jackson county case. The stipulation provided: Petitioner and Respondent are jointly agreed, that pending a final hearing in the matter herein, all corporate assets in a certain entity known as Jovial, Inc., a corporation organized and lawfully operating in the State of California, shall be in the exclusive custody and control of Petitioner wife. Respondent further agrees forthwith, to do any and all things necessary to effectuate possession and control of corporate assets to Petitioner wife, upon execution of this Stipulation by counsel for the respective parties herein.

Petitioner and Respondent jointly agree, pending final disposition and hearing in the matter herein, that all joint checking, savings and financial accounts shall be immediately transferred to Petitioner wife. Respondent agrees to such transfer, forthwith, upon the execution of this Stipulation by counsel for the respective parties.

The petition was filed in Ray County on June 18, 1992. Seven days later, on June 25, the judge entered a temporary order implementing the stipulation. Two days earlier, on June 23, the Jackson county judge had entered his order, in accordance with his previous conference with the attorneys. On June 26, the Jackson county judge met with Mirabile, Moroney and the opposing attorney in chambers. The judge told the respondents that he had learned about the Ray county filings and order, and that something "smelled." The respondents denied any wrongdoing.

The attorney for Leahy's ex-wife filed a complaint against Moroney based on this sequence of events. The Circuit Bar and Advisory Committees, after testimony by all involved counsel, found probable cause. Joseph Leahy refused to pay the Jackson county child support order until he was held in contempt in October 1992, four months after the Ray county order and while it was in effect.

On April 14, 1993, nearly nine months after issuing the order—and after the disciplinary hearings began—the Ray county court, on its "own motion for the reason that there is some suggestion that there was impropriety in the issuance of the Temporary Order," rescinded its order. The Leahys neither appealed this Ray county decision nor took any further action in that case. The Leahys reconciled and now live together in the state of California....

III.

The Master found that respondents initiated a frivolous, sham proceeding for legal separation, with the actual purpose of avoiding collection of a child support judgment in violation of Rules 4-3.1, 4-3.3 and 4-8.4(b) and (c). Under Rule 4-3.1, it is professional misconduct for an attorney to bring a frivolous proceeding. Rule 4-3.3 details a lawyer's duty of candor toward a tribunal, and Rule 4-8.4 provides that conduct involving dishonesty, fraud, deceit or misrepresentation is professional misconduct. The respondents counter that they had a duty to follow their clients' instructions.

Attorneys generally must follow their clients' instructions, but only within the limits of the law. "The client has ultimate authority to determine the purposes to be served by legal representation, within the limits imposed by law and the lawyer's professional obligations." Comment, Rule 4-1.2. The knowing failure to pay child support without good cause is a crime. Section 568.040 RSMo 1994. Fraudulent conveyances of assets are void. Section 428.020 RSMo

1986 (repealed Aug. 28, 1992). The Rules of Professional Responsibility prohibit other improper conduct. Rule 4-8.4. An attorney may not assist or induce a client to engage in criminal or fraudulent or other improper conduct, Rule 4-8.4(a), but a lawyer may discuss the legal consequences of any course of conduct with a client. Rule 4-1.2.

The Master concluded that the respondents crossed this line, finding only the complainant's testimony credible, and finding unbelievable most of the other witnesses (including the circuit judge and the present Mrs. Leahy, both of whom testified only by deposition). The Master found suspicious that the respondents filed the legal separation so quickly after the Jackson county order and that the respondents and their clients were close friends. According to the Master, the contempt order against Joseph Leahy, and his contumacious refusal to pay child support, demonstrated that the respondent attorneys intended to use the Ray county filings to assist or induce the Leahys in avoiding the child support obligation. Ultimately, however, the Master recommended public sanctions less than disbarment, but the CDC recommends that respondents be disbarred.

This Court disciplines attorneys in order to protect the public and to maintain the integrity of the profession. To disbar an attorney, it must be clear that the attorney is not fit to continue in the profession; disbarment is reserved only for clear cases of severe misconduct.

The evidence does not support any sanction. In disciplinary proceedings, the CDC must prove the charges by a preponderance of the evidence. In this case, the CDC has not proved the charges of professional misconduct by a preponderance of the evidence.

The CDC argues that Moroney and Mirabile knew that the legal separation was frivolous and a sham. To the contrary, the Leahys testified that they actually separated, that they told their attorneys that they desired a legal separation, and that they, in fact, complied with the terms of the Ray county order. The respondent attorneys testified that they believed the separation was real. Lawyers are responsible for pleadings and other documents prepared in litigation, but need not have personal knowledge of matters asserted in documents submitted to courts because such documents contain assertions of the client, not the lawyer. See comment, Rule 4-3.3. Lawyers must make an inquiry reasonable under the circumstances. Rule 55.03(b).

Emphasizing that the Master found all this testimony incredible, the CDC argues that this credibility finding indicates that respondents acted fraudulently. The Master's determinations of credibility are advisory only and do not constitute evidence of professional misconduct. In this case, the CDC may not meet its burden of proof merely by showing inconsistencies in the testimony of the respondents and their clients. True, this Court has considered false statements to a disciplinary tribunal as an aggravator in imposing sanctions, but only where the CDC offered sufficient additional evidence to support the charges. *In re Waldron*, 790 S.W.2d 456, 461 (Mo. banc 1990).

The CDC also argues that the respondents have failed to rebut or explain the suspicious circumstances surrounding the filings, and that this constitutes circumstantial evidence of fraud. A charge of professional misconduct does not create a rebuttable presumption of professional misconduct.

It is professional misconduct for a lawyer to engage in conduct involving fraud. Rule 4-8.4(c); see also Rule 4-9.1 (defining fraud). Fraudulent intent may be shown by "badges of fraud," one of which is "inability to pay debts as they become due." The Master and the separate opinion both emphasize that the Ray county judge ordered Leahy to pay his present wife all his "claimed" income. The Ray county order did not convey all of Leahy's income but rather $7,000 of his $16,250 monthly income. Leahy was solvent at all relevant times. As the later contempt judgment held, Leahy—while subject to the Ray county order—was able to pay his child support obligations because he controlled the income his personal services produced.

On the key issue, the respondents and their clients testified consistently and adamantly that the clients truly desired a legal separation, and under the terms in the stipulation. The CDC's evidence does not overcome this clear, consistent evidence. Most importantly, the Ray county judge testified, by deposition, that the respondent attorneys told him of the Jackson county order at their first appearance in Ray County. In fact, the Ray county judge testified that he and the Jackson county judge discussed the cases shortly after both orders were entered, and months later at a judicial conference. The Ray county judge's deposition shows that the respondent attorneys did not perpetuate a fraud on the Ray county court. The Ray county judge testified that he, in fact, agreed with the position of Joseph Leahy in the Jackson county proceeding.

The CDC also invokes a judgment, where another Jackson county judge determined that, for purposes of service of process, Joseph Leahy resided at the same address in California as Joyce Leahy, in October 1992, during the period of alleged separation. First, there is absolutely no evidence that Mirabile knew anything about this judgment. Second, Moroney, who actually opposed this judgment, had a reasonable basis in fact to believe that the Leahys were still separated in October, because their living arrangements were, by all accounts, complex during the nine-month life of the Ray county order of legal separation.

The CDC points to other evidence suggesting that the Leahys still lived together after the petition was filed, including evidence that Joyce Leahy moved to the Los Angeles area, where Joseph Leahy was living. Both respondents testified that they were advised by their clients that they were separated. Mirabile testified that when he called Joyce Leahy at her Missouri address, she answered. Mirabile's contemporaneous billings were to Joyce Leahy at her Missouri address, never at the California address where the CDC claims they lived together. That the Leahys reconciled by the summer of 1993 is not inconsistent with separation a year earlier.

The Master and the CDC infer collusion because Moroney and Mirabile are friends and were also friends of their clients. Absent some other restriction, attorneys may represent their close friends.

The Master found that the order of contempt against Joseph Leahy—issued four months after the Ray county filings—shows that their purpose was to avoid the Jackson county child support order. There is no evidence that the respondents encouraged Joseph Leahy to refuse to pay his child support, nor any proof that he was ever unable to pay the child support (as he candidly testified he had the resources to pay it). The contempt order only shows that Joseph Leahy did not want to pay the child support, and does not constitute evidence of misconduct on the part of the respondents.

The CDC also suggests that the fact that Joseph Leahy appealed the child support order demonstrates that Moroney and Mirabile tried to help him avoid the obligation. An attorney does not commit professional misconduct by filing a non-frivolous appeal. The question here is whether the respondents knew, or should have known after an inquiry reasonable under the circumstances, that they were filing a fraudulent, sham petition for legal separation. See Rule 55.03(b). There is no question that Joseph Leahy did not want to pay the child support, fought the order, and was ultimately held in contempt for nonpayment. This does not demonstrate that the respondents unethically assisted him in avoiding the obligation.

The CDC proves that Moroney angrily stated to the Jackson county judge, the day before he filed a petition for legal separation, that his client would be better off divorced and that if he had been his attorney at the time, the corporation would have been created with Joyce Leahy as the owner. An attorney may discuss the legal consequences of any course of conduct with a client, so long as the attorney does not assist or induce a client to engage in criminal, fraudulent, or other improper conduct. In this case, the preponderance of the evidence does not support the charges of professional misconduct.

IV.

Given the balance of evidence in these discipline cases, this Court dismisses the informations against both Moroney and Mirabile.

Opinion concurring in part and dissenting in part by Judge John C. Holstein:

I reluctantly concur in the dismissal of the information against attorney Mirabile. However, I respectfully dissent as to dismissal of the information regarding attorney Moroney.

The majority opinion correctly notes that the Master's findings are merely advisory, but it is also true that such findings are helpful to this Court. *In re Griffey*, 873 S.W.2d 600, 601 (Mo. banc 1994). Typically, the one before whom a witness testifies is in a far better position to determine the credibility of the witness and the weight to be given to the testimony than a tribunal reviewing only the cold record. *Davis v. Research Medical Center*, 903 S.W.2d 557, 568 (Mo. App. 1995). In the era when factual findings in a judge-tried case were, as here, reviewed de novo, Judge Lamm summed up this principle artfully:

> Truth does not always stalk boldly forth naked, but modest withal, in a printed abstract in a court of last resort. She oft hides in nooks and crannies visible only to the mind's eye of the judge who tries the case. To him appears the furtive glance, the blush of conscious shame, the hesitation, the sincere or flippant or sneering tone, the heat, the calmness, the yawn, the sigh, the candor or lack of it ... *Creamer v. Bivert*, 214 Mo. 473, 113 S.W. 1118, 1120 (1908).

In the present case, the Master specifically found that respondents' testimony was not credible, that respondents were aware of their clients' intent to file for separation only to avoid the collection of child support, and that respondents actively participated in carrying out that evil intention. There is a great danger in being too quick to reject the determination of witness credibility found by a Master who both heard and saw the witnesses testify in person. For that and the following reasons, I would find facts consistent with those of the Master at least with regard to Mr. Moroney.

The majority opinion correctly points out (and it should come as no surprise) that respondents and their clients testified that the Leahys truly desired a legal separation and respondents truly believed their clients so desired. Witnesses accused of intentional wrongdoing rarely affirm the accusations on the witness stand.

Although a charge of professional misconduct does not create a rebuttable presumption of professional misconduct, Missouri courts have been willing to look to "badges of fraud" when fraudulent intent underlying a transaction is being proven. These "badges" include (1) a conveyance to a spouse, (2) inadequate consideration, (3) transactions different from the usual method of transacting business, (4) transfers in anticipation of suit or execution, (5) retention of possession by the debtor, (6) the transfer of all or nearly all of debtor's property, (7) insolvency caused by the transfer; and (8) failure to produce rebutting evidence when circumstances surrounding the transfer are suspicious. A concurrence of several badges of fraud in one transaction allows an inference of fraudulent intent and has been held to create a presumption thereof. Far from being arcane, the badges of fraud are rooted in everyday experience and provide a practical aid to the factfinder in the search for the truth regarding whether fraud has occurred.

Joseph Leahy's transfer of all his control of Jovial, Inc., and all of the couple's joint accounts to Joyce as well as his agreement to pay Joyce and their children one hundred percent of his monthly income is a textbook example of nearly all the badges of fraud. It is a conveyance to a spouse. It certainly differed from the usual method of dividing marital property and resolving marital disputes. The stipulation amounted to a transfer of all or nearly all of Leahy's assets. Had Leahy's scheme been effective, no assets would have been available for the Jackson County child support judgment. The Master was "incredulous that Joseph Leahy would fight a bitterly contested dissolution action over a period of months with his ex-wife over an increase in child support, yet in less than one day would agree to pay to his current wife the full amount of his claimed $7,000.00 monthly income for support and maintenance, assign to her control over all assets solely in his name, and transfer to her all interest in all joint checking, savings and financial accounts."

Additionally, the Ray County transaction was clearly made in anticipation of an order from the Jackson County Circuit Court. Joseph's deceptive enterprise in the Ray County Circuit Court began only after the Jackson County judge indicated his intention to impute over sixteen thousand dollars of monthly income to Joseph. This transaction in anticipation of the resolution of the Jackson County case is a more obvious badge of fraud than anticipated by Nance or Riccardi.

Joesph Leahy's stipulations in Ray County divested him not only of all his income and existing financial accounts, but also of Jovial, Inc., his principal income-producing asset. Moreover, after giving away virtually everything, Joseph could be considered insolvent. *See, e.g.*, section 276.401(17); *Adams v. Richardson*, 337 S.W.2d 911, 916 (Mo. 1960) (defining "Insolvency"). Indeed, this appeared to the Master to be Joseph's purpose in consenting to the Ray County order. That the fraudulent transaction giving rise to this proceeding took the form of a judgment rather than a deed or sale is of no legal consequence. A collusive judgment is a form of fraudulent conveyance if intended to defraud creditors and may be vacated.

Given the many badges of fraud that accompanied the Leahys' Ray County stipulation, I find as a matter of fact that the Leahys had a fraudulent purpose in initiating that proceeding and entering into the stipulation. My conclusion might be different if the obvious fraudulent circumstances were rebutted by persuasive evidence from a disinterested or neutral source indicating a genuine intent to separate. Examples of evidence by a neutral or disinterested source might include documentary evidence that, at some point, Joseph and Joyce lived separately. Perhaps third parties with nothing at stake in the proceeding might have testified to marital problems they perceived to have existed between the Leahys at any time before June 16, 1992. At any rate, the testimony of the four alleged co-conspirators, however consistent with each other and adamant, is wholly unpersuasive.

The evidence suggesting that respondents knew of their clients' fraudulent intent and assisted them, by bringing a baseless separation proceeding, in carrying out their scheme is also necessarily circumstantial.

The strongest evidence against Moroney arises out of the timing of significant events in the two lawsuits. After learning of the Jackson County judge's intent to impute significant income to Joseph and remarking that his client would be better off were he to divorce and renounce his corporate holdings, respondent Moroney spoke first to Joyce, not his client. That evening, Moroney met at length with Joseph and Mirabile. Moroney had suggested Joyce retain Mirabile, having immediately decided to separate from her husband given this recent financial adversity. The very next day, Moroney was present at the filing of Joyce's fraudulent petition and he filed the stipulation and joint motion. It is difficult to believe an attorney could ever be satisfied that his client truly had decided in good faith to seek a legal separation and to give away virtually all of his assets in less than a day. The circumstance becomes even more unbelievable when the recent turn in the Jackson County litigation is considered.

Although attorneys may generally represent their friends, the close relationship between Moroney, Joseph, Mirabile, and Joyce is another element that makes the possibility of bad faith more likely. Additionally, details of respondents' testimony before the circuit bar committee and Advisory Committee differed from their testimony before the Master. "[T]he putting together of trivial circumstances may furnish persuasive evidence of fraud." I find respondent Moroney knowingly participated in bringing a baseless lawsuit before the Ray County Circuit Court, which contained false statements of fact about the marriage of Joseph and Joyce Leahy. Further, I find that the purpose of that lawsuit was principally to help Joseph avoid his obligation to support his daughter by a previous marriage despite his ability to do so. Thus, Moroney's conduct violates Rules 4-3.1, 4-3.3 and 4-8.4 and subjects him to appropriate punishment up to and including disbarment.

The majority appears to place great significance on the statements made by the Ray County judge that he knew of the Jackson County lawsuit. I do not agree with the significance of that evidence for two reasons. First, the extent of the judge's knowledge is unclear. Indeed, that judge eventually saw fit to rescind his order in the matter on his own motion. Second, the opinion of the Ray County judge does not change the effect his order would have had upon Joseph's ex-wife and daughter in their efforts to collect child support.

Had the separate maintenance case not been dismissed and had the matter come here as a fraudulent conveyance case, any reasonable person would immediately recognize the Leahys' scheme for what it surely was, a fraudulent use of the court process to avoid child support. A lawyer with full knowledge of the circumstances Moroney had at hand should at least be held to the same standard as a reasonable person in recognizing that fraud was afoot. Without other contradictory information, a lawyer might, but is not duty bound, to believe the statements of a client. But the lawyer-client relationship does not suspend the lawyer's need to exercise common sense in evaluating the client's intent to commit a fraud, particularly where the lawyer's assistance is the means of effectuating that intent. In the past, lawyers with marginal ethics might advise a client on how to avoid the claims of creditors through fraudulent conveyances. Here the lawyer, Moroney, went well beyond giving advice. He actually assisted in advancing the client's transparently fraudulent plan. This Court should not place its imprimatur on a lawyer's contrived ignorance or countenance such reckless conduct by a member of the bar.

With respect to respondent Mirabile, the evidence that he knew the Leahys' ulterior motive in filing the Ray County matter is not as strong or clear as that implicating Moroney. Unlike Moroney, Mirabile was essentially brought into this situation by a colleague, not by an emotional, vindictive client. The extent of Mirabile's knowledge of Joseph's underlying legal controversy in Jackson County is unclear. Mirabile was, therefore, more likely an unwitting participant in the Leahys' scheme. While his lack of diligence in inquiring into the details of his client's circumstances is troubling, it is not usually a cause for substantial discipline.

For these reasons, I reluctantly concur in the majority's finding with respect to respondent Mirabile. I dissent from that portion of the opinion finding that Moroney should not be disciplined. At minimum, Moroney should be suspended from the practice of law indefinitely.

Questions

1. With which opinion do you agree in this case? Why?
2. At the core of the case is the "sham" separation. The majority concludes that there is insufficient evidence that the separation was not genuine. Part of the problem here is that, in many states, the law is unclear re-

garding the elements of a legal separation. Here the court noted that the parties actually lived apart, but what if they hadn't? During difficult economic times or to facilitate parenting, even divorced couples may continue to share a house. Would sharing living quarters preclude a judgment of legal separation? In most states, grounds for a legal separation are not stated separately from those of divorce. Even in states that do define separation, spouses may not be required to have residences. For example, D.C. Code § 16-904(c) (2008) defines separation as pursuing "separate lives, sharing neither bed nor board" but provides that a couple may be separated even though they "reside under the same roof."

In this case, the law of Missouri simply did not make clear what would constitute a sham separation. Other contexts might provide more guidance. For example, in the tax context, to deduct alimony a couple must not be "members of the same household." IRS § 71. Accordingly, in *Del Vecchio v. Commissioner*, 32 T.C.M. (CCH) 1153 (1973), an ex-husband whose economic circumstances forced him to move back into his ex-wife's residence could not deduct alimony payments even though the couple did not live as husband and wife in any other respects. In the immigration context as well, courts will look through form to the substance of a relationship to determine whether a divorce, annulment, or marriage is a "sham" for the purposes of avoiding immigration laws.

3. Suppose your client (Wife) has retained you to advise her on a plan to transfer various jointly held marital assets out of her husband's name and into her name. Her husband is incapacitated and in a nursing home. The plan is to transfer these assets so that Husband will qualify for Medicaid and also to use his former assets to help support him. Your research indicates that, while some courts refer to these plans as fraudulent in nature, they nonetheless recognize the divorces as valid for the purposes of qualifying for public assistance simply because the statutes do not otherwise prohibit this approach. *L.M. v. State, Div. of Med. Assistance & Health Servs.*, 659 A.2d 450, 451 (N.J. 1995)(reversing administrative decision denying Medicaid to husband after his wife of 53 years obtained divorce in order to qualify him for Medicaid).

   Would you accept this representation? What more would you want to know? How would you counsel Wife on this plan? What if you are unsure that Wife will really use the extra assets she would receive under this plan to care for Husband? What is Husband is comatose?

4. One of the canons of the 1968 Model Code of Professional Conduct states that "An attorney should avoid even the appearance of impropriety." This canon introduces the section of the code on conflict of interests. In more

recent times, the appearance of impropriety standard has been relaxed in order to avoid over-broad disqualifications (though the standard has been made an enforceable rule for judges in the 2007 ABA Model Code of Judicial Conduct, Rule 1.2). As an aspirational standard for attorneys, however, avoiding the appearance of impropriety is a fine principle to practice. Assume that Mirabile & Moroney did not actually plan to set up a sham divorce in order to affect child support. How could they have structured their representation in order to avoid the appearance of impropriety?

5. One of the incidents that led to this difficulty for the attorneys was attorney Maroney's angry response to the judge's decision on child support. Model Rule 1.2(b) states that "A lawyer's representation of a client, including representation by appointment, does not constitute an endorsement of the client's political, economic, social or moral views or activities." Yet attorneys often identify strongly with their client's causes, taking actions against their clients quite personally and emotionally. In family law, clients may even expect attorneys to be as angry and upset by the actions of others as is the client. There is a fine line between appropriate zeal and empathy and losing one's independent professional judgment. Consider AAML Standard 7.1 and the comments to that standard in Appendix A. Do you think Maroney stepped over the line? What can you do to insure that you do not become over-identified with the client's cause?
6. The court here was divided on Mirabile's duty to investigate the fraudulent intent of his client. The rules of professional conduct give very little guidance regarding your duty to verify a client's story. Model Rule 3.1 comment 2 indicates that lawyers must "inform themselves about the facts of their clients' cases and the applicable law." To what degree can you simply believe your client? Do you have any obligation to investigate their statement?

   Rule 11 of the Federal Rules of Civil Procedure or a state counterpart to that rule provides more guidance. Rule 11 provides that an attorney's signature is that attorneys' certification that factual contentions have or will have evidentiary support "to the best of the person's knowledge, information, and belief, formed after an inquiry reasonable under the circumstances." Where facts cannot be obtained without the use of formal discovery, an attorney may designate factual allegations as ones that are subject to discovery. However, the Advisory Committee's comment warns that this ability to flag unsupported factual allegations "does not relieve litigants from the obligation to conduct an appropriate investigation into the facts that is reasonable under the circumstances; it is not a license to join parties, make claims, or present defenses without any factual basis or justification." 146 F.R.D. at 585. The test is one of objective reasonableness:

the nature of the legal claim, the nature of the factual claims, the ease of obtaining objective verification, your relationship with your client, the time available, the credibility of the client's version of the facts, and many other facts may influence the determination of reasonableness.

Suppose you represent a Father in an action for modification of his child support obligation. You are assisting Father in filling out the form for calculating child support. Father believes a modification is appropriate because his income has dropped, his expenses have increased, and he believes that Mother's earnings have increased substantially. Previously, Father worked during the week at a local manufacturing facility. He has been laid off from that job and now works for a construction company. He often must work on weekends, which is also when he has parenting time with his children. He has his sister care for the children while he works and pays her $10 an hour. You have asked him for verification of his income and expenses and he explains that he works on a cash basis only and has no independent verification. Can you simply accept your client's statement of income and expenses? What if your client's lifestyle seems to indicate that he is earning substantially more than he is representing?

7. Just as ethically troublesome as avoiding frivolous filings on behalf of your client is dealing with other attorneys who have filed frivolous pleadings. What if you are aware of an attorney who routinely counsels his clients to obtain protective orders immediately upon filing a divorce petition? What are your ethical duties and options in defending your clients against these protective orders?

Reflective Journaling: Communicating with Clients about Confidentiality and Candor

Given the exceptions to confidentiality and privilege, what should you say to your clients about your duty of confidentiality? Consider these two contrasting views on the question and think about your clients.

Compare:

> [A] study showed that many lawyers rarely fully advise their client of these rules [about exceptions to confidentiality] and that many clients significantly misunderstand [them].... Lawyers owe it to the public to do a better job explaining confidentiality in light of the study's findings of widespread public misunderstanding. The best place to do this is where the lawyer meets the public, i.e. during the initial interview. Because a proper client understanding of fees and confidentiality are

> important to establishing and maintaining trust and competence, we suggest that lawyers carefully plan how to explain them to their clients. It may be useful to distribute a written explanation of the rules on confidentiality and the lawyer's fee structure before the initial interview. A written explanation of confidentiality allows the lawyer to cover both the ethical rule on confidentiality and the attorney-client privilege rule in that jurisdiction. This allows the lawyer to provide a full explanation to the client in a more efficient manner than a mini-lecture at the beginning of the interview, when the client may not be listening intently.[8]

with:

> [S]uch a warning is going to impede, if not wholly frustrate, the already difficult task of establishing a relationship of trust and confidence with the client.... The question in the client's mind is "Can I really trust you?" And the client will not be reassured by a lawyer who invites full disclosure and at the same time cautions the client about the possible betrayal of his confidences.... The lawyer who gives a Miranda warning is not the client's champion against a hostile world; on the contrary, she presents herself at the outset as an agent of that hostile world.... [I]t is important to recognize that the frightened and confused client who is given a lawyer-client Miranda warning may well be innocent. As Professor Stephen A. Saltzburg has observed, "Good persons (or persons with good claims) may shrink from the attorney who gives Miranda warnings as quickly as bad persons (or persons with bad claims)." Note too that the lawyer-client Miranda warning must be given before any serious lawyer-client discussions can begin—that is, before the lawyer can possibly make an informed judgment about the client's guilt or innocence."[9]

Reflect in writing on when and what you will say to clients about your duty of confidentiality and the limits of that duty. For a discussion of more views on this subject, see Clark D. Cunningham, *How to Explain Confidentiality?*, 9 Clinical L. Rev. 579 (2003).

---

8. Robert Cochran, John DePippa & Martha Peters, Counselor-at-Law: A Collaborative Approach to Client Interviewing and Counseling 70–71 (Second ed. 2006).

9. Monroe H. Freedman & Abbe Smith, Understanding Lawyers' Ethics 155 (2nd ed. 2002).

Research Assignment

As you know, state standards on confidentiality and its exceptions vary considerably across the states. Research your own state's law to determine the exceptions to confidentiality, the application of the crime-fraud exception to privilege, and whether an attorney is subject to any duties to report abuse under mandated reporter statutes for elder or child abuse.

To Learn More

In addition to the articles and web resources cited in this chapter, the following articles are helpful to understanding the attorney's duty of candor:

Gerald B. Wetlaufer, *The Ethics of Lying in Negotiation*, 76 Iowa L. Rev. 1219 (1990).

(an excellent starting point for considering the duty of candor in negotiations, the article explores various forms of lies and deceptions used in negotiation and argues that while some of these may at times be effective, they are nevertheless unethical).

Lisa Lerman, *Lying to Clients,* 138 U. Pa. L. Rev. 659 (1990).

(as the title implies, the article explores the situations in which attorneys lie to their clients. Based on the author's interviews with attorneys, the article examines lawyer deception of their clients, both directly and through a third party. The article discusses the ethics and costs of this deception and makes suggestions for reforms in legal practice).

Douglas R. Richmond, *Lawyers' Professional Responsibilities and Liabilities in Negotiations,* 22 Geo. J. Legal Ethics 249 (2009).

(a primer on the attorney's duties of communication and candor with clients, opponents and the courts).

Chapter Seven

Representing Children and the Interests of Children

Learning Objectives for This Chapter

After you have read this chapter and completed the assignments you should be able to:

- Identify the roles attorneys play in child representation.
- Clarify your role in any given representation involving children.
- Identify and resolve conflicts of interest in child representation.
- Identify the skills and knowledge necessary for effective child representation and have a plan for acquiring and maintaining the necessary level of competence.
- Clarify your duty of confidentiality in any given child representation and explain that duty to a child client.
- Clarify your relationship with other persons or entities in actions involving children.
- Identify the ethical and legal restrictions on evidence gathering when representing children.

A. The Child's Right to an Attorney

Children's legal interests may arise in settings like any other client: in tort actions, contractual planning, or in disputes with educational institutions or employers. In addition, children may be the subject of specialized legal proceedings, such as delinquency, dependency, adoption, or custody actions. In many instances, the child's parents or guardians will engage your services to represent their child.

When a parent seeks your assistance for their child, you must clarify your relationship with the parent. The child client may have a diminished capacity to direct the representation and, unlike many other settings in which you are representing an individual with diminished capacity, here the person financing the representation (the parent) also has the legal right to exercise control and guidance over your client. Thus, when representing a child's interests in a tort action for example, you may take your direction from the parent, presuming that the parent has the legal right to help to direct their child's representation and is in the best position to determine what actions will best protect their child's interests.

However the status of parental rights to assert the legal rights of their children is not always clear. Children are not competent to sue or be sued and must have a parent or guardian bring actions on their behalf. But that procedural requirement does not necessarily mean that the parent has a substantive right to direct the child's representation. The question of the right of a parent to direct a child's representation was was at issue before the Supreme Court recently in *Winkelman et al v. Parma,* 550 U.S. 516 (2007). There, parents of a child with autism sought to appeal an administrative determination in an action under the Individuals with Disabilities Education Act (IDEA). The court of appeals had dismissed the action because the child was not represented by an attorney and the non-lawyer parents were not authorized by statute to appear on behalf of their children.

While only criminal defendants have the constitutional right to self-representation, courts routinely permit individuals to represent themselves in civil cases. A lay person representing others, however, violates rules against unauthorized practice of law. If the parents had been suing to vindicate their own rights, there would have been little concern regarding the absence of an attorney. However, the court of appeals found that the parents did not have independent rights and were advocating on behalf of their child's rights only. As non-lawyers, without an express statutory authorization to advocate in an appellate court on the behalf of their children, the parents were engaged in the unauthorized practice of law. However, the parents argued that their constitutional right to the care, custody, and control of their child would be deprived if they were not able to appear in court on their son's behalf without an attorney they could not afford to hire. Rather than address the power of parents to advocate in court on behalf of their children's legal rights, the court concluded that the IDEA creates independent, enforceable rights for parents in the special education of their children. Since the parents were enforcing their own rights, they were simply representing themselves *pro se* and the status of a parent's right to represent their child's independent legal rights remains an open question.

Parents undoubtedly do not have the right to direct their child's legal representation when the interests of the parents conflict with the child, as in cases in which there are allegations of abuse or neglect. In those instances, the parent's interests may skew with their parental decision-making. As Professor Moore noted in commenting on the uncertain status of the parent in directing a child's representation:

> [l]awyers must be highly sensitive to the particular context in which the representation occurs. For example, in delinquency cases, courts and commentators generally agree that because it is the child whose due process rights are implicated, it is the child alone who decides, in consultation with the attorney, how the representation will proceed. Similarly, parents are not likely to be granted any decision-making authority in child custody cases or cases involving claims of parental misconduct because it is the very fact of a conflict of interests between parents and child which creates the need for separate representation on behalf of the child. In the absence of either authoritative law or a developing consensus among lawyers in the field, lawyers should at least consult with both parents and child (where feasible) to determine if a plan of decision making can be adopted that will be satisfactory to all concerned.[1]

As a general rule, you must not assume that the parent may direct the representation unless and until you have first satisfied yourself that the law allocates this decision-making to the parent in this case or that the child is incapable of directing your representation.[2]

In other circumstances, you will be engaged to represent a child not by a parent or guardian but by court appointment or as a public attorney. In one of the most common situations of child representation, delinquency actions, the United States Supreme Court has recognized that a child has the right to independent representation when facing incarceration. "The juvenile needs the assistance of counsel to cope with problems of law, to make skilled inquiry into the facts, to insist upon regularity of the proceedings, and to ascertain whether he has a defense and to prepare and submit it."[3] Aside from juvenile delinquency, the right of children to counsel is secured primarily through leg-

1. Nancy J. Moore, *Conflicts of Interests in the Representation of Children*, 64 Fordham L. Rev. 1819, 1853 (1996).

2. For an excellent discussion of the role of parents in juvenile delinquency cases and practical advice on working with parents and children in these cases, see Kristin Henning, *It Takes a Lawyer to Raise a Child?: Allocating Responsibilities among Parents, Children, and Lawyers in Delinquency Cases*, 6 Nev. L.J. 836 (2006).

3. *In re* Gault, 387 U.S. 1 (1967).

islation. The United States Supreme Court in *Lassiter v. Department of Social Services*, 452 U.S. 18 (1981), held that that due process might, in an individual case, require appointed counsel but that as a categorical matter there is a presumption against the right to counsel absent a threat to physical liberty.[4] However, the court also noted that where legislation mandates counsel, this legislative decision substitutes for the court's balancing test and creates a liberty interest to be protected by due process.[5] Statutes provide courts with the discretion to appoint counsel for children in a variety of circumstances. For example, in proceedings governed by the Indian Child Welfare Act, courts have discretion to appoint counsel for Indian children when this representation is in the best interests of the child.[6] At the state level, legislation may provide a right to counsel for children in contested adoption proceedings[7] or in cases involving termination of parental rights.[8] Thus, in those states in which legislation requires appointment of counsel for children, that right is constitutionally protected.

The key policy question here is when a legislature or court should appoint an attorney for a child. This question has generated over a decade of debate and controversy. Advocates for child representation in a broad range of circumstances argue that appointing attorneys for children "when their disposition or welfare is at stake is the most significant and practical reform that can be made in the area of children and the law."[9] Those taking this approach emphasize that appointing an attorney for children protects their dignity as well as their rights and interests and improves decision-making by keeping a child-centered focus.[10] The United Nations Convention on the Rights of the Child supports this position. Article 12 of the Convention requires states to provide children

---

4. *Id.* at 27. *But see* Kenny A. v. Perdue, 356 F. Supp. 2d 1353, 1359 (N.D. Ga. 2005)(finding that children in termination of parental rights proceedings have a constitutional right to counsel).

5. *See* Battishill v. Ark. Dep't of Human Servs., 82 S.W.3d 178, 180 (Ark. Ct. App. 2002) (Arkansas statutes providing for right to counsel in abuse and neglect proceedings creates due process right in all cases).

6. *See* 25 U.S.C. §1912(b) (2000).

7. *See, e.g.,* Okla. Stat. Ann. §7505-1.2 (2004).

8. *In re* Williams, 805 N.E.2d 1110 (Ohio 2004) (because child is considered a party to parental rights termination action, the child has right to legal counsel).

9. Henry H. Foster, Jr. & Doris J. Freed, *A Bill of Rights for Children,* 6 Fam. L.Q. 343, 356 (1972). *See, also,* Linda D. Elrod, *Client-Directed Lawyers for Children: It is the 'Right' Thing to Do,* 27 Pace L. Rev. 869, 872 (2007).

10. Barbara Ann Atwood, *Representing Children: The Ongoing Search for Clear and Workable Standards,* 19 J. Am. Acad. Matrim. Law 183, 195-96 (2005).

"the opportunity to be heard in any judicial and administrative proceedings affecting the child, either directly, or through a representative."[11]

Others are more cautious. In custody matters, for example, where the best interests of the child is the controlling standard, appointment of an attorney for a child may skew decisions by "elevating the expressed wishes of the child to a degree of prominence and weight in the ultimate calculus that is at odds with the current law. With a lawyer forcefully articulating the child's preference with all of the rhetorical devices available to a trained advocate, that position inevitably will assume far greater weight than it would if merely expressed by the child himself or herself."[12] Some scholars express concern that giving children more rights to influence the outcome in custody or abuse and neglect proceedings is not healthy for these children.[13]

Question for Discussion

In most civil cases, particularly outside the context of abuse and neglect actions, the decision to appoint an attorney for a child is a discretionary one. How do you advocate for or against appointment of a child's attorney in any given case? Section 12 of the Uniform Act provides a non-exclusive list of factors the court may consider in determining whether to appoint attorneys for children in custody actions. Read this section and try to identify the types of situations in which you would argue that an attorney for the child would improve the decision making and process. Think about other factual circumstances in which an attorney would not be appropriate.

> (b) In determining whether an appointment under subsection (a) is appropriate, the court shall consider the circumstances and needs of the child, the court's need for information and assistance, the financial burden on the parties and the cost of available alternatives for resolving the issues in the proceeding, and any factors indicating a particularized need for representation, including:
>
> (1) any desire for representation or participation expressed by the child;

---

11. Convention on the Rights of the Child, G.A. Res. 44/25, U.N. GAOR, 44th Sess., U.N. Doc. A/Res/44/25 (Nov. 20, 1989).

12. Martin Guggenheim, *The Making of Standards for Representing Children in Custody and Visitation Proceedings: The Reporter's Perspective*, 13 J. Am. Acad. Matrim. Law 35, 53-54 (1995).

13. Robert E. Emery, *Hearing Children's Voices: Listening-and Deciding-Is an Adult Responsibility*, 45 Ariz. L. Rev. 621, 622 (2003).

(2) any inappropriate adult influence on or manipulation of the child;
(3) the likelihood that the child will be called as a witness or be questioned by the court in chambers and the need to minimize harm to the child from the processes of litigation;
(4) any level of acrimony that indicates a lack of objectivity of the parties regarding the needs of the child;
(5) any interference, or threatened interference, with custody, access, visitation, or parenting time, including abduction or risk of abduction of the child;
(6) the likelihood of a geographic relocation of the child that could substantially reduce the child's time with:
(A) a parent;
(B) a sibling; or
(C) another individual with whom the child has a close relationship;
(7) any conduct by a party or an individual with whom a party associates which raises serious concerns for the safety of the child during periods of custody, visitation, or parenting time with that party;
(8) any special physical, educational, or mental-health needs of the child that require investigation or advocacy; and
(9) any dispute as to paternity of the child.

B. Role Confusion in Child Representation

Some states have a model of representation of children that requires that attorneys be appointed to represent the child as a "guardian ad litem" or "attorney ad litem." Many states use a "hybrid" model in which attorneys appointed in these cases are expected to both represent the child's wishes and also the best interests of the child and to both advocate for the child and assist the court.

Despite numerous calls for greater clarity of role, in the majority of states, models of representation remain confused, broad, and conflicting. The resulting conflicts make the attorney's job in these cases extremely difficult. The rules of professional conduct of every state require that attorneys pursue their client's lawful objectives, (Model Rule 1.2) yet an attorney in many states must, if the child's best interests demand, advocate for a result the child does not wish.[14] In cases of conflicting duties, attorneys may ask the court to represent separate counsel for the child. Some states have held that, where an attorney raises such a request and the child is sufficiently mature to direct the representation, the court must appoint a separate attorney to represent the child.[15] Other courts simply conclude that the attorney should inform the court of the child's preferences, but is not required to advocate for that preference. Where a state adopts a "hybrid" role such as this, attorneys and courts alike (not to mention the children involved) may be operating under confused and even conflicting role conceptions.

This hotpotch of representation schemes is partly a result of federal mandates. As a condition of receiving federal funds for child abuse and treatment programs, the federal Child Abuse Prevention and Treatment Act[16] requires states to appoint a "guardian ad litem" for a child. In over half the states, that representation must be provided by attorneys.[17] While all major organizations oppose the "hybrid" model of representation, the American Academy of Matrimonial Lawyers opposes the "best interest" attorney as well, taking the position that an attorney should never be appointed to advocate for a particular outcome on behalf of a child if the child is incapable of directing the representation.[18]

The Uniform Representation of Children in Abuse, Neglect and Custody Proceedings Act (Uniform Act) requires appointment of either an attorney for the child or a "best interests" attorney in any action in which abuse or neglect allegations arise.[19] Comments to the Uniform Representation of Children in Abuse, Neglect, and Custody Proceedings Act explains the role of best interests attorney in this way:

---

14. *See, e.g.*, *In re* Marriage of Rolfe, 699 P.2d 79, 86 (Mont. 1985); Veazey v. Veazey, 560 P.2d 382, 390 (Ala. 1977); *In re* Marriage of Barnthouse, 765 P.2d 610, 612 (Colo. Ct. App. 1988) (approving attorney's conduct in recommending against following the child's wishes), *cert. denied*, 490 U.S. 1021 (1989).

15. In the Interest of A.T. and T.P., 744 N.W.2d 657 (Iowa Ct. App. 2007); *In re* Williams, 101 Ohio St. 3d 398, 2004 Ohio 1500, 805 N.E.2d 1110 1113–14 (Ohio 2004).

16. 25 U.S.C. § 1912(b)(2000).

17. *Representation of Children in Court Survey*, (October 2004)(table of statutes prepared for NCCUSL as background in drafting the Uniform Act), *available at* http://www.law.upenn.edu/bll/archives/ulc/RARCCDA/Oct2004MtgSurvey.pdf.

18. American Academy of Matrimonial Lawyers, *Revised Standards for Attorneys for Children in Custody or Visitation Proccedings*,J. Am. Acad. Matrim. Law (2009), forthcoming.

19. National Conference of Commissioners on Uniform State Laws, Uniform Representation of Children in Abuse, Neglect, and Custody Proceedings Act (2007), *available at* http://www.law.upenn.edu/bll/archives/ulc/rarccda/2007_final.pdf.

> "Best interests attorney" is a term of art that was introduced by the ABA in developing the Custody Standards and signifies an independent legal representative for a child client who advocates positions in the proceeding that will serve the child's interests even if those positions are not identical with the child's expressed views. In other respects, however, the best interests attorney performs the same duties of representation that are performed by the child's attorney, including the duty to provide advice and counsel to the child and the duty to inform the court of the child's expressed objectives if the child so desires. See Sections 11 and 13. Several jurisdictions have authorized attorneys to function in the same capacity as best interest attorneys but have denominated them differently. See, e.g., Vernon's Tex. Code Ann. Family Code § 107.021 (amicus attorney); Mich. Comp. Laws Ann. 712A.17d (West 2006) (lawyer-guardian ad litem); 750 Ill. Comp. Stat. Ann. § 5/506 (West 2006) (child representative).[20]

Professor Martin Guggenheim has identified three core criticisms of the role of best interest attorney:

> First, best interests advocacy liberates lawyers to choose the outcome to seek without any certainty that what is being sought is what the child wants (or even what is best for the child). Second, best interests lawyering is too different from the core meaning of what lawyers are or should be. As ABA leaders recently explained: "It is the role of the judge, not the lawyer, to decide best interest after hearing from all of the parties."[21] Permitting "the lawyer to decide what is in the child's best interest and [to] make that recommendation to the Court," proponents of the new ABA Neglect and Abuse Standards explain, "places the lawyer in an uncomfortable position akin to testifying, outside their area of expertise, while denying others in the proceeding the opportunity to cross-examine the presenter."[22] Finally, allowing lawyers to advocate for the results they themselves have chosen risks contam-

---

20. *Id.*, at Section 2.

21. Letter dated July 27, 2009 from Bob Rothman, Larry Fox, Joanne Epps, Dave Weiner, and Trish Refo to the ABA House of Delegates regarding the ABA Model Act Governing the Representation of Children in Abuse, Neglect and Dependency Proceedings.

22. *Id.*

> inating the proceeding by making the child's lawyer more important to the result than is appropriate.[23]

Given these concerns the AAML has taken a position that no one - attorney or lay person alike - should be in a position of advocating for a child's "best interests." This position does not deny the value of professionals who assist the court in investigating the circumstances of a child or even testifying (and being subject to cross examination) as to their opinion regarding the best interests of that child. However, as Professor Guggenheim notes:

> Authorizing someone to *give* an opinion is one thing; authorizing her to marshal forces in support of that opinion to increase the likelihood that the court will follow it is entirely different. Of all the arguments against permitting lawyers to engage in best interests advocacy, this should be counted as the strongest. The one thing lawyers are very good at is making a case for the position they are advocating. Lawyers routinely accomplish this by selectively highlighting facts. They emphasize those that support their position; they strive to obfuscate those that do not. They search for witnesses who will help advance their theory; they turn away those that don't. Their purpose becomes to persuade the fact-finder to rule in their favor. In other words, they litigate strategically. And the best of them are very good at doing so.[24]

The conflict between representing the child or the child's best interest is not the only role tension that attorneys representing children have to negotiate. There is a third role that attorneys often are called upon to play when acting as a child's representative: that is, a judicial agent of the court. Many courts continue to demand that attorneys appointed as guardians *ad litem* combine the advocacy and judicial functions, with the judicial role taking precedence.[25]

---

23. Martin Guggenheim, *The AAML's Revised Standards for Representing Children in Custody and Visitation Proceedings: The Reporter's Perspective*, J. Am. Acad. Matrim. Law (2009), forthcoming.

24. Id.

25. *See, e.g.*, Cok v. Cosentino, 876 F.2d 1, 3 (1st Cir. 1989) (*per curiam*); Myers v. Morris, 810 F.2d 1437, 1465 (8th Cir. 1987), *cert. denied*, 484 U.S. 828 (1987); Kurzawa v. Mueller, 732 F.2d 1456, 1458 (6th Cir. 1984); Widoff v. Wiens, 45 P.3d 1232, 1235–36 (Ariz. Ct. App. 2002); Kennedy v. State, 730 A.2d 1252, 1255 (Me. 1999) (quoting State *ex rel* Bird v. Weinstock, 864 S.W.2d 376, 384 (Mo. Ct. App. 1993)); Tindell v. Rogosheske, 428 N.W.2d 386, 387 (Minn. 1988).

The problem with blending the judicial role with a children's representation role is that the role of judicial agent and the role of attorney are quite opposite in many respects. Judges are required to be neutral, disinterested and passive; attorneys represent a particular client's objectives with "warm zeal." In the hybrid role, the attorney may become a witness,[26] summarizing investigations and reporting witness statements—a situation that not only ignores the rules of evidence but places the attorney in a position of violating prohibitions on attorneys appearing as witnesses in cases in which they are acting as an advocate.[27]

Finally, attorneys appointed as guardians ad litem, especially in states in which this role is also filled by trained non-lawyer volunteers, may be asked to fill a variety of other roles. Attorneys may find themselves acting as a de facto custody evaluator or informally facilitating visitation or mediating disputes between adults. While representing a child's best interest may require actions that overlap these roles, attorneys should resist being placed in a formal role other than as the attorney for the child or the child's best interest and should clarify any misunderstanding regarding their role. Advisory Task Force Comments to the Minnesota Rules of Guardian Ad Litem Procedure highlight some of these other roles and responsibilities that are inappropriate for attorneys representing children or their best interests:

> The provision of direct services to the child or the child's parents is generally beyond the scope of the guardian ad litem's responsibilities. Therefore, except in special circumstances, the appointing court should not order the guardian ad litem, and the guardian ad litem should not undertake, to provide such direct services. Providing such direct services could create a conflict of interest and/or cause a child or family to become dependent upon the guardian ad litem for services that should be provided by other agencies or organizations. The guardian ad litem may locate and recommend services for the child and family, but should not routinely deliver services.
>
> Specifically, a guardian ad litem should not: (a) provide "counseling" or "therapy" to a child or parent; (b) foster a friendship or "big brother/big sister" relationship with a child or parent by inviting the

26. On the role of reports and guardians ad litem as witnesses, see generally, Leinenbach v. Leinenbach, 634 So.2d 252 (Fla. App. 1994) (trial court erred in relying on report of guardian ad litem where father was not afforded opportunity to rebut contents of report); Sanfillippo v. Sanfillippo, 637 S.W.2d 77 (Mo. App. E.D. 1982)(A court may not admit into evidence a GAL's report which contains hearsay or opinions that would not otherwise be admissible).

27. Model Rule of Prof'l Conduct 3.7 (2008).

> child or parent into the home of the guardian ad litem, routinely entertaining the child or parent at the movies, or giving money or gifts to the child or parent; (c) give legal advice or hire an attorney for the child or parent; (d) supervise visits between the child and parent or third parties, except as ordered by the court; (e) routinely provide transportation for the child or parent, except as ordered by the court; (f) provide child care services for the child; (g) make placement arrangements for the child or remove a child from the home; or (h) provide a "message service" for parents to communicate with each other.[28]

Even when the role of the attorney for the child is clear in any given case, confusion can result from circumstances in which attorneys shift roles between representing parents, children, or the state. The Colorado Supreme Court recently issued an order stating that it would not allow "attorneys to practice as both respondent parents' counsel and in the capacity of guardian ad litem." As the court observed, this shifting role pressures attorneys to under-represent children in order to preserve relationships.

> [One] court has observed that the shifting of roles tends to benefit the litigant who has the right to appear in court and is in a position to pressure counsel to obtain a desired result. Where an attorney is representing the respondent in one case but is the guardian ad litem in the next, subtle compromises are made to insure a working relationship when the roles of counsel are reversed. Since the children are almost never in attendance at court hearings and the historical trend has been for guardians ad litem to infrequently visit their children, the children's interest is too often not adequately represented. By removing this subtle conflict of interest, [this] court has observed that the quality of representation of parents and children has been improved.[29]

Given the diversity of roles required or expected of the attorney for the child, how do you go about clarifying your role? In the absence of clear guidance from state law, the best way to insure that your role is clear and defined is to

---

28. Minnesota Supreme Court Rules of Guardian Ad Litem Procedure, Advisory Task Force Comments, CO-95-1475 (1997), *available at* http://www.courts.state.mn.us/rules/adlitem.html.

29. Chris Melonakis & William Delisio, *A Report to the Chief Justice of the Colorado Supreme Court Pursuant to Chief Justice Directive 98-02* 14 (2003) *available at* http://www.17th judicialdistrict.com/Report%20Final.pdf.

request a court order that not only designates the role in which you are appointed, but also identifies for how long you are expected to serve that role, and outlines the rights and duties of your role. States have been moving toward more defined standards of practice for attorneys for children. Read, for example, with the very specific checklist of duties provided by the Georgia aspirational standards in Appendix B. Does this list help to clarify the attorney role?

Problem for Discussion

Suppose you have been appointed as an attorney for a child in a hotly contested divorce action. Allegations of abuse and neglect have been raised by each parent against the other. You have interviewed your thirteen-year-old female client and have discovered that she wants very much to live with her father. She discounts all of the allegations of abuse and neglect except to say that her mother "does scream a lot" and sometimes is "too strict." She does not appear to have any significant objection to living with her mother, but would simply prefer to live with her father because she "is closer to him" and he "understands her better." All your investigation from teachers, medical care professionals, neighbors and relatives on both sides of the family points to a father who sets no limits for his daughter, pampers her with an endless stream of material goods, and is generally permissive to the point of neglectful. When you raise some examples of her father's neglect—as when she was gone for 24 hours and he did not search for her or notify anyone of her absence—she insists that this is because he knows that she is mature enough that he can trust her.

What further steps might you take to discuss your client's preference? Given your state's definition of attorney for the child in dependency actions, what would be your responsibility to the client to advocate for her preference? If you believe her preference is unwise, to what extent may or should you attempt to influence the child's preference?

Research Assignment

Research the standards for appointment of attorneys for children in your state. In what types of proceedings are attorneys required? When is appointment discretionary? What is the role of attorneys in these proceedings? Has your court promulgated standards of practice for attorneys for children?

C. Regulation of Competence in Child Representation

In addition to negotiating the ambiguity of a role that often challenges child representation, many attorneys who primarily work in the child welfare system must also work with extreme resource limitations. Many attorneys appointed to represent children operate in a chronically underfunded system. Hourly rates for contract attorneys in child representation rarely exceed $75 an hour, and many jurisdictions have caps on total fees of less than $1,000 per case.[30] A recent study of attorneys in child welfare actions found that more than 40% of all respondents have more than 100 cases and almost 20% of all respondents have over 200 cases.[31] Among child law specialists, over 70% have more than 100 cases and 20% have more than 300 cases.[32]

Underfunding places attorneys for whom child representation is their full-time practice in a near-constant battle to maintain their ethical duties of competence and diligence. Low fees and high caseloads may even create pressures for dishonesty in billing practices.[33] Comment 2 to Model Rule 1.3 states that "[a] lawyer's work load must be controlled so that each matter may be handled competently." ABA Formal Opinions, issued in response to Congressional efforts to drastically cut funding for legal services in 1981,[34] and again in 1996,[35] emphasize that attorneys have an affirmative duty to restrict the size of their caseloads and that underfunding of representation does not excuse attorneys for indigent clients from their duty of competence and diligence. An ABA Formal Opinion in 2006, directed primarily to the public defender community, but generally applicable to all attorneys facing excessive caseloads, directs attorneys to decline these excessive representations.[36]

---

30. See the collection of statutory fee standards collected in Appendix D, Jean Koh Peters, *How Children Are Heard in Child Protective Proceedings, in the United States and Around the World in 2005: Survey Findings, Initial Observations, and Areas for Further Study*, 6 Nev. L.J. 966, 1082–83 (2006).

31. Howard Davidson & Erik S. Pitchal, *Caseloads Must Be Controlled So All Child Clients Can Receive Competent Lawyering* 6 (working paper, Oct. 2006), *available at* http://ssrn.com/abstract=943059.

32. *Id.* at 7.

33. Lewis v. Comm. for Pub. Counsel Servs., 739 N.E.2d 706, 708 (Mass. App. Ct. 2000) (Attorneys who represented children were fined for charging in excess of the statutory rate.).

34. ABA Comm. on Ethics and Prof'l Responsibility, Formal Op. 347 (1981).

35. ABA Comm. on Ethics and Prof'l Responsibility, Formal Op. 96-399 (1996).

36. ABA Comm. on Ethics and Prof'l Responsibility, Formal Op. 06-441 (2006).

The opinion recognizes that, when these representations come through court appointment, the matter is not simply one of just saying no. Model Rule 6.2 directs that attorneys should not seek to avoid appointment unless there is good cause. While seeking to avoid excessive appointments is a necessary first step, if appointed by the court nonetheless, attorneys may pursue any available means of review of the court's order. In the final analysis, however, it is the court's decision as to whether an attorney can competently represent an appointed client, and an attorney will be subject to contempt for further refusals to continue with the representation.[37] In these situations, attorneys are left to do the best they can, providing triage lawyering while continuing to advocate for improvements in the system.

With high caseloads and few resources, some attorneys have difficulty in providing children the most basic of representation—meeting with the child client, keeping the child client informed of legal proceedings, and conducting even a basic investigation of the case. One must wonder at the fact that state standards of practice for guardians ad litem must instruct attorneys to meet their clients. Yet surveys of child representatives reveal that not all attorneys do complete even this basic representation task.[38]

In a system in which competence is under pressure, how does the court insure accountability for attorneys appointed to represent children? In other areas of legal practice, one of the most powerful deterrents to negligent representation is liability. However, in many states, because the attorney appointed to represent a child serves a hybrid function of attorney for the child's interest and also agent of the court, attorneys are granted immunity from liability. Consider the following excerpt from an opinion in which the court reasoned that the role of the attorney guardian ad litem is such that they should have quasi-judicial immunity from civil liability:

---

37. *See* ABA Comm. on Ethics and Prof'l Responsibility, Formal Op. 06-441 (2006); Tenn. Opinion Attorney General 02-107 (October 1, 2002); *see also* State *ex rel.* Picerno v. Mauer, 920 S.W.2d 904, 910 (Mo. Ct. App. 1996)(holding attorney in contempt for failing to comply with court's order to proceed with hearing); Iowa Sup. Ct. Bd. of Prof'l Ethics & Conduct v. Hughes, 557 N.W.2d 890, 894 (Iowa 1996) ("[I]gnoring a court order is simply not an appropriate step to test the validity of the order under our Code of Professional Responsibility.").

38. A 2000 study of Colorado GALs indicated that in 41% of cases, the GAL did not meet with the child. Daniel P. Gallagher, *Child Abuse and Neglect Cases in the Colorado Courts 1996–2000: A Reassessment* 2 (2002), *available at* http://www.cde.state.co.us/artemis/scl_8/SC92C432002INTERNET.pdf.

State ex rel Bird v. Weinstock

864 S.W.2d 376 (Mo. Ct. App. 1993)

[In this case, an attorney was appointed as a guardian ad litem for children who were the subject of a contentious custody action. The father of the children had filed a negligence actions against the guardian ad litem. The guardian ad litem claimed that as an officer of the court he was entitled to immunity from the father's suit and brought this action for a writ of prohibition directing the trial judge to dismiss the negligence case.]

In support of his claim of what can properly be termed "quasi-judicial" immunity, Guardian points out that the Missouri Supreme Court has adopted the common law doctrine of judicial immunity, explaining the rationale as follows:

> Judicial immunity exists "not for the protection or benefit of a malicious or corrupt judge, but for the benefit of the public, [in] whose interest it is that the judges should be at liberty to exercise their functions with independence and without fear of consequences."

State ex rel. Raack v. Kohn, 720 S.W.2d 941, 944 (Mo. banc 1986)....

Typically, those to whom immunity has been extended represent the interests of society as a whole. The conduct of their official duties may adversely affect a wide variety of individuals, each of whom may be a potential source of future controversy. Immunity has thus been extended to forestall an atmosphere of intimidation that would conflict with their resolve to perform their functions in a principled fashion. Appointed counsel's principal responsibility is to serve the individual interests of his client. In fact, an indispensable element of his performance is the ability to act independently of the state and to oppose it in adversary litigation. In essence, although the Court acknowledged that there might be other policy bases for extended immunity to appointed counsel, such an extension could not be justified strictly on the basis of function because defense counsel and the court are not on the same side.

In contrast, at least in custody matters, the guardian ad litem has traditionally been viewed as functioning as an agent or arm of the court, to which it owes its principal duty of allegiance, and not strictly as legal counsel to a child client. In essence, the guardian ad litem role fills a void inherent in the procedures required for the adjudication of custody disputes. Absent the assistance of a guardian ad litem, the trial court, charged with rendering a decision in the "best interests of the child," has no practical or effective means to assure itself that all of the requisite information bearing on the question will be brought before it untainted by the parochial interests of the parents. Unhampered by the ex parte and other restrictions that prevent the court from conducting its own investigation of the facts, the guardian ad litem essentially functions as the court's investigative agent, charged with the same ultimate standard that must ultimately govern the court's decision—i.e., the "best interests of the child." Although the child's preferences may, and often should, be considered by the guardian ad litem in performing this traditional role, such preferences are but one fact to be investigated and are not considered binding on the guardian. Thus, the obligations of a guardian ad litem necessarily impose a higher degree of objectivity on a guardian ad litem than is imposed on an attorney for an adult.

This traditional role of the guardian ad litem may properly be contrasted with the view that the role of the guardian is to act solely as attorney or legal counsel to the child. This view contemplates a strict attorney-client relationship with the child wherein the guardian is expected to act strictly as an advocate for the child's preferences. This is essentially the view espoused by Father. He asserts that §452.423 codifies the guardian ad litem's status as that of a court appointed attorney for the child which, he asserts, is incompatible with Guardian's claimed status as a judicial officer.

Contrary to Father's contention, our review of these provisions, the balance of §452.423 and §210.160, and Missouri case law concerning the contemplated role of a guardian ad litem in child custody actions leads us to conclude that the role envisioned for the guardian ad litem in Missouri is a hybrid of the traditional and attorney-client roles, although closer to the traditional role than the strict attorney-client or advocate role.

Viewed in isolation, the use of the term "legal representative," the authorization to subpoena and examine witnesses and offer testimony, and the requirement that the guardian ascertain the child's wishes, feelings, attachments and attitudes could be viewed as indicative of a legislative intent that the guardian ad litem is to function as attorney for the child. On the other hand, none of these features of the statute are inherently inconsistent or incompatible with the traditional view of the guardian ad litem's role. The term "legal representative" is ambiguous. A "representative" may be one acting "in place of" as well as "on behalf of." Although the trial activities of subpoenaing and examining witnesses and offering testimony must ordinarily be performed by an attorney, there is no express requirement that the guardian perform these activities personally. In fact, both §§452.423.5 and 210.160.5 allow the court to designate non-attorney volunteer advocates to assist in the performance of the guardian ad litem duties "for the court," (emphasis added) with access to a court appointed attorney guardian ad litem if the circumstances require. Although the guardian ad litem is required to ascertain the child's wishes, feelings, attachments and attitudes, there is no direction that the guardian advocate such wishes and feelings even if the guardian concludes that the child's desires are not in its best interest. See §452.423.2(2) RSMo Supp. 1992.

Missouri courts have consistently held that the duty of a guardian ad litem is to protect the best interests of the child. *In re G*, 389 S.W.2d 63, 66 (Mo. App. 1965). It is the guardian ad litem's duty to stand in the shoes of the child and to weigh the factors as the child would weigh them if his judgment were mature and he was not of tender years. *In Interest of J.L.H.*, 647 S.W.2d 852 (Mo. App. 1983). The court is not bound by the opinion or recommendation of the guardian ad litem. *Brooks v. Division of Children's Services*, 411 S.W.2d 276, 282 (Mo. App. 1967). Nevertheless, under our statutory scheme for adjudication of custody disputes, it is imperative that the guardian ad litem investigate and present its perspective to the trial judge, thereby enabling the court to render a decision in accordance with the statutory standard of "best interests of the child." *In Interest of J.L.H.*, 647 S.W.2d at 860–61; §§452.375.2, 452.410.1 RSMo Supp 1992. Our review of these and other cases addressing the role of the guardian ad litem in custody disputes confirms that Missouri courts have consistently adhered to the traditional view that the guardian's principal allegiance is to the court. Although the best interests of the child are always paramount, the guardian's relationship to the child is not strictly that of attorney and client....

We hold that the same policies that led the Missouri Supreme Court to recognize judicial immunity in *State ex rel. Raack v. Kohn*, 720 S.W.2d 941, 944 (Mo. banc 1986) compel the extension of quasi-judicial immunity to statutorily mandated guardians ad litem in child custody proceedings. As other courts have observed:

> Indeed, the need for an independent guardian ad litem is particularly compelling in custody disputes. Often, parents are pitted against one another in an intensely personal and militant clash. Innocent children may be pawns in the conflict. To safeguard the best interests of the children, however, the guardian's judgment must remain impartial, unaltered by the intimidating wrath and litigious penchant of disgruntled parents. Fear of liability to one of the parents can warp judgment that is crucial to vigilant loyalty for what is best for the child; the guardian's focus must not be diverted to appeasement of antagonistic parents. See *Ward v. San Diego County Dep't of Social Serv.*, 691 F. Supp. 238, 240 (S.D. Cal. 1988).

Short by Oosterhous v. Short, 730 F. Supp. 1037, 1039 (D. Colo. 1990).

Further, in Missouri, permitting suits against guardians ad litem would be incompatible with the court's exclusive power of removal. The filing of the suit, irrespective of the merits of the contentions advanced, would instantly create a conflict of interest between the guardian and the child, thus necessitating withdrawal or, as occurred in this case, suspension of the guardian's participation. Thus, assuming standing exists, either parent or the child could accomplish indirectly what we have previously held they cannot accomplish directly—i.e., removal of a guardian whose views of the child's best interests do not coincide with their own.

Extension of judicial immunity to guardians ad litem in custody matters does not, as Father contends, thereby remove all accountability. There are numerous mechanisms in place to prevent abuse and misconduct. Attorney guardians remain subject to the Rules of Professional Conduct. The civil immunity we acknowledge in this case attaches only to conduct within the scope of the guardian's duties. *Short by Oosterhous*, supra, 730 F.Supp. at 1039. The appointing court is required by statute to supervise the guardian's faithful performance and to discharge him if he fails to perform competently. §§452.423.3, 210.160.3 RSMo Supp. 1992.

The allegations of negligence advanced in this case fall squarely within the scope of Guardian's duties as court appointed guardian ad litem. Accordingly, we find that Guardian is absolutely immune from liability for the conduct alleged in Father's petition.

Questions

1. Do you agree with the court's approach to immunity? Without civil liability to provide a check on the competence of guardians ad litem, what other mechanisms are available? Do you think these would be as effective? A number of states follow the *Weinstock* approach and provide absolute immunity for guardians ad litem or best interests attorneys for actions within the scope of their authority. *Cok v. Cosentino*, 876 F.2d 1, 2 (1st Cir. 1989) (per curiam); *Myers v. Morris*, 810 F.2d 1437, 1467 (8th Cir. 1987), *cert. denied*, 484 U.S. 828 (1987); *Kurzawa v. Mueller*, 732 F.2d 1456, 1458 (6th Cir. 1984); *Sarkisian v. Benjamin*, 820 N.E.2d 263, 266 (Mass. App. Ct. 2005); *Tindell v. Rogosheske*, 428 N.W.2d 386, 387 (Minn. 1988); *Billups v. Scott*, 571 N.W. 2d 603, 607 (Neb. 1997); *Fleming v. Asbill*, 483 S.E.2d 751, 754–55 (S.C. 1997); *Delcourt v. Silverman*, 919 S.W.2d 777, 786 (Tex. App. 1996), *cert. denied*, 520 U.S. 1213 (1997); *Paige K.B. v. Molepske*, 580 N.W.2d 289, 295 (Wis. 1998). Other states provide only qualified immunity, holding guardians ad litem liable for acts that exceed ordinary negligence. *See, e.g.*, Ore. Rev.

Stat. §419A.170(4) (2007) (providing qualified immunity to court appointed special advocate for acts in good faith within scope of duties); Vernon's Texas Code Ann. Family Code §107.009 (2004)(qualified immunity for child's attorney). n Maryland, attorneys, whether representing children or the best interests of children, are held to standard of ordinary care and diligence. *Fox v. Wills*, 890 A.2d 726 (Md. 2006); Md. Code §1-202 (2008). Which approach makes the most sense to you?

2. The court notes that the attorney guardian ad litem has a dual role, as both traditional guardian and as attorney for the child. Should immunity apply only when the guardian ad litem is acting in the former capacity? What if a guardian ad litem gives bad advice to a child or misses a crucial investigation that directly harms the child? Shouldn't the child have some recourse? Some courts take a functional approach to the question, providing immunity for attorneys when they are advocating for the child's best interest but not if the attorney is acting as a traditional attorney for the child. *Carrubba v. Moskowitz*, 877 A.2d 773 (Conn. 2005); *Marquez v. Presbyterian Hospital,* 608 N.Y.S.2d 1012 (N.Y. Sup. Ct. 1994). Do you agree with this approach?
3. As the *Weinstock* opinion suggests, immunity protects attorneys from being used by parties to manipulate and prolong a dispute. It also serves to encourage attorneys to serve as child representatives pro bono by lowering the risks of malpractice and discipline. How else might one lower the risk of vindictive lawsuits by parents?
4. The court notes, in its discussion of standing, that the guardian is stepping into the parent's shoes. How are attorneys best suited to this role? Would a better solution be to appoint a mental health professional or even another family member to act as the child's decision maker?

D. Communication and Counseling in Child Representation

If family representation in general presents challenges to competency, child representation does so even more. Attorneys need a unique and broad range of skills and knowledge to communicate with and counsel children effectively. The roles that are played by children's lawyers include traditional core lawyering tasks, such as analyzing the application of the law to the child's situation, developing legal alternatives and strategies, and carrying out those strategies in negotiations and courtroom advocacy. However, the unique needs of counseling and instructing the client in these circumstances also require a sophisticated understanding of children, families, and cultures. This knowledge is drawn from the expertise of other professionals, such as psychologists or other child-focused professionals. Moreover, knowledge is not enough—there is a specialized skill dimension in communicating with children and families that attorneys in this field must develop. Finally, children's lawyers must be able to marshal the many interdisciplinary resources necessary to provide services to support the children and families with whom they are working. This ability is the core of social work expertise. Children's lawyers may have expertise in one of these tasks areas but will require training to supplement the remaining areas.

Initially, attorneys must master the unique procedural and substantive law involved in child representation. However, beyond doctrinal knowledge, one of the most important areas of competence is understanding and interacting with the child client. As we saw in Chapter Two, ordinarily, an attorney must take direction from the client regarding objectives of the representation. Even with clients who have diminished capacity, attorneys have a duty to maintain as normal an attorney-client relationship as possible. Yet it is difficult to avoid paternalism when representing a child. "Although ethical and legal standards call for attorneys to represent children as zealously as they would adults, the lingering strains of *parens patriae* ideology sometimes cause children's attorneys to abandon adversarial efforts in paternalistic deference to the court's efforts to intervene in the child's life."[39]

Avoiding paternalism requires respecting the autonomy and dignity of the child and taking time to become familiar with the client's world:

> As an attorney handling an oil and gas matter will have knowledge of geology, an attorney in a medical negligence case will know something about medicine or an attorney dealing in commercial transactions will have a knowledge of business, an attorney dealing with children should know something about childhood development.[40]

Knowledge of child development is only the beginning however. Communicating with the oil and gas client is unlikely to require any specialized training in understanding the client's communication. These clients are adults who are more likely to come from a similar cultural perspective as the attorney. They are generally better able to unambiguously express their interests and perspectives to the attorney than are most child clients.

---

39. American Bar Association Juvenile Justice Center, et. al., A Call For Justice 16 (2002).

40. Robert M. Murphy, *Child Protection for the Non-Specialist: A Random Overview of Issues*, 6 Okla. B.J. 495, 497 (2004).

For the attorney representing the child, however, ascertaining the child's wishes, feelings, attachments, and attitudes requires specialized training in communicating with children and an understanding of the context in which they are communicating. For example, a child's orientation is to the present and the concrete.[41] Thus, if the attorney asks a first-grade child "Are you in school?" the child may very well answer, "No" because the child is not at that moment in school. If such misunderstandings regarding basic information are common, misunderstanding the child's wishes, feelings and attitudes is nearly inevitable if attorneys lack training in communicating with the child.

There are three components to effective communication with children. First, attorneys must know how their communication with children will be affected by a child's development. Second, attorneys representing children must be sensitive to the impact of class and culture on the representation. In dependency actions in particular, attorneys are likely to come from a vastly different cultural context than their clients.[42] Attorneys must be able to bridge the gulf of age and education differences with their child clients, but class and race differences are common as well. The majority of children in child welfare cases are children of color living in poverty.[43] The significance of these differences should not be underestimated. As Professor Appell instructs us:

> These disparities go both to the heart of attorney-client communication and the attorneys' competence to represent their clients. That is because these disparities create the risk that children's attorneys will not appreciate, or even apprehend, the social dimensions of the presenting legal problems. An attorney's lack of familiarity with a child's culture and social systems may, in turn, lead the attorney to discount the child's stated preferences. Thus, attorneys may not understand the consequences of the various available outcomes or decisions they may make. For example, the attorney may not be aware that a counseling center to which a child is referred is in rival gang territory. Similarly, children's attorneys may not see or understand factors contributing to or even causing other legal problems relating to housing, employment, immigration, or other family issues. The fact that children's law

41. Charmaine Brittain & Deborah Esquibel Hunt, Helping Children in Protective Services: A Competency-Based Handbook 132 (2d. ed. 2004); Anne Graffam Walker, Handbook on Questioning Children (1999).

42. Annette Ruth Appell, *Representing Children Representing What?: Critical Reflections on Lawyering for Children*, 39 Colum. Hum. Rts. L. Rev. 573, 608–09 (2008).

43. *Id.*

> offices are litigation-focused and less likely to engage in community outreach and education further removes attorneys from their clients.[44]

A third component—interpersonal communication skills—is equally important. Learning communication skills requires modeling, practice, and opportunities for feedback and re-practice in context. Attorneys undertaking child representation should seek out opportunities to observe experienced and effective children's attorneys in practice.

In addition to knowledge and communication skills, child representation calls upon attorneys to be able to marshal community resources on behalf of their client. As the American Bar Association Standards of Practice for Lawyers Representing a Child in Abuse and Neglect Cases suggest, attorneys must be able to know how to locate, communicate, and cooperate with experts, must have access to "[i]nformation on accessible child welfare, family preservation, medical, educational, and mental health resources for child clients and their families, including placement, evaluation/diagnostic, and treatment services," and must understand the agencies providing these services.[45] Yet, many attorneys are reluctant to take a system's view of the children they represent, feeling that "[t]his isn't law, it's social work."[46] For example, in *State Public Defender v. Iowa District Court for Polk County*,[47] an attorney who contracted with the public defender's office was granted the statutory $45 an hour pay for time spent helping his client, a mother in a termination case, find housing.[48] The public defender's office challenged the pay, arguing that it was the provision of "social services, not legal services."[49] The court disagreed, noting that finding housing for the mother was a logical part of the overall strategy to avoid termination of the mother's parental rights.[50]

Competent communication with children requires overcoming paternalistic biases, acquiring both knowledge and skills in child communication, and practicing law in a broad sense of service and problem solving, rather than merely advocacy. To what extent do you feel that law school has prepared you for these skills?

---

44. *Id.* at 609–10 (footnotes omitted).

45. American Bar Association Standards of Practice for Lawyers Representing a Child in Abuse and Neglect Cases (1996) at I-2(8).

46. Jane Aiken & Stephen Wizner, *Law as Social Work*, 11 Wash. U. J.L. & Pol'y 63, 63 (2003).

47. 620 N.W.2d 268 (Iowa 2000).

48. *Id.* at 269–70.

49. *Id.* at 269.

50. *Id.*

Practice Portfolio: A Plan for Competence

Research your state and local court's requirements for training (if any) for children's attorneys. Finally, explore resources for acquiring these necessary qualifications. Consider local organizations and continuing education providers. Examine the programs available through national child advocacy organizations. In particular, you may wish to examine the training the Court Appointed Special Advocates (CASA) program provides for its lay volunteers in abuse and neglect actions (http://www.casanet.org/training/index.htm) as well as the certification program of the National Association of Counsel for Children. (http://www.naccchildlaw.org). Prepare a plan for acquiring the knowledge and skills necessary to be an effective child representative. Include in your plan the goals of the training, the resources you would access, estimated costs, and a timeline.

E. Confidentiality

An attorney must keep confidential information relating to the representation of their client, including child clients. However, attorneys representing children may find that confidentiality issues arise more often and are more difficult than in many other representation settings. First, as Chapter Five explores, attorneys have discretion to reveal confidential information without their client's consent in a variety of circumstances, but most commonly in order to prevent death or serious bodily injury. Moreover, under Model Rule 1.14 as adopted by the majority of states, an attorney may disclose information reasonably necessary to protect a client with diminished capacity from substantial physical, financial or other harm.

Yet exercising this discretion to reveal information a child has provided to an attorney can have serious consequences. Disclosure of a child client's communications can represent yet one more betrayal of trust in a lifetime of betrayal experienced by a child who has been victimized by abuse or neglect. Even in a custody dispute, a child's information regarding preferences for custody arrangements can, if revealed directly, exacerbate the child's feelings of guilt and responsibility. Thus, even if you have the discretion to reveal a child client's information, you should weigh carefully the costs of disclosure and find the method of using or disclosing your child client's information that best protects both your client and your client's trust in you.

The rules of professional conduct also allow disclosure of confidential client information when required by law or court order. Increasingly, in the area of child representation, attorneys may find themselves subject to the obligation to report certain confidential information when child abuse or neglect is suspected. The Child Abuse Prevention and Treatment Act[51] requires all states to enact statutes that provide for the reporting of known and suspected child abuse and neglect in order to qualify for federal grant monies. Some states have specific categories of mandated reporters, which may or may not include attorneys. Other states simply require all persons to report suspected child abuse, but some of these states expressly exempt attorneys.[52] Michigan is one such state that protects attorney-child communications strictly.[53] As one commentator explains:

> The Michigan choice was that children needed someone to confide in since they have no one else, typically not even a therapist, who is permitted by law to keep their secrets if those secrets include a suspicion of harm or risk of harm to the children. The parade of horrors of children disclosing abuse to their lawyers who could not report the abuse without the child's permission was thought remediable or worth the cost. Through the lawyer-child counseling process, the lawyer-GAL might obtain the child's permission to disclose the secret or encourage the child to talk with and disclose to others.[54]

Confidentiality is especially difficult to negotiate when an attorney serves as a judicial agent/guardian ad litem and as an attorney for the child. Guardians ad litem are often expected to act as the "eyes and ears of the court," investigating facts and preparing reports and providing recommendations to the court, regardless of the child's desire to keep information confidential. Moreover, in some jurisdictions, these attorneys may even be called upon to testify. Yet, Model Rule 3.7 provides that an attorney may not be a witness in a proceeding in which he or she is representing a party. The Uniform Act recommends that the role of judicial agent should be confined to "best interest advocates" (who need not be attorneys) but is never appropriate for attorneys, even attorneys appointed as "best

51. 42 U.S.C. §§5101–5106 (1997).

52. Lisa Hansen, *Attorney's Duty to Report Child Abuse*, 19 J. Am. Acad. Matrimonial Law. 59, 69 (2004)(providing chart describing various state reporting requirements); Jennings Lockie, *Salt in the Wounds: Why Attorneys Should Not Be Mandated Reporters of Child Abuse*, 36 N.M. L. Rev. 125, 127–28 (2006) (noting that seven states require attorneys to report child abuse and fifteen states require reports from any person who learns of abuse).

53. Mich. Comp. Laws §712A.17d(1)(a) (West 1998); Mich. Stat. Ann. §27.3178 (598.17d(1)(a)) (1998).

54. Don Duquette, *Legal Representation for Children in Protection Proceedings*, 34 Fam. L.Q. 441, 460 (Fall 2000).

interest attorneys."* Nonetheless, in many jurisdictions, attorney guardians ad litem might testify or submit reports and recommendations to the court.

In these jurisdictions, the law may not apply either the duty of confidentiality or the attorney-client privilege to the information these attorneys obtain. Rather, the attorneys may be required by the terms of the court order appointing them to provide a range of otherwise-confidential information to the court. In some states, statutes[55] or court decisions[56] require attorneys acting as guardians ad litem to disclose any information to protect the child's best interests. In these states, the attorney has neither duty nor discretion to keep confidential information provided by the child and the child may not assert attorney-client privilege to prohibit the attorney's testimony.[57]

Problems for Discussion

1. Suppose you have been appointed as a guardian ad litem in a custody action in which both parents have made claims of abuse and neglect. Their daughter Felicia is an intelligent, independent and fiercely angry 12-year-old girl. You have asked her questions about what she likes best about living with one or the other parent and other questions designed to elicit her preference and attachments and she continually responds "I dunno" or "It doesn't matter." When pressed to explain, she tells you that she plans on running away and living with a friend in California. You believe, given the level of detail in her plans, that she will indeed do so.

---

* Uniform Act, *supra* n.9 at Section 14.

55. *See, e.g.*, Del. Code Ann. tit. 29, § 9007A(c) (2003) ("The attorney guardian ad litem's duty is to the child. The scope of the representation of the child is the child's best interests. The attorney guardian ad litem shall have the duty of confidentiality to the child unless disclosure is necessary to protect the child's best interests.").

56. This may be required by state statute; *see also In re* Christina W., 639 S.E.2d 770, 778 (W. Va. 2006) ("[W]hile a guardian ad litem owes a duty of confidentiality to the child[ren] he or she represents in child abuse and neglect proceedings, this duty is not absolute. Where honoring the duty of confidentiality would result in the child[ren]'s exposure to a high risk of probable harm, the guardian ad litem must make a disclosure to the presiding court in order to safeguard the best interests of the child[ren]."); Roy T. Stuckey, *Guardians Ad Litem as Surrogate Parents: Implications for Role Definition and Confidentiality*, 64 Fordham L. Rev. 1785, 1792 (1996).

57. Ross v. Godwah, 131 N.H. 291, 554 A.2d 1284 (N.H. 1988). *But see*, Sharonda B. v. Herrick, No. 97C 225 1998 U.S. Dist. LEXIS 9433 (N.D. Ill. 1998) (allowing assertion of privilege); *In re* Maraziti, 559 A.2d 447, 450 (N.J. Super. Ct. App. Div. 1989)(same).

How do you respond? If she does run away, may/must you disclose that information to anyone?

Suppose you were instead appointed to represent Freedom in a delinquency case and she has indeed run away. She calls you and tells you her whereabouts but instructs you to tell no one. You believe that she would be better off—both in the delinquency case and generally—if her parents were notified. What do you do?

2. One of your clients is Mary Married. Mary is married to Harry Married. Mary has two daughters from a previous relationship, ages 10 and 16, who have lived with Harry and her. Mary has left Harry and, with her daughters, is temporarily living with her sister. Mary has asked for your help in obtaining an ex parte, temporary order of protection against Harry, who has physically and sexually assaulted Mary on more than one occasion. You do so. However, on the day before the hearing for the final order of protection, Mary tells you that she has changed her mind and intends to return to Harry, as he has apologized and she fears her ability to care for herself and her daughters without him. You counsel her regarding this choice, help her make a safety plan, and your representation ends with the dismissal of her motion for a full order of protection.

   Two weeks later, Mary's oldest daughter Dolores calls, leaving you a hysterical voice message asking if she has to stay with her mother, as her step father has been sexually abusing her. She says her mother has been pretending like she doesn't know. She asks for your help and says that if she has to return to Harry's home, she will run away.

May you:

Report the abuse to the state child abuse hot line?
Call up Mary and tell her what Dolores has told you?
Assist Dolores in obtaining a protective order against her step father?

Portfolio Problem: Discussion Confidentiality

Interview an attorney who regularly represents children to discover how he or she explains confidentiality to a child client in understandable terms. Learn how and to what degree the attorney explains the exceptions to confidentiality to child clients and how doing so affects the attorney's ability to establish his or her client's trust. Share what you have learned and reflect on the extent to which the method the attorney uses is one that would be comfortable for you.

To Learn More

In addition to the articles and web resources cited in this chapter, the following books are helpful to exploring further the ethical issues presented by child representation:

William Wesley Patton, Legal Ethics in Child Custody and Dependency Proceedings—A Guide for Judges and Lawyers (Cambridge Press 2006).

> Explores ethical issues in representing children in custody and abuse and neglect actions, including alternative dispute resolution in child protection practice, motion and trial practice, and appellate procedures. Issues are examined from the perspective of children's counsel, parents' counsel, government attorneys, and judges. An appendix contains a mock California child abuse dependency petition with background facts followed by an analysis of the ethical issues raised by the case.

Jean Koh Peters, Representing Children in Child Protective Proceedings: Ethical and Practical Dimensions (LexisNexus, Third ed. 2007).

> Research driven and practice oriented, this comprehensive text provides a model for representation of children that includes methods for assuring cultural competence and respect for autonomy of children, as well as practical tips for negotiating the many stages of dependency actions. The book provides comprehensive research regarding national and international standards for child representation.

Jennifer L. Renne & Claire Sandt, Legal Ethics in Child Welfare Cases (ABA 2004).

> Based on an article series that appeared in the *ABA Child Law Practice*, the text addresses ethical issues for lawyers representing parents, children, and child welfare agencies in child abuse/neglect and termination of parental rights proceedings. Issues include: Quality Representation; Protecting client confidences; Representing a client with diminished capacity; Handling conflicts of interest; Interacting with other parties; Ethical issues in litigation; and Special issues for Guardians ad Litem. The National Child Welfare Resource Center on Legal and Judicial Issues offers free training and technical assistance on issues covered in the book.

Charmaine R. Brittain and Deborah Esquibel Hunt, eds., Helping in Child Protective Services: A Competency-Based Casework Handbook (Oxford, Second ed. 2004).

A deskbook for child protection workers, the text is not designed for attorneys but provides excellent overview of social work processes, techniques for interviewing children and families, child development, medical evaluation of abuse and neglect and other information necessary for effective legal representation in this field.

Chapter Eight

Litigation Ethics

Learning Objectives for This Chapter

After you have read this chapter and completed the assignments you should be able to:

- Identify the tensions that sometimes exist between an adversarial ethic and the constructive resolution of family law disputes.
- Prepare to respond to clients who wish you to engage in adversarial excess.
- Prepare to respond to attorneys who engage in abusive tactics.
- Identify risks in using evidence your client has obtained.
- Identify the standards regarding communication with represented persons and the difficulties presented by that standard in representing family members.
- Identify risks presented by dealing with a pro se litigant and steps you can take to reduce that risk.

A. The Adversary Ethic and Representation of Families

The adversary ethic is deeply rooted in American law and lawyer ethics, though it has become increasingly tempered by other values. The 1968 American Bar Association Model Code of Professional Responsibility stated a primary value of adversarial representation in Canon 7: "A lawyer shall represent a client zealously within the bounds of the law." An ethical consideration within that section states that when "serving as advocate, a lawyer should resolve in favor of his client doubts as to the bounds of the law."[1] This ethic required an attorney to make the client's interests primary, over any other interest save the law itself. Thus, the required zealousness is described as that which is "within

1. Model Code of Prof'l Responsibility EC 7-3 (1980).

the bounds of the law." Certainly the consideration of the interests of third parties was minimally expressed in the code. The code warned that a lawyer must not "intentionally fail to seek the lawful objectives of his client ... through reasonably available means permitted by law."[2]

The more current ABA Model Rules of Professional Conduct retained much of this commitment to the role of attorney as partisan advocate. While, other values, such as candor to tribunals and the professional and personal independence of the attorney were given some greater weight, the notion of an adversary ethic at the core of the attorney's role remains strong. While the rules did not retain the language of Canon 7 in the text of the rules, Comment 1 to Rule 1.3 suggests that "[a] lawyer must act with commitment and dedication to the interests of the client and with zeal in advocacy upon the client's behalf. A lawyer is not bound, however, to press for every advantage that might be realized for a client." Where the rules did shift the balance toward increased obligations to third parties and to the courts, they were subject to considerable criticism as threatening fundamental aspects of the attorney-client relationship.[3] Moreover, the duties to non-clients in the rules are rarely the source of genuine change in the culture of law, given their ambiguity and under-enforcement. [4]

In the context of resolving family disputes, the belief in zealous advocacy as a primary value in legal representation is often troublesome. As the preamble to the AAML Bounds of Advocacy notes:

> ... the emphasis on zealous representation of individual clients in criminal and some civil cases is not always appropriate in family law matters. Public opinion (both within and outside the AAML) has increasingly supported other models of lawyering and goals of conflict resolution in appropriate cases. A counseling, problem-solving approach for people in need of help in resolving difficult issues and conflicts within the family is one model; this is sometimes referred to as "constructive advocacy."

Despite this recognition that adversarial partisanship needs to be balanced with the needs of human relationships, what exactly the correct balance should be is open to question.

---

2. Model Code of Prof'l Responsibility DR 7-101(A)(1) (1980).

3. Theodore Schneyer, *Professionalism as Politics: The Making of a Modern Legal Ethics Code,* in Lawyers' Ideals/Lawyers' Practices: Transformations in the American Legal Profession, 95, 113–17, 122–23, 127–30 (Robert L. Nelson et al. eds., 1992).

4. *See, e.g.*, Judith L. Maute, *Sporting Theory of Justice: Taming Adversary Zeal with a Logical Sanctions Doctrine*, 20 Conn. L. Rev. 7, 20–21 (1986).

Moreover, even an attorney fully committed to a practice oriented to holistic problem-solving will face scorched-earth adversaries. A recent study of negotiating behaviors among attorneys in various practice areas found that "Family law had the highest percentage of unethical adversarial lawyers ... compared to all other practice areas."[5] The authors of the study suggest that this disproportionate representation of unethical adversarial practice in family law may be explained by a constellation of factors: the emphasis on the adversarial system in legal culture, the wishes of clients who push negative behavior, and the emotional context of family law disputes. The authors also speculate that easy cases are handled pro se, leaving only the highest conflict cases for legal representation. Finally, the authors suggest that many family law cases may be handled by generalist attorneys who are unprepared for the unique emotional demands of this practice field.

Since adversarial excess seems all too common in this field, this chapter will examine some of the issues of adversarial balance and excess that arise in the context of family law litigation: threats and other hardball tactics, and the problems raised by improper evidence gathering.

1. Threats and Other Hardball Tactics

Rule 4.4 expressly states that "[A] lawyer shall not use means that have no substantial purpose other than to embarrass, delay, or burden a third person." Yet the adversarial ethic seems to lead some attorneys to believe that these tactics are necessary and useful in family law disputes.

Are hardball tactics an effective approach to advocacy? Empirical research indicates that they are not. Consider this summary of the research on the styles used by successful negotiators:

> Most successful negotiators are able to combine the most salient traits associated with the cooperative/problem-solving and the competitive/adversarial styles. They endeavor to maximize client returns, but attempt to accomplish this objective in a congenial and seemingly ingenuous manner. They look for shared values in recognition of the fact that by maximizing joint returns, they are more likely to obtain the best settlements for their own clients. Although successful negotiators try to manipulate opponent perceptions, they rarely resort to truly deceitful tactics. They know that a loss of credibility will un-

5. Andrea Kupfer Schneider and Nancy Mills, *The Ineffective Family Lawyer*, in Innovations in Family Law Practice 13, 19 (Kelly Browe Olson & Nancy Ver Steegh, eds. 2008).

> dermine their ability to achieve beneficial results. Despite the fact successful negotiators want as much as possible for their own clients, they are not "win-lose" negotiators who judge their results, not by how well they have done, but by how poorly they think their opponents have done. They realize that the imposition of poor terms on opponents does not necessarily benefit their own clients. All factors being equal, they want to maximize opponent satisfaction. So long as it does not require significant concessions on their part, they acknowledge the benefits to be derived from this approach. The more satisfied opponents are, the more likely those parties will accept proposed terms and honor the resulting agreements.
>
> These eclectic negotiators employ a composite style. They may be characterized as competitive/problem-solvers. They seek competitive goals (maximum client returns), but endeavor to accomplish these objectives through problem-solving strategies. They exude a cooperative approach and follow the courtesies of the legal profession. They avoid rude or inconsiderate behavior, recognizing that such openly adversarial conduct is likely to generate competitive/adversarial responses from their opponents. They appreciate the fact that individuals who employ wholly inappropriate tactics almost always induce opposing counsel to work harder to avoid exploitation by these openly opportunistic bargainers. Legal negotiators who are contemplating the use of offensive techniques should simply ask themselves how they would react if similar tactics were employed against them.[6]

The AAML Bounds of Advocacy urge attorneys to adopt this constructive advocacy approach. As the comments introducing the section on Professional Cooperation and the Administration of Justice point out, "candor, courtesy and cooperation: (1) facilitate faster, less costly and mutually accepted resolution of disputes; (2) reduce stress for lawyers, staff and clients; (3) reduce waste of judicial time; and (4) generate respect for the court system, the individual attorney and the profession as a whole." Read in particular AAML Standards 7.1—7.3 and the comments in Appendix A.

In negotiations in particular, tactics can easily step over the line. We have considered the problems of misrepresentation in negotiations in chapter six; another common tactic to gain advantage in negotiations is the use of threats.

6. Charles B. Craver, *Ethics: How to Be Deceptive Without Being Dishonest/How to Be Assertive Without Being Offensive*, 38 S. Tex. L. Rev. 713, 729–30 (1997).

To a certain extent, threats are a necessary part of settling any legal dispute: the threat of going to trial to resolve a dispute is often the prime inducement to settle. When is a threat over the line? The only express direction regarding threats in the rules of professional conduct was that found in the 1968 Model Code of Professional Responsibility, DR 7-105(A). That rule prohibited a lawyer from bringing or threatening criminal charges if the sole purpose was to gain an advantage in a civil matter. The rule was not incorporated into the Model Rules of Professional Conduct because it was considered overbroad and vague. Nonetheless, half of the states retained the provision when they adopted the Model Rules. Even without the rule, other provisions of the rule have been applied in various circumstances of threats: most commonly, Model Rule 3.4 (Fairness to Opposing Party and Counsel), Model Rule 4.1 (Truthfulness in Statements to Others), Model Rule 4.4 (Respect for Rights of Third Persons), and Model Rules 8.4(b), (d) and (e) (Misconduct—especially "conduct prejudicial to the administration of justice").

How do you negotiate the line between legitimate pressure tactics in a settlement and unlawful or unethical threats? Courts may consider a number of factors in evaluating an attorney's threats. Threatening the possibility of criminal action is more likely to be proper if the criminal matter and the civil claim relate to one another. Thus threatening to refer a child support case to the prosecutor for criminal nonsupport or criminal contempt as a way of pressuring settlement of a civil action to recover past due child support is more likely to be considered acceptable pressure than making the same threat in order to induce settlement of a debt entirely unrelated to child support.

The risk of discipline increases significantly whenever a threat is combined with misrepresentation or a frivolous claim. Threatening criminal action to induce settlement is not appropriate where the facts do not support either the criminal charge or the civil claim. An attorney is far more likely to incur discipline or liability if the threats are baseless.[7]

Moreover, even if there is a strong basis for suggesting that a criminal charge might arise, the lawyer should not attempt to exert improper influence over the criminal process, or suggest that she has such influence. For example, in *In re* Ray, 651 N.W.2d 727 (Wis. 2002) a lawyer representing a father seeking to reestablish joint custody of his children after his former spouse moved them out of state told the mother's sister and sister's friend that they would go to jail for interfering with the custody order or for conspiracy to kidnap. The sister's

7. State *ex rel.* Oklahoma Bar Ass'n v. Worsham, 957 P.2d 549 (Okla. 1998) (lawyer's threat of criminal prosecution without basis in fact or law is violation of disciplinary rule that prohibits assertion of frivolous claims and rule regarding truthfulness).

friend was so intimidated that she turned herself in to the local sheriff. The court suspended the attorney for violating the attorney's oath to refrain from "offensive personality." An especially important consideration in weighing the legitimacy of the threat is the fairness of the demand the threat is pressuring. If the demand is for a sum that exceeds the clients actual financial losses (perhaps with no allocation for less quantifiable types of damage such as emotional distress) the threat is more likely to be considered excessive. If any part of the sum demanded appears to include a price simply for keeping quiet, the threat to pursue criminal charges would most certainly be extortion.

The directness of the threat appears also to be a factor. Merely raising the criminal implications of conduct is not as likely to be considered improper as is making an actual threat. For example, the Oregon court declined to discipline an attorney who sent a letter to a hit-and-run driver in which he contrasted his client's generous offer to settle with the driver's own criminal behavior. The court was influenced by the attorney's statement, "I am not telling you this to threaten you." *In re McCurdy*, 681 P.2d 131 (Or. 1984).

You should never threaten to report something that you have a legal duty to report (e.g., reporting another attorney's violation of the rules that raises your duty to report under Model Rule 8.3) or make promises that would otherwise violate the law (e.g., destruction of evidence or suborning perjury). These statements violate the rules of professional conduct because by merely threatening, you imply that you will not follow through on your legal duty to report if you obtain the result you desire.

While the few cases relating to threats tend to focus on threats of criminal prosecution, in the family law field, threats of civil litigation can be equally problematic if the threat is to obtain custody of a child in order to gain advantage in a financial settlement. AAML Standard 6.2 and comments suggest that attorneys should never use children as a bargaining chip in gaining financial leverage.[8] Family law attorneys find that putting a statement in their retainer agreements regarding this restriction on their advocacy can help to deter clients from suggesting this course of action.

In recent years, with the advent of daytime talk-show exposés and internet video postings, threats to take matters to the public media represent another opportunity for negotiation tactics. Model Rule 3.6 prohibits attorney's state-

8. *See* Scott Altman, *Lurking in the Shadow*, 68 S. Cal. L. Rev 493, 530 (1995)(reviewing empirical studies suggesting that threats to trade custody for financial advantage are not uncommon in divorce litigation and arguing that these threats can "coerce, exploit, traumatize children, impoverish women, and demonstrate inappropriate attitudes toward important relationships.").

ments to the media where those statements are substantially likely to materially prejudice a proceeding. Consider also AAML Standard 2.9 and comments in Appendix A, which suggest that, given the private nature of family law litigation, it is rarely appropriate to discuss a client's case with the media and that these discussions will routinely prejudice the case. On the other hand, if the prejudice to which Rule 3.6 refers is the effect on the decision maker, extrajudicial statements may be less likely to prejudice the outcome in family law cases since most of these actions are decided by judges rather than juries.[9] However, a broader reading of prejudicial would suggest that trial publicity is rarely appropriate in a family law setting given the sensitive private nature of these matters and the likelihood of harm to children and other third persons.

For most attorneys, the question is not how to avoid these unethical and abusive tactics, it is how to respond to these tactics when others use them. It is far too easy to respond in kind. Remember Mark Twain's warning: "Don't wrestle with pigs. You both get dirty and the pig likes it." If joining in the mud slinging is not effective, how do you respond? Consider how you would deal with the actions of the attorney in the following case:

In re Nathan

671 N.W.2d 578 (Minn. 2003)

This disciplinary action arises out of the misconduct of the respondent, Dale C. Nathan, in a child custody matter and a CHIPS proceeding.... Nathan was admitted to practice law in Minnesota in 1965. Nathan has been admonished twice before. Nathan's misconduct in these matters falls into three general categories. The first is a pattern of harassing and frivolous conduct; the second is a pattern of violating, threatening to violate and assisting others in violating court orders and confidentiality statutes; and the third is making unfounded derogatory statements about judges and false statements to others. We will consider Nathan's conduct in the child custody and CHIPS matters in turn.

Child Custody Matter

In late 1999 or early 2000, Nathan began representing a mother in a child custody matter arising out of a paternity proceeding. The father was seeking unsupervised visitation of the child and the mother sought to prevent unsupervised visitation. The pattern of harassing and frivolous litigation that the referee found Nathan engaged in was pervasive in this matter.

---

9. Restatement (Third) of the Law Governing Lawyers § 109 cmt. b (2000) (noting little likelihood that extrajudicial statements will become improper basis for decision if matter to be decided by judges instead of juries).

Nathan sent the guardian ad litem several harassing letters. In one letter he called her "worse than worthless" and threatened to "deal with her accordingly." In another letter addressed to her, he threatened to inform others involved in the case that she was not "truthful or impartial and cannot be trusted." Nathan also wrote letters to the judge complaining that the guardian ad litem was biased. Because of Nathan's conduct, an attorney was appointed to represent the guardian ad litem. Nathan then sent the guardian ad litem's attorney a letter threatening to publish the guardian ad litem's letters to him and the judge on Nathan's website "as examples of outrageous actions by a court-appointed quasi-expert."

Nathan engaged in a similar pattern of conduct towards the individual appointed as the visitation investigator. The judge ordered the parties to split the cost of hiring the investigator and to cooperate with her by giving her access to all necessary records and individuals. In a letter to the investigator, Nathan stated that he would not pay for her services, as he believed that the judge's order was "premature and unjustified." Nathan was also upset because he learned that during a supervised visitation session the investigator asked the child to refer to her father as "Dad." Nathan stated that this was "not acceptable" and threatened to discontinue visitation. Three days later, Nathan sent the investigator another letter, stating that she could not have direct contact with the mother or any member of her family. That letter included several derogatory statements about the investigator's professional reputation and threatened to publish a description of her actions on Nathan's website.

In addition to threatening to violate the court order to cooperate with and pay for the investigator, the referee found that Nathan violated and assisted his client in violating other court orders in this matter. After the judge adopted the investigator's visitation recommendation and ordered a transition from supervised to unsupervised visitation, the mother did not bring the child to a scheduled supervised visitation. The father's attorney moved for a contempt hearing and the mother went into hiding and did not appear. In an affidavit, the mother stated that she did not appear on Nathan's advice, and that throughout the time she was in hiding with the child, Nathan advised her not to turn herself in. The father did not see the child again for over a year.

The judge asked Nathan multiple times to disclose his client's location and whether his client was in the state. Nathan stated that he advised his client not to appear but refused to give the legal basis for that advice. Nathan repeatedly refused to disclose any information relating to his client's location, citing attorney-client privilege. The judge found Nathan in contempt. Nathan still refused to disclose the location of his client and was incarcerated for 54 days. Nathan never complied with the court's order.

[Discussion of additional misconduct omitted]

CHIPS Proceeding

Nathan represented the mother of four children in a CHIPS proceeding in which Ramsey County sought to terminate the mother's parental rights to the two youngest children. The referee found that Nathan engaged in a pattern of harassing and frivolous litigation, violated and threatened to violate court orders and confidentiality statutes and rules, made baseless derogatory statements about judges, and made false statements.

The pervasive nature of the harassing and frivolous litigation and the threats to violate and violations of court orders and confidentiality statutes and rules in this matter are closely linked. Nathan sent a letter to the psychologist hired by the county demanding that she provide a written response to 31 questions. Nathan wrote: "If you do not provide satisfactory bases for your allegations, I will publish your letter on my website." Nathan also harassed the social worker in the case. In a memorandum to the court Nathan wrote: "What is happening in this case is madness. It is uncivilized. [The mother] is being denied custody of her children ... by an out-of-control power crazed social worker on the basis of a report by a psychologist.... The person who is crazy is [the psychologist]." Nathan also repeatedly called the social worker a racist, including a statement in a memorandum to the court of appeals. Nathan continued with a similar course of conduct toward all involved in the case. For example, Nathan asked the court to order the foster parent of one of the children to send the child to the school of the mother's choice and threatened to sue the foster parent if the court did not grant his request.

As a result of Nathan's conduct and threats to disclose information, the judge issued a protective order restraining "Nathan from making public any part of the juvenile protection case record in this case without first obtaining a court order." The judge also ordered Nathan to pay $1,500 in sanctions and restrained him from further harassing any witnesses or parties. After the judge issued this order Nathan sent him a letter threatening to publish an article about the case "regardless of the consequences to me." Nathan then published an article on his website describing the case entitled The Young Sex Perverts and placed an ad in the newspaper directing individuals to the article. Nathan also sent letters to the assistant county attorney and others threatening to violate the protective order. In a memorandum responding to a contempt motion that followed, Nathan admitted that he published materials in violation of the court order because "[o]ccasionally, it is necessary to violate a court order or even a law in order to correct serious injustices."

The court found Nathan in contempt for violating the protective order and ordered him to remove all information regarding the case from his website, fined him $500, and again restrained him from publishing any information regarding the case. Two days later Nathan sent the judge a letter stating that if the judge did not schedule a hearing and provide 10 items of relief he was requesting, he would publish an article in area newspapers. Enclosed was an article entitled The Young Sex Perverts with the judge's name prominently displayed below the title. Nathan published the article in the St. Paul Pioneer Press as a paid advertisement on November 3, 2000, shortly before election day.

The final piece of harassing and frivolous conduct in this matter is a federal lawsuit Nathan filed against the social worker, judge, assistant county attorney, psychologist, and one of the foster parents, among others, alleging their actions violated 42 U.S.C. § 1983 (2000). The defendants moved for summary judgment, and the federal district judge granted the motion and awarded the psychologist $2,607.09 in attorney fees.

[The court suspended the attorney indefinitely, with no right to reapply for reinstatement for six months and, among other sanctions, ordered that if the attorney were reinstated to the practice of law, he would be placed on supervised probation for two years following reinstatement, with the terms and conditions of probation to be determined at the time of reinstatement.]

Questions

1. How would you have responded if you had been an attorney involved in litigation with this attorney? In many cases, going to the court for an order can help, but here the attorney was willing to violate court orders. How do you protect your client from attorneys such as this?
2. Some attorneys simply refuse to undertake representations when other attorneys who engage in this type of conduct are involved. Suppose you were representing a client in a case and had entered your appearance when the opposing party engaged the services of an attorney like Nathan. Would you be justified in withdrawing from the representation because of the opposing attorney's reputation for making litigation difficult? Doesn't this simply reward bullies?
3. Could you ask a court to disqualify an attorney from representation for this type of conduct? The power to disqualify an attorney is part of a court's inherent power to control the conduct of litigation in its court, much like the court's contempt powers. Courts do not ordinarily disqualify attorneys for general violations of the rules of conduct, especially because they are reluctant to deny a client their choice of attorney. What arguments might you make to convince a court that disqualification is necessary and appropriate?
4. Unethically aggressive attorneys would be out of business if there were no clients hiring them. However, clients sometimes come to attorneys seek-

ing aggressive, even hostile, representation and believe that these attorneys will best represent their interests. These clients may become confused or even angry when their attorneys are on friendly terms with opposing counsel. How do you identify and moderate these client expectations?

5. Perhaps the most difficult issues regarding tactical ethics is when the children are involved in the cross-fire of adversarial tactics. When representing a parent in a family law matter, attorneys do not ordinarily owe a legal duty to the children[10]; however, the interests of the children in that family are more than peripheral third parties. Most family law attorneys believe that they owe at least a moral, if not a legally enforceable, duty to the children. AAML Standard 6.1 in Appendix A. In particular the AAML Bounds of Advocacy provide that, "An attorney should not permit a client to contest child custody, contact or access for either financial leverage or vindictiveness." AAML Standard 6.2. When parents want to use their children as an adversarial weapon, how do you effectively counsel them regarding this tactic?

2. Evidence Gathering

Fact investigation is an integral part of any family representation. One difficult dilemma attorneys in many family law cases must face is "how much is enough?" This is especially an issue in cases involving children, where the best interests factor turns on a seemingly unlimited scope of historical facts and expert predictions regarding the future. In general, it is up to you to determine how much investigation beyond the minimum is necessary in any given case. Your decision will be guided by the facts you already have, your client's willingness and ability to finance further discovery, the time available, and local rules governing the discovery process.

Attorneys have a legitimate concern that a failure to undertake extensive fact investigation may lead to liability.[11] However, fact investigation is also the

10. Lamare v. Basbanes, 636 N.E.2d 218 (Mass. 1994)(attorney for defendant father in a child abuse proceeding owed no duty to the children such that liability would arise upon the father's abduction and murder of the children); Rhode v. Adams, 957 P.2d 1124 (Mont. 1998)(mother's attorney owed no duty to children such that they could be joined as parties to father's civil rights action against attorney for violation of due process) ; Strait v. Kennedy, 13 P.3d 671 (Wash. Ct. App. 2000)(attorney owed no duty of care to the children of his client (mother) due to his failure finalize mother's divorce before she died, with the consequence that children were not entitled to as large a share of mother's estate).

11. Gursey, Schneider & Co. v. Wasser, Rosenson & Carter, 109 Cal. Rptr. 2d 678 (Cal. App. 2001) (client's forensic accountants have a cause of action for indemnity against client's former family lawyers as a result of $2.5 million arbitration award for overlooking assets).

most likely area in which to find attorneys abusing the adversarial system—using discovery as a tool of obstruction and harassment of opponents and as a method of churning their cases in order to charge more fees. Model Rule 4.4 prohibits using methods of gathering evidence that violate the legal rights of a third person or engaging in behaviors with no substantial purpose other than delay or harassment. Likewise, AAML Standards 7.1 through 7.14 and their comments warn against many of the more common abusive practices. In particular, note the litany of abusive practices described in one comment:

> avoidance of compliance with discovery through overly narrow construction of interrogatories or requests for production; objection to discovery without good faith basis; improper assertion of privilege; production of documents in a manner designed to hide or obscure the existence of particular documents; direction to parties and witnesses not to respond to deposition questions without adequate justification; requests for unnecessary information that does not bear on the issues in the case; and requests for sanctions before making a good faith effort to resolve legitimate discovery disputes.[12]

Parties in family law disputes might themselves want to assist in the fact gathering process, and you certainly will want them to do so in many instances. However, you must take care that your client's fact gathering does not violate the law or the rights of others. Suppose for example that Wife has retained you to represent her in her divorce action. Throughout the case you ask her to deliver certain information regarding the marriage property and other items of interest. One day Wife gives you photocopies of Husband's financial records. Do you ask how she obtained the photocopies?

There is considerable risk in your using this evidence without being aware how it was obtained. The exclusionary rule does not generally apply in civil cases in most jurisdictions because the exclusionary rule is meant to apply to curb government abuse, not private violations.[13] Nonetheless, introducing the evidence illegally obtained may result in discipline or liability. Model Rule 8.4(c) prohibits an attorney from engaging in conduct involving dishonesty, fraud, deceit or misrepresentation and this rule may be applied to an attorney who uses evidence wrongfully obtained, regardless of whether the law allows

---

12. Comment to AAML Standard 7.8, *infra* Appendix A.

13. Rogers v. Williams, 633 A.2d 747 (Del. Fam. Ct. 1993); *In re* Moore, 885 S.W.2d 722 (Mo. Ct. App. 1994); Del Presto v. Del Presto, 235 A.2d 240 (N.J. Super. Ct. App. Div. 1967); Sackler v. Sackler, 203 N.E.2d 481 (N.Y. 1964).

that use.[14] Moreover, if your client has violated the law in obtaining evidence, they may be inclined to suggest that they did so at your direction.

The use of wiretap evidence is especially fraught with risk. Many state laws and federal wiretapping statutes have been held to apply to interspousal wiretaps. The consequences for you if your client produces this evidence are, at best, that the court will exclude the evidence.[15] At worst, you may find yourself subject to discipline or liability.[16] The Electronic Communications and Privacy Act of 1986, which includes Wiretap Act,[17] and the Stored Communication Act,[18] were enacted with domestic surveillance in mind. Consider the application of the Wiretap Act in the following case:

United States v. Wuliger

981 F.2d 1497 (6th Cir. 1992), *cert denied* 510 U.S. 1191 (1994)

Defendant William T. Wuliger appeals the judgment of conviction and sentence for multiple violations of Title III of the Omnibus Crime Control and Safe Streets Act of 1968, ("Title III" or the "Act"), 18 U.S.C. §§2510–2520.... Defendant filed a motion to acquit after verdict which was denied. The District Court fined defendant $5,000 and placed him on probation for two years provided that he surrender his license to practice law and serve a thirty-day home detention. Execution of the sentence, other than the fine, was stayed pending disposition of this appeal. For the reasons stated below, we reverse the defendant's conviction and remand the case to the District Court for a new trial consistent with this opinion.

Defendant, an Ohio attorney, was retained on April 4, 1989 by David Ricupero to represent him in a divorce action commenced by Ricupero's wife, Polly Ricupero, a.k.a. Polly Wilhelm. During a one-week period in mid-March of 1989, Mr. Ricupero intercepted and recorded all telephone calls at the Ricupero's marital home without Mrs. Ricupero's prior knowledge or consent by installing

14. North Carolina State Bar, Opinion 192 (1995) (attorney may not listen to or use tape recording of conversation obtained in violation of wiretapping laws in domestic relations action); Standing Committee on Legal Ethics of Virginia State Bar, Opinion 1448 (1992) (Attorney may not advise client to make surreptitious recording of conversation for purposes of generating evidence in child abuse case. Even if evidence would be admissible, conduct was unethical as involving fraud, deceit and misrepresentation).

15. Stamme v. Stamme, 589 S.W.2d 50 (Mo. Ct. App. 1979).

16. Leach v. Byram, 68 F. Supp. 2d 1072 (D. Minn. 1999) and United States v. Wuliger, 981 F.2d 1497 (6th Cir. 1992).

17. 28 U.S.C. §2510 et seq. (2000).

18. 18 U.S.C. §§2701–2711 (2000).

a wiretap device. Conversations between Mrs. Ricupero and her priest, her marriage counselor, her attorney and many of her friends were recorded. Mr. Ricupero was not a party to any of these communications.

These tapes were made in violation of Title III which criminalizes unauthorized, unconsensual wiretapping. Section 2511(1)(a) is the basis for liability and provides that "any person who intentionally intercepts [or] endeavors to intercept ... any wire, oral, or electronic communication" shall be fined or imprisoned not more than five years. Title III also makes any use or disclosure of the contents of a communication obtained in violation of section 2511(1)(a) illegal, 18 U.S.C. §2511(1)(c)-(d).

Mr. Ricupero gave these tapes to the defendant for use in the divorce proceedings and represented that he had recorded the telephone conversations with his wife's knowledge. When the defendant became aware that the tapes of the conversations were in fact made without the knowledge or consent of Mrs. Ricupero is disputed. The defendant had his secretary transcribe the tapes and had a law clerk prepare written summaries of their contents.

On April 10, 1989, a hearing was held in an Ohio state court on Mrs. Ricupero's charges of domestic violence by Mr. Ricupero. During the defendant's cross-examination of Mrs. Ricupero he used the written summaries of the transcripts in an attempt to impeach her testimony. This was the first time Mrs. Ricupero obtained actual knowledge that her husband had tapped the telephones. Counts 1 and 2 of the indictment charged the defendant with intentionally using and disclosing the contents of a wire communication in violation of Title III at this hearing. The defendant was acquitted of both of these charges.

The defendant was convicted on counts 4, 6 and 8 of the indictment for using the contents of the non-consensual recordings in violation of section 2511(1)(d) on three subsequent occasions. The first was the May 24, 1989 deposition of Mrs. Ricupero. The defendant brought several audio tapes and folders filled with the written transcripts to the deposition. The defendant relied on the contents of the tapes to ask Mrs. Ricupero pointed questions about statements she allegedly made or that others made to her in telephone conversations recorded during March 1989. He also played the tapes themselves numerous times. Mrs. Ricupero's attorney, Carl Murway, objected to the use of the tapes and their contents, but allowed the deposition to continue.

The defendant next used the contents of the tapes at the May 26, 1989 deposition of John Wilhelm, the man with whom Mrs. Ricupero was involved at the time and to whom she is now married. Relying on the transcripts, the defendant asked Mr. Wilhelm about a specific conversation he and Mrs. Ricupero allegedly had in March 1989 which had been recorded. Once again Mrs. Ricupero's attorney objected to this use of the tapes.

The third occasion on which the defendant used the contents of the recordings was the July 8, 1989 state court divorce hearing. The defendant used tape derived information to cross-examine Mrs. Ricupero on whether she had hidden marital money from her husband prior to the divorce.

The defendant admits that he intentionally used the contents of the recordings on these three occasions. He argues that his conduct was not criminal under the Act. The defendant alleges several errors in the court below....

II. [State of Mind Requirements]

A. Knowledge or Reason to Know of the Violation...

[W]e find that the District Court committed plain error in its instructions to the jury on the government's burden of proof under section 2511(1)(d). This section provides that:

> any person who ... intentionally uses, or endeavors to use, the contents of any wire, oral, or electronic communication, knowing or having reason to know that the information was obtained through the interception of a wire, oral, or electronic communication *in violation of this subsection* [shall be fined or imprisoned].

18 U.S.C. §2511(1)(d) (emphasis added)....

Section 2511(1)(a) provides in pertinent part that: "Any person who intentionally intercepts or endeavors to intercept any wire communication shall be guilty of a criminal offense."

The charge required the jury to find only that the defendant knew or had reason to know that the information was derived from a wire interception. It did not require the jury to find that the defendant knew or had reason to know that the interception itself was in violation of Title III. As we interpret this section, however, knowledge or reason to know of the illegality is an element of this offense...

[We look to] the significance of the *mens rea* requirement in our criminal law. "The contention that an injury can amount to a crime only when inflicted by intention is no provincial or transient notion. It is as universal and persistent in mature systems of law as belief in freedom of the human will and a consequent ability and duty of the normal individual to choose between good and evil." *Liparota v. United States*, 471 U.S. 419, 425, 85 L. Ed. 2d 434, 105 S. Ct. 2084, 2088 (1985)(quoting *Morissette v. United States*, 342 U.S. 246, 250, 72 S.Ct. 240, 243, 96 L.Ed. 288 (1952)). The Court further noted that "[c]ertainly far more than the simple omission of the appropriate phrase from the statutory definition is necessary to justify dispensing with an intent requirement." *Id.* (quoting *United States v. United States Gypsum Co.,* 438 U.S. 422, 438, 98 S.Ct. 2864, 2874, 57 L.Ed.2d 854 (1978))....

[I]n *Fultz v. Gilliam*, 942 F.2d 396 (6th Cir.1991), a case construing sections 2511(1)(c) and (d) of the Act, this Court assumed that knowledge of illegality was an essential element of these offenses. While discussing the scope of these sections the Court stated that "[b]y prohibiting all intentional uses and disclosures of unauthorized interceptions by an individual with knowledge of the violation, subsections (1)(c) and (d) strengthen subsection (1)(a) by denying the wrongdoer the fruits of his conduct." *Id.* at 401 (emphasis added).

The government cites *Fultz* to support the well accepted rule that ignorance or mistake of the law is no defense, in this case, to a violation of the Wiretap Act. The government seems to be arguing that by recognizing a knowledge of illegality requirement, this Court would be creating a mistake of law defense. This position is mistaken. If the defendant claimed ignorance that the use of nonconsensual recordings was illegal, that claim would be one of mistake of law. However, whether or not the defendant knew or had reason to know the interception in this case was nonconsensual and thus, illegal, is a question of fact....

Under these instructions, the government did not have the burden of proving that the defendant knew or had reason to know that the recordings were nonconsensual.... We find that by failing to instruct the jury that it had to find the defendant knew or had reason to know that the recordings were made in violation of the Act, the defendant was deprived of his only defense. The court's instructions were tantamount to directing a verdict against the defendant and amounted to plain error.

B. Reason to Know Standard...

[T]he defendant argues that due to an attorney's professional obligations, attorneys are entitled to a special instruction on the "reason to know" standard. The defendant asserts that as an advocate his role is not to pre-judge the merits of his client's factual allegations. Mr. Ricupero represented to the defendant that the tapes were made with his wife's knowledge, in which case they would not violate Title III. The defendant argues that he should be able to rely on the factual representations of his client regardless of his personal opinion as to the client's credibility. He points to his professional duty to present any evidence or theory which is arguably viable, subject to standards of good faith and reasonableness. Because he proceeded on the belief his client was telling the truth, the defendant contends he had no "reason to know" Mrs. Ricupero did not in fact consent to the recordings.

There is nothing in the Act which affords attorneys special treatment. Accordingly, we find that the defendant was not entitled to a special instruction on the reason to know standard solely because he used the tapes in his role as attorney. However, an attorney's professional duties may be a factor in determining whether there is reason to know that recorded information, given by the client, was illegally obtained. Although an attorney must not turn a blind eye to the obvious, he should be able to give his clients the benefit of the doubt. This countervailing duty is one the jury may take into account in deciding whether defendant had reason to know.

III. [Exceptions]

The defendant argues that the trial court erred in failing to recognize various exceptions to the application of Title III and thus failed to instruct the jury on the defenses provided by these alleged exceptions.... We find that the District Court correctly refused to recognize the asserted exceptions to the Act, and uphold the Court's decision to refuse defendant's proposed instructions.

A. Impeachment Exception to Section 2515

[The court rejects an argument that, in civil domestic cases, the court should apply an exception used by some courts in criminal prosecutions that allows use of wiretap evidence for impeachment purposes]

B. Interspousal Exception

Next, the defendant contends that the trial court's failure to instruct on the conflicting interpretations of Title III, concerning the existence of an interspousal wiretapping exception to section 2511(1)(a), was error. The unlawfulness of interspousal wiretapping has been a settled point of law in this Circuit since our decision in *United States v. Jones*, 542 F.2d 61 (6th Cir.1976) ... Concededly, in *Simpson v. Simpson*, 490 F.2d 803 (5th Cir.), *cert. denied,* 419 U.S. 897, 95 S.Ct. 176, 42 L.Ed.2d 141 (1974), the Fifth Circuit held that section 2511(1)(a) was not intended to prohibit purely interspousal wiretaps placed on telephones in the marital home. The *Jones* Court rejected this view. Unlike the Fifth Circuit, this Court was unwilling to look beyond the language of section 2511(1)(a) which clearly expresses a blanket prohibition on all electronic surveillance (except under circumstances specifically enumerated in the statute). We are bound to follow *Jones.* There is no interspousal exception to the Act....

The defendant alleges that in his research he discovered the Simpson case, and cases indicating that Ohio domestic relations courts were allowing the use at trial of interspousal wiretap recordings or of information derived therefrom. E.g., *Beaber v. Beaber*, 41 Ohio Misc. 95, 322 N.E.2d 910 (Ohio Com.Pl., 1974). He submits that because of this precedent, he believed that the tapes Mr. Ricupero made were legal and therefore the existence of these cases bore on his knowledge or reason to know whether the tapes were made in violation of the Wiretap Act.

Due to this mistake, the defendant contends that he did not possess the requisite knowledge to violate section 2511(1)(d). In *Fultz*, 942 F.2d at 396, we addressed a very similar issue under section 2511(1)(c) which prohibits disclosure of the contents of an intercepted communication, by an individual knowing or having reason to know that the information was obtained through an interception in violation of Title III. The defendant in *Fultz* asserted that "not even the Circuit Courts are in agreement whether interspousal wiretapping is a violation of the Federal Wiretapping Act or is excluded." *Id.* at 404. The Court rejected the defendant's argument that he lacked the requisite mental state because the argument was premised on a mistake of law, which has long been recognized as no defense to a criminal prosecution. See *Cheek v. United States,* 498 U.S. 192,——, 111 S.Ct. 604, 609, 112 L.Ed.2d 617 (1991).

We interpret the defendant's proposed instruction as a request for a mistake of law defense and, therefore, find that the District Court did not err in refusing to give it.

C. Good Faith Defense

Next, the defendant claims that there is a statutory "good faith" defense which authorized his conduct. To support his theory, he cites section 2520(d), which provides in pertinent part that:

> a good faith reliance on ... a court warrant or order, a grand jury subpoena, a legislative authorization, or a statutory authorization ... is a complete defense against any ... criminal action brought under this chapter....

18 U.S.C. §2520(d). The defendant then asserts that because the Ohio Code of Professional Responsibility is both a court order and a legislative authorization, he is entitled to an acquittal since he "relied on" the Code in deciding whether or not to use the tapes. Nothing in the Code "authorizes" the defendant to violate Title III in carrying out his professional duties. The defendant's reliance on section 2520 is mistaken; it is not applicable to this case. This defense was intended in part to protect telephone companies or others who cooperate under court order with law enforcement officials. *Jacobson v. Rose,* 592 F.2d 515, 522–23 (9th Cir.1978), *cert. denied,* 442 U.S. 930, 99 S.Ct. 2861, 61 L.Ed.2d 298 (1979)....

Under section 2511(1)(d), the government must prove beyond a reasonable doubt that the defendant knew or had reason to know that the recordings he used were obtained in violation of the Act. The District Court's failure to instruct the jury properly on the requisite mental element of section 2511(1)(d) amounted to plain error. Accordingly, we REVERSE the defendant's conviction and REMAND the case for a new trial consistent with this opinion.

Discussion

1. This case provides a frightening example of the range of risks one faces when using wiretap evidence. After conviction at the first trial, the dis-

trict court fined Wuliger $5,000 and placed him on two years probation on the condition that he serve a 30-day home detention and surrender his license to practice law. On January 22, 1992, the Supreme Court of Ohio indefinitely suspended Wuliger. *In re Wuliger*, 583 N.E.2d 1317 (Ohio 1992). He was reinstated February 3, 1993. *In re Wuliger*, 606 N.E.2d 961 (Ohio 1993). In a subsequent civil suit later filed by the wife, the attorney escaped liability because the divorce degree included a broad release of the parties and their lawyers. The court held that the language of the release covered a suit for violation of The Wiretap Act. *Ricupero v. Wuliger, Fadel & Beyer*, 1994 WL 483871 (N.D. Ohio. 1994).

2. The act prohibits "use" of illegally obtained recordings, but would that include using the information gained from those tapes as leverage in negotiations? See *Leach v. Byram*, 68 F. Supp. 2d 1072 (D. Minn. 1999) (threat to use to tapes to impeach credibility considered "use"). What about using the information from the recordings as a tool to guide further discovery without express reference to the recordings?
3. Do wiretap acts prohibit a parent's recording of conversations between their child and the other parent? Case law points to conflicting answers. See *Platt v. Platt*, 951 F.2d 159 (8th Cir. 1989); *Campbell v. Price*, 2 F. Supp. 2d 1186 (E.D. Ark. 1998); *Pollock v. Pollock*, 154 F.3d 601 (6th Cir. 1998). Which rule seems more appropriate to you?
4. Much of the law regarding electronic surveillance has moved on from telephone wiretapping to computer surveillance. What if, instead of intercepting phone calls in this case, Mr. Ricupero had copied emails from his wife's computer? While the Electronic Communications Privacy Act (ECPA) does provide an exclusionary rule for intercepted electronic communication, most courts examining this issue have determined that interception under the ECPA must occur contemporaneously with transmission.[19] Because most email communications would not be captured as they are transmitted, but later copied from the computer's hard drive, this rule would not apply to exclude using these emails in evidence.[20] At this point another federal law may come into play. The Computer Fraud and Abuse Act of 1984[21] (CFAA). This Act provides liability if a person "intentionally accesses a computer without authorization or exceeds authorized access, and thereby obtains ... information from any protected computer

19. Fraser v. Nationwide Mut. Ins. Co., 352 F.3d 107, 113 (3d Cir., 2003).

20. Evans v. Evans, 610 S.E.2d 264 (N.C. App. 2005); White v. White, 781 A.2d 85 (N.J. Super. Ch. Div. 2001).

21. 18 U.S.C. § 1030 (2000).

if the conduct involved an interstate or foreign communication."[22] Given the ways in which information is transmitted through the internet, accessing a spouse's computer to obtain confidential emails or to track website visits, may well fall within the scope of this Act.

The most difficult issue in applying the Act to spousal computer surveillance is in determining whether one has "authorization" to access the computer. While the Act has not yet been applied in the marital context, cases from employment settings are instructive. For example, in *United States Bioservices Corp. v. Lugo,* 595 F. Supp. 2d 1189 (D. Kan. 2009), employees of a pharmaceutical company obtained confidential information on their work computers, e-mailed it to their personal e-mails, and later disclosed it to their new employer. The court held that their actions could not constitute access to protected computer "without authorization" under Computer Fraud and Abuse Act (CFAA) because they had access to the computers as part of their job. However, the court did find that the employer stated a claim for the employees having "exceeding authorized access" under CFAA, because they had accessed reports that were outside scope of their duties and e-mailed confidential information to their personal accounts.

What would you want to know about Mr. Ricupero's copying of his wife's email in order to determine whether he had violated CFAA? Even if you determine that he had not violated the Act, how comfortable are you in using these emails?

5. Your firm represents MaryAnn Jones in what has become a particularly contentious marital dissolution. During the representation, Ms. Jones brings in copies of text messages from her husband's cell phone. The text messages are between he and his priest, marriage counselor, attorney, and a woman with whom Ms. Jones believes the husband is having an affair. Ms. Jones told you that her husband consented to the taping. She wants you to use them to discredit her husband in court. The texts are indeed very powerful and damaging to the husband's case. What should you do?
6. The opposite of the issue of wrongfully gathering evidence is destroying evidence. Rule 3.4(a) provides that an attorney may not materially alter, destroy, or conceal a document or other material having potential evidentiary value or unlawfully obstruct another party's access to evidence. The spoliation doctrine allows the fact finder to draw an adverse evidentiary inference against the party who destroyed evidence when the party had a duty to retain that evidence. Destruction or alteration of evidence can

22. *Id.*

raise possibilities of criminal liability. However these doctrines only apply after the evidence has been destroyed. What steps can you take to prevent the destruction of evidence?

Research and Portfolio Problem: Discovery Forms and Procedures

Laura W. Morgan, *Marital Cybertorts: The Limits of Privacy in the Family Computer,* 20 J. Am. Acad. Matrimonial Law. 231, 249–50 (2007) advises that:

> The courts do not like "self-help discovery," even when it does not break the law.... All family law attorneys should advise their clients never to install spyware on a computer the other spouse uses. All family law attorneys should also adhere to the rules of civil procedure and evidence, which now contain specific rules for electronic evidence.... Courts are more than willing to allow parties access to relevant electronic evidence in divorce cases, and to enter orders preventing the spoliation of evidence.

In some family law actions in most jurisdictions, formal discovery is carefully controlled with a range of mandatory disclosures. Research the court rules for your jurisdiction to learn what the discovery process entails for a dissolution with children. Then prepare a checklist for discovery and a set of standard forms, paying particular attention to include electronic communication. If your jurisdiction requires mandatory discovery, there may be standard form interrogatories provided by the courts. Research form books and practice guides for your jurisdiction. See if the family law section of your state or local bar association provides guides or forms. Remember that a form is never a substitute for having read the law and understood your client's case.

3. Communication with Represented Parties

Model Rule 4.2 prohibits attorneys from communicating with persons represented by counsel. Moreover, attorneys may not use clients or others as conduits for communicating with these persons. This rule respects the important role an attorney's representation plays in the adversary system and prevents actions that could undermine that role. Yet, in family law disputes, your clients are very likely to continue to communicate with one another on a regular basis. Divorcing couples may need to negotiate regarding ongoing financial obligations; parents will need to communicate regarding their children; the members of a family business will need to continue to work together to wind up the business. These clients need your counsel regarding those communications. In providing this counsel, when might you be seen as using the client as a tool for improperly communicating with a represented party? When should you request the permission of the other attorneys regarding a communication with their clients?

Consider the following ethics opinion on the subject:

State Bar of California Standing Committee on Professional Responsibility and Conduct

Formal Opinion No. 1993-131

Issue:

Attorney represents husband in pending dissolution action. Wife is separately represented by counsel. Husband wishes to communicate directly with his wife without either counsel present regarding the merits of the dissolution to attempt to resolve various disputed issues. Husband seeks guidance from his attorney regarding the content of and strategy to be pursued during such communication. To what extent, if any, may the attorney give such guidance to husband without violating rule 2-100 of the California Rules of Professional Conduct.

Discussion:

The question posed is not unique. It is most often encountered in legal disputes which involve on-going relationships between the opposing parties such as in family law and employment disputes. However, the question can arise whenever parties to a dispute, negotiation, business transaction or other matter are each represented by separate counsel, and desire to communicate between themselves without their counsel present regarding the merits of the dispute, but desire the assistance of their counsel in doing so.

Rule 2-100 of the California Rules of Professional Conduct states in pertinent part:

> While representing a client, a member shall not communicate directly or indirectly about the subject of the representation with a party the member knows to be represented by another lawyer in the matter, unless the member has the consent of the other lawyer.

Rule 4.2 of the American Bar Association, Model Rules of Professional Conduct is similar.

This rule and its predecessors have a history of being strictly enforced in California. The Supreme Court of California has found the rule necessary to preserve the attorney-client relationship and the proper functioning of the administration of justice. According to the Supreme Court of California, the rule is designed to shield opposing parties not only from an attorney's approaches which are intentionally improper, but from approaches which are well intended but misguided. *Abeles v. State Bar*, 9 Cal.3d 603, 609; 510 P.2d 719 (1973). The rule is designed to permit an attorney to adequately function in the proper role of an attorney and to prevent the opposing attorney from impeding that performance. The rule anticipates that if a party's counsel is present when an opposing attorney communicates with that party, counsel can correct any elements of error in the communication or correct the effect of the communication by calling attention to counteracting elements which may exist. *Mitton v. State Bar*, 71 Cal.2d 525, 534 455 P.2d 753 (1969).

The extent to which the Supreme Court of California finds this rule fundamental to the proper functioning of the attorney-client relationship and the administration of justice is illustrated by the strict manner in which the court has enforced the rule by the imposition of discipline. Two examples are illustrative in this regard.

In *Abeles v. State Bar*, *supra*, 9 Cal.3d at pp. 609–10, Abeles was publicly reprimanded for having communicated with an adverse party whom Abeles knew to have an attorney of record in pending litigation, even though the opposing party told Abeles that he was not in fact represented.

In *Turner v. State Bar*, 36 Cal.2d 155, 222 P.2d 857 (1950) Turner was suspended from the practice of law for three months for violating the rule. Turner represented defendants in litigation in which plaintiffs were separately represented. After judgment was entered in favor of plaintiffs, an appeal was filed in which the defendants were represented by new counsel. While the matter was on appeal, Turner was requested by his former clients and their new attorney to finalize settlement terms that had been worked out between the parties themselves. Turner did so without the involvement of opposing counsel. The Supreme Court of California found that Turner had acted as more than a "scrivener" in finalizing the settlement terms and therefore violated the rule by becoming substantively involved with plaintiffs without the knowledge of plaintiffs' counsel. The fact that Turner was no longer attorney of record for defendants in any proceeding was irrelevant. As long as Turner was an attorney for defendants, knew adversity existed between the defendants and plaintiffs, and knew plaintiffs were represented by counsel, his communications with plaintiffs without their counsel present were improper.

The above authorities leave no doubt that an attorney cannot communicate upon the merits of a dispute *directly* with an opposing party known to be represented by counsel. However, in addition to prohibiting direct communication, rule 2-100 also prohibits *indirect* communication between an attorney and an opposing party represented by counsel. It is the prohibition against indirect communication that is invoked whenever clients seek counsel from their attorneys regarding communication the clients intend to have with opposing parties. Counseling clients regarding such communication can violate rule 2-100.

One course of action for an attorney whose client wishes to communicate with a represented opposing party is for the attorney to attempt to dissuade the client from such and, to the extent it occurs, assure that the attorney is not involved in and provides no guidance to the client in preparing for the communication. This was the course of action that was recommended in American Bar Association Formal Opinion No. 75 (1932) and American Bar Association Informal Opinion No. 524 (1962). These old opinions were, however, withdrawn when the American Bar Association adopted Rule 4.2 of the American Bar Association, Model Rules of Professional Conduct. It is now recognized that attorneys need not discourage clients from direct communication with one another and that such communication can be beneficial. (See, e.g., Discussion to rule 2-100 ["Rule 2-100 is not intended to prevent the parties themselves from communicating with respect to the subject matter of the representation...."]; Formal Opinion No. 1991-2 of the Bar Association of the City of New York Committee on Professional and Judicial Ethics (April 30, 1991) ([lawyers are not obligated to discourage direct client-initiated communication between represented parties].) In fact, by discouraging direct communication between the parties themselves, an attorney may be failing to act competently by foreclosing opportunities to efficiently settle or resolve the dispute.

Obviously, there is a line to be drawn between these two extremes, i.e., the attorney directly communicating with an adverse party represented by counsel on the one hand, and the attorney refusing to be involved at all in any communication his or her client has with an opposing party represented by counsel. Where this line is drawn is more easily determined in some cases than others.

For example, any direct communication on the merits of a dispute in writing, by telephone, face-to-face or otherwise between an attorney and an opposing party known by the attorney to be represented by counsel is prohibited unless opposing counsel consents. Direct communication is not prohibited, however, between attorneys and opposing parties known to be unrepresented by counsel. Whether an opposing party is known to be represented by counsel is determined by what a reasonable attorney should have known rather than what the attorney actually knows. A party is known to be represented if the party has an attorney of record even if the party insists that he or she is unrepresented. (See, e.g., *Abeles v. State Bar*, *supra*, 9 Cal.3d at pp. 606–607, 610.)

To be prohibited, communication must be upon the "subject of the representation." Although any communication with an opposing party represented by counsel should be limited[23], the rule prohibits only that communication which involves the merits of a dispute.

The parties have the right to communicate with each other without their counsel present. Information obtained by a client from an opposing party represented by counsel where there has been no prohibited direct or indirect communication under rule 2-100 may properly be communicated by the client to the attorney and used by the attorney as is otherwise appropriate.

What the rule prohibits and permits is less clear in those situations where the client consults the attorney in anticipation of the client's future communication with a represented opposing party. In determining what is appropriate in such circumstances, counsel should be guided by the overriding purpose of rule 2-100, which is to prohibit one side to a dispute from obtaining an unfair advantage over the other side as a result of having ex-parte access to a represented party.

When the content of the communication to be had with the opposing party originates with or is directed by the attorney, it is prohibited by rule 2-100. Thus, an attorney is prohibited from drafting documents, correspondence, or other written materials, to be delivered to an opposing party represented by counsel even if they are prepared at the request of the client, are conveyed by the client and appear to be from the client rather than the attorney. An attorney is also prohibited from sending the opposing party materials and simultaneously sending copies to the party's counsel. Providing copies to opposing counsel does not diminish the prohibited nature of the communications with the opposing party.

An attorney is also prohibited from scripting the questions to be asked or statements to be made in the communications or otherwise using the client as a conduit for conveying to the represented opposing party words or thoughts originating with the attorney.

When the content of the communication to be had with the opposing party originates with and is directed by the client, it is permitted by rule 2-100. Thus, an attorney may confer with the client as to the strategy to be pursued in, the goals to be achieved by, and the general nature of the communication the client

23. As recognized in the discussion following rule 2-100, there are a number of authorities which authorize communication between an attorney and a person who would otherwise be subject to the rule. Where such authorities apply, they may override the prohibitions of rule 2-100.

intends to initiate with the opposing party as long as the communication itself originates with and is directed by the client and not the attorney.

Rule 2-100 specifically contemplates that communication between an attorney and an opposing party represented by counsel is appropriate with the consent of the opposing counsel. Therefore, prudent attorneys concerned about anticipated communication between parties on disputed issues should attempt to reach an understanding with opposing counsel as to the standards that will apply to counsel's involvement in such communication.

Questions

1. Suppose your client has asked you to draft a divorce settlement proposal for them to review. You know that if you do so, the client will share the proposal with their spouse. Would drafting the proposal for the client violate Model Rule 4.2? Would you have any obligation to disclose the document to opposing counsel?
2. What about speaking with children? Note that AAML Standard 6.3 suggests that "When issues in a representation affect the welfare of a minor child, an attorney should not initiate communication with the child, except in the presence of the child's lawyer or guardian ad litem, with court permission, or as necessary to verify facts in motions and pleadings." The rule prohibiting contact with represented persons has been variously applied to attorneys appointed as guardians ad litem for children. Some authorities have held that the attorneys in these circumstances are not bound by the rule. *State ex rel. Children, Youth & Families Dep't v. George F.*, 964 P.2d 158, 163 (N.M. Ct. App. 1998). Authorities in other states apply to children's attorneys the same prohibitions on communication with represented parties as any other attorney. Wash. Sup. Ct. Guardian Ad Litem R. 4(a) (requiring permission of attorney for represented persons)). D.C. Bar, Ethics Op. 295 (2000),; NYSBA Comm. on Prof'l Ethics, Op. No. 656 (1993), 1993 WL 555956 (citing similar ethics opinions from Wisconsin, Arizona, and North Carolina). Suppose you are representing a child in a state in which your authority under the rules is unclear. How do you proceed if you wish to communicate directly with the represented adults in the case?

B. The Pro Se Opponent

Pro se litigation is very common in family law matters, with "some reports indicating that eighty percent or more of family law cases involve at least one pro se litigant."[24] Increasingly states are providing assistance to pro se litigants, especially in divorce cases, in order to address congested court dockets. A number of states have rules of civil procedure designed to facilitate pro se divorce litigation.[25] Pro se litigation is especially common in cases in which the law is designed to be accessible without attorneys, such as in protective order actions. You may regularly find yourself facing an unrepresented party and that unrepresented party may look to you for legal questions and preparation of necessary documents.

Despite the routine nature of facing a pro se litigant, only one rule of professional conduct expressly addresses the attorney's duty in this context. Model Rule 4.3 prohibits a lawyer from stating or implying disinterest and requires the lawyer to make reasonable efforts to correct any misunderstandings held by the unrepresented party about the lawyer's role.[26] The previous ABA Model Code of Professional Responsibility provided more specific guidance,[27] prohibiting, in particular, giving advice to unrepresented litigants and some state's rules have retained that prohibition. Similarly, AAML Standard 3.2 provides that an attorney "should not advise an unrepresented party." Read the suggested disclaimer in the comments to that standard in Appendix A.

The one type of advice that you should give an unrepresented person is the advice to seek counsel. Some courts have held that you must give this advice to unrepresented parties in ceertain instances. For example, the New York court held in *In re Michelman*, 616 N.Y.S.2d 409, 411–12 (N.Y. App. Div. 1994) that an attorney representing adoptive parents must advise the biological mother of the need for independent counsel. You could also direct an unrepresented party to sources for obtaining help, such as court provided pro se websites or classes.

Beyond the advice to obtain counsel, rules in most states prohibit any other advice to unrepresented parties. The solution of asking your client to communicate necessary paperwork to the opposing party does not necessarily solve

---

24. Russell Engler, *And Justice for All—Including the Unrepresented Poor: Revisiting the Roles of the Judges, Mediators, and Clerks*, 67 Fordham L. Rev. 1987, 2047 (1999).

25. *See, e.g.*, Ariz. R. Civ. P. 55(b)(1)(ii)(2008); Fla. R. Fam. Law R. Proc. 12.750 (2009); Minn. Gen. R. Prac. 110.01-.09 (2008).

26. Board of Overseers v. Dineen, 500 A.2d 262, 265 n.2 (Me. 1985), *cert. denied*, 476 U.S. 1141, 106 S.Ct. 2248, 90 L.Ed.2d 694 (1986) (lawyer representing only one spouse in divorce action must take reasonable steps to prevent other spouse from believing that lawyer represents that person's interests as well).

27. Model Code of Prof'l Responsibility DR 7-104(A)(2) (1969) (lawyer must not "give advice to a person who is not represented by a lawyer, other than the advice to secure counsel, if the interests of such person are or have a reasonable possibility of being in conflict with the interests of his client").

the ethical quandary. A lawyer may not funnel advice to the opposing party through his own client.[28]

The difficulty with this prohibition on advice is that the line between providing information and giving advice is not a clear one. For example, attorneys necessarily tread close to that line whenever they draft a document and then ask a non-client to sign that document. ABA Informal Op. 1140 (1970) concluded that, "As long as these documents are not accompanied by or coupled with the giving of any advice to the defendant, they would constitute only communication … and … would be ethical." However, often a non-client will want to ask a question about the document. Would an attorney be "giving advice" by answering questions or describing what that document does? It would depend on the question of course. Answers to innocuous question of fact or procedure such as "Should I sign with my married or maiden name?" "Does this agreement include the XYZ account?" or "How long will it take for the court to hear this?" are likely permissible. However, anything close to the line of "What does this mean?" or "Should I do this?" is going to fall in the category of advice. One way to think about the line between information and advice is to ask whether the question you are answering could only be answered one way, without the exercise of judgment. Another consideration is whether the question relates to the rights or alternatives of the unrepresented person. Any communication with pro se parties should be undertaken with the utmost caution, and especially so in circumstances in which the rules of professional conduct consider joint representation to be a *per se* conflict of interest.

If the opposing party does not secure representation, you have no duty to maintain a position of neutrality. Suppose, for example, you have been asked to file a civil action against an individual on behalf of your client. You are aware that the claim is likely barred by the statute of limitations. May you nonetheless file the claim? An ABA Formal Ethics Opinion 94-387 suggested that you have no duty either to the opposing party or to the court to refrain from filing the action or to raise the issue of the statute of limitations, as that is a defense and may be waived by a defendant. You may not, of course, misrepresent the facts regarding the dates in such a way as to mislead on the issue. Would you feel comfortable filing this action on behalf of your client?

In some settings, the law provides higher duties on attorneys facing to *pro se* opponents to avoid overreaching and to inform the unrepresented persons of the need for independent counsel. Probably the clearest setting in which this is

28. Ky Bar Assoc. Ethics Op. E-365 (March 11, 1994).

true is in the representation of one party to a prenuptial agreement. Because spouses are generally held to have a fiduciary duty to one another, an attorney who helps one spouse take advantage of their unrepresented partner is not really helping to protect the client's interests. Helping the unrepresented party to understand why independent counsel is important is vital to the stability of any agreement you negotiate. Equally important and difficult is educating your own client regarding the need for fairness and balance in furthering his goals in the agreement. Consider the comments of the Washington court regarding dealing with an unrepresented party in drafting a prenuptial agreement:

> An attorney in this situation is presented with a number of choices. He or she may endeavor, if the client consents, to prepare a contract which is designed to meet the [test] of economic fairness for the economically subservient party. Whether or not the client consents to the preparation of a contract which attempts to achieve economic fairness for the economically subservient party, the attorney should explain to that unrepresented party *why* it is so important that he or she seek the advice of independent counsel. That which is obvious to attorneys and judges may not be obvious to the unrepresented and economically subservient party. Every marriage eventually will terminate by one of two means: by marital dissolution or by the death of a spouse during marriage. What is indeed being sought is a divorce settlement and a death settlement. The purpose of independent counsel is more than simply to explain just how unfair a given proposed contract may be; *it is for the primary purpose of assisting the subservient party to negotiate an economically fair contract.* The desire of the economically dominant party to preserve the bulk of his or her wealth, and for some reasonable degree of certainty in the event of divorce, is not necessarily entirely inconsistent with the goal of economic fairness for the disadvantaged party. It is not conducive to marital tranquility to ask a party who comes into the marriage destitute to leave the marriage equally destitute, or worse, perhaps many years later, and perhaps at a time when age, health and forgone career opportunities dictate that he or she can no longer acquire assets by virtue of employment, to leave the marriage in a far worse position than if the marriage had never taken place. *Both* parties to a prenuptial contract need to understand the underlying premises which dictate the need for independent counsel.
>
> .... In *Friedlander v. Friedlander*, 80 Wn.2d 293, 301, 494 P.2d 208 (1972) the court stated that a prenuptial contract freely and intelligently made is generally regarded as conducive to marital tranquility

> and the avoidance of disputes about property in the future. To the extent that the parties negotiate an economically fair contract, we fully agree. The same cannot be said of a contract which fails the [economic fairness test]. An attorney who represents either party to a prenuptial contract should seriously consider the implications of RPC 2.1 (In rendering advice, a lawyer may refer not only to law but to other considerations such as moral, economic, social and political factors, that may be relevant to the client's situation.). A client is not well served by an unenforceable contract. Marital tranquility is not achieved by a contract which is economically unfair or achieved by unfair means.[29]

Helping your client to understand that there is little benefit to be gained in taking advantage of an opponent's lack of representation (or poor representation) is probably some of the hardest counseling you may have to undertake. You may find that the best way to set the tone is to communicate consistently your philosophy of representation in your advertising, your initial interview, your engagement letter or retainer agreement, and, most importantly, in your actions in representation.

Practice Portfolio: Explaining Documents to an Unrepresented Person

You may find yourself in a position in which you find it necessary or useful to draft documents for an unrepresented opposing party to sign. For example, in a divorce action, your client's spouse may be willing to waive service. May you draft the waiver for the spouse to sign? ABA Informal Ethics Opinion 1269 (1973) suggested that this would not be improper so long as you did not advise the spouse. Could you explain what the waiver is? Why the spouse should sign it? Write a letter to accompany this document.

To Learn More

In addition to the articles and web resources cited in this chapter, the following resources are helpful to addressing issues of ethics in family litigation:

---

29. *In re* Marriage of Foran, 67 Wn. App. 242, 254; 834 P.2d 1081, 1088–89 (Wash. App. 1992).

Civility and Professionalism Standards

A number of bar associations and professional organizations have adopted voluntary civility guidelines that you may find useful as guides to practice in representing family members in litigation. Most of these guidelines are available online. A collection links to the various codes can be found at the websites of :

The National Center for State Courts
http://www.ncsconline.org/wc/courtopics/statelinks.asp?id=45&topic=JudEth.

The American Bar Association Center for Professional Responsibility
http://www.abanet.org/cpr/professionalism/profcodes.html.

In particular, you may find helpful the ABA Section on Family Law's Civility Standards, online at http://www.abanet.org/family/reports/standards_civility.pdf.

John C. Mayoue, *Balancing Competing Interests in Family Law: How to Handle Alternative Relationships, Third-Party Interests, Interspousal Torts, Privilege, and Privacy Issues,* Second Edition (ABA 2003).

This text deals with three aspects of third-party interests in family law. First the text addresses civil and evidentiary issues affecting marital relationships, including privileges against self-incrimination, applicable testimonial privileges between divorcing spouses and clergy, counselors or accountants, and offers an analysis of federal and state wiretapping laws in the context of domestic relations. Second, the text explores the impact of third parties, such as employed experts, persons against whom spouses can assert tort claims, and persons with interests in marital privacy. It also considers third-party privacy and substantive rights in the discovery process. Finally, the text discusses how non-traditional and alternative relationships are treated by the law. Appendices provide state-by-state charts comparing various evidentiary standards and third-party rights.

Chapter Nine

Alternative Dispute Resolution

Learning Objectives for this Chapter

After you have read this chapter and completed the assignments you should be able to:

- Explain why alternatives to litigation are important in family representation and be motivated to learn more about forms of alternative dispute resolution used in family representation in your region.
- Identify key differences between representing a client in adversarial proceedings and representing a client in mediation.
- Describe the key characteristics of collaborative divorce.
- Explain the ethical issues raised by collaborative divorce agreements.
- Describe factors important to counseling a client in choosing and engaging in dispute resolution process.

A. Mediation

Because of the high relationship costs of litigation in family law disputes, alternatives to litigation have become increasingly important. Indeed, less than two percent of family cases are ultimately decided by a judge.[1] A number of processes have emerged to help to facilitate resolution of family law disputes outside of litigation. These alternatives include arbitration, mediation, collaborative negotiation, and many variations on these processes. Family law arbitration[2] shares many characteristics with litigation, in that it provides a

1. Eleanor E. Maccoby & Robert J. Mnookin, Dividing The Child: Social And Legal Dilemmas Of Custody 137, 141 (1997).

2. To learn more about family law arbitration, see George K. Walker, *Family Law Arbitration: Legislation and Trends*, 21 J. Am. Acad. Matrimonial Law. 521 (2008).

neutral third-party decision maker who enforces the process and controls and limits the scope of information and communication, much as the rules of evidence and procedure control and limit the communication in litigation. Mediation, however, is quite different in orientation and process.

The Model Standards of Practice for Family and Divorce Mediation define mediation as:

> A process in which a mediator, an impartial third party, facilitates the resolution of family disputes by promoting the participants' voluntary agreement. The family Mediator assists communication, encourages understanding and focuses the participants on their individual and common interests. The family mediator works with the participants to explore options, make decisions and reach their own agreements. [3]

In many family disputes, you may choose to advise your clients that mediation may reduce animosity, speed resolution, and help parties to learn to communicate constructively with one another. In child custody disputes in particular, custody arrangements crafted by the parties through mediation will often lead to increased involvement by both parents in the child's life after litigation, more durable agreements, reduced costs and increased client satisfaction.[4] In fact, mediation has become so integral a component of dispute resolution in many family law cases that many states now require mediation for divorce or custody disputes.[5]

Counseling clients regarding the availability of alternative dispute resolution mechanisms in general and mediation in particular is an important part of your initial consultation with clients in family representation. Rule 2.1, by its terms, is the only rule in the Model Rules that addresses the lawyer's role as "Advisor." Comment 5 to Model Rule 2.1 suggests that "When a matter is likely to involve litigation, it may be necessary under Rule 1.4 to inform the client of forms of dispute resolution that might constitute reasonable alternatives to litigation." While the language is only vaguely directive, in many states attorneys must discuss alternatives to litigation with their clients as a matter of court

---

3. Model Standards of Practice for Family and Divorce Mediation, Overview and Definitions (2000) *infra* Appendix C.

4. Andrew Schepard, *Kramer vs. Kramer Revisited: A Comment on The Miller Commission Report and the Obligation of Divorce Lawyers for Parents to Discuss Alternative Dispute Resolution with Their Clients*, 27 Pace L. Rev. 677, 682–84 (2007).

5. Jane C. Murphy & Robert Rubinson, *Domestic Violence and Mediation: Responding to the Challenges of Crafting Effective Screens*, 39 Fam. L.Q. 53 (2005)(appendix reviews statutes of the 50 states indicating whether the statute contains a domestic violence exception).

rule[6] or as part of the disciplinary code.[7] Even if your state does not generally require this discussion,[8] as a family law attorney, you should consider counseling clients regarding mediation as a standard of best practice.[9]

The required discussion should inform the client of what mediation is, how it differs from litigation and negotiation, and the advantages and disadvantages of mediation for that particular client. [10] However, in situations in which bargaining power is skewed or a client's decision-making capacity is diminished, as might be present in situations of domestic violence, you may want to advise against voluntary mediation or request an exception or of a delay of mandatory mediation.[11]

> In order to make informed decisions about participation in mediation, families should consider factors such as the following: the pattern of domestic violence; the frequency and severity of the violence; the health and mental health status of the parties; the likely response of the primary perpetrator; the quality of the mediation process actually available; whether the parties are represented; the presence of children; relative financial resources; and preferred decision making approach. If it occurs, mediation should be conducted by an experienced and specially trained mediator who institutes tailored safety precautions and procedures. At a minimum, these should include written ground rules, inclusion of lawyers and support persons; separate arrivals and departures, and use of separate caucusing.[12]

If an attorney is representing a client in mediation, the same rules regarding conflicts of interest apply as if the attorney were representing the client in litigation or negotiation. Thus, attorneys may not simultaneously represent

---

6. *See, e.g.*, Mo. Sup. Ct. R. 17.02(b)(2009)(requiring attorneys to advise clients of ADR availability).

7. *See, e.g.*, Va. R.P.C. R. 1.4 & comt. 1a (2008)(attorneys must discuss alternatives to litigation that might be more appropriate to the client's goals).

8. *See generally*, Marshall J. Berger, *Should an Attorney be Required to Advise a Client of ADR Options?*, 13 Geo. J. Legal Ethics 427, Appendix I–II (2000) (comprehensive listing of court rules, state statutes and ethics provisions).

9. *See* Nicole Pedone, *Laywer's Duty to Discuss Alternative Dispute Resolution: In the Best Interest of Children*, 36 Fam. & Conciliation Cts. Rev. 65 (1998).

10. *See* Mary Kay Kisthardt, *The Use of Mediation and Arbitration for Resolving Family Conflicts: What Lawyers Think About Them*, 14 J. Am. Acad. Matrim. Law. 353, 374 (1997).

11. Nancy Ver Steegh, *Yes, No and Maybe: Informed Decision Making About Divorce Mediation in the Presence of Domestic Violence*, 9 Wm. & Mary J. Women & L. 145 (2003).

12. Nancy Ver Steegh, *Family Court Reform and ADR: Shifting Values and Expectations Transform the Divorce Process*, 42 Fam. L.Q. 659, 665–66 (2008).

adverse parties to a mediation any more than they would adverse parties to litigation. Yet sometimes parties may come to an attorney seeking assistance in crafting an agreement between them in a mediated negotiation. In these instances, you may choose to act as a mediator for the parties. This is certainly permissible, though that was not always clearly so.

For years, the Model Rules attempted to find a standard for appropriate practice by attorneys as intermediaries. Model Rule 2.2 provided that attorneys could assist multiple clients in crafting agreements or solving problems. However, the conditions attached to the rule were so restrictive, it precluded many of the situations in which an attorney would be most useful, limiting the role of attorney to little more than scrivener. Intermediation was permitted only if the attorney reasonably believed that the matter could be resolved "on terms compatible with the clients' best interests, that each client will be able to make adequately informed decisions in the matter, and that there is little risk of material prejudice to the interests of any of the clients if the contemplated resolution is unsuccessful."

So limited was the role contemplated by Model Rule 2.2 that in 2002, the ABA deleted that rule entirely and adopted Model Rule 2.4 "Lawyer Serving as Third-Party Neutral." This rule recognizes that attorneys may serve as mediators, arbitrators, or in other roles serving "persons who are not clients of the lawyer to reach a resolution of a dispute or other matter that has arisen between them." The rule requires only that the lawyer clarify his or her role, so that individuals do not believe that the attorney third-party neutral is acting as a representative for any party. See AAML Standard 8.3 in Appendix A. The ethical problems arise when attorneys attempt to shift from one role to the other or never clarify and communicate the role they are to play.

If you choose to offer mediation services as part of your practice, the ethical issues when acting as a mediator are diverse. Competence is a fundamental issue. Mediation requires separate training and, in many states professional certification, so that you should only undertake mediation when they have the necessary training and experience. See AAML Standard 8.1 in Appendix A. The ethical duties of mediators in family law cases are beyond the scope of this text, but a good introduction to these issues can be found by reviewing the 2000 Model Standards of Practice for Family and Divorce Mediation in Appendix C. Those standards, drafted by a symposium of representatives from a variety of family law and dispute resolution organizations were promulgated by the Association of Family and Conciliation Courts and adopted in 2001 by the American Bar Association House of Delegates.

Most attorneys will be more likely to represent clients in mediation than actually conduct the mediation themselves. Representing clients in mediation requires, at a minimum, training in interest-based negotiation. However, even with training, cooperative, interest-based bargaining may be sufficiently foreign to some attorneys that they may conclude that they simply lack the aptitude or attitude to successfully represent clients participating in mediation processes:

> ... the zealous advocate will likely prove a failure in mediation, where creativity, focus on the opposing sides' interests, and a broadening, not narrowing of issues, may be more valued skills.... Some have suggested the settlement function is sufficiently different from the adversarial function requiring different individuals, with different personalities and orientations as well as ethics. Thus, as courts struggle with such legal issues as what it means to attend a settlement proceeding "in good faith," representatives of parties (which is the term I prefer to the term "advocates") have to consider how to become effective in a different forum. A different orientation to the client and to the "adversary" may be essential in the kind of creative option generation and problem-solving that is essential in a mediation setting.[13]

Your duties in representing a client in mediation begin with helping the client to choose a mediator. While models of mediation vary, the most typical family mediation is built on a model of facilitative mediation.[14] Facilitative mediation is process focused rather than outcome oriented. The mediator assist individuals to communicate with one another to jointly solve the problems that have brought them to mediation. Rather than having the mediation revolve around each party's position, mediation communication grounds itself in each person's interests. Key to choosing a mediator is insuring that the mediator is well-trained and effective in these key skills. Many states provide certification standards for family mediators.

Attorneys should ask mediators about their training, approach and experience. The Model Standards of Practice for Family and Divorce Mediation recommend that:

13. Carrie Menkel-Meadow, *Ethics in Alternative Dispute Resolution: New Issues, No Answers from the Adversary Conception of Lawyer's Responsibilities*, 38 S. Tex. L. Rev. 407, 427–28 (1997).

14. For a thorough discussion of the various models of family mediation, see Ann Milne, Jay Folberg, & Peter Salem, *The Evolution of Divorce and Family Mediation: An Overview*, Divorce and Family Mediation: Models, Techniques, and Applications, 14–17 (Jay Folberg, Ann L. Milne and Peter Salem, eds. 2004).

> Effective mediation requires that the family mediator be qualified by training, experience and temperament; that the mediator be impartial; that the participants reach their decisions voluntarily; that their decisions be based on sufficient factual data; that the mediator be aware of the impact of culture and diversity; and that the best interests of children be taken into account. Further, the mediator should also be prepared to identify families whose history includes domestic abuse or child abuse.[15]

Some mediators try to maintain a strictly neutral stance toward the legal, financial or emotional wisdom of the party's proposed solutions, offering no expert evaluation of proposals. In some states, mediators are required to forgo neutrality in order to advance the best interests of the child in child custody mediations.[16] Of course, if a mediator is to truly facilitate the process, they will have to offer some routes to evaluation, even if it is simply questions designed to help the parties test the practicality or wisdom of their ideas. However, other mediators use a more explicitly evaluative approach in mediation. These mediators may propose their own solutions rather than having the parties generate all solutions. They may evaluate the parties' solutions in light of their expert prediction of how those outcomes compare to the results that might be achieved through judicial resolution. When mediators take this approach, attorneys must carefully consider the qualifications of the mediator to provide substantive expertise and the possibility of bias, as these concerns are significantly magnified in the presence of evaluative mediation.

In addition to these more traditional models of mediation, a variety of other less-traditional models may be appropriate for certain clients or problems. Some mediators with mental health expertise may offer therapeutic or "transformative" mediation, in which the goal of the mediation is to improve the re-

---

15. Model Standards of Practice for Family and Divorce Mediation, Appendix C.

16. Kansas Supreme Court Rules Relating to Mediation: Standards of Practice for Lawyer Mediators in Family Disputes (2008), *available at* http://www.kscourts.org/Rules/.

Standard IV(D) provides:

D. The mediator has a duty to ensure that the participants consider fully the best interests of the children, that they understand the consequences of any decision they reach concerning the children. The mediator also has a duty to assist parents to examine the separate and individual needs of their children and to consider those needs apart from their own desires for any particular parenting formula. If the mediator believes that any proposed agreement of the parents does not protect the best interests of the children, the mediator has a duty to inform them of this belief and its basis. The mediator shall terminate the mediation if the mediator believes the agreement of the parents does not protect the best interests of the children.

lationship skills of the parties, with a settlement of the dispute being an incidental outcome of that improvement. Other mediators may offer hybrids of arbitration and mediation, in which they will serve to recommend outcomes to the parties or the court if the parties are unable to come to agreement in the mediation process. Helping a client to choose the right mediator requires understanding how these models of mediation work and when one model might be preferable to another.

Having chosen a mediator, you must next prepare the client for mediation. Mediation requires that you allocate to the client a greater sharing of decision-making responsibility than is envisioned by the Model Rule 1.2 means/ends distinction. In some states, attorneys are not allowed to participate in mediation processes or discretion may be given to the mediator to exclude attorneys. Even when you will be present in the mediation, however, your responsibility is to empower the client to be able to participate effectively in the process.

One of the most difficult aspects of this preparation is helping the client to understand how different the language and demeanor of the attorney and client must be in this setting as compared to an adversarial setting. Clients must understand that respectful listening and collaborative problem solving are essential to this process, as opposed to adversarial posturing and partisan advocacy. You must not only explain your own attitudes and behaviors in mediation but must prepare the client to approach mediation in the same way.

A key to this preparation is helping your client to understand and prepare for dealing with conflicts. Conflict can be threatening: situations can be tense, outcomes are uncertain, and relationships fragile. But conflict can also be productive, when it provides a vehicle for addressing issues, releasing tension, stimulating creative problem solving, and ultimately strengthening relationships and improving outcomes.

You will need to help your client understand what he or she is fighting about and how he or she might approach that conflict. In terms of the subject matter of the conflict, Mediator Christopher W. Moore describes five different "spheres of conflict" that may characterize what people fight about: interest, structural, value, relationship and data conflicts.[17] Interest conflicts are caused by perceived or actual competitive interests. Those interests might be substantive, procedural or psychological interests. Being able to identify those interests and recognize when they are the cause of conflict can be a powerful problem solving tool. Structural conflicts are caused by destructive patterns of behavior or interaction, unequal power or resources, time constraints, or other en-

17. Christopher W. Moore, The Mediation Process 27 (2nd ed. 1986).

vironmental factors that interfere with cooperation. Addressing these structural conflicts is critical to insuring a fair mediation or negotiation process. Value conflicts are caused by belief systems and differing criteria for evaluating ideas or behavior. Realistic problem solving must take these intrinsic values into account. Relationship conflicts are caused by strong emotions (usually negative) or may be the result of poor communication skills. Family conflicts are nearly always going to involve some degree of relationship conflict. In many instances, relationship conflicts are most productively addressed in mediation, which can provide a structure for dealing constructively with emotions and improving communication. Finally, data conflicts are caused by missing, inaccurate or conflicting information, or differing interpretations or assessments of the data. Third party decision-makers can be especially helpful in breaking impasses over data conflicts.

Once you have helped your client identify the types of conflict involved in the dispute, you next need to think about how your client might address that conflict. Is your client likely to go into the mediation with a competitive mindset—determined to direct the process and determine the outcome? Would your client be more likely to cooperate and try to find ways to achieve win-win solutions as possible? How likely is your client to compromise and give up some points? Would your client do so simply to avoid having to deal with conflict? Does your client appear to have insight into the perspectives and attitudes of the other parties in the conflict? How is your client likely to express her emotions in the mediation? To prepare your client for mediation, you must not only understand your client's communication style and attitudes toward conflict, you must help your client understand how these aspects of their personality will impact the mediation.

An additional issue to consider in preparing the client for mediation is the protection of confidentiality. If statements made in mediation could later be used in court as evidence, this might create incentives for tactical abuse of the process. Thus, most states provide some form of protection for the confidentiality of mediation statements. [18] Like other communications privileges, these protections extend only to statements made in mediation and not to information otherwise discoverable or admissible. Discovery rules in most family courts ordinarily include standard, broad required disclosures from both sides and, given the breadth of issues in most family disputes, it is difficult to con-

18. Kelly Browe Olson, *Lessons Learned from a Child Protection Mediation Program: If at First You Succeed and then You Don't…*, 41 Fam. Ct. Rev. 480 (2003); Ellen E. Deason, *Secrecy and Transparency in Dispute Resolution: The Need for Trust as a Justification for Confidentiality in Mediation: A Cross-Disciplinary Approach*, 54 Kan. L. Rev. 1387 (2006).

ceive of information that would not be within the scope of discovery. However, the ability to misuse the mediation process as a tactical tool for adversarial discovery still exists for the parties, though much of this can be avoided with an experienced and well-trained mediator and a well-prepared client.

One of the most important roles for attorneys in representing clients in mediation is that of preparing and reviewing an agreement. If you do not participate in the mediation itself, you should caution your clients to refrain from signing any agreements until you have had an opportunity to review those agreements. Even if you are participating in the mediation, the final settlement agreement should be concluded after the mediation has closed, so that the parties can testify regarding the agreement, facilitating its acceptance by the court and later enforcement.

Many excellent resources exist to help you learn how to prepare your clients for mediation or collaborative negotiation processes; some of these are listed at the end of this chapter. Your jurisdiction likely has mediator training programs available as well. Even if you do not plan on becoming a mediator yourself, attending these programs can help you better represent your client in mediation as well as providing skills that are transferable to other dispute resolution processes.

Research Assignment

Family law mediation varies dramatically from state to state and even among different courts within a state. Locate the laws governing family law mediation in your local court. Is mediation mandatory in some cases? Are there exceptions for domestic violence? Are mediators subject to certification or licensure? Do they have standards of practice? What is the scope of confidentiality in mediation? You may find that the answers to these questions require research in state statutes, state or local court rules or individual court orders.

Portfolio Problem: Preparing the Client for Mediation

You represent Mother in an action to modify child custody. Mother and Father were married thirteen years ago and divorced eight years ago. They have a daughter, Diane, who is currently ten years old. Before their divorce they entered into a separation agreement which was later incorporated but not merged into their judgment of divorce. They agreed to joint legal custody of their daughter with primary physical custody to Mother, who lived in Chicago, and liberal visitation to Father, who resides in Michigan. Both Mother and Father have remarried and each has a child of their new marriage.

Nearly two years ago, Mother, who was a member of the Army National Guard, was deployed to the Middle East for what she was told would be a period of at least one year (it was closer to two years). When Father learned of this, he petitioned for custody of Diane. Mother had argued that her new husband should have physical custody of Diane during her absence. The court stayed the proceedings under the provisions of the Servicemembers Civil Relief Act, 50 U.S.C. §§501–596, which requires a court, upon application of a person in military service, to stay any proceeding in which the person is involved during the period of such duty, unless the person's ability to participate in the lawsuit is unaffected by his or her military service. However, the court issued a temporary order of custody placing Diane with her father. At the end of the school year, the child moved to Michigan to reside with her father, who lived with his new wife and their daughter. Recently, in contemplation of her return from active military duty, Mother engaged your services to petition the Family Court for reinstatement of the original custody arrangement. Father has petitioned to modify the temporary custody order to award primary physical custody to him, with substantial visitation to Mother.

The law in your state requires a petitioner seeking to modify an existing custody order to demonstrate that since the order was entered there has been a significant change in circumstances such that a change in the custody arrangement is in the child's best interests. Where a significant change in circumstances is established, the court uses a multi-factor balancing test to consider the child's best interests in establishing the custody arrangement. Factors include: maintaining stability for the child, the child's wishes, the home environment with each parent, each parent's past performance, relative fitness, ability to guide and provide for the child's overall well-being, and the willingness of each parent to foster a relationship with the other parent.

Mother and Father are both excellent parents. Both have demonstrated stable employment, adequate income, suitable homes, and an unwavering commitment to their child's well-being. The shared custody arrangement that Mother and Father followed before Mother's deployment worked well for everyone involved.

In his father's home, Diane resides full time with her stepmother and half sister. Diane has a good relationship with her stepmother and has developed a strong bond with her sister. She has also formed relationships with her stepmother's relatives in Michigan. Since Diane has been living with Father for the past 16 months, she has done well academically, has actively participated in organized sports, and has made friends with local children.

Mother legally separated from her second husband during her deployment and has moved. She shares custody of their son and has an amicable relationship with her husband, with whom Diane also has a good relationship. Diane's grandparents, with whom she is close, reside near Mother, as do other maternal relatives.

Mother recognizes that Father does a good job with Diane and wants him involved. She is quite willing to share legal custody, but would like to go back to the same physical custody arrangement they had before her deployment. She is frustrated that her service to her country should cost her custody of her child and bristles at her ex-husband's suggestion that she resign from the military. In fact, the balance between the couple's careers was at least part of the tension in their marriage. She is unsure whether she will be called for another oversees deployment soon. If she is called up, she could make her wishes known to remain in the states and ask for a deferment; however, she is concerned about the impact this would have on her career advancement. In fact, she has mentioned that she was considering volunteering for another overseas assignment in the near future, but she is waiting to see how this custody matter proceeds.

In your jurisdiction, mediation for a minimum of two hours is required in child custody disputes. Attorneys are not generally permitted to participate in these mediations. You have identified a mediator with whom both you and your client are comfortable. Now you must prepare your client for mediation. Prepare a checklist of issues you will want to cover with your client in preparing her for the mediation. You can find many generic checklists for preparing for mediation on the web that you may want to use as a starting point, but be sure that your checklist guides you through the steps you need to take in preparing **this** client.

B. Collaborative Law

Collaborative law practice represents the newest development in alternative dispute resolution in family law practice. Just as there are many approaches to the process called mediation, one can find an even greater variety of practice arrangements that are called "collaborative law." Attorneys may advertise and provide representation that they call "collaborative" or "cooperative," but that process may be based on strategic, positional bargaining or may envision litigation as one possible aspect of the representation.

For the purposes of this examination of the ethical issues in collaborative law process, collaborative law practice will be assumed to require two separate agreements: a limited scope representation agreement between each attorney and client and a separate agreement among both the attorneys and clients that commits all to engage in collaborative processes and requires both attorneys to withdraw should the collaborative process break down.

Little formal regulation of the ethical aspects of these agreements has emerged to this point. Three states have statutes expressly regulating collaborative law. California's statute merely defines the practice and notes that it is a permissible approach in family law cases. [19] North Carolina and Texas each have more detailed statutes, providing requirements for collaborative law agreements and rules governing confidentiality and evidentiary privileges for collaborative law processes. [20] The Texas statute also mandates a duty of candor in collaborative law processes.[21] More regulation is likely to emerge as the practice of collaborative law grows. The National Conference of Commissioner on Uniform State Laws is working on a Collaborative Law Act.[22]

1. Client Consent to Collaborative Lawyering[23]

One aspect of the collaborative law process is the initial agreement between each attorney and his or her client that the attorney will provide representation limited to collaborative negotiation and that the client consents to the attorney's withdrawal should that process break down. As discussed in Chapter Two, these limited scope representation agreements are ethically permissible subject to two qualifications: the attorney must communicate with the client suf-

19. Cal Fam. Code § 2013 (West 2007) permits (but provides no substantive regulation of) a "Collaborative law process" in specified family law matters. The statute defines collaborative law as a "process in which the parties and any professionals engaged by the parties to assist them agree in writing to use their best efforts and to make a good faith attempt to resolve disputes ... on an agreed basis without resorting to adversary judicial intervention." Likewise, the North Carolina statute identifies the four-way agreement and withdrawal provision as essential to the process. *See* N.C. Gen. Stat. § 50-72 (2006)("A collaborative law agreement must be in writing, signed by all the parties to the agreement and their attorneys, and must include provisions for the withdrawal of all attorneys involved in the collaborative law procedure if the collaborative law procedure does not result in settlement of the dispute.").

20. N.C. Gen. Stat. § 50-70 to 50-79 (2006); Tex. Fam. Code Ann. §§ 6.603 & 153.0072 (Vernon 2005).

21. Tex. Fam. Code Ann. § 6.603(c)(Vernon 2005)("A collaborative law agreement must include provisions for:

(1) full and candid exchange of information between the parties and their attorneys as necessary to make a proper evaluation of the case").

22. http://www.nccusl.org.

23. For a more extended version of this section, see Barbara Glesner Fines, *Ethical Issues in Collaborative Lawyering*, 21 J. Amer. Acad. Matrimonial Law. 141 (2008).

ficiently to allow the client to make an informed choice regarding collaborative divorce and the attorney must also exercise independent professional judgment regarding the advisability of this collaborative method.

Attorneys should take great care in counseling their clients regarding the collaborative law agreement. As a matter of prudence, the client's informed consent should be in writing, but attorneys must recognize that having a client sign a representation agreement is not proof that the client has given informed consent. Just as attorneys have an ethical obligation to counsel clients regarding other alternatives to litigation, so attorneys should fully explain the collaborative law process and the risks and benefits of that process compared to other options. Clients should understand that, not only does the process differ from litigation or mediation, but that the outcomes and goals of the representation may differ as well. It is especially important that the client understand the costs of obtaining new representation should the collaborative process fail. Clients should understand that collaborative agreements create pressure to settle, as well as opportunities to abuse the process by disqualifying both attorneys by refusing to settle.

In addition to the client's informed consent, the attorney's independent assessment of the appropriateness of this process for any given client is critical to the "reasonableness" of limiting the scope of representation to negotiated settlement only. Attorneys should not only help clients to determine whether collaborative practice is appropriate for their divorce, but should exercise their independent professional judgment in screening clients for collaborative practice. The risk of abuse of the process must be given careful and serious consideration. For example, just as there is an ongoing debate over the suitability of mediation in cases involving domestic violence, the imbalance of power, manipulation, and fear that are part of the domestic violence dynamic may make collaborative practice impossible.

Differential financial resources are also a consideration. Collaborative law, with its team of two attorneys and additional professionals as necessary to facilitate settlement, can require a significant investment. This investment is no more, perhaps, than litigation costs, but if the negotiation is unsuccessful, this investment is lost and the litigation costs remain. Where one party has limited resources, the opportunity for that client to be able to participate in a collaborative law practice may depend on modifying the rules. Thus, for example, if a client is represented by a legal aid attorney in the collaborative law process and the negotiations are unsuccessful, would the entire legal aid office then be disqualified from representing the client in litigation? This would mean the client would essentially be left without counsel entirely. Emerging regulation of collaborative law processes must address these circumstances of power imbalance and determine whether the process can be modified to address these concerns.

2. Required and Prohibited Withdrawal in Collaborative Law Agreements

A second lens through which to view these limited representation agreements is that of ethical withdrawal. Here again, there are a wide variety of models of collaborative law practice. While nearly all collaborative lawyers insist that the requirement that both attorneys withdraw if the process is unsuccessful, there is a group of attorneys who practice "cooperative" law in which they use the interest-based, cooperative methods of collaborative law but, failing to reach settlement, they then proceed to represent their clients in litigation.[24] For purposes of this analysis, the mandatory withdrawal will be treated as an essential aspect of collaborative law.

The attorney-client retention agreements provide a client's advance consent to the lawyer's withdrawal under certain conditions. These might include bad faith tactics by the client, withdrawal by the opposing attorney or client from the collaborative law process, or a breakdown in the negotiation process. Would an attorney's withdrawal be required in the absence of this agreement? State ethics rules governing withdrawal generally follow the pattern of Model Rule 1.16. Under that rule, withdrawal is only mandatory if the client fires the attorney, the attorney is violating the rules of professional conduct, or the attorney becomes unable to practice.[25]

Permissive withdrawal is permitted only under limited circumstances. One such circumstance is whenever there would be no materially adverse effect to the client. However, this basis for permissive withdrawal would not apply in a collaborative law agreement since withdrawal does work a significant detriment to the client—indeed, it is the very threat of this withdrawal that provides the "engine" that encourages continued negotiation. Other justifications

---

24. John Lande & Gregg Herman, *Fitting the Forum to the Family Fuss: Choosing Mediation, Collaborative Law, or Cooperative Law for Negotiating Divorce Cases*, 42 Fam. Ct. Rev. 280, 282 (2004).

25. Rule 1.16(a) provides: "Except as stated in paragraph (c), a lawyer shall not represent a client or, where representation has commenced, shall withdraw from the representation of a client if: (1) the representation will result in violation of the rules of professional conduct or other law; (2) the lawyer's physical or mental condition materially impairs the lawyer's ability to represent the client; or (3) the lawyer is discharged." Model Rules of Prof'l Conduct, R. 1.16(a)(2009).

for permissive withdrawal include circumstances in which a client insists on pursuing an objective that the lawyer considers repugnant or imprudent (here, the client insists on adversarial or uncooperative negotiation), or when the client fails to fulfill an obligation to the lawyer after being given reasonable warning (here the client fails to fulfill the obligation to engage in collaborative processes).[26] Under this analysis, the attorney's withdrawal upon the breakdown of the collaborative process would be permissible, especially given the client's advance agreement to that outcome. Of course, there is a difference between the attorney being permitted to withdraw by the rules and being required to withdraw because of the agreement with the client, but to the extent the client is always able to fire the attorney, it seems well within the client's authority to require an attorney to withdraw.

3. Conflicts of Interest and Four-way Agreements

While collaborative law could conceivably proceed with each client entering into a limited scope representation agreement and no express agreement across the table, the more common description of the collaborative law process provides that both attorneys and clients agree to a cooperative ethic and to withdrawal in the event of breakdown of the process. It is this aspect of the collaborative law process that has caused the most ethical concerns. In the Colorado ethics opinion finding collaborative law unethical, it was the four-way agreement with a mandatory withdrawal provision that the Colorado ethics opinion found to constitute a conflict of interest and an impermissible restraint on and attorney's independent professional judgment.[27]

The concern that four-way agreements violate conflicts rules rests in the notion that the attorney, by becoming contractually obligated to an opposing client and his or her attorney, has created a situation in which the attorney's representation may be materially limited by the lawyer's responsibilities to a third person. By disqualifying himself from adversarial representation, the collaborative attorney has, according to the Colorado ethics opinion, materially interfered with his "independent professional judgment in considering alternatives" or has "foreclose[d] courses of action that reasonably should be pursued on behalf of the client." The Colorado opinion found particularly troubling that the power to force a withdrawal lies in the hands of an opponent.

---

26. Model Rules of Prof'l Conduct, R. 1.16(b)(2009).

27. Colorado Ethics Op. 115: Ethical Considerations in the Collaborative and Cooperative Law Contexts (Feb. 24, 2007).

Disqualification from future litigation is not contingent upon any good faith erosion of the collaborative process. If the process does not result in an agreement between the parties, regardless of the good or bad faith participation of any party to the process, the four way agreement requires the collaborative Law practitioner to withdraw. The process is particularly susceptible to abuse in this respect.

In contrast to the Colorado opinion, the ABA's ethics opinion found no inherent conflict of interest in this four-way agreement because the clients involved had already agreed with their attorneys to the attorney's withdrawal.[28] Nonetheless, just as attorneys should carefully consider whether to counsel their clients to consent to a limited scope representation agreement, so too attorneys should carefully assess the reasonableness of counseling their clients to enter into a four-way agreement. Attorneys should consider whether the opposing attorney and client are able to enter into the collaborative law process fairly and with minimal risk of failure of the process. An attorney should ordinarily advise against entering into a collaborative process, if the attorney is aware that the bargaining across the table is likely to be colored by "puffery"[29] "strategic positioning" and other attitudes toward the process that, while permitted by the rules of professional conduct, are nonetheless destructive of the overall collaborative process. Likewise, where the power balance or emotional stability of the parties is such that a collaborative process is unlikely to be fair or stable, collaborative agreements would be unreasonable.

In the absence of more defined regulations of collaborative law practice, attorneys wishing to represent their clients in this process will need to be extremely diligent in their evaluation of their clients, the opposing attorneys and parties, and of their own skills and motivations in order to provide ethical representation. Attorneys must insure clear communication and carefully drafted agreements. Collaborative law practice presents an exciting variation on the growth of consensual, cooperative dispute resolution processes in the family law field. If attorneys participating in the process continue to maintain a careful scrutiny of their ethical obligations in the practice, the public will be well-served by having available this option.

---

28. ABA Comm. on Ethics and Prof'l Responsibility, Formal Op. 07447 (2007).

29. ABA Comm. on Ethics and Prof'l Responsibility, Formal Op. 06-439 (2006) ("the ethical principles governing lawyer truthfulness do not permit a distinction to be drawn between the caucused mediation context and other negotiation settings. The Model Rules do not require a higher standard of truthfulness in any particular negotiation contexts. Except for Rule 3.3, which is applicable only to statements before a "tribunal," the ethical prohibitions against lawyer misrepresentations apply equally in all environments.").

Questions For Discussion

1. In what kinds of cases or for what types of clients would collaborative law work best? In which cases would you find the process inadvisable?
2. A variety of organizations provide training and support for attorneys interested in the process, as well as public education regarding collaborative law. Some of these organizations also provide client referrals. Both attorneys and other professionals such as therapists or financial planners may belong to these organizations. What ethical issues are raised by an attorney's participation in these organizations? See Model Rules 5.4, 7.2

Reflective Journaling: Your Attitudes Toward Conflict

There is a subtle ethical concern in counseling clients regarding approaches to dispute resolution you should consider. It is not uncommon to hear attorneys describe their interest in collaborative law as having arisen because they were "burned out" or couldn't stand the adversarial process any longer.[30] In other words, some attorneys practice collaborative law for themselves as much as for their clients. While these attorneys may reject adversarial representation in family law litigation, they must nonetheless respect the value of these approaches for some clients. If attorneys practicing collaborative law allow their own personal distaste for litigation to cloud their judgment regarding the suitability of collaborative law for their clients, they may be "selling" a dispute resolution approach to their clients.[31] This would not result in a client's informed consent to a reasonable limitation on the scope of representation.

Just as it is important in preparing your client for mediation to understand his approach to conflict, so too you must understand your own preferences in considering how you will represent clients in any form of dispute resolution. Think about different situations in which you have had to deal with conflict—from friendly disagreements in low-stakes decisions to high-tension, high-stakes conflicts. How would you describe your approach to conflict? When is

---

30. *See* Christopher M. Fairman, *A Proposed Model Rule for Collaborative Law*, 21 Ohio St. J. on Disp. Resol. 73, 73 (2005); Stuart Webb, *Collaborative Law: An Alternative for Attorneys Suffering from "Family Law Burnout,"* Matrim. Strategist 7 (July 2000).

31. One commentator has suggested that "The danger is that a lawyer committed to the collaborative law process may lack the capacity, even unconsciously, to provide a client with a fair representation of the risks and benefits of utilizing such a process." *See* Larry Spain, *Collaborative Law: A Critical Reflection on Whether a Collaborative Orientation Can Be Ethically Incorporated into the Practice of Law*, 56 Baylor L. Rev. 141, 161 (2004).

your approach effective? When do you think it is less effective? How else might you approach conflict to improve your ability to resolve conflict?

In addition to reflecting on past experience, there are several tools you might consider to help you become more aware of your responses to conflict. One tool is a conflict style inventory. Thomas Kilmann Conflict Mode Instrument (http://www.kilmann.com/conflict.html); Kraybill Conflict Style Inventory (http://www.riverhouseepress.com/Conflict_Style_Inventory.htm).

Using the Myers-Briggs Type Indicator and its four personality preferences (extraverted-introverted, sensing-intuitive, thinking-feeling, and judging-perceiving) may also provide insight for your reflection. Don Peters, *Forever Jung: Psychological Type Theory, The Myers-Briggs Type Indicator and Learning Negotiation*, 42 Drake L. Rev. 1 (1993). Professor Len Riskin has suggested that mindfulness meditation may be an effective method of developing insights into your own responses to conflict. Leonard L. Riskin, *The Contemplative Lawyer: On the Potential Contributions of Mindfulness Meditation to Law Students, Lawyers and Their Clients*, 7 Harv. Negot. L. Rev. 1 (2002).

Write a short reflection on your approach to conflict and your role as an attorney in resolving family disputes.

To Learn More

In addition to the articles and web resources cited in this chapter, the following books are helpful to achieving the competence necessary to represent families in alternative dispute resolution processes:

Roger Fisher, William Ury and Bruce Patton, Getting to Yes (2d ed. 1991).

> The classic text on negotiation. This is essential reading for understanding the basics of dispute resolution that ground not only principled negotiation, but mediation and collaborative law processes. The book is concise and straightforward. The authors have produced many fine books since then that you may want to explore (for example, Fisher, Beyond Reason: Using Emotions as You Negotiate; Ury, Getting Past No or Stone, Patton, Heen & Fisher, Difficult Conversations: How to Discuss what Matters Most). None of these books are directly addressing family disputes, but all are helpful to understanding the basic principles behind principled negotiations.

Harold I. Abramson, Mediation Representation: Advocating in a Problem Solving Process (NITA 2004).

Designed for attorneys representing clients in mediation, rather than a guide for the mediators themselves, this text emphasizes a creative problem solving approach to mediation. The text explores the attorney's key roles in mediation: advising your clients about the mediation option, negotiating an agreement to mediate with other attorneys, preparing cases and clients for the mediation session, and appearing in the pre-mediation conferences, mediation sessions, and post-sessions. The text has checklists, sample forms, and other helpful guides.

Jay Folberg, Ann L. Milne and Peter Salem, Divorce and Family Mediation: Models, Techniques, and Applications (2004).

A comprehensive text focusing on family and divorce mediation. The editors have gathered articles from authors from broad range of disciplines. The text examines the facilitative, transformative, therapeutic and hybrid models of mediation of family disputes. Several chapters address strategies for addressing common issues in mediation, and the unique concerns of children and domestic violence. While addressed primarily to mediators from a range of disciplines, the text will provide attorneys with a sophisticated understanding of approaches to mediation in family disputes that will guide their representation of clients.

Kelly Browe Olson and Nancy Ver Steegh, eds., Innovations in Family Law Practice (2008)

Chapters on collaborative law practice, cooperative negotiation agreements, and unbundling. The authors survey these new developments in family law representation. Appendices provide samples forms and checklists to guide the practitioner.

Appendix A

American Academy of Matrimonial Lawyers Bounds of Advocacy

Goals for Family Lawyers*

Preface

The idea for the Bounds of Advocacy was conceived in November 1987 by James T. Friedman of Chicago, Illinois, then President of the American Academy of Matrimonial Lawyers. The original Bounds of Advocacy was then drafted, discussed, debated and approved during the terms of former Presidents Friedman, Leonard L. Loeb of Wisconsin, Donn C. Fullenweider of Texas and Sanford S. Dranoff of New York.

After ten years, new ethical issues have arisen. With the idea of addressing new concerns and updating the original report, Presidents George S. Stern of Georgia and Miriam E. Mason of Florida jointly appointed our Committee. The Committee wishes to thank all of these presidents for their encouragement and support during the lengthy process of developing the Original Bounds of Advocacy and in producing this revision.

The majority of the Committee that drafted these revisions consists of the same Fellows who wrote the original version, with the continued assistance of the same Reporter. This revision is offered to ensure that the aspirational goals of the AAML continue to respond to changes in society and the various court systems and approaches to family law matters.

Had any of us not served on this committee, this work would be different. Special praise is due Steve Sessums, our chair. Steve's dedication to the project never flagged. His uncanny ability to help our disparate group find consensus continues to amaze. A special acknowledgement is due Rob Aronson, our representative from academia. Rob contributed the knowledge of an ethics expert and the perspective of someone who has not practiced divorce law. He admirably performed the daunting task of finding logic in, and adding structure to, our often random ideas.

The committee thanks the Academy for giving us another opportunity to ponder and discuss problems important to our clients and us. This project was challenging, enlightening, and, at times, humbling. This publication, we hope, will serve to advance the debate about what we, as family lawyers, do.

November, 2000

Stephen Sessums, Chair, Tampa, Florida
Gaetano Ferro, New Canaan, Connecticut
Joan Kessler, Milwaukee, Wisconsin
Diana Richmond, San Francisco, California
Barbara Salomon, Denver, Colorado
Gary Silverman, Reno, Nevada
David Walther, Santa Fe, New Mexico
Errol Zavett, Chicago, IllinoisREPORTER: Robert Aronson, Seattle, Washington

Preliminary Statement

The primary purpose of the Bounds of Advocacy: Goals for Family Lawyers is to guide matrimonial lawyers confronting moral and ethical problems. Existing codes often do not provide adequate guidance to the matrimonial lawyer. The ABA's Model Rules of Professional Conduct ("RPC") are addressed to all lawyers, regardless of the nature of their practices. This generally means that, with rare exceptions, issues relevant only to a specific area of practice cannot be dealt with in detail or cannot be addressed at all. Many Fellows of the American Academy of Matrimonial Lawyers have encountered instances where the RPC provided insufficient, or even undesirable, guidance. Most attorneys—and presumably all Academy Fellows—are able to distinguish "black" (unethical or illegal conduct) from "white" (ethical and proper practice). These Goals are therefore directed primarily to the "gray" zone where even experienced, knowledgeable matrimonial lawyers might have concerns, and constitute an effort to provide clear, specific guidelines in areas most important to matrimonial lawyers.

Conduct permitted by the RPC cannot form the basis for state bar or court discipline. Hence, the Goals here established for matrimonial lawyers use the terms "should" and "should not," rather than "must," "shall," "must not" and "shall not." Because the Bounds of Advocacy aspires to a level of practice above the minimum established in the RPC, it is inappropriate to use the Goals to define the level of conduct required of lawyers for purposes of malpractice liability or state bar discipline.

Some Goals elaborate upon RPC rules or relate those Rules to issues confronting matrimonial lawyers. Each Goal is followed by a Comment. The Comments are intended to explain, provide examples of conduct addressed and, in some instances, suggest limitations of the application of the Goal.

Few human problems are as emotional, complicated or seem so important as those problems people bring to matrimonial lawyers. The break-up of a marriage will be felt not only by the couple but also by other family members and often by friends and others with personal or business relationships with the parties. The problems and expense of the divorce system can be daunting.[1]

Family law disputes occur in a volatile and emotional atmosphere. It is difficult for matrimonial lawyers to represent the interests of their clients without addressing the interests of other family members. Unlike most other concluded disputes in which the parties may harbor substantial animosity without practical effect, the parties in matrimonial disputes may interact for years to come. In addition, many matrimonial lawyers believe themselves obligated to consider the best interests of children, regardless of which family member they represent. A 1988 survey of Academy Fellows indicated that the harm done to children in an acrimonious family dispute was seen as the most significant problem for which there is insufficient guidance in existing ethical codes.

The matrimonial lawyer serves many functions. Often the appropriate role is to be a skilled litigator, the person who can help clients achieve their goals in court or in arbitration. The lawyer has always had additional roles as well. The matrimonial lawyer's job includes discussing with the client the available

1. Concern for the problems and expense of the divorce system has caused an increasing number of parties to attempt to navigate the process without the assistance of a lawyer. *See* Bruce D. Sales et al., *Self-Representation in Divorce Cases,* 1993 ABA Standing Comm. on Delivery of Legal. Serv. 34 (study of Maricopa County (Phoenix) Arizona found in 1990 that no lawyer was involved in 52% of divorce cases, and at least one party represented herself or himself in about 90% of divorce cases). The study followed a similar study of Maricopa County divorces that found pro se representation in the period 1980–85 rose from 24% to 47%. Stephen R. Cox & Mark Dwyer, *A Report on Self-Help Law: Its Many Perspectives,* 1987 ABA Special Comm. On Delivery of Leg. Serv. 34. See also Robert B. Yegge, *Divorce Litigants Without Lawyers,* 28 Fam. L.Q. 407 (1994); *Responding to the Needs of the Self- Represented Divorce Litigant,* 1994 ABA Standing Comm. on the Delivery of Legal Serv. 5.

personal and financial choices that must be made. Many lawyers now serve as mediators or represent clients in mediation. Others represent clients in arbitration, or serve as neutral arbitrators.

Litigation demands some of the lawyer's very highest skills, those traditionally associated with effective courtroom advocacy. These Bounds of Advocacy reflect the availability of additional ways to resolve disputes. When litigation is employed, the matrimonial lawyer should conduct it constructively because the parties to a matrimonial case will often find it necessary to interact with each other for years after they leave the courtroom. Advocacy skills may also be used to the client's advantage in arbitration or mediation. An effective advocate's stock in trade is the power to persuade.

The traditional view of the matrimonial lawyer (a view still held by many practitioners) is of the "zealous advocate" whose only job is to win.2 However, the emphasis on zealous representation of individual clients in criminal and some civil cases is not always appropriate in family law matters. Public opinion (both within and outside the AAML) has increasingly supported other models of lawyering and goals of conflict resolution in appropriate cases. A counseling, problem-solving approach for people in need of help in resolving difficult issues and conflicts within the family is one model; this is sometimes referred to as "constructive advocacy." Mediation and arbitration offer alternative models. Mediation is a method of resolving disputes in which a trusted neutral attempts to facilitate a compromise between the parties. Arbitration involves the hiring of a respected neutral to hear both sides, then make a decision that will resolve the controversy.

Matrimonial lawyers should recognize the effect that their words and actions have on their client's attitudes about the justice system, not just on the "legal outcome" of their cases. As a counselor, a problem-solving lawyer encourages problem solving in the client. Effective advocacy for a client means considering with the client what is in the client's best interests and determining the most effective means to achieve that result. The client's best interests include the well being of children, family peace, and economic stability. Clients look to attorneys' words and deeds for how they should behave while involved with the legal system. Even when involved in a highly contested matter, divorce attorneys should strive to promote civility and good behavior by the client towards the parties, the lawyers and the court.

In recent years, an increasing number of individual lawyers and associations have observed a widening gap between the minimum level of ethical conduct mandated by the RPC and the much greater level of professionalism to which all attorneys should aspire. Some attorneys have ignored the caveat that the Rules do not "exhaust the moral and ethical considerations" that characterize the practice of law at the highest level.[2] Local and state bar associations, along with a number of state and federal courts, have adopted codes of professionalism attempting to raise the level of practice above the ethical minimum necessary to avoid discipline.

These Bounds reaffirm the attorney's obligation to competently represent individual clients. These Bounds also promote a problem-solving approach that considers the client's children and family as well. In addition, they encourage efforts to reduce the cost, delay and emotional trauma and urge interaction between parties and attorneys on a more reasoned, cooperative level.

In drafting these Bounds of Advocacy, the Committee observed a number of conventions:

1. Whenever the Goals or comments refer to "an attorney," "lawyer" or "matrimonial lawyer," the reference is to an attorney practicing family law, exclusively or in an individual case. This area of practice is described in many ways, including "divorce," "domestic relations" and "family law." In the absence of a universally accepted designation, the choice was the term used by the AAML—"matrimonial law."

2. The conduct of attorneys, in general, is covered in the RPC or CPR. Therefore, an effort was made to avoid repetition of rules and principles already addressed in the CPR and RPC. For example, the basic conflicts of interest requirements are addressed in the CPR and RPC. These Bounds address only those conflicts where additional guidance was deemed desirable, or where the RPC and CPR do not adequately address the unique requirements of family law practice. For that reason these Bounds do not address the matrimonial lawyer's obligation of honesty and candor in dealing with the Court since that obligation is adequately covered by other bodies of law.

3. Citation to legal authority has been kept to a minimum. However, to indicate the basis and provide some support for the Goals and Comments, some footnotes have been added to this version of the Bounds of Advocacy. Where it is appropriate to cite an official code, references are to the ABA Model Rules of Professional Conduct. It is recognized that some jurisdictions retained the Code of Professional Responsibility and others significantly amended the ABA Model RPC. Other states retained the CPR format with amendments to comport with the substance of the RPC. And the ABA may soon adopt amendments to the Model RPC. In all situations, attorneys should consult the applicable code in their jurisdictions, along with relevant statutory and case law.

---

2. American Bar Association, Model Rules of Professional Conduct, (Hereafter "RPC"), Scope section.

(4) The fact that some clients, lawyers and judges are women and some are men is reflected in these Bounds. References to gender have been eliminated where possible. In those instances where elimination of gender-specific pronouns would be unduly awkward, sometimes the masculine and sometimes the feminine is used.

Attorney as Counselor and Advocate

A person comes to a matrimonial lawyer with human problems that have legal aspects. Problems arising from the breakup of a family are particularly emotional and affect the family. The matrimonial lawyer's role spans a spectrum of services, from counseling to litigation. Choices include mediation, arbitration and other problem-solving methods. The matrimonial lawyer's approach to resolving problems is crucial to the future health of the family. The matrimonial lawyer has a critical, demanding counseling role in addressing these problems. Just as a physician diagnoses the causes of the patient's pain and counsels the patient about a variety of treatments before undertaking surgery, the matrimonial lawyer serves an analogous role.

These AAML Bounds of Advocacy reflect a shift toward the role of constructive advocacy, a counseling, problem-solving approach for a family member in need of assistance in resolving difficult issues and conflicts within the family.

1. Competence and Advice

1.1 An attorney is responsible for the competent handling of all aspects of a representation, no matter how complex.

Comment

Matrimonial matters almost always involve issues beyond questions of divorce, custody and support, such as property, tax, corporations, trusts and estates, bankruptcy, and pensions. All matrimonial lawyers should possess enough knowledge to recognize the existence of potential issues in the myriad legal areas relevant to the representation.[3] That knowledge is not limited to

---

3. *See, e.g.*, Martin v. Northwest Washington Legal Services, 43 Wn.App. 405, 717 P.2d 779 (1986) (Lawyer and firm found to be negligent, giving rise to viable malpractice claim, in failing to inquire about, discuss, or seek division of client's husband's military pension; expert testimony and affidavits established the duty of a reasonably competent attorney to make such an inquiry into division of military pension in a dissolution case where the attorney was on notice that one of the parties was a member of the Armed Services).

legal information. For example, custody and visitation cases require knowledge of child development and, at times, understanding of mental and emotional disorders.

An attorney may properly undertake a matter for which he lacks the necessary experience or expertise if "in good faith he expects to become qualified through study and investigation, as long as such preparation would not result in unreasonable delay or expense to his client."[4] Proper handling might include engaging (with the client's consent) persons knowledgeable in other fields to assist in gathering the knowledge and information necessary to represent the client effectively.[5] An attorney who cannot obtain competence through reasonable study and preparation should seek to withdraw or, with the client's consent, associate with or recommend a more expert lawyer.[6]

1.2 An attorney should advise the client of the emotional and economic impact of divorce and explore the feasibility of reconciliation.

Comment

The divorce process can exact a heavy economic and emotional toll. The decision to divorce should never be made casually. An attorney should discuss reconciliation and whether the client has considered marriage counseling or therapy. If the client exhibits uncertainty or ambivalence, the lawyer should assist in obtaining help.

A lawyer's role in family matters is to act as a counselor and advisor as well as an advocate. The RPC specifically permit the lawyer to address moral, economic, social and political factors, which may be relevant to the client's situation.[7] "Where consultation with a professional in another field is itself something a competent lawyer would recommend, the lawyer should make such a recommendation."[8] Although few attorneys are qualified to do psychological counseling, a discussion of the emotional and monetary repercussions of divorce is appropriate.

---

4. RPC 1.1

5. *See, e.g., In re* Yetman, 552 A.2d 121 (N.J. 1989) (failure of lawyer who had no experience in estate matters to refer complex matter to another lawyer violated the lawyer's duty of competence; once it became clear that a case the attorney originally thought was simple became more complicated, case should have been turned over to new counsel).

6. *See* **Goals 2.4 and 4.6** as to the issue of the client's refusal to give consent or inability to pay for costs. Nothing in this Comment should be construed to require the attorney to advance costs.

7. RPC 2.1.

8. ABA Comment, RPC 2.1.

If the client wishes to reconcile, the matrimonial lawyer should attempt to mitigate litigation-related activities that might prejudice the effectiveness of counseling and marital harmony. It is important, however, for the attorney to be mindful that a "breathing spell" afforded by counseling could harm the client's interests. The other spouse may take advantage of the delay for financial or other advantage. The lawyer should warn the client of these risks and recommend precautions to protect the client in the interim.

1.3 An attorney should refuse to assist in vindictive conduct and should strive to lower the emotional level of a family dispute by treating all other participants with respect.

Comment

Some clients expect and want the matrimonial lawyer to reflect the highly emotional, vengeful personal relationship between spouses. The attorney should counsel the client that discourteous and retaliatory conduct is inappropriate and counterproductive, that measures of respect are consistent with competent and ethical representation of the client, and that it is unprofessional for the attorney to act otherwise.

Although the client has the right to determine the "objectives of representation," after consulting with the client the attorney may limit the objectives and the means by which the objectives are to be pursued.[9] The matrimonial lawyer should make every effort to lower the emotional level of the interaction among parties and counsel. Some dissension and bad feelings can be avoided by a frank discussion with the client at the outset of how the attorney handles cases, including what the attorney will and will not do regarding vindictive conduct or actions likely to adversely affect the children's interests. If the client is unwilling to accept the attorney's limitations on objectives or means, the attorney should decline the representation.

---

9. RPC 1.2. *See also* ABA Comment to Rule 1.2: "[A] lawyer is not required to pursue objectives or employ means simply because a client may wish that the lawyer do so.... The terms upon which representation is undertaken may exclude specific objectives or means. Such limitations may exclude objectives or means that the lawyer regards as repugnant or imprudent."

1.4 *An attorney should be knowledgeable about different ways to resolve marital disputes, including negotiation, mediation, arbitration and litigation.*

ADR

Comment

Many clients favor a problem-solving model over litigation. It is essential that matrimonial lawyers have sufficient knowledge about alternative dispute resolution to understand the advantages and disadvantages for a particular client and to counsel the client appropriately concerning the particular dispute resolution mechanism selected.[10] For example, an attorney who represents a client in mediation should understand the differences between the traditional litigation role and the role of the consulting attorney in mediation.

Effective litigation skills are essential to the problem solving process, regardless of whether a particular dispute is finally resolved through litigation, mediation or arbitration.

1.5 *An attorney should attempt to resolve matrimonial disputes by agreement and should consider alternative means of achieving resolution.*

Comment

The litigation process is expensive and emotionally draining. Settlement may not be appropriate or workable in some cases due to the nature of the dispute or the animosity of the parties. Litigation is the best course in those cases.

In matrimonial matters, a cooperative resolution of disputes is highly desirable. Matrimonial law is not a matter of winning or losing. At its best, matrimonial law should result in disputes being resolved fairly for all parties, including children. Major tasks of the matrimonial lawyer include helping the client develop realistic objectives and attempting to attain them with the least injury to the family. The vast majority of cases should be resolved by lawyers negotiating settlements on behalf of their clients.

---

10. *See* ABA Comment to RPC 2.1: "Matters that go beyond strictly legal questions may also be in the domain of another profession. Family matters can involve problems within the professional competence of psychiatry, clinical psychology or social work; ... Where consultation with a professional in another field is something a competent lawyer would recommend, the lawyer should make such a recommendation." For example, it may be appropriate for a professional with counseling training to deal with custody or visitation issues, whereas a financial expert might be needed to deal with division of property questions.

Parties are more likely to abide by their own promises than by an outcome imposed on them by a court.[11] When resolution requires complex trade-offs, the parties may be better able than the court to forge a resolution that addresses their individual values and needs. An agreement that meets the reasonable objectives of the parties maximizes their autonomy and their own priorities. A court-imposed resolution may, instead, maximize legal principles that may seem arbitrary or unfair within the context of the parties' family. An agreement may establish a positive tone for continuing post-divorce family relations by avoiding the animosity and pain of court battles.[12] It may also be less costly financially than a litigated outcome. Parents who litigate their custody disputes are much more likely to believe that the process had a detrimental effect on relations with the divorcing spouse than parents whose custody or support disputes are settled.[13] These issues should be discussed with the client.

---

11. *See* Jessica Pearson & Nancy Thoennes, The Benefits Outweigh the Costs in Divorce Mediation: Readings, at p.94 (ABA 1985) ("[S]uccessful mediation clients are less likely to report problems with their court orders and more likely to report that their spouses are in total compliance"). See also Daniel J. Guffman, *For Better or Worse, Till ADR Do Us Part: Using Antenuptial Agreements to Compel Alternatives to Traditional Adversarial Litigation*, 12 Ohio St. J. on Disp. Resol. 175 (1996).

12. There is substantial evidence of the destructive effect of divorce conflict on the children. *See, e.g.*, Paul Amato, *Life-span Adjustment of Children to Their Parents' Divorce*, in 4 The Future of Children: Children and Divorce (David & Lucille Packard Found. 1994); Johnston, J.R. Kine & J.M. Tschann, *Ongoing Postdivorce Conflict: Effects on Children of Joint Custody and Frequent Access*, 59 Amer. J. of Orthopsych. 576–592 (1989); L.A. Kurdek & B.Berg, *Correlates of Children's Adjustment to Their Parents' Divorces*, in Children and Divorce (Kurdek ed. 1983); R. Emery, *Interparental Conflict and the Children of Discord and Divorce*, 92 Psych. Bull. 310–330 (1982). In addition, divorce litigation has an adverse effect on the parental relationship. See J. Kelly & M.A. Duryee, *Women's and Men's Views of Mediation in Voluntary and Mandatory Settings*, 30 Fam. and Conciliation Ct. Rev. 43–49 (1992); J.B. Kelly, L. Gigy & S. Hausman, *Mediated and Adversarial Divorce: Initial Findings From a Longitudinal Study*, in Folberg & A. Milne (eds.), Divorce Mediation: Theory and Practice (N.Y. 1988).

13. *See* Stephen C. Bowman, *Idaho's Decision on Divorce Mediation*, 26 Idaho L. Rev. 547, 549–550 (1989/1990): "Compliance with child support orders has been shown to be fifty percent higher when achieved through voluntary agreement rather than when court-ordered." (Citing William A. Waddell, *Improving Child Support Payments*, 8 Mediation Quarterly 57, 63 (Sept. 1985)). *See also* Howard Irving & Michael Benjamin, Family Mediation: Contemporary Issues (Sage Publ. 1995) ("Common sense suggest that such satisfaction (with mediation processes) should be related to greater compliance with the terms of the agreement, as it was in a number of studies (Bahr, 1981; Emery & Wyer, 1987); Irving & Benjamin, 1992; Johnson et al., 1985; Person & Thoennes, 1985; Waldron et al. 1984)").

A settlement may be achieved by negotiation between the lawyers (either with or without the parties being present), by mediation, or by the parties themselves with advice and information from their lawyers. The matrimonial lawyer's task includes informing the client about the availability and nature of mediation or other alternatives to traditional negotiation or litigation.

2. Communication and Decision Making Responsibility

In no area of law is the relationship of trust between attorney and client more important than in matrimonial law. Clients come to matrimonial lawyers when there is a significant problem in the family relationship. Emotions often render rational decision-making difficult. Clients seek the advice and judgment of their matrimonial attorneys, even about non-legal matters. Therefore, issues of communication and decision-making in the attorney-client relationship arise frequently.

2.1 An attorney should accord clients respect.

Comment

One predicate to a successful attorney-client relationship is the attorney's treating the client with respect. This attitude should also be conveyed to the attorney's staff.

Courts sometimes seek meetings in chambers with counsel in the absence of the parties. If the proposed chambers conference relates to the substantive settlement of issues in the case, counsel should ask if the client may participate in the conference, but if the local rule, practice, custom or habit is to have such conferences without the client present, counsel may participate in such a conference and advocate the client's interests.

2.2 An attorney should provide sufficient information to permit the client to make informed decisions.

Comment

The client should have sufficient information to participate intelligently in deciding the objectives of the representation and the means by which they are to be pursued, to the extent the client is willing and able to do so. Clients vary in their ability and willingness to participate in decision-making. Regardless of the extent of participation, they are entitled to be fully informed. Failure of the attorney to provide complete information may result in criticism, disciplinary action, or a lawsuit.[14] Although relevant information should be conveyed promptly, in rare instances, "a lawyer may be justified in delaying transmission of information when the client would be likely to react imprudently to an immediate communication."[15]

A difficult question is whether the matrimonial lawyer should provide, either voluntarily or upon request, a negative opinion of opposing counsel, the judge, or the law. For example, should the client be told that a case is assigned to a judge who has demonstrated prejudice against men or women or who has difficulty with complex tax or financial issues, or that the other lawyer seems incapable of settlement and invariably ends up in difficult trials? Although lawyers must use their best judgment in individual cases, some general guidelines are: (1) do not lie or in any way tell the client less than the whole truth; (2) answer specific questions ("If we go to court, how is the judge likely to rule?" or "What are the risks?") as diplomatically but as completely as possible; (3) do not criticize the court, opposing counsel, or the system unless necessary for the client to make informed decisions or to understand delays or the necessity of responding to conduct of the court or opposing counsel. Unnecessary criticism of the court, the legal system or opposing counsel undermines the effectiveness and enforceability of judgments and harms the reputation of all lawyers and judges.

Lawyers who are unwilling to give a client bad news or a realistic assessment of the case may create other problems. It is important to maintain a proper balance between accurately advising the client and avoiding unnecessary criticism of other participants in the process.

2.3 An attorney should keep the client informed of developments in the representation and promptly respond to communications from the client.

Comment

The duty of keeping the client reasonably informed and promptly complying with reasonable requests for information[16] includes the attorney or a staff member promptly responding to telephone calls, normally by the end of the next business day. The attorney should routinely: send the client a copy of all pleadings and correspondence, except in unusual circumstances; provide no-

---

14. *See, e.g.*, Matter of Knobel, 699 N.E.2d 1142, 1145 (Ind. 1998) ("By failing to explain the status of his clients' representations to them so that they could make informed decisions, the respondent violated [Ind.] Prof.Cond.R. 1.4(b)").

15. ABA Comment, RPC 1.4.

16. RPC 1.4(a).

tice before incurring any major costs; provide notice of any calendar changes, scheduled court appearances, and discovery proceedings; communicate all settlement offers, no matter how trivial or facetious; advise of major changes in the law affecting the proceedings; and provide reports of major changes in case strategy.

Frequent communication with the client on important matters (1) empowers the client, (2) satisfies the client's need for information about the progress of the case, (3) helps build a positive attorney-client relationship, and (4) helps the client understand the amount and nature of the work the attorney is performing, thereby reducing concern that nothing is happening and that the attorney's fees are not being earned.[17] While the attorney should understand that a pending divorce is usually the most important matter in the life of the client, the client should understand that a successful lawyer has many clients, all of whom believe their case to be the most important.

2.4 An attorney should share decision-making responsibility with the client, but should not abdicate responsibility for the propriety of the objectives sought or the means employed to achieve those objectives.

Comment

The conduct and resolution of a divorce case may require making many decisions, from the most mundane (which word to use in a letter) to the most significant (whether to litigate or accept a proposed settlement). During the course of the representation, decision-making authority may reside with the client, the attorney, or both.

It is appropriate as part of the lawyer's counseling function to assist the client in reframing the client's objectives when to do so would be in the client's best interests. A lawyer may counsel a client not only as to the law, but also as to "other considerations such as moral, economic, social and political factors that may be relevant to the client's situation."[18]

---

17. *See, e.g.*, Matter of Knobel, 699 N.E.2d 1142, 1145 (Ind. 1998) ("We find that the respondent violated Ind. Professional Conduct Rule 1.4(a) by failing to keep his clients informed about the status of their [marital] actions and by failing to respond to their requests for information").

18. RPC 2.1. *See* In re Marriage of Bonds, 71 Cal.App.4th 290, 83 Cal.Rptr.2d 783, 810 (1999) (stressing the importance of independent consultation and advice regarding prenuptial agreement because "the heightened emotions and optimism which often precede marriage may hinder people from considering what may be in their long-term best interests. After all, marriage itself has been referred to as the 'triumph of hope over experience'."), *re-*

Thus, although the lawyer is entitled to make "decisions not affecting the merits of the cause or substantially prejudicing the rights of a client,"[19] the attorney and client should jointly make significant choices, such as whether to file a costly motion of uncertain success, or whether to retain certain experts. Even when the client has ultimate decision-making authority, the attorney should provide counsel and advice.

The attorney must abide by the client's decisions as to the objectives of the representation, subject to the rules of ethics or other law.[20] Further, the lawyer should consult with the client as to the means by which those objectives are to be pursued. "In questions of means, the lawyer should assume responsibility for technical and legal tactical issues" (e.g., choosing forum, type of pleadings, or judicial remedy), "but should defer to the client regarding expenses to be incurred and concern for third persons who might be adversely affected."[21]

Examples:

1. The client insists that the real problem in the marriage was his mother-in-law and asks the matrimonial lawyer to bring that to the court's attention during the trial. The lawyer knows that the facts, which seem so important to the client, are irrelevant under the rules of the forum and counter-productive at trial. The lawyer must rely on her judgment and explain to the client why this is not an appropriate, let alone persuasive, argument. The risk is that the client, unhappy with the ultimate result, may claim that if the lawyer used the argument the client wished, the case would have been won. That is a risk inherent in the practice of law.
2. In a jurisdiction where the wife has a claim for maintenance which the lawyer believes will succeed, the husband offers to pay a larger share of the assets if the wife will waive the right to maintenance, which, under local law, will terminate at the death of either party or at the wife's remarriage. If the client stays unmarried, she will benefit far more from maintenance than the additional assets. Which should she accept? The matrimonial lawyer's role is to educate the client and allow her to make the choice.
3. The guilt-ridden husband offers the wife virtually all of the assets and a support order that will leave him all but penniless. The wife tells her attorney to draft the appropriate documents to finalize his offer. The wife's attorney should

---

view granted and opinion superseded by 981 P.2d 40, 87 Cal.Rptr.2d 410 (1999); In re Foran, 67 Wash.App.2d 242, 834 P.2d 1081 (1992) ("A client is not well served by an unenforceable contract. Marital tranquility is not achieved by a contract which is economically unfair or achieved by unfair means").

19. CPR, EC 7-7.

20. RPC 1.2(a).

21. ABA Comment, RPC 1.2.

fully inform her of the risks of such a one-sided settlement (continual post-judgment litigation, practical unenforceability). If the client insists on a settlement posture that the attorney believes blatantly unrealistic, she should put her advice in writing and may, if she chooses, then carry out the client's instructions. The lawyer representing the husband should try to persuade his client to offer less. If the husband insists, the lawyer should consider: (1) putting in writing all of the reasons why the husband's offer is very detrimental to him and that the attorney strongly advises against it; (2) advising that the client obtain the advice of another lawyer, a counselor, or a responsible friend or family member; and (3) withdrawing.

2.5 *When the client's decision-making ability appears to be impaired, the attorney should try to protect the client from the harmful effects of the impairment.*

Comment

The economic and emotional turmoil caused by marital disputes often affects a client's ability to make rational decisions in his own best interest. The lawyer who reasonably believes the client to be incompetent should seek appointment of a guardian.[22] A client who is not incompetent, but whose ability to make reasonable decisions is impaired, creates difficult problems for the lawyer.

A client may be impaired although not incompetent as a result of substance abuse or another physical or psychological condition. A lawyer with reasonable cause to believe that the client's impairment will interfere with the representation should send the client for evaluation to determine whether the client is legally competent. The attorney may withdraw from the representation of a client who will not undergo the evaluation.

The lawyer is not compelled to follow irrational or potentially harmful directives of a client, particularly one who is distraught or impaired, even if the client is legally competent. The lawyer should oppose any client's illegal or improper decision ("I don't care what the court says, I won't pay her a cent").

22. *See* RPC 1.14 and ABA Comment. Under RPC 1.14(b), "[a] lawyer may seek the appointment of a guardian or take other protective action with respect to a client only when the lawyer reasonably believes that the client cannot adequately act in the client's own interest." *But cf.* RPC 1.14(a) providing that the lawyer "shall, as far as reasonably possible, maintain a normal client-lawyer relationship with the client." *See also* ABA Comment to RPC 1.14: "In many circumstances, however, appointment of a legal representative may be expensive or traumatic for the client." And, the matrimonial lawyer must always be certain that the client's best interests, rather than the lawyer's personal moral or religious views, motivate the lawyer's conduct.

The attorney should attempt to dissuade the client before accepting any obviously detrimental decision. The attorney should consider consulting others who might have a stabilizing influence on the client such as the client's therapist, doctor or clergy. It would normally be improper for the attorney to seek appointment of a guardian in such a situation because to do so may be expensive, traumatic and adversely affect the client's interest.[23]

When rejection of the attorney's advice is likely to adversely affect the client's interests, the attorney should document both the advice and the client's refusal to follow it. Such documentation emphasizes the risk to the client and protects the attorney from subsequent allegations of complicity in the conduct or failure to properly advise the client of the risks involved. In appropriate cases, the attorney may withdraw from representation.

2.6 An attorney should not permit a client's relatives, friends, lovers, employers, or other third persons to interfere with the representation, affect the attorney's independent professional judgment, or, except with the client's express consent, make decisions affecting the representation.

Comment

Third persons often try to play a part in matrimonial cases. Frequently, the client asks that one or more of these people be present at conferences and consulted about major decisions. The potential conflicts are exacerbated when the third person is paying expenses or the attorney's fee. Neither payment of litigation expenses nor sincere concern about the welfare of the client makes those third persons clients. To the extent specifically authorized by the client, the lawyer may discuss choices with third parties, provided all concerned are aware that such discussions may waive any attorney-client privilege.[24] While it is important for persons going through a divorce to receive advice and support from those they trust, the client, with the advice of the attorney, should make the decisions by which the client must ultimately live.

Both the client and the person paying for the representation must be informed at the outset that nothing related by the client in confidence will be disclosed without the client's consent. The duty to protect confidential infor-

23. ABA Comment, RPC 1.14.

24. *See, e.g.*, Crenshaw v. Crenshaw, 646 So.2d 661 (Ala. 1994) (attorney-client privilege does not exist when client to attorney communications are made in the presence of a third party whose presence is not necessary for successful communication between the attorney and the client).

mation also requires that the attorney raise the issue of the effect on confidentiality of the parents, friends, lovers, children or employers' being present. Usually, the presence of a third person not necessary to the rendition of legal services waives the attorney-client privilege.[25] For this and other reasons, an attorney should discourage family members and other third persons from participating in client conferences. In addition to the potential loss of confidentiality, a more accurate account of the client's desires and best interests can usually be obtained when no third persons are present.

Examples:

1. An attorney represents an elderly woman. The son of the client, who is paying the attorney's fee, instructs the attorney to establish a trust to manage the client's assets. The attorney must ignore the son's request and explain the attorney's obligation to act only as requested by the client. In addition to acting only after consultation with and consent by the client, the attorney may not accept payment from the son unless he can avoid interference with the client-lawyer relationship and preserve the confidentiality of communications with the client.[26] Even if the son's wishes are not necessarily adverse to the client's interests, the attorney must assure that he has independently determined the best course for the client. The client should be directed to make her own decisions regarding the representation whenever possible.
2. The minor daughter of an old friend asks the lawyer to find a jurisdiction that will allow her to marry without parental consent. The lawyer is personally convinced that the marriage will be disastrous for the daughter and feels strong obligations to her parents to prevent her from doing something foolish. Under current ethical rules, as well as under these Bounds, the lawyer may not inform the parents or act in any way contrary to the client's stated desires. However, it is appropriate for the lawyer to point out practical, moral, and other non-legal considerations and to attempt to convince the child that the proposed course of action is not in her best interests.[27] It is also appropriate for the lawyer to decline to represent the child or provide the information.

---

25. *See, e.g.*, Dietz v. Doe, 131 Wash.2d 835, 850, 935 P.2d 611, 619 (1997) ("Waiver may occur when the communication is made in the presence of third persons on the theory that such circumstances are inconsistent with the notion that the communication was ever intended to be confidential"); State v. Post, 32 Ohio St. 3d 380, 513 N.E.2d 754 (1987) (client's disclosure to third party of communications made pursuant to attorney-client privilege breaches confidentiality underlying privilege and constitutes waiver).

26. RPC 1.8(f). *Accord,* DR 5-107(A)(1).

27. *See* RPC 2.1 and Comment. *See also* Samuel M. Davis, *The Role of Attorney in Child Advocacy,* 32 U. Louisville J. Fam. L. 817, 829 (1994) ("In the attorney's role as counselor,

2.7 An attorney should not allow personal, moral or religious beliefs to diminish loyalty to the client or usurp the client's right to make decisions concerning the objectives of representation.

Comment

Attorneys would not be human without personal beliefs about issues affecting family law practice. No lawyer should be expected to ignore strongly held beliefs. But the matrimonial lawyer may only limit the objectives of the representation if the client consents after consultation.[28] The client even has the right to be consulted about the means by which the objectives are to be pursued, matters normally within the lawyer's discretion.[29] Therefore, the lawyer should withdraw from representation if personal, moral or religious beliefs are likely to cause the attorney to take actions that are not in the client's best interest. If there is any question as to the possible effect of those beliefs on the representation, the client should be consulted and consent obtained. **See 2.4 & Comment**

2.8 An attorney should discourage the client from interfering in the spouse's effort to obtain effective representation.

Comment

Clients who file or anticipate the filing of a divorce proceeding occasionally telephone or interview numerous attorneys as a means of denying their spouse access to effective representation. The attorney should discourage such practices, and should not assist the client, for example, by responding to the client's

---

the attorney is in a position to advise and help the child to understand not only what the child's choices are but also the potential consequences of those choices"); Robyn Marie-Lyon, *Speaking for a Child: The Role of Independent Counsel for Minors,* 75 Calif. L. Rev. 681, 695 (1987); Katherine Hunt Federle, *The Ethics of Empowerment: Rethinking the Role of Lawyers in Interviewing and Counseling the Child Client,* 64 Fordham L. Rev. 1655, 1691 (1996) ("When the attorney perceives the client as competent and she values client autonomy, she should treat the child as she would an adult and advise the child fully and candidly about her case. The lawyer should not manipulate or coerce the child into choosing a particular course of action or usurp the client's decision-making authority.... Additionally, the attorney should acknowledge her responsibility to counsel the child about non-legal matters and should make the client aware of other professional treatment services.").

28. RPC 1.2(c).

29. RPC 1.2(a). *See* ABA Comment: "In questions of means, the lawyer should assume responsibility for technical and legal tactical issues, but should defer to the client regarding such questions as the expense to be incurred and concern for third persons who might be adversely affected.

request for a list of matrimonial lawyers, if improper motives are suspected. When the client has already contacted other lawyers for the purpose of disqualifying them, the client's attorney should attempt to persuade the client to waive any conflict so created.

2.9 An attorney should not communicate with the media about an active case under most circumstances. An attorney should not communicate with the media about a case, a client or a former client without the client's prior knowledge and consent, except in exigent circumstances when client consent is not obtainable.

Comment

Statements to the media by an attorney representing a party in a family law matter may be inappropriate because family law matters tend to be private and intimate. They are not the business of anyone but the parties and their family. Public discussion of a case tends to obstruct settlement, cause embarrassment, diminish the opportunity for reconciliation and harm the family, especially the children. Statements to the media by an attorney representing a party in a matrimonial matter are also potentially improper because they tend to prejudice an adjudicative proceeding.[30]

An attorney's desire to obtain publicity conflicts with the duty to the client. If contacted by the media, the attorney should respond by saying: "I cannot give you information on that matter because it deals with the personal life of my client." The attorney, as an officer of the court, has duties to both the courts and the client. The parties, subject to order of the court, have a right to discuss their case if they so desire, despite the advice of their counsel. However, a lawyer's statements may have the effect of influencing an adjudicative body presently sitting or to be convened in the future. An attorney may withdraw if the client disobeys instructions not to speak publicly about the case.

It is no excuse that the opposing party, his counsel or agents, first discussed the matter with the media. However, if necessary to mitigate recent adverse publicity, the attorney may make a statement required to protect the client's legitimate interests. Any such statement should be limited to information essential to mitigate the recent adverse publicity.[31]

---

30. *See* RPC 3.6 and Comment.

31. *See* RPC 3.6(c), providing that a lawyer "may make a statement a reasonable lawyer would believe is required to protect a client from the substantial undue prejudicial effect of recent publicity not initiated by the lawyer or the lawyer's client. A statement made pur-

An attorney should never attempt to gain an advantage for the client by providing information to the media to embarrass or humiliate the opposing party or counsel.

3. Conflict of Interest

Conflict of interest dilutes a lawyer's loyalty to the client.[32] A lawyer's loyalty may be diluted by personal interests (financial security, prestige, and self-esteem) and interests of third persons (family, friends, business associates, employer, legal profession, and society as a whole). A conflict exists if the representation of a client "may be materially limited by the lawyer's responsibilities to another client or to a third person, or by the lawyer's own interests."[33] The key to preventing unintentional violations of the conflict of interest rules lies in anticipating the possibility that a conflict situation will develop.

The influences that might dilute a matrimonial lawyer's loyalty to a client are unlimited.[34] The interests of children, relatives, friends, lovers, employers and the opposing party, along with a perceived obligation to the court and the interest of society, may be compelling in a given case. In family law matters, where "winning" and "losing" in the traditional sense often lose their meaning, determination of the appropriate ethical conduct can be extremely difficult.

3.1 An attorney should not represent both husband and wife even if they do not wish to obtain independent representation.

Comment

The temptation to represent potentially conflicting interests is particularly difficult to resist in family disputes. Often the attorney is the "family lawyer"

---

suant to this paragraph shall be limited to such information as is necessary to mitigate the recent adverse publicity." *See also* Cal. St. RPC Rule 5-120.

32. ABA CPR Ethical Consideration 5-1 provides:

The professional judgment of a lawyer should be exercised, within the bounds of the law, solely for the benefit of his client and free of compromising influences and loyalties. Neither his personal interests, the interests of other clients, nor the desires of third persons should be permitted to dilute the loyalty to his client.

33. RPC 1.7(b).

34. *See generally* Kristi Saylors, *Conflicts of Interest in Family Law*, 28 Fam. L.Q. 451 (1994).

and previously represented husband, wife, family corporations, and even the children.[35] Representing husband and wife as an intermediary is not totally prohibited by the RPC.[36] However, it is impossible for the attorney to provide impartial advice to both parties. Even a seemingly amicable separation or divorce may result in bitter litigation over financial matters or custody. A matrimonial lawyer should not attempt to represent both husband and wife, even with the consent of both.[37]

The attorney may be asked to represent family members in a non-litigation setting. If separation or divorce is foreseeable or if one of the parents desires defense to a charge of battery, the lawyer may see her role as counselor or negotiator for all concerned. This temptation should be resisted.[38]

Representation of both spouses should be distinguished, however, from *mediation* of a dispute where the attorney represents neither of the spouses.[39] See 8.1–8.4. While 8.4 permits the attorney-mediator to give advice "that would enable the parties to make reasonably informed decisions," the mediator must remain impartial, indicate that the participants are free to reject the advice, and advise the participants that the mediator represents neither of them, so they should seek independent legal advice.

---

35. ABA Comment to RPC 1.7. For example, an attorney representing a husband with respect to his corporation would be precluded from representing his wife against him in an unrelated dissolution of marriage or custody proceeding.

36. However, the ABA Comment to Rule 2.2 states:

In considering whether to act as intermediary between clients, a lawyer should be mindful that if the intermediation fails the result can be additional cost, embarrassment and recrimination. In some situations the risk of failure is so great that intermediation is plainly impossible. For example, a lawyer cannot undertake common representation of clients between whom contentious litigation is imminent or who contemplate contentious negotiations. More generally, if the relationship between the parties has already assumed definite antagonism, the possibility that the clients' interests can be adjusted by intermediation ordinarily is not very good.

Rule 2.2 does not apply to a lawyer acting as arbitrator or mediator between or among parties who are not clients of the lawyer, even where the lawyer has been appointed with the concurrence of both parties.

37. *See, e.g.*, Walden v. Hoke, 189 W.Va. 222, 227, 429 S.E.2d 504, 509 (1993)(unethical for lawyer to represent husband and wife at any stage of separation and divorce proceeding, even if simple or uncontested and with full disclosure and informed consent); Board of Bar Overseers of the Bar v. Dineen, 500 A.2d 262 (Maine 1985).

38. This Goal does not apply in adoption proceedings or other matters where the spouses' positions are not adverse.

39. Cf. RPC 2.2 (permitting intermediation *between two clients* only under extremely narrow circumstances that would not include a dispute between two family members).

Because the attorney-mediator represents neither party, the attorney-mediator may not appear in court on behalf of either. It is the consensus of Academy members, however, that an attorney-mediator who has assisted the participants in reaching a mutually determined agreement, may appear in court "on behalf of the agreement," solely for the purpose of filing it. Any of the parties may be represented by counsel of their choice at such a proceeding.

3.2 An attorney should not advise an unrepresented party.[40]

Comment

Once it becomes apparent that another party intends to proceed without a lawyer, the attorney should, at the earliest opportunity, inform the other party in writing as follows:[41]

1. I am your spouse's lawyer.
2. I do not and will not represent you.
3. I will at all times look out for your spouse's interests, not yours.
4. Any statements I make to you about this case should be taken by you as negotiation or argument on behalf of your spouse and not as advice to you as to your best interest.
5. I urge you to obtain your own lawyer.[42]

3.3 An attorney should not simultaneously represent both a client and a person with whom the client is sexually involved.

Comment

A matrimonial lawyer is often asked to represent a client and the client's lover. Joint representation may make it difficult to advise the client of the need to recover from the emotional trauma of divorce, the desirability of a prenup-

---

40. *See* Walden v. Hoke, 189 W.Va. 222, 228, 429 S.E.2d 504, 510 (1993) (regardless of how simple, amicable, and uncontested the divorce may be, the preparation of documents for the opposing party raises the possibility of prejudice and presents the appearance of impropriety).

41. *See* RPC 4.3.

42. *See* ABA Comment, RPC 4.3 ("During the course of a lawyer's representation of a client, the lawyer should not give advice to an unrepresented person other than the advice to obtain counsel."). *Accord,* DR 7-104(A)(2). *See* Pa. Bar Op. 96-145 (1996) (lawyer representing wife in divorce action may comply with unrepresented husband's request for a meeting to review financial information; but lawyer must not state or imply that she is disinterested, give legal advice to the husband, and must correct any misunderstanding husband may have about her role in the negotiation).

tial agreement, or the dangers of early remarriage. The testimony of either might be adverse to the other at deposition or trial. In addition, the client may desire to waive support payments because she believes she is going to marry her lover. The inherent conflicts in attempting to represent both the client and her lover render such representation improper. Even when the client's new partner is not represented by the attorney, but wishes to participate in consultations and other aspects of the representation, the attorney must be alert to the danger of the client's undermining her own best interests in an effort to accommodate her new partner.

3.4 An attorney should not have a sexual relationship with a client, opposing counsel, or a judicial officer in the case during the time of the representation.

Comment

Persons in need of a matrimonial lawyer are often in a highly vulnerable emotional state. Some degree of social contact (particularly if a social relationship existed prior to the events that occasioned the present representation) may be desirable, but a more intimate relationship may endanger both the client's welfare and the lawyer's objectivity.[43]

Attorneys are expected to maintain personal relationships with other attorneys, but must be sensitive to the threat to independent judgment and the appearance of impropriety when an intimate relationship exists with opposing counsel or other persons involved in the proceedings.

4. Fees

Many divorce clients have never before hired an attorney and are vulnerable because of fear and insecurity. Matrimonial lawyers and their clients may

---

43. To an increasing degree, states have adopted specific limitations on attorney-client sexual relations. *See, e.g.*, Calif. RPC Rule 3-120 (1998); Florida RPC Rule 4-8.4(i) (1998); Minn. RPC Rule 1.8(k) (1998); Wisc. RPC SCR 20:1.8(k)(2) (1998). In addition, a number of state court decisions have found that an attorney's sexual relations with a client constitutes "moral turpitude," justifying the imposition of disciplinary sanctions despite the absence of an express rule banning such conduct. *See, e.g.*, Matter of DiSandro, 680 A.2d 73, 75 (R.I. 1996); People v. Good, 893 P.2d 101, 103 (Colo. 1995) ("Because the lawyer stands in a fiduciary relationship with the client, an unsolicited sexual advance by the lawyer debases the essence of the lawyer-client relationship"); *In re* Heard, 136 Wash.2d 405, 963 P.2d 818 (1998). See Jennifer Tuggle Crabtree, Comment, *Does Consent Matter? Relationships Between Divorce Attorneys and Clients*, 23 J. Legal. Prof. 221 (1999).

not have the long-standing relationship out of which business lawyers and their clients often evolve an understanding about fees.

It is not unusual for a party to a divorce to lack sufficient funds to pay an attorney. This lack of resources, various strictures against contingent fee contracts, the unwillingness of some courts to redress the economic imbalance between the parties with fee awards, and the tendency of overwrought clients to misunderstand the fee agreement or to blame their attorneys for undesirable results, can make payment extremely difficult.

These factors help to explain why the records of fee dispute committees indicate that the number of disputes arising from family law cases is several times greater than those from any other category. Thus, financial arrangements with clients should be clearly explained, agreed upon and documented.

4.1 Fee agreements should be in writing.[44]

Comment

At the outset the matrimonial lawyer should tell the client the basis on which fees will be charged[45] and when and how the attorney expects to be paid.[46] In

---

44. Matrimonial lawyers and clients would normally enter into a mutually executed fee agreement. However, some attorney-client relationships would justify the attorney's drafting a letter confirming an oral agreement. Such a confirming letter would be permissible under this Goal, provided that the client indicates approval in writing.

45. When appropriate, this information might include the fact that total fees and costs cannot be predicted. RPC 1.5(a) provides that the factors in determining a reasonable fee include:

(1) the time and labor required, the novelty and difficulty of the questions involved, and the skill requisite to perform the legal service properly;

(2) the likelihood, if apparent to the client, that the acceptance of the particular employment will preclude other employment by the lawyer;

(3) the fee customarily charged in the locality for similar legal services;

(4) the amount involved and the results obtained;

(5) the time limitations imposed by the client or by the circumstances;

(6) the nature and length of the professional relationship with the client;

(7) the experience, reputation, and ability of the lawyer or lawyers performing the services; and

(8) whether the fee is fixed or contingent.

46. *See* RPC 1.5(b). According to the Comment to RPC 1.5:

It is not necessary to recite all the factors that underlie the basis of the fee, but only those that are directly involved in its computation. It is sufficient, for example, to state that the basic rate is an hourly charge or a fixed amount or an estimated amount, or to identify the factors that may be taken into account in finally fixing the fee. When developments occur during the representation that render an earlier estimate substantially inaccurate, a revised

some jurisdictions, fee agreements must be in writing.[47] Written fee agreements should delineate the obligations of the attorney and the client. Agreements should specify the scope of the representation. Fee agreements should be presented in a manner that allows the client an opportunity to consider the terms, consult another attorney before signing and obtain answers to any questions to fully understand the agreement before entering into it. The written fee agreement should be entered into when the representation is initiated or as soon as possible thereafter.

Examples of Scope Provisions:

a. Our representation will include advising, counseling, drafting, negotiating, investigating, analyzing and handling this family law matter to a final resolution, whether by negotiated settlement or, if necessary, by trial and adjudication by a court. Depending on the specifics of your case, its resolution may include: custody, visitation, and support of your children; classification of assets as "marital" or "non-marital;" the valuation and division of marital property; the determination of maintenance for you or for your spouse; and determining whether the attorney's fees and costs incurred may be shifted from you to your spouse, or vice versa.

b. Our representation will be limited to settlement or trial of the issue of ________. We have not agreed to undertake any appeal of any order entered.

c. Our representation will be limited to assisting in settlement through negotiation and mediation. If attempts at settlement are unsuccessful and litigation is instituted, our representation will cease. You agree to then retain trial counsel to represent you thereafter.

---

estimate should be provided to the client. A written statement concerning the fee reduces the possibility of misunderstanding.

47. *See, e.g.*, Calif. Bus. & Prof. Code §6148(a) (requiring that the fee agreement be in writing whenever it is reasonably foreseeable that the total expense to the client will exceed $1000); D.C. RPC 1.5(b) ("When the lawyer has not regularly represented the client, the basis or rate of the fee shall be communicated to the client, in writing, before or within a reasonable time after commencing the representation"); N.J. RPC 1.5(b); DeGraaf v. Fusco, 660 A.2d 9 (N.J. Super. Ct., App. Div. 1995) (error not to instruct jury that Rule 1.5(b) requires lawyers to put fee agreement in writing). Conn. RPC 1.5(b) (fee agreement, including substantial detail concerning the scope of the matter and client responsibility for costs and expenses, must be in writing); Alaska Ethics Op. 95-4 (1995) (written statement of costs required); Cf. Kaplan v. Pavalon & Gifford, 806 F.Supp. 192 (N.D. Ill. 1992), *aff'd* 12 F.3d 87 (7th Cir. 1993) (fee-sharing agreement void because not reduced to writing). See generally, Lawrence A. Dubin, *Client Beware: The Need for a Mandatory Written Fee Agreeement Rule*, 51 Okla. L. Rev. 93 (1998).

4.2 *An attorney should provide periodic statements of fees and costs.*

Comment

When the fee arrangement is based on an hourly rate or similar arrangement, this information can be part of the necessary communications concerning the case addressed in **2.3 and Comment.** The statement should be sufficiently detailed to apprise the client of the time and charges incurred.[48] In addition, the matrimonial lawyer should comply with fee regulations in the lawyer's jurisdiction that may be more detailed or restrictive in requiring information about fees and costs.

4.3 *All transactions in which an attorney obtains security for fees should be properly documented.*[49]

Comment

All security agreements should be arms-length transactions. When taking mortgages on real property from a client, the client should be independently represented. If an attorney takes personal property as security, it must be appraised, photographed and identified by a qualified appraiser to establish concretely its precise identity and value. The attorney should then secure it in a safe place (usually a safe deposit box) where there is no danger that it can be removed, substituted or lost.[50]

---

48. *See, e.g.*, In re Marriage of Pitulla, 491 N.E.2d 90 (Ill.App. 1986) (client entitled to evidentiary hearing concerning portion of dissolution judgment requiring payment of attorney's fees; court noted that client's repeated requests for itemization of fees had been denied by attorney, and the court held that the client's right to know services lawyer performed and time spent on the case is implied in every lawyer-client contract).

49. As stated in the Comment to RPC 1.5: "A lawyer may accept property in payment for services, such as an ownership interest in an enterprise, providing this does not involve acquisition of a proprietary interest in the cause of action or subject matter of the litigation contrary to Rule 1.8(j). However, a fee paid in property instead of money may be subject to special scrutiny because it involves questions concerning both the value of the services and the lawyer's special knowledge of the value of the property." Some jurisdictions do not permit an attorney to take a security interest in a client's property. In those jurisdictions that do permit such a security interest, the attorney should be sensitive to the need of the client for use of the property involved. In matrimonial law matters where marital property is the subject of litigation, the potential for conflict is increased.

50. *See* RPC 1.15.

4.4 *An attorney's fee should be reasonable, based on appropriate factors, including those listed in RPC 1.5(a).*

Comment

Lawyers should charge reasonable fees for services performed pursuant to a valid fee agreement. Although the starting point in determining a reasonable fee is often the lawyer's hourly rate multiplied by the hours spent on the case, a number of other factors may be relevant in determining an appropriate fee in a particular representation. RPC 1.5(a) lists many of those factors.

Clients, as consumers, should be able to negotiate fee agreements that best suit their needs and circumstances. In addition to fees based solely on hourly rate, a fee agreement may provide for a contingent fee, or one based on "value," a specified result, or some combination of factors. No single factor is appropriate in all family law cases since both clients and the nature of the representations vary greatly. Therefore, it is important at the outset for the attorney to explain the factors to be used in determining the fee, provide the fee agreement in writing (see **4.1**), and, particularly when factors in addition to the attorney's hourly rate will be considered, afford the client an opportunity to obtain independent advice about the proposed fee arrangement.

Some jurisdictions have prohibited fees in domestic relations cases that were in any way based on the results obtained in the case, holding that such fees constituted contingent fees. Courts in other jurisdictions have held that the fact that an hourly fee is enhanced on the basis of results obtained does not necessarily make it a contingent fee.[51] This Goal would permit "results" fees. Under RPC 1.5(a), the factors to be considered in determining the reasonableness of a fee include "the amount involved and the results obtained." A fee that is based on an hourly rate, but may be enhanced by a specified result is not the same as a traditional contingent fee, which provides that the attorney will receive a specified percentage of any recovery. If the client loses, the attorney receives no fee at all.

A fee based on the attorney's usual hourly rate, but enhanced by achieving a specified result, may be justified in a given case by any combination of the following circumstances: the complexity of the case; the shortness of the time between the attorney's retention and impending proceedings; the difficult, ag-

---

51. *See, e.g.*, Head v. Head, 66 Md.App. 655, 505 A.2d 868 (1986) (fee based in part on results obtained and not on percentage of any amount recovered or saved was not contingent); *In re* Marriage of Malec, 205 Ill.App.3d 273, 287–88, 562 N.E.2d 1010, 150 Ill.Dec. 207 (1990) (consideration of results achieved does not necessarily make fee agreement contingent).

gressive nature of the opposing party and counsel; a particular attorney's unique ability to settle a case quickly and avoid lengthy and acrimonious trial proceedings; and a substantial risk that the representation will be unsuccessful due to unfavorable factual or legal context. A fee based in part on results obtained is permissible under this Goal so long as the specified "result" does not include obtaining a divorce, custody or visitation provisions, or the amount of alimony or child support awarded (see **4.5**), and if the fee is: (1) reasonable under the circumstances; (2) in addition to the attorney's usual hourly rate; (3) based on factors clearly stated in writing and provided to the client at the outset of the agreement; and (4) agreed to in writing by the client at the outset of the representation after full consultation and an opportunity to seek independent legal advice.

4.5 An attorney should not charge a fee the payment or amount of which is contingent upon: (i) obtaining a divorce; (ii) custody or visitation provisions; or (iii) the amount of alimony or child support awarded. An attorney may charge a contingent fee for all other matters, provided that:

(a) the client is informed of the right to have the fee based on an hourly rate; and
(b) the client is afforded an opportunity to seek independent legal advice concerning the desirability of the contingent fee arrangement.

Comment

This Goal continues the absolute prohibition of fees contingent upon securing a divorce or a specified amount of alimony or child support, and makes clear that the prohibition includes custody or visitation proceedings. In other matters relating to a divorce, however, the policy bases for the prohibition do not apply. Therefore, this Goal provides that an attorney should be able to enter into a contingent fee agreement with an informed client who reasonably believes such an arrangement is in the client's best interests.

Although attorneys and informed clients are generally able to determine that a contingent fee arrangement is more beneficial to the client than one based, for example, on an hourly rate, there has long been a total ban on contingent fees in domestic relations cases. The primary basis for the prohibition in divorce cases is that the arrangement would "put strong economic pressure on the lawyer to assure that reconciliation did not occur."[52] In addition, the

52. Charles Wolfram, Modern Legal Ethics §9.4.4, at p.539 (West 1986) (citing cases).

rationale that contingent fee arrangements are necessary in other civil cases to enable indigent litigants to obtain counsel is believed not to be applicable in divorce cases.[53] The spouse in possession of marital assets will usually have little difficulty in obtaining representation, while the other spouse is assumed to be protected by the court's authority to compel the spouse with the greater assets to pay attorney's fees.[54]

A third basis for the ban on contingent fees is that it may "disrupt the pattern of wealth distribution that the court intended in making the award," unless the existence of the contingent fee is made known to the court in advance.[55] And, to the extent that the contingent fee applies to the amount of a property settlement and not to support or alimony, the attorney may be tempted to advocate more for the former, even if not in the best interests of the client and any children.[56]

At the same time, however, the complete ban on contingent fees at all stages of domestic relations cases,[57] particularly when interpreted strictly,[58] and coupled with decisions holding that fees based in any way on the results obtained in the case are prohibited contingent fees,[59] is unsupported by the above poli-

---

53. *Id.* At p.540, *citing* McDearmon v. Gordon & Gremillion, 247 Ark. 318, 445 S.W.2d 488 (1969).

54. *See, e.g.*, Pfohl v. Pfohl, 345 So.2d 371 (Fla. Ct. App. 1977) (wife ordered to pay $30,000 for husband's attorney's fees in dissolution action where wife had over $4 million in assets compared to husband's $200,000); Finley v. Finley, 422 N.E.2d 289 (Ind. Ct. App. 1981) (husband ordered to pay $350,000 in wife's attorney's fees); Werk v. Werk, 416 So.2d 483 (Fla. Ct. App. 1982) (order for wife to pay $10,000 in fees to husband's attorney affirmed where husband had been excluded from business and home owned by wife so that he was without income or support). *See generally* Wenona Y. Whitfield, *Where the Wind Blows: Fee Shifting in Domestic Relations Cases,* 14 Fla. St. U. L. Rev. 811–813 (1987) (collecting cases).

55. Wolfram, supra note 53, at p.540.

56. *See, e.g.*, Levine v. Levine, 206 Misc. 884, 135 N.Y.S.2d 304 (1954).

57. *See* RPC 1.5(d)(1).

58. *See, e.g.*, Fletcher v. Fletcher, 227 Ill.App.3d 194, 591 N.E.2d 91, 93, 169 Ill.Dec. 211 (1992) ("Contingent fees are not allowed in dissolution cases when contingent upon obtaining the dissolution or based upon the financial aspects of the dissolution"); Licciardi v. Collins, 180 Ill.App.3d 1051, 1061, 536 N.E.2d 840, 847–848, 129 Ill.Dec. 790, 797 (1989) (illegal contingent fee agreement in a dissolution case bars recovery even under a theory of quantum meruit): "[W]e believe the public policy behind the rule so important that, as long as an attorney's services are employed with respect to the division of marital property, the rule bars contingent fees therefor whether or not a judgment of dissolution has or has not been entered when the attorney is retained."

59. *See, e.g.*, In re Marriage of Malec, 205 Ill.App.3d 273, 562 N.E.2d 1010, 150 Ill.Dec. 207 (1990) (agreement in which client offered to pay $1,000,000 if certain results were obtained held to be illegal contingent fee agreement).

cies. Such a ban also undermines the freedom of attorneys and informed clients to enter into fee arrangements that best suit the nature of particular cases and the interests of both.

A contingent fee arrangement might be preferable to an hourly rate for some divorce clients. For example, although courts may have the *power* to compel the spouse with the greatest assets to pay attorney's fees, they often do not do so. Therefore, if the client is unlikely to pay the attorney's fee unless the client receives a substantial award, the client's ability to obtain quality legal representation may be dependent upon the availability of a contingent fee agreement.

In addition, the amount of effort involved in a difficult case might result in an hourly fee that the client could only afford if he or she won. And yet, it is in just such a case that the client would need an experienced attorney, who would be unlikely to undertake a risky case, solely on the basis of the attorney's hourly rate. At the same time, the client might be reluctant to commit to the attorney's hourly rate in a complex and costly case, without a way of assuring there will be adequate funds from which to pay the fee.

Due to the prohibition on contingent fees (and cases holding a "results" fee to constitute a contingent fee), a lawyer may feel compelled to enter into an hourly fee arrangement with a client who subsequently loses the case after a substantial effort. The result in the case and the client's inability to pay may cause the lawyer to feel compelled ethically to reduce the fee. Such a result would seem to be both ethical and desirable. It would also be indistinguishable as a matter of policy from a contingent fee agreed to at the outset of the attorney-client relationship.

For these reasons, this Goal limits the prohibition of contingent fees to those aspects of divorce cases supported by the historic policy bases. In other matters, informed clients should have the same ability to choose a contingent fee arrangement as clients in other civil matters. Jurisdictions that completely ban all contingent fees should be urged to adopt a rule similar to this Goal.

4.6 An attorney may withdraw from a case when the client fails to honor the fee agreement.

Comment

The fee agreement should set forth the circumstances under which the matrimonial lawyer will be permitted to withdraw for non-payment. Before withdrawing, the attorney must take reasonable steps to avoid foreseeable prejudice to the rights of the client, allowing time for employment of other counsel, and delivering to the client papers and property to which the client is entitled.[60][61]

---

60. *See* RPC 1.16(d).

However, the attorney should not seek to withdraw from a case on the eve of trial unless there was a clear prior understanding that withdrawal would result from non-payment.[61]

4.7 An attorney may properly take all steps necessary to effect collection, including mediation, arbitration or suit, from a client who fails to honor the fee agreement.[62]

Comment

Lawyers are entitled to be paid reasonable fees for services performed pursuant to a valid fee agreement. Alternatives to litigation should be used unless they are unlikely to be effective.

5. Client Conduct

A client is entitled to know what laws govern divorce and the consequences of those laws on a dissolution of marriage. A matrimonial lawyer should advise a client about the repercussions of any matrimonial litigation, including factors that are likely to be considered in economic and custody determinations. However, the lawyer should avoid assisting the client in using the counseling process to engage in fraudulent conduct.

5.1 An attorney should not condone, assist, or encourage a client to transfer, hide, dissipate, or move assets to improperly defeat a spouse's claim.

Comment

It is improper for an attorney to "counsel a client to engage, or assist a client, in conduct that the lawyer knows is criminal or fraudulent, but a lawyer may discuss the legal consequences of any proposed course of conduct with a client...."[63] Whether the client proposes opening a secret out-of-state bank account, moving assets to an offshore trust, or having a family member hold sums of cash for

---

61. RPC 1.16(b) provides that a lawyer may withdraw if she can do so "without material adverse effect on the interests of the client, or if: ... (4) the client fails substantially to fulfill an obligation to the lawyer regarding the lawyer's services and has been given reasonable warning that the lawyer will withdraw unless the obligation is fulfilled."

62. It should be noted that states vary concerning the circumstances in which a lawsuit will be permitted. Thus, for example, a lawsuit to obtain fees would be invalid in California unless the client first had an opportunity to arbitrate.

63. RPC 1.2(d).

the purpose of concealment, the advice to the client must be the same: "Don't do it." A client's efforts, outside the presence of his or her spouse, to transfer assets beyond the reach of the court may indicate an improper motive. The attorney should suggest including the spouse in the discussions. Refusal by the client may well indicate an improper purpose, which the attorney should refuse to assist.

Hiding assets to defeat a spouse's claim is a fraud upon the client's spouse and likely to result in a fraud upon the court.[64] The client must also be advised not to conceal data about property, fail to furnish relevant documents, insist on placing unrealistic values on properties in, or omit assets from, sworn financial statements.

On the other hand, "[t]here is a critical distinction between presenting an analysis of legal aspects of questionable conduct and recommending the means by which a crime or fraud might be committed with impunity."[65] It may sometimes be difficult to determine whether a client's questions concerning legal aspects of predivorce planning are asked to facilitate an improper purpose. Although the attorney should initially give the client the benefit of any doubt, later discovery of improper conduct mandates that the attorney cease such assistance and may require withdrawal from representation.[66]

5.2 An attorney should advise the client of the potential effect of the client's conduct on a child custody dispute.

Comment

Predivorce conduct of the parents may significantly affect custody decisions, as well as the children's adjustment to the divorce itself. The client is entitled to advice where there is a custody issue. Conduct conforming to such advice often will benefit both the children and the client's spouse, independent of any custody dispute. Suggesting that the client spend more time with the child and consult, from time to time with the child's doctor, teacher, and babysitter, is

---

64. Such conduct may also constitute a fraud upon the client's children. See, e.g., In re Shaeffer, 824 S.W.2d 1 (Mo. 1992) (attorney's representation of a marital dissolution client's girlfriend in a "friendly suit" against the client for the purpose of transferring money from the client to the girlfriend without the knowledge of the client's adult children found to be prejudicial to the administration of justice and reflect adversely on attorney's fitness to practice law).

65. ABA Comment, RPC 1.2. The Comment also provides that the attorney "is required to give an honest opinion about the actual consequences that appear likely to result from a client's conduct. The fact that a client uses advice in a course of action that is criminal or fraudulent does not, of itself, make a lawyer a party to the course of action."

66. *See* RPC 1.16(a) & (b); ABA Comment, RPC 1.2.

appropriate. It is also proper to describe the potential harmful consequences to the children (and to the client legally) of prematurely introducing the children to a new romantic partner, substance abuse, abusive or derogatory behavior toward the other parent, or other inappropriate behavior.

Predivorce planning is an ideal opportunity to advise the client on ways to make the divorce transition easier for the children. For example, the lawyer might describe ways for the parents in concert to inform the children of the divorce and to reassure the children that both parents will always be there for them. The lawyer might describe programs available in the client's community to aid both parents and children in adjusting to divorce. Most important, predivorce planning is an opportunity to orient the client toward consideration of the children's needs first and toward the desirability of working out a cooperative parenting plan.

The lawyer should describe how mediation of child custody disputes might assist in effecting a cooperative parenting plan. It is appropriate to tell the client that children suffer from parental conflict and that a child custody dispute involving the searching inquiry of a custody evaluation and rigors of a trial is likely to be harmful to every member of the family.

The lawyer should consider whether the custody claim will be made in good faith. If not, the lawyer should advise the client of the harmful consequences of a meritless custody claim to the client, the child, and the client's spouse.[67] If the client persists in demanding advice to build a spurious custody case or to use a custody claim as a bargaining chip or as a means of inflicting revenge (**see 6.2 and Comment**), the lawyer should withdraw.[68]

6. Children

One of the most troubling issues in family law is determining a lawyer's obligations to children. The lawyer must competently represent the interests of the client, but not at the expense of the children. The parents' fiduciary obligations for the well being of a child provide a basis for the attorney's consideration of the child's best interests consistent with traditional advocacy and client loyalty principles. It is accepted doctrine that the attorney for a trustee or other fiduciary has an ethical obligation to the beneficiaries to whom the fidu-

67. *See* RPC 2.1 and previous discussion indicating that it is proper for an attorney to refer to moral, economic and social, as well as legal, factors relevant to the client's situation.

68. RPC 1.16 **requires** that the attorney withdraw if the representation "will result in violation of the rules of professional conduct or other law," and **permits** withdrawal if the client "insists upon pursuing an objective that the lawyer considers repugnant or imprudent."

ciary's obligations run.[69] Statutory and decisional law in most jurisdictions imposes a fiduciary duty on parents to act in their child's best interests.[70] For this analysis to be of benefit to practitioners, however, a clearer mandate must be adopted as part of the ethical code or its official interpretations.

6.1 An attorney representing a parent should consider the welfare of, and seek to minimize the adverse impact of the divorce on, the minor children.

Comment

Although the substantive law in most jurisdictions concerning custody, abuse and termination of parental rights is premised upon the "best interests of the child," the ethical codes provide little (or contradictory) guidance for an attorney whose client's expressed wishes, interests or conduct are in direct conflict with the well-being of children. This Goal emphasizes that the welfare of each family member is interrelated.

Matrimonial lawyers should counsel parties to examine their wishes in light of the needs and interests of the children and the relationship to other family members. In so doing, the matrimonial lawyer is not only advising the client to adhere to applicable substantive law, but is also reminding the client that the family relationship continues.

Parents owe a continuing fiduciary duty toward each other,[71] as well as toward their children, to serve their children's best interests. In many in-

---

69. *See, e.g.*, Ruden v. Jenk, 543 N.W.2d 605, 610 (Iowa 1996) (attorney owes duty to administrator of estate as to legal aspects of assignments of deceased beneficiary's interest); Disciplinary Proceedings Against Noble, 100 Wash.2d 88, 101, 667 P.2d 608, 615 (1983) (Stafford, J., concurring and dissenting in part) (as a fiduciary, attorney owed highest degree of "good faith, care, loyalty, and integrity, as well as the obligation to fully, timely, and honestly inform beneficiaries of all facts which would aid them in protecting their respective interests").

70. ABA Comment to RPC 1.14. *See also* ABA Comment to RPC 1.2: "Where the client is a fiduciary, the lawyer may be charged with special obligations in dealings with a beneficiary."

71. *See, e.g.*, Ann. Cal. Fam. Code §721(b) (1998) ("[I]n transactions between themselves, husband and wife are subject to the general rules governing fiduciary relationships" and which impose "a duty of the highest good faith and fair dealing on each spouse, and neither shall take any unfair advantage of the other."). *See* In re Marriage of Cottin, 63 Cal.App.3d 139, 133 Cal.Rptr. 583 (1976) (husband owed fiduciary duty to disclose all community assets in marital settlement agreement); In re Marriage of Modnick, 33 Cal.3d 897, 906, 191 Cal.Rptr. 629, 663 P.2d 187 (1983) ("[A] duty arises from the fiduciary relationship that exists between spouses with respect to the control of community property."); In

stances, parents should subordinate their own interests to those of their children. Matrimonial lawyers and parents alike should collaboratively seek parenting arrangements that eliminate fractious contact between parents, minimize transition or transportation difficulties and preserve stability for the children.

Children do not benefit from involvement in their parents' divorce. The attorney should warn the client against leaving papers from the attorney out where children can read them and to avoid talking about the case when children can overhear.

If the parents are in conflict and disagree about custody and other parenting issues, the attorney should consider, with the cooperation of the other parent's attorney, sending the parties to a neutral mental health professional who is a family therapist. The goal of this referral is to resolve their disputes through counseling with the help of that mental health professional. The referring agreement should include confidentiality for all contacts with the therapist and exclusion of that therapist as a witness in the divorce case.

The attorney should discourage the client and refuse to participate in multiple psychological evaluations of children for the purpose of finding an expert who will testify in their favor. Repeated psychological evaluations of children are contrary to the children's best interest.[72]

---

re Marriage of Eltzroth, 67 Or.App. 520, 525–26, 679 P.2d 1369, 1372–73 (1984) ("Oregon courts have long recognized that a husband and a wife do not deal at arms' length and have imposed a fiduciary duty of the highest degree in transactions between them.... Husband had a duty to deal with his wife fairly and to make a full and frank disclosure of all circumstances materially bearing on the contemplated agreement, including a full disclosure of marital assets").

72. While the lawyer may not limit the objectives of the representation without the client's consent, RPC 1.2(a), the means by which those objectives are pursued are normally within the lawyer's discretion, RPC 1.2(a). According to the Comment to RPC 1.2(a), however: "In questions of means, the lawyer should assume responsibility for technical and tactical issues, but should defer to the client regarding such questions as the expense to be incurred and concern for third persons who might be adversely affected." In most cases, the lawyer's explanation of the benefits of therapy and the harm in involving the child unnecessarily in the divorce and obtaining repeated evaluations, coupled with the parent's concern for the child's welfare, should be sufficient to obtain the client's consent to the lawyer's adherence to this Goal.

6.2 An attorney should not permit a client to contest child custody, contact or access for either financial leverage or vindictiveness.

Comment

Tactics oriented toward asserting custody rights as leverage toward attaining some other, usually financial, goal are destructive. The matrimonial lawyer should counsel against, and refuse to assist, such conduct. Proper consideration for the welfare of the children requires that they not be used as pawns in the divorce process. Thus, for example, in states where child support is determined partly on the basis of the amount of time a parent spends with the child, the lawyers should negotiate parenting issues based solely on considerations related to the child, then negotiate child support based on financial considerations. If despite the attorney's advice the client persists, the attorney should seek to withdraw.

6.3 When issues in a representation affect the welfare of a minor child, an attorney should not initiate communication with the child, except in the presence of the child's lawyer or guardian ad litem, with court permission, or as necessary to verify facts in motions and pleadings.

Comment

Issues affecting a child's welfare may arise before, during, and after legal proceedings. There is a risk of harm to the child from an attorney's contacts and attempts to involve the child in the proceedings. Advice to or manipulation of the child by a parent's lawyer has no place in the lawyer's efforts on behalf of the parent. Information properly to be obtained from a child regarding the parents and the parents' disputes should be obtained under circumstances that protect the child's best interests.[73]

---

73. *See, e.g.*, Pa. Bar Op. 95-134 (1996) (lawyer for parent in child custody proceeding may interview unrepresented child only if, after sensitive consideration, lawyer determines that advantages of interview outweigh any risk of harm to child; lawyer should consult with parent, carefully consider content of interview, and explain lawyer's role to child; and, if child is represented by guardian ad litem, child advocate or attorney, lawyer must secure representative's permission).

6.4 An attorney should not bring a child to court or call a child as a witness without full discussion with the client and a reasonable belief that it is in the best interests of the child.[74]

Comment

Taking sides against either parent in a legal proceeding imposes a large emotional burden on a child. Some children do not want to express a preference in child custody disputes; they want their parents to resolve the issue without calling them. Other children want their views expressed, and their views may be highly relevant to the outcome of the dispute. All participants in a family law proceeding (including attorneys for all parties, any party's therapist, child custody evaluator, and the judge) should strive to permit a child's views and information to be expressed in a manner that least exposes the child to the rigors of the courtroom. The attorney should weigh carefully the risks and benefits to the child of testifying, including consulting with appropriate experts as to the potential for harm.

Where a child's information is material on an issue other than custody, counsel should explore whether the same information can be introduced from another source, rendering the child's testimony cumulative and unnecessary.

6.5 An attorney should disclose information relating to a client or former client to the extent the lawyer reasonably believes necessary to prevent substantial physical or sexual abuse of a child.

Comment

Under current RPC 1.6(b)(1), an attorney may reveal information reasonably believed necessary "to prevent the client from committing a criminal act that the lawyer believes is likely to result in imminent death or substantial bodily harm."[75] Many states permit the attorney to reveal the intention of the client

---

74. In some jurisdictions, the child may be required, have the right, or be permitted to testify or appear in court proceedings. In such jurisdictions, this Goal would not apply. See Kathleen Nemechek, Note, *Child Preference in Custody Decisions: Where We Have Been, Where We Are Now, Where We Should Go,* 83 Iowa L. Rev. 437 (1998) (surveying the law in different jurisdictions). *Compare* Texas Family Code § 153.009 (court "shall" interview a child ten years or older if requested by a party); Tenn. Family Code § 36-6-106(7) ("The court shall consider all relevant factors including the following where applicable: ..."The reasonable preference of a child of twelve (12) years of age or older. The court may hear the preference of a younger child upon request.").

75. RPC 1.6(b)(1). The ABA Comment to Rule 1.6 states:

The lawyer's exercise of discretion requires consideration of such factors as the nature

to commit any crime and the information necessary to prevent it. The rules do not appear to address, however, revelation of conduct that may be severely detrimental to the well being of the child, but is not criminal. Also, while engaged in efforts on the client's behalf, the matrimonial lawyer may become convinced that the client or a person with whom the client has a relationship has abused one of the children. Under traditional analysis in most jurisdictions, the attorney should refuse to assist the client. The attorney may withdraw if the client will not be adversely affected and the court grants any required permission. Disclosure of risk to a child based on past abuse would not be permitted under this analysis, however.

Notwithstanding the importance of the attorney-client privilege, the obligation of the matrimonial lawyer to consider the welfare of children, coupled with the client's lack of any legitimate interest in preventing his attorney from revealing information to protect the children from likely physical abuse, requires disclosure of a substantial risk of abuse and the information necessary to prevent it. If the client insists on seeking custody or unsupervised visitation, even without the attorney's assistance, the attorney should report specific knowledge of child abuse to the authorities for the protection of the child.[76]

As stated in the Comment to the ABA Ethics 2000 Commission's proposed revision of RPC 1.6(b)(1):

> Although the public interest is usually best served by a strict rule requiring lawyers to preserve the confidentiality of information relating to the representation of their clients, the confidentiality rule is subject to limited exceptions. In becoming privy to information about a client, a lawyer may foresee that the client intends serious harm to another person. However, to the extent a lawyer is required or permitted to disclose a client's purposes, the client will be inhibited from revealing facts which would enable the lawyer to counsel against a

---

of the lawyer's relationship with the client and with those who might be injured by the client, the lawyer's own involvement in the transaction and factors that may extenuate the conduct in question. Where practical, the lawyer should seek to persuade the client to take suitable action. In any case, a disclosure adverse to the client's interest should be no greater than the lawyer reasonably believes necessary to the purpose.

76. See Robert Aronson, *What About the Children? Are Family Lawyers the Same (Ethically) As Criminal Lawyers?*, 1 Journ. of Inst. for Study of Leg. Ethics 141 (1996); Robin Rosencrantz, *Rejecting "Hear No Evil Speak No Evil": Expanding the Attorney's Role in Child Abuse Reporting*, 8 Geo. J. Legal Ethics 327 (1995). Goal 6.5 and the Comment reflect the collective judgment of the Fellows of the Academy and should be followed to the extent possible under the law of the jurisdiction. If the law of the jurisdiction prohibits such disclosure, this Goal does not apply.

wrongful course of action. The public is better protected if full and open communication by the client is encouraged than if it is inhibited. Paragraph (b)(1) recognizes the overriding value of life and physical integrity and permits disclosure reasonably necessary to prevent reasonably certain death or substantial bodily harm. Substantial bodily harm includes life-threatening or debilitating injuries and illnesses and the consequences of child sexual abuse. Such harm is reasonably certain to occur if it will be suffered imminently or if there is a present and substantial threat that a person will suffer such harm at a later date if the lawyer fails to take action necessary to eliminate the threat.[77]

It may also be appropriate to seek the appointment of a guardian ad litem or attorney for the child or children.[78] The entire thrust of the family law system is intended to make the child's well-being the highest priority. The vindictiveness of a parent, the ineffective legal representation of the spouse, or the failure of the court to perceive on its own the need to protect the child's interests do not justify an attorney's failure to act. However, even the appointment of a guardian or lawyer for the child is insufficient if the matrimonial lawyer is aware of physical abuse or similarly extreme parental deficiency. Nor would withdrawal (even if permitted) solve the problem if the attorney is convinced that the child will suffer adverse treatment by the client.

6.6 ***An attorney should not make or assist a client in making an allegation of child abuse unless there is a reasonable basis and evidence to believe it is true.***

Comment

An attorney who is made aware of abuse by a party (or someone closely associated with a party) is permitted, if not obligated, to provide that information during divorce or custody proceedings (see **6.5**). While reporting the existence of child abuse is crucial, however, a claim that a parent has abused a child is ugly and leads to the most unpleasant and harmful litigation in the field of family law. Such claims draw the child into testing or some other form of examination, which itself may be traumatic. The harm to both the accusing and accused parent will almost always be very great.

---

77. *See also* Restatement of the Law Third, The Law Governing Lawyers, Proposed Final Draft No.2 §117A (ALI 1998).

78. In some jurisdictions, however, such an effort might be prohibited as conduct adverse to the client and based on confidential information.

Desperate or angry spouses sometimes cannot resist the temptation to use such a strong weapon as an abuse charge. Use of such charges to obtain an unfair advantage in the dispute is inexcusable. If a client insists on making such a claim that the lawyer believes unjustified, the lawyer should withdraw from further representation. The lawyer should use all available information and resources—including evaluation by a doctor, therapist, or other health professional—to be sure there is a reasonable basis and substantial supporting evidence for such a charge. Even when the allegation is believed to be justified, it should be made in a manner least harmful to any children and least likely to inflame the dispute.

7. Professional Cooperation and the Administration of Justice

Candor, courtesy and cooperation are especially important in matrimonial matters where a high emotional level can engulf the attorneys, the court and the parties. Allowing the adverse emotional climate to infect the relations between the attorneys and parties inevitably harms everyone, including the clients, their children and other family members. Although lawyers cannot ensure that justice is achieved, they can help facilitate the administration of justice.

Combative, discourteous, abrasive, "hard ball" conduct by matrimonial lawyers is inconsistent with both their obligation to effectively represent their clients and their role as problem-solvers. Good matrimonial lawyers can be cordial and friendly without diminishing effective advocacy on behalf of their clients. In fact, candor, courtesy and cooperation: (1) facilitate faster, less costly and mutually accepted resolution of disputes; (2) reduce stress for lawyers, staff and clients; (3) reduce waste of judicial time; and (4) generate respect for the court system, the individual attorney and the profession as a whole.

7.1 An attorney should strive to lower the emotional level of marital disputes by treating counsel and the parties with respect.

Comment

Some clients expect and want the matrimonial lawyer to reflect the highly emotional, vengeful relationship between the spouses. The attorney should explain to the client that discourteous or uncivil conduct is inappropriate and counterproductive, that measures of respect are consistent with competent and ethical representation of the client, and that it is unprofessional for the attorney to act otherwise.

Ideally, the relationship between counsel is that of colleagues using constructive problem-solving techniques to settle their respective clients' disputes consistent with the realistic objectives of each client. Examples of appropriate measures of respect include: cooperating with voluntary or court-mandated mediation; meeting with opposing counsel to reduce issues and facilitate settlement; promptly answering phone calls and correspondence; advising opposing counsel at the earliest possible time of any perceived conflict of interest; and refraining from attacking, demeaning or disparaging other counsel, the court or other parties.

The attorney should make sure that no long-standing adversarial relationship with or a personal feeling toward another attorney interferes with negotiations, the level of professionalism maintained, or effective representation of the client. Although it may be difficult to be courteous and cooperative when opposed by an overzealous lawyer, an attorney should not react in kind to unprofessional conduct. Pointing out the unprofessional conduct and requesting that it cease is appropriate.

7.2 *An attorney should stipulate to undisputed relevant matters, unless inconsistent with the client's legitimate interests. If the client's permission is required, the attorney should encourage the client to stipulate to undisputed matters.*

Comment

The attorneys' stipulation to undisputed matters avoids unnecessary inconvenience and wasted court time. The attorney seeking a stipulation should do so in writing, attempting to state the true agreement of the parties. Other counsel should promptly indicate whether or not the stipulation is acceptable.

7.3 *An attorney should not deceive or intentionally mislead other counsel.*

Comment

Attorneys should be able to rely on statements by other counsel. They should be able to assume that the matrimonial lawyer will correct any misimpression caused by an inaccurate or misleading prior statement by counsel or her client. Although an attorney must maintain the client's confidences, the duty of confidentiality does not require the attorney to deceive, or permit the client to deceive, other counsel.[79] When another party or counsel specifically requests

79. RPC 4.1 provides that a lawyer shall not knowingly: "(a) make a false statement of material fact or law to a third person; or (b) fail to disclose a material fact to a third per-

information which the attorney is not required to provide and which the attorney has been instructed to withhold or which may be detrimental to the client's interests, the attorney should refuse to provide the information, rather than mislead opposing counsel.

Examples

1. The matrimonial lawyer is approached by opposing counsel, who asks: "Although my client realizes there is no hope for reconciliation, he is desperate to know whether his wife is seeing another man. Is she?" The attorney knows that the wife has been having an affair. It would be proper for the attorney to indicate an unwillingness or inability to answer that question, but it would be improper either to suggest that the client has not had an affair, or to tell opposing counsel lurid details on the condition that they not be disclosed.[80]

2. The attorney believes that the opposing party has engaged in activity that the party would not want made public. It is improper to bluff the other side into settlement by hinting that the matrimonial lawyer will use damaging evidence of the conduct if that evidence does not exist. It is also improper to threaten public disclosure if the evidence exists, but would likely be inadmissible or irrelevant at trial.

7.4 An attorney should neither overstate the authority to settle nor represent that the attorney has authority that the client has not granted.

Comment

In either case presented in the Goal, the attorney has improperly induced reliance by other counsel that could damage the attorney-client relationship.

---

son when disclosure is necessary to avoid assisting a criminal or fraudulent act by a client, unless disclosure is prohibited by rule 1.6." As noted in the Comment to Goal 6.5, jurisdictions differ concerning the scope of the exception to the duty of confidentiality for client criminal conduct or fraud. An attorney may be permitted to reveal confidences necessary to avoid a future crime or fraud, and, in some jurisdictions, a past fraud committed during the course of the representation or with the lawyer's assistance. Even if a jurisdiction would not permit disclosure of past crimes or frauds, the attorney would be obligated to advise the client to rectify the fraud. If the client refuses, the attorney must withdraw from the representation. RPC 1.16(a); 8.4(c). *See* RPC 1.2 and ABA Comment: "A lawyer may not continue assisting a client in conduct that the lawyer originally supposes is legally proper but then discovers is criminal or fraudulent. Withdrawal from the representation, therefore, may be required."

80. *See* RPC 1.6.

A matrimonial lawyer who is uncertain of his authority—or simply does not believe that other counsel is entitled to know such information—should either truthfully disclose his uncertainty, or state that he is unwilling or unable to respond at all.

7.5 An attorney should not induce or rely on a mistake by counsel as to agreed upon matters to obtain an unfair benefit for the client.

Comment

The need for trust between attorneys, even those representing opposing sides in a dispute, requires more than simply avoiding fraudulent and intentionally deceitful conduct. Misunderstandings should be corrected and not relied upon in the hope that they will benefit the client. Thus, for example, the attorney reducing an oral agreement to writing not only should avoid misstating the understanding, but should correct inadvertent errors by other counsel that are inconsistent with prior understandings or agreements. Whether or not conduct or statements by counsel that are not necessarily in her client's best interests should be corrected may not always be clear and will depend on the particular facts of a case. The crucial consideration should be whether the attorney induced the misunderstanding or is aware that other counsel's statements do not accurately reflect any prior agreement. It is thus unlikely that tactical, evidentiary or legal errors made by opposing counsel at trial require correction.[81]

Examples

1. In an effort to compromise a dispute over maintenance (alimony), the parties agree that payments be made that are deductible by the husband and taxable to the wife. While reviewing the agreement, the attorney for the wife realizes that the language will not create the tax consequences both sides had assumed and will, in fact, benefit his client because the payments will be treated neither as deductible alimony to the husband nor taxable to the wife. The matrimonial lawyer should disclose this discovery to opposing counsel.

If, however, counsel's mistake goes to a matter not discussed and agreed upon—either explicitly or implicitly, the obligation to the client precludes disclosure of the mistake without the client's permission. Thus, if alimony was agreed upon without any discussion of tax consequences, the wife's lawyer would not

---

81. *But cf.* RPC 3.3(a)(3) (duty to disclose to the court "legal authority in the controlling jurisdiction known to the lawyer to be directly adverse to the position of the client and not disclosed by opposing counsel").

be obligated to provide the language necessary to make payments tax deductible by the husband and includable by the wife.

2. The lawyer for the wife prepares a stipulation erroneously providing for the termination of maintenance upon the remarriage of either party. If the husband asks his attorney if it is really true that by his remarriage he can terminate his liability to pay any further maintenance, the attorney should correct the mistake in the stipulation or a judgment entered upon it. The lawyer should bring it to the attention of opposing counsel.[82]

7.6 An attorney who receives materials that appear to be confidential should refrain from reviewing the materials and return them to the sender, as soon as it becomes clear they were inadvertently sent to the receiving lawyer.

Comment

There are many circumstances in which an attorney receives materials that were inadvertently sent by another attorney or party. Such instances have been increasing due to the use of e-mail, the ability to send simultaneous faxes to multiple persons, and the sheer volume of materials provided through discovery in complex cases. If the materials are not harmful or confidential, no issue is raised. If, however, the materials were not intended to be provided and contain confidential information, the temptation to use them to the client's benefit is great.

The courts' and ethics committees' treatment of inadvertent disclosure of confidential materials is not uniform. Some courts have followed the ABA Standing Committee approach (below) that the materials should be returned unread. Other courts have taken the position that any unforced disclosure of attorney-client privileged communications destroys confidentiality and terminates the privilege, not only for the communications disclosed, but also for all related communications.[83]

A number of courts have taken an intermediate approach, holding that the right of receiving counsel to make use of inadvertently sent materials depends on a number of factors. For example, one court indicated that it would look

---

82. *See* RPC 4.1; 8.4.

83. *See, e.g., In re* Sealed Case, 877 F.2d 976, 980 (D.C. Cir. 1989): "[I]f a client wishes to preserve the privilege, it must treat the confidentiality of attorney-client communications like jewels—if not crown jewels. Short of court compelled disclosure, [citation omitted] or equally extraordinary circumstances, we will not distinguish between various degrees of 'voluntariness' in waivers of attorney-client privilege."

to five factors in determining whether a document had lost its privilege: "(1) The reasonableness of the precautions taken to prevent inadvertent disclosure in view of the extent of the document production; (2) the number of inadvertent disclosures; (3) the extent of the disclosure; (3) any delay and measures taken to rectify the disclosures; (5) whether the overriding interests of justice would be served by relieving the party of its error."[84]

Regardless of how courts might resolve the issue of the extent to which voluntary (though unintended) disclosure waives confidentiality for purposes of attorney-client privilege, the *ethical* issue concerning the proper conduct of the receiving attorney remains. This Goal is consistent with ABA Formal Opinions in providing that once the inadvertence is discovered, the receiving attorney should not further examine the materials and should return them to the sending lawyer.[85]

In providing that the receiving lawyer was ethically obligated to return inadvertently sent confidential materials, the ABA Committee relied on the following factors: "(i) the importance the Model Rules give to maintaining client confidentiality, (ii) the law governing waiver of the attorney-client privilege, (iii) the law governing missent property, (iv) the similarity between the circumstances here addressed and other conduct the profession universally condemns, and (v) the receiving lawyer's obligations to his client."

This Goal is also consistent with 7.5 that an attorney should not rely on a mistake by opposing counsel, but should instead correct inadvertent errors. And, since the decision whether to rely on inadvertent errors by another counsel is one of "means," the error is "appropriate for correction between the lawyers without client consultation."[86]

---

84. Hartman v. El Paso Natural Gas Co., 107 N.M. 679, 763 P.2d 1144, 1152 (1988). *See also* Mendenhall v. Barber-Greene Co., 531 F.Supp. 951, 959 (N.D. Ill. 1982): "Mendenhall's lawyer (not trial counsel) might well have been negligent in failing to cull the files of the letters before turning over the files. But if we are serious about the attorney-client privilege and its relation to the client's welfare, we should require more than such negligence by counsel before the client can be deemed to have given up the privilege."

85. ABA Formal Opinion 92-368 (1992) provides that once the inadvertence is discovered, the receiving attorney should notify the sending lawyer of receipt of the documents and should abide by that lawyer's instructions as to their disposition. See also ABA Formal Opinion 94-382 (1994).

86. ABA Formal Opinion 92-368 (1992). The ABA Committee relied on the following analysis from Informal Opinion 86-1518 (1986) (Notice to Opposing Counsel of Inadvertent Omission of Contract Provision) as equally applicable to the inadvertent receipt of confidential materials:

The opinion concluded that "[the sending client's] lawyer had no duty to notify [the sending client] of the error under Model Rule 1.4 because the client has no decision to make. Nor was the lawyer barred by the confidentiality provisions of Model Rule 1.6 from

Examples

1. The wife's lawyer receives an e-mail addressed to the husband from the husband's lawyer. In many cases that would be sufficient to indicate that the wife's lawyer was an unintended recipient. If, however, the receiving lawyer has a reasonable basis to believe a copy was intended for him, he may read the message unless and until it becomes evident that the message was unintentionally sent to him.
2. The lawyer for the husband has sought discovery of numerous documents from the wife relating to issues in the case. In response to the document request, the wife's attorney sends over ten large boxes of materials. While reviewing the documents, the husband's lawyer discovers in a seemingly unrelated file, a letter from the wife's attorney to the wife that begins: "As to your question about your use of drugs prior to your marriage to Husband...." Unless the husband's lawyer has a reasonable basis to believe the letter was provided intentionally, was relevant, and was not otherwise confidential, the lawyer should stop reading and return the letter to the wife's attorney.

7.7 An attorney may use materials intentionally sent from an unknown or unauthorized source unless the materials appear to be confidential. Confidential materials should be deposited with the court and a ruling sought.

Comment

Attorneys occasionally receive papers from outside of the expected sources. Such materials may have been sent anonymously. The materials should be treated differently depending on both their source (if known) and apparent nature.

Clearly confidential or privileged material, regardless of the sender, should be returned to the other lawyer, preferably unread. If the materials are the subject of a proper discovery request but were improperly withheld, the receiving

---

informing the other side because this disclosure was "impliedly authorized" by the representation. Because under Model Rule 1.2 the lawyer has the authority to decide the technical means to carry out the representation and because the client's right under the same Model Rule to committed and dedicated representation is not unlimited, the opinion concluded that the "error is appropriate for correction between the lawyers without client consultation.".... While Informal Opinion 86-1516 is not on all fours with the instant situation, its charitable view toward inadvertence, its unwillingness to permit parties to capitalize on errors, its recognition of a limitation on client decision-making authority and its respect for the role of counsel all support the position advanced in this opinion as to counsel's proper conduct upon the inadvertent receipt of confidential information.

lawyer should deposit them with the court and seek a ruling as to their proper disposition.[87]

Documents not clearly confidential may be used by the receiving attorney. For example, a lawyer receiving an unmarked envelope containing statements of undisclosed accounts in the name of the other party may use the materials. A receiving lawyer who believes the materials were intentionally withheld from a response to a proper discovery request should report the fraud to the court.

7.8 An attorney should cooperate in the exchange of information and documents. An attorney should not use the discovery process for delay or harassment, or engage in obstructionist tactics.

Comment

As a basic rule of courtesy and cooperation, attorneys should try to conduct all discovery by agreement, never using the discovery process to harass other counsel or their clients. This principle applies both to attorneys attempting to obtain discovery and to those from whom discovery is sought.[88] The discovery rules are designed to eliminate or reduce unfair surprise, excessive delay and expense, unnecessary and futile litigation, and the emotional and financial cost of extended and overly adversarial litigation. In addition, pretrial discovery often results in settlements more beneficial than protracted litigation. In no area of the law are these benefits more important than in matrimonial law, where the necessity of future dealings between the parties and the interest in protecting the emotional and psychological stability of chil-

---

87. ABA Formal Opinion 94-382 (1994) deals with the situation where the confidential materials were intentionally sent by a person not authorized to send them. For the most part, the Committee applied the same analysis as in Formal Op. 92-368 (1992) (discussed in the Comment to Goal 7.6). However, the opinion indicates that if the receiving lawyer has a legitimate claim that the documents should have been, but were not, produced by an adverse party in response to pending discovery requests, the receiving lawyer may seek to obtain from a court a definitive resolution of the proper disposition of the materials. *See, e.g., In re* Shell, 1992 W.L. 275426 (E.D. La. 1992) (ordering that such documents not be used by receiving party unless they "were the subject of a proper discovery request and were improperly withheld by adverse parties").

88. *Cf.* RPC 3.4(d). Protection of the client and sound pretrial practice often dictate that information be obtained under oath. Nothing in this Goal or Comment is intended to suggest that cooperation in the exchange of information should be informal when that is not appropriate.

dren necessitate avoiding unnecessary litigation and acrimony. It is in the interest of all parties (including the client) to assist, rather than resist, legitimate discovery.

Consistent with this view of discovery in family law cases as information gathering rather than as adversarial weapon, a number of jurisdictions have now adopted codes of professional courtesy and have imposed mandatory disclosure requirements on all divorcing spouses.[89] In many states the fiduciary responsibility for interspousal disclosure is confirmed explicitly by statute, rule, or in approved discovery request forms.[90]

It is in the interest of all counsel and the parties to avoid improper tactics. In a misguided effort to advance the interests of their clients, attorneys may be tempted to wear down the opposing party or counsel by means of oppressive "hardball" discovery tactics. These tactics do not advance the *legitimate* interests of clients and are clearly improper. Improper discovery conduct under this Goal includes: avoidance of compliance with discovery through overly narrow construction of interrogatories or requests for production; objection to discovery without good faith basis; improper assertion of privilege; production of documents in a manner designed to hide or obscure the existence of particular documents; direction to parties and witnesses not to respond to deposition questions without adequate justification; requests for unnecessary information that does not bear on the issues in the case; and requests for sanctions before making a good faith effort to resolve legitimate discovery disputes.

Counsel's behavior during depositions is as important as behavior before the court. Because most cases are settled rather than tried to a court, the deposition process may be a party's only measure of acceptable behavior when solving the problems of the parties, currently and in the future. Attorneys therefore should conduct themselves in deposition with the same courtesy and respect for the legal process as is expected in court. For example, they should not conduct examinations or engage in other behavior that is purposely offensive, demeaning, harassing, intimidating, or that unnecessarily invades the privacy of anyone. Attorneys should attempt to minimize arguments during deposition, and if sensitive or controversial matters are to be the subject of deposition questioning, when not contrary to the client's interests, the deposing

89. *See, e.g.*, Colo. R. Civ. P. 26.2; Ann. Cal. Fam. Code §721 (1998); E.D. Wis. Local Rule 7.07; D. Ariz. Rule 2.5 (requiring use of uniform interrogatories).

90. *See, e.g.*, Colo. R. Civ. P. 33 and 34; Ann. Cal. Fam. Code §721 (1998); E.D. Wis. Local Rule 7.07.

attorney should consider discussing such matters in advance to reach any appropriate agreements.

With the focus of discovery being the legitimate pursuit of information rather than strategic confrontation, attorneys should not coach deponents by objecting, commenting, or otherwise acting in a manner that suggests a particular answer to a question, or object for the purpose of disrupting or distracting the questioner or witness. Objections should only be made in the manner and on grounds provided by applicable court rules. Attorneys should not intentionally misstate facts, prior statements or testimony. Such conduct increases the animosity without legitimate purpose.

Although not required under this Goal, the Fellows of the Academy believe that a *mandatory* disclosure provision would best promote the cooperative, problem-solving approach of the Bounds of Advocacy. Therefore, the Academy recommends adoption in each state of a mandatory discovery provision.[91]

7.9 An attorney should grant to other counsel reasonable extensions of time that will not have a material, adverse effect on the legitimate interests of the client.

Comment

The attorney should attempt to accommodate counsel who, because of schedule, personal considerations, or heavy workload, requests additional time to prepare a response or comply with a legal requirement. Such accommodations save the time and expense of unnecessary motions and hearings. No lawyer should request an extension of time to obtain an unfair advantage.

7.10 An attorney should clear times with other counsel and cooperate in scheduling hearings and depositions.

Comment

Good faith attempts by attorneys to avoid scheduling conflicts tend to avoid unnecessary delays, expense to clients and stress to attorneys and their staff. In return, other counsel should confirm the availability of the suggested time within a reasonable period and should indicate conflicts or unavailability only when necessary. As prior consultation concerning scheduling is a courtesy measure, it is proper to schedule hearings or depositions without agreement

---

91. *See, e.g.*, Colo. R. Civ. P. 26.2; E.D. Wis. Local Rule 7.07.

if other counsel fails or refuses to respond promptly to the time offered, raises unreasonable calendar conflicts or objections, or persistently fails to comply with this Goal.

7.11 An attorney should provide notice of cancellation of depositions and hearings at the earliest possible time.

Comment

Adherence to this Goal will avoid unnecessary travel, expense and expenditure of time by other counsel, and will also free time for the court for other matters. The same principles apply to all scheduled meetings, conferences and production sessions with other counsel.

7.12 An attorney should submit proposed orders promptly to other counsel before submitting them to the court. When submitted, other counsel should promptly communicate approval or objections.

Comment

Proposed orders following a hearing should generally be submitted at the earliest practicable time.

7.13 An attorney should not seek an ex parte *order without prior notice to other counsel except in exigent circumstances.*

Comment

There are few things more damaging to a client's confidence in his lawyer, or to relationships between lawyers, than for a party to be served with an *ex parte* order about which his lawyer knows nothing.[92] Even where there are exigent circumstances (substantial physical or financial risk to the client), or where local rules permit *ex parte* proceedings, notice to, or the appearance of, other counsel usually will not be able to prevent appropriate relief from issuing.

---

92. Even when authorized by law, *ex parte* proceedings present the potential for unfairness since "there is no balance of presentation by opposing advocates." ABA Comment, RPC 3.3(d). The lawyer for the represented party has a duty to make disclosure of "material facts known to the lawyer which will enable the tribunal to make an informed decision, whether or not the facts are adverse." RPC 3.3(d). Fairness and professional courtesy call for notice to other counsel as well.

7.14 An attorney should not attempt to gain advantage by delay in the service of filed pleadings or correspondence upon other counsel.

Comment

When pleadings or correspondence are mailed or delivered to the court, copies should normally be transmitted on the same day and in the same manner to all other counsel of record. An identical method need not be employed, so long as delivery on the same day will be achieved. For example, if the court is one block from counsel's office and opposing counsel's office is 50 miles away, it would be acceptable to hand deliver a document to the court and to fax it to counsel so that it arrived on the same day.

Attorney as Mediator or Arbitrator

8. Mediator

8.1 An attorney should act as a mediator only if competent to do so.

Comment

No lawyer should act as the mediator of marital disputes without adequate education, training or experience.[93] There are many ways to acquire the necessary knowledge and skill, including law school training programs, AAML mediation training certification, continuing legal education, formal training programs, and informal training by peers. The neutral role as mediator involves different skills and orientation than the matrimonial lawyer's role in representing clients, and to act competently as mediator requires study and training.

A matrimonial lawyer may be a better mediator because the lawyer may be in the best position to understand the likely outcome of litigation and is best able to ensure the understanding and validity of a mediated agreement. Mediation involves skills that, like trial advocacy, require study and training.

---

93. *See* Draft Standards of Practice for Lawyer Mediators in Family Disputes (preamble) (ABA 1986); Standards of Conduct for Mediators IV (Americcan Arbitration Assn., ABA, and Society of Professionals in Dispute Resolution, 1994). It is assumed in this Standard that the attorney does not represent either of the parties to the dispute. *Cf.* RPC 2.2 (intermediaries).

8.2 An attorney acting as a mediator in a marital dispute should remain impartial.

Comment

The primary responsibility for resolution of a marital dispute rests with the participants. A neutral person trying to help people resolve disputes in an amicable way should help the parties reach an informed and voluntary settlement. At no time should a mediator coerce a participant into agreement or make a substantive decision for a participant. The mediator should remain completely impartial in assisting the participants in reaching agreement, permitting neither manipulative nor intimidating practices. If the mediator suspects that any of the participants are not capable of participating in informed negotiations, the mediator should postpone mediation and refer those participants to appropriate resources.

Although the mediator should not have a vested interest in any particular terms of a settlement, the mediator should "be satisfied that agreements in which he or she has participated will not impugn the integrity of the process"[94] and are fundamentally fair. If the mediator is "concerned about the possible consequences of a proposed agreement, and the needs of the parties dictate, the [mediator] must inform the parties of that concern. In adhering to this Standard, the [mediator] may find it advisable to educate the parties, to refer one or more of the parties for specialized advice, or to withdraw from the case."[95] The mediator should assist the clients not only in treating each other fairly, but also in considering the interests of unrepresented parties, and in particular the interests of their children. Thus, Standard VII.B. of the Academy of Family Mediators' Standards of Practice for Divorce and Family Mediation provides: "The mediator has a responsibility to promote the participants' consideration of the interests of children and other persons affected by the agreement. The mediator also has a duty to assist parents to examine, apart from their own desires, the separate and individual needs of such people."

---

94. Society of Professionals in Dispute Resolution, Ethical Standards of Professional Responsibility, Standard 6 (1986).

95. Donald T. Weckstein, *In Praise of Party Empowerment—And of Mediator Activism*, 33 Willamette L. Rev. 501, 537 (1997).

8.3 *An attorney acting as a mediator in a marital dispute should urge each party to obtain independent legal advice.*

Comment

At the outset, the mediator should encourage both parties to obtain independent legal advice. Doing so will help ensure that the participants have the opportunity to understand the implications and ramifications of available options. Parties in mediation who have consulting attorneys have the benefit of advice focused on their own interests and can participate with more confidence in the process. Review of a proposed mediated settlement agreement with a party's consulting attorney affords that party the opportunity to reflect on the fairness of the agreement before signing it and helps ensure that the party understands the agreement and enters into it voluntarily.

8.4 *An attorney acting as a mediator in a marital dispute should only give advice that will enable the parties to make reasonably informed decisions.*

Comment

The mediator should have the knowledge and experience necessary to provide relevant information and advice to help the participants make reasonable, informed decisions.[96] Participants informed about applicable legal principles are able to make thoughtful decisions to resolve their disputes. Some information, such as the tax consequences of certain transactions, legal principles about the characterization of assets, and the need for formal parenting plans, is neutral and beneficial to both parties. A mediator with sufficient experience and expertise may provide such information. Otherwise, the mediator should assist the participants in obtaining expert information when such information is necessary for an informed agreement.[97]

---

96. "The mediator may provide information about the process, raise issues, and help parties explore options. The primary role of the mediator is to facilitate a voluntary resolution of a dispute. Parties shall be given the opportunity to consider all proposed options." American Arbitration Association/American Bar Association/Society of Professionals in Dispute Resolution, Model Standards of Conduct for Mediators, Comment to Standard I. (1995).

97. "A mediator cannot personally ensure that each party has made a fully informed choice to reach a particular agreement, but it is a good practice for the mediator to make the parties aware of the importance of consulting other professionals, where appropriate, to help them make informed decisions." *Id.*

The extent to which a mediator should provide *advice* (as opposed to information) is a controversial issue.[98] On the one hand, it is difficult for the mediator to maintain impartiality while providing advice to one of the participants. Also, in some circumstances providing advice might be seen as constituting legal representation, which is inappropriate for a mediator and might bring into play the conflict of interest rules.[99] There is the danger that the participants will perceive advice from the mediator as a directive that they must follow. On the other hand, the participants may be unable to make informed decisions without some guidance. They may seek that guidance from a lawyer-mediator rather than obtain outside expert advice on every issue that arises. Such advice may be necessary to ensure that the rights and legitimate interests of the participants and their children have been dealt with in a fair and informed manner.

Guidelines attempting to distinguish between providing permissible information and impermissible advice appear largely semantic and virtually unenforceable. And, to the extent that they prohibit advice that would assist the participants in making informed, fair decisions, such rules are undesirable from a policy standpoint. Therefore, this Goal provides that it is permissible for a mediator to provide advice under the following guidelines.[100]

---

98. *See, e.g.*, AMERICAN BAR ASSOCIATION FAMILY LAW SECTION TASK FORCE, Standard VII E. (July 1997): "The mediator should facilitate the parties' understanding of the applicable doctrines and practices of family law before reaching an agreement. The mediator may define the legal issues that may influence the parties' resolution of their dispute, but should refrain from giving the parties legal advice based upon the mediator's interpretation of the law as applied to the facts of their situation."

99. *See, e.g.*, RPC 2.2 (intermediation).

100. *See* Donald T. Weckstein, *In Praise of Party Empowerment—And of Mediator Activism*, 33 Willamette L. Rev. 501 (1997):

[It] is important to note that the accepted definitions of mediation do not preclude the mediator from offering suggestions, recommendations, opinions, information, predictions, or even advice and proposals. The key criterion is a mediator's facilitation of self-determination by the disputants. Rather than interfering with the self-determination of parties to resolve their own dispute, activist interventions by the mediator may enhance the parties' empowerment by educating them and by aiding their realistic understanding of the alternatives to agreement. It is imperative, however, that in employing activist interventions, the mediator not attempt to decide the dispute, direct a resolution, or coerce the parties into accepting a solution. For the process to remain a mediation, the parties must retain their power to reject the mediator's analysis or information. Therefore, the mediator's activist intervention must be offered only as an educational aid to give the parties a better information base on which to reach or reject voluntary agreement.

See also Robert B. Moberly, *Mediator Gag Rules: Is it Ethical for Mediators to Evaluate or Advise?*, 38 S. Tex. L. Rev. 669, 672 (1997) ("If a mediator decides to evaluate, I argue that he or she ought to be required to provide the parties with information sufficient for them

A mediator choosing to provide advice or evaluation should tell the participants they are free to reject it.[101] "Evaluations, particularly of a predictive nature, generally should be resorted to only after other more facilitative measures have failed to break an impasse."[102] The mediator should, if possible, offer suggestions in the guise of questions, rather than definitive statements, because doing so is less coercive.[103]

Whether a mediator should provide advice may depend on the information provided to the participants at the start of the mediation. At the outset, the mediator should explain to the parties the different roles of lawyers and mediators, the desirability of consulting independent legal advice, the risks of reaching an agreement without such advice, and the inapplicability of the lawyer-client privilege.[104] The mediator should provide in writing to all participants a statement such as the following:

1. Although I am a lawyer, I am not acting as a lawyer for either of you. You are not my clients. I do not represent either of you. I will help you reach a fair,

---

to make reasonably informed decisions about their rights and responsibilities"); comments of Leonard Riskin in Symposium, *Standards of Professional Conduct in Alternative Dispute Resolution,* 1995 J. Disp. Resol. 95, 100 (1995) ("if the parties intelligently decide that they want the narrow evaluative mediation, ... the mediator ought to evaluate and it's ethical ... evaluation can enhance self-determination."). John Feerick, Chair of the AAA/ABA/SPIDR Standards Commission, has stated that the Commission's draft standards "do not prohibit mediators from taking on an evaluative role per se in mediation," although he cautions against a "loss of neutrality in the process." John D. Feerick, *Standards of Conduct for Mediator and Annotated Comparisons,* 38 S. Tex. L. Rev. 455, 459 (1997). And the director of a law school mediation clinic states: "I think it is misguided to argue that a mediator with knowledge of the law should not share her knowledge with the parties in a law-based mediation—especially if the parties are pro-se.... When settling their disputes, disputants must be permitted to invoke legal norms if they choose to, and the mediator must take steps to ensure that the parties' choices are knowing and informed." James H. Stark, *Preliminary Reflections on the Establishment of a Mediation Clinic,* 2 Clinical L. Rev. 457, 487 (1996). *See* Nancy H. Rogers & Craig A. McEwen, Mediation: Law, Practice, Policy, Ch.10 at pp.12–13 (1994) ("advice" may be given in a nonpartisan way; and providing only "information" may harm a participant if it is wrong, incomplete, or given in a manner that in reality or appearance detracts from impartiality).

101. "The mediator may ... offer opinions about the strengths and weaknesses of a case.... It is acceptable for the mediator to suggest options in response to parties' requests, but not to coerce the parties to accept any particular option." Order of the Supreme Court of Minnesota Promulgating Amendments to the Minnesota General Rules of Practice (Aug. 8, 1997).

102. Weckstein, *supra* note 101, at 552.

103. *Id.* at 520.

104. *Cf.* RPC 2.2.

informed agreement. I will give you advice about how the law might affect your decisions and aspects of your agreement, but I will not favor either of your interests, or provide advice that is beneficial to one of you but detrimental to other participants.

2. You should obtain independent advice from someone who is looking out only for your interests. You should consult your own attorney before signing any agreement reached during this mediation.

3. I cannot act as a lawyer for either of you during the course of the mediation, even for unrelated matters. After the mediation is completed, I will not be able to act as a lawyer for either of you as to any issues involved in the mediation.

9. Arbitrator

9.1 An attorney should act as an arbitrator only if competent to do so.

Comment

No lawyer should act as the arbitrator of marital disputes without adequate education and training.[105] There are many ways to acquire the necessary knowledge of arbitration and skill as an arbitrator, including law school training programs, AAML arbitration training workshops, continuing legal education, formal training programs, and experience as an arbitrator in other areas of the law. A matrimonial lawyer is likely to be a better arbitrator of matrimonial disputes than nonlawyers or lawyers who practice in different fields because of the matrimonial lawyer's understanding of the nuances of family law and experience with the likely outcome of matrimonial litigation.

9.2 An attorney acting as an arbitrator should comply with all relevant rules applicable to judges, including the Code of Judicial Conduct.

Comment

Because arbitrators act in a quasi-judicial role, they have been afforded immunity protection akin to that of judges. Judicial immunity protects judges to the extent that they " … are not liable to civil actions for the[ir] judicial acts, even when such acts are in excess of their jurisdiction, and are alleged to have

---

105. *See, e.g.*, Code of Professional Responsibility for Arbitrators of Labor-Management Disputes, §§B.1 & C.1.a (Nat'l Academy of Arbitrators, American Arbitration Assn., Federal Mediation and Conciliation Service) (hereafter "CPR for Arbitrators"); Code of Ethics for Arbitrators in Commercial Disputes IV.B. (American Arbitration Assn., ABA Special Comm., 1977) (hereafter "Code of Ethics for Arbitrators").

been done maliciously or corruptly."[106] In fact, the Court in *Stump v. Sparkman* went on to hold: "A judge will not be deprived of immunity because the action he took was in error, was done maliciously, or was in excess of his authority; rather, he will be subject to liability only when he has acted in the 'clear absence of all jurisdiction'."[107]

Arbitral immunity has its base in judicial immunity. The extension of judicial immunity to arbitrators began in the 1880's, and remains firmly a part of our jurisprudence. In 1884, the principle of arbitral immunity was eloquently articulated: "an arbitrator is a quasijudicial officer under our laws, exercising judicial functions. There is as much reason in his case for protecting and insuring his impartiality, independence and freedom from undue influence, as in the case of a judge or juror."[108]

Whereas mediators are treated more like attorneys for conflict of interest analysis, arbitrators are treated more like judges.[109] This distinction is important because judges are generally held to a higher ethical standard than attorneys. For example, the former CPR admonition to avoid even the appearance of impropriety (Canon 9) has been deleted from the RPC.[110] Under Canon 2 of the CJC, however, a *judge* "should avoid impropriety and the appearance of impropriety in all of the judge's activities."[111]

Therefore, an attorney requested to serve as an arbitrator in a matrimonial proceeding may wish to consider some actions not necessarily routinely done in the role of an advocate. For example, disclosure of any prior relationship, social or professional, with any of the parties, attorneys or witnesses will increase the confidence of the participants in the objectivity of the arbitrator.[112] Any conflict of interest that exists at the inception of the arbitration, or that

---

106. Stump v. Sparkman, 435 U.S. 349, 356, (1978).

107. *Id.*, 435 U.S. at 356–357.

108. Hoosac Tunnel Dock & Elevator Co. v. O'Brien, 137 Mass.424 (1884). *See also* Int'l Union United Auto Workers v. Greyhound Lines, Inc., 701 F.2d. 1181, 1186 (6th Cir, 1983); Claxarano v. Liebowitz, 550 F. Supp. 1389, 1390 (S.D. N. Y. 1982). *See generally*, Nolan & Abrams, Vol II, Industrial Relations Law Journal, number 2, p.228 (1989).

109. *See e.g.*, RPC 1.12 ("Former Judge or Arbitrator").

110. *See* Comment to ABA MRPC 1.10.

111. *See* also CJC Canons 3(C)(1), 3(E)(1) ("A judge shall disqualify himself or herself in a proceeding in which the judge's impartiality might reasonably be questioned") (1990); CPR for Arbitrators 2.B.3 ("might reasonably raise a question as to the arbitrator's impartiality"). An analysis of the CJC as it applies to arbitrators can be found in J. Lapinski & A. Jorgensen, *Arbitrator's Ethics—The Role of the Judicial Code of Ethics in Arbitration,* 13 Arb. Q. of the NW 18 (1992).

112. *See* CPR for Arbitrators §2.B; Code of Ethics for Arbitrators Canon II.A.(1)&(2). See also Nassau County (New York) Ethics Op. No. 89-16 (1989) (lawyer-arbitrator who has

comes into existence during the proceedings should also be disclosed. In addition, unless all parties consent after disclosure, a former arbitrator may not subsequently represent anyone in connection with the matter in which he or she "participated personally and substantially."[113] Care should be taken to decide only those matters included in the arbitration agreement or other document referring the matter to arbitration. Like judges, arbitrators should be cautions about participating in settlement discussions because the appearance of objectivity may be lost even if the arbitrator in fact remains uninfluenced by the positions taken by the parties in settlement discussions.

---

previously arbitrated a dispute involving one of the parties in a present dispute should disclose the prior dealing).

113. RPC 1.12(a).

Appendix B

Guidelines for Georgia's Attorney Guardians *Ad Litem* in Child Deprivation Cases (2000)

These Guidelines were developed in partnership with the American Bar Association Center for Children and the Law and the Georgia Supreme Court Child Placement Project. The full text of the report accompanying these guidelines is available online at http://www.childwelfare.net/mrb/projects/gal_guide.html

The Three Main Areas of Focus for the Georgia Guidelines

1) Every child should be represented in all deprivation cases at each stage from the initial removal to permanency.

2) One attorney GAL should be assigned per family through permanency, with active and continued involvement in the case until permanency is achieved.

3) Communication must be improved among all groups/stakeholders, with defined roles for all the participants.

Specific Guidelines for Each Hearing Stage

Preparation and Organization for Cases

In addition to Georgia law, the GAL should be knowledgeable of the following to be effective:

- DFCS policies and procedures;
- Basic child development/attachment issues;
- Legal proceedings surrounding GAL issues;
- Federal regulations relating to DFCS and foster care;
- Adoption process/benefits available;
- Substance abuse, addiction, and recovery stages;
- Basic child abuse tenets:

1) standards for interview process,
2) cycles of abuse,
3) basic psychology of victim behavior.

GAL should keep a file with the following contents:

- All pleadings;
- Interview notes;
- Hearing notes;
- Copies of all exhibits submitted at hearings or in court;
- Copies of all court orders;
- Copies of the home study, caseplans, health and psychological reports, CASA reports, and school reports.

The GAL should maintain the file in such a way that a new GAL could pick up representation of child immediately, if necessary.

Complaint

The complaint is the first document filed with the court to initiate a deprivation case. The complaint will allege abuse or neglect of a child or children. It is generally filed by a Department of Family and Children Services (DFCS) caseworker, although complaints may be filed by any person against a child's primary caretaker. While we recognize that some counties do not appoint GALs at the complaint stage, courts are urged to appoint GALs as early as possible to these cases to best protect children.

In some jurisdictions, the actions in the lists will be handled by other participants, particularly DFCS or court staff. They are included in the GAL list because it is in the best interests of the child that these actions be taken, and if no one else takes the initiative, the GAL should at least raise the issue.

When a complaint is filed, the GAL should or make sure the following is done:

- Strive to be appointed as the child representative before 72-hour hearing;
- Identify and investigate parents of the child;
- Identify which parties, if any, should receive service by publication if the case proceeds to the adjudicatory hearing;
- Read any available reports (e.g., police, DFCS intake, psychological evaluation);
- Interview appropriate parties first, then make contact with the child;
- Provide business card or contact information to the child and all relevant parties;
- Explore any record of prior involvement with this child or child's family;
- Identify issues for the 72-hour hearing;

- Obtain a copy of the complaint;
- Check to see if any extended family members are available, willing, and/or appropriate to take custody;
- Investigate and identify preventive services and diversion;
- Look for prior DFCS records.

72–Hour Hearing

This emergency hearing is held within 72 hours of a child's removal from the home. It is critical that this hearing be timely and thorough. Time is of the essence in child abuse and neglect cases, and any opportunity to prevent a child's case from continuing its path into the system should be seized. Once a child is removed from the home, it becomes logistically and practically more difficult to help a family resolve its problems; thus, all guidelines developed for this hearing seek to prevent the child from unnecessarily entering the system and to ensure faster permanency for the child who does enter the system.

At the 72-hour hearing, the GAL should do or should make sure the following is done:

- Raise the issue of failed or successful attempts to provide reasonable notice to all parties, including father(s);
- Identify/verify parties, including the parents with current addresses, contact numbers, and Social Security numbers;
- Request a copy of all previous orders, such as substance abuse, child support, paternity tests, if appropriate;
- Begin identifying and investigating services, preventive measures, extended family, home studies of relatives and psychological evaluations;
- Assist with finding temporary placement, if appropriate;
- If a putative father is available, aid him in understanding and then assuming his role in the proceedings, advise as to legitimation procedure or paternity testing, when appropriate;
- Determine if anyone has ordered a birth certificate; if no one has done so, request one;
- Confirm that the parents received notice of their right to legal representation, with separate representation for each parent, when necessary;
- Once the putative father has representation, explore the issues of involvement with the child, child support, extended family support and the question of terminating or surrendering rights to child/ren, if appropriate;
- Ask for an appointment of a CASA, when appropriate, and identify what issues the CASA will be addressing;
- Fully inquire into visitation options, when appropriate;

- Fully inquire into whether any criminal charges exist arising from the incident which may have brought the child into care;
- Start the process of building the record;
- When there are multiple children, ensure that each is represented without any conflict of interest;
- Ask, on record, if the agency will file a petition;
- Ask, on record, for the GAL to be involved in development of the 30-day caseplan;
- Request the date for the adjudicatory hearing;
- Following the 72-hour hearing, follow up on the outcome and next steps for the case.

Caseplan

The caseplan is the roadmap for how the case should proceed for the future. It is a document created by the caseworker and submitted to the court for approval. Once approved, the document resides in both the court and DFCS case file as well as going to the parent(s). The caseplan lays out what has to be done to resolve this case. It should be created, when appropriate, in participation with the parent(s) of the child. The caseplan will be reviewed every 3 to 6 months. Optimally, it should be distributed at the end of the dispositional hearing; however, DFCS has 30 days after that hearing to get a copy to the parents.

For the caseplan, the GAL should do or should make sure the following is done:

- Make recommendations for the caseplan, as appropriate;
- Receive notice of caseplan family conference or meeting;
- Request scheduling of this meeting at 72-hour hearing;
- Attend the caseplan meeting or, if attendance is not possible, send a designee;
- Receive or request a copy of the caseplan;
- Ensure that the caseplan relates to reasons for removal;
- Ensure that the findings of fact relate to the caseplan;
- Ensure that the steps relate to the caseplan problems and goals;
- Ensure that the caseplan reflects timelines and details for who is personally responsible under each provision of the caseplan;
- Ensure every goal and step is clearly defined;
- Sign off on the caseplan.

Petition

The petition is a document outlining the facts and allegations of the deprivation case. The petition is filed by the DFCS representative or the petitioner in preparation for the adjudicatory hearing. If the child is removed from the parents, the petition must be filed within 5 days after the 72-hour hearing.

For the petition, the GAL should do or should make sure the following is done:

- Review petition for content;
- Find out what witnesses are going to be present;
- Urge the agency to file the petition, when appropriate;
- If agency does not file a petition, consider filing a petition if necessary (note: if petition is filed by the GAL, one must request a new GAL due to a conflict of interest);
- If the petition is filed by the GAL, share appropriate information with the new GAL;
- Ask DFCS to file before a specified date, when appropriate.

Adjudicatory Hearing

The adjudicatory hearing is the trial of the facts. The outcome of adjudication controls whether the state may intervene over the objections of the family. The standard of proof is clear and convincing evidence.

For the pre-trial conference or prior to adjudicatory hearing, the GAL should do or should make sure the following is done:

- Request pre-trial conferences, when appropriate;
- Review first placement/best placement material, as applicable;
- At a minimum, meet with the child;
- Meet with the child's parent(s) with permission and with the parents' attorney present, if appropriate;
- At those meetings, reiterate your role and responsibilities for the child and the parent(s);
- When explaining your role to the child, use developmentally appropriate language;
- Review the petition;
- Investigate the allegations as they relate to the well-being of the child/ren;
- Identify and talk to all appropriate parties;
- Explore the extended family and other placement options;
- Develop recommendations for progress or resolution of the case;
- Work with the CASA volunteer by sharing information and concerns;
- Talk with the parent(s)' attorneys separately, if appropriate;
- Review the DFCS file and other materials such as school, medical, and child care records;
- If necessary, conduct formal discovery for the case to discover other materials such as school, medical, and child care records;
- Visit the child's home, if warranted, and visit the foster or relative placement home, using CASA or designee as appropriate;

- Issue subpoenas for witnesses, as needed, for trial;
- Where the child is a potential witness, work with the agency or SAAG to develop a strategy to minimize stress on the child;
- Inquire into the medical/psychological treatment for the parent(s) and child/ren, when appropriate;
- Request other process diversions, when appropriate, such as mediation or further pre-trial conferences;
- Observe, or have designee observe, the parent-child visit, when appropriate;
- Require the child to be present for all hearings unless excused in advance (note: if one is serving as the child's attorney, instead of GAL, the child must be present unless it would be detrimental to the child);
- Discuss the court process with the child.

At the adjudicatory hearing, the GAL should do or should make sure the following is done:

- Assure that if the child/client meets with the judge in chambers, the parent(s) have waived their right to be present;
- Contest any request for a continuance unless it is due to a legal reason, an unavoidable reason, or a continuance is in the best interest of the child;
- If using the child hearsay exception, be aware that the child may be subject to cross-examination and should be available to the court;
- Work with the agency to develop a strategy when the child is a potential witness;
- Explore alternative methods for the child to testify (e.g., video or closed circuit);
- Thoroughly examine all stipulations, address all issues of evidence, and ensure that the stipulations give support to an adequate caseplan;
- Call witnesses and/or issue subpoenas, when appropriate;
- Be prepared to cross-examine witnesses;
- Be prepared and willing to make objections;
- Make recommendations as needed;
- Provide admissible evidence (e.g., no hearsay unless using an exception, no ex parte communications, no contact with the judge by the GAL without others present or knowingly absent);
- Offer appropriate motions and/or objections to preserve issues for appeal;
- Actively consult with any lay guardian, designee, or CASA;
- Bring to the court's attention if child's wishes differ with best interests.

Dispositional Hearing

Disposition is the stage of the juvenile court process in which, after finding that the child is deprived and is within the jurisdiction of the court, the court determines who should have custody and control of the child. This hearing is usually held immediately following the adjudicatory hearing. All parties present at the adjudicatory hearing need to be present at the dispositional hearing.

At the dispositional hearing, the GAL should do or should make sure the following is done:

- Encourage and engage in appropriate concurrent planning;
- Offer input in final caseplan preparation;
- Review the caseplan to see if it is still appropriate in light of the adjudicatory hearing;
- Address the following issues: placement, services (e.g., transportation, parenting classes, housing, etc.), timeframes, medical needs, educational/IEP needs, and counseling needs;
- Address the following issues surrounding visitation: parents, siblings, others as appropriate, meaningful opportunities, time-frames, frequency, unsupervised visitation considered on an ad hoc basis, early start to visitation, and alternate resources for frequent visits (e.g., church, extended family, CASA, etc.);
- Work with other parties to facilitate creative/alternative visitation plans to maintain parent/child relationship;
- Review first placement/best placement material, when appropriate;
- Review the caseplan on the record so that the judges can clearly explain the goals, timelines, future hearing dates, notice, and full disclosure to the parent(s);
- Ensure a clear understanding of caseplan steps and goals to all involved;
- Identify and meet with foster parents, if appropriate;
- Raise the issue of foster parents receiving notice of hearings;
- Develop a rapport with the child, help ensure foster home placement is the best option;
- Obtain pre-placement information of the placement family and location;
- Request protective orders as appropriate (e.g., parents for substance abuse);
- Ensure early and adequate provision of services;
- Ensure that the orders are clear and specific, using language that the parents can understand;
- Ensure that specific deadlines are set;
- Refer to Child Support Recovery;

- Make clear to the parents that the caseplan has now been ordered by the court;
- Explore independent living programs for older children;
- Explore relative resources.

In aggravating circumstances and non-reunification (e.g., cases of abandonment, crimes, torture, etc.), the GAL should do or make sure the following is done:

- Be involved in early exploration of placement;
- Follow up on the filing of a non-reunification pleading (note: if you as the GAL file a non-reunification pleading, you must step down as GAL and have a new GAL assigned);
- Strategize with DFCS to ensure swift action on the case;
- Investigate extended family placement, utilizing in-state as well as out-of-state relatives;
- Be knowledgeable and able to assist with the Interstate Compact Placement Contract (ICPC), if appropriate;
- Be prepared to ask for or submit an "expedited" ICPC order within 45 days or court review;
- Make sure next court date is set, as well as the date by which the agency must file its pleadings;
- Establish the pattern for frequency of review hearings.

Review Hearings

Review hearings are court proceedings that take place after disposition in which the court reviews the status of the case. In many counties, this hearing is delegated to citizen review panels who do a full review of the case and make recommendations to the judge. The judge will then review the same case on paper with the panel's recommendations and will issue an order incorporating those recommendations, if appropriate. Reviews examine progress made by the parties since the conclusion of the dispositional hearing and provide an opportunity for correction and revision of the case plan. The purpose of review hearings is to make sure that the case progresses, that the child spends as short a time as possible in temporary placement, and that the entire process is monitored for accountability.

At review hearings, the GAL should do or should make sure the following is done:

- Monitor the frequency of the reviews to ensure they are adequate;
- Suggest next hearing dates to ensure that case gets frequent, necessary reviews.

For citizen review panels, the GAL should do or should make sure the following is done:

- Receive notice of panel meeting;
- Attend when warranted;
- If necessary, provide crucial information in writing to the panel;
- Review the report of the panel and request judicial or in-court review as needed;
- Provide input to the panel or, at minimum, provide a written report;
- At a minimum, visit with the child at or before each review.

For judicial reviews, the GAL should do or make sure the following is done:

- Receive notice of the court date;
- Attend each review;
- Review the report and then object or explain as needed;
- Discuss extending/expanding visitation rights, if appropriate;
- Assist with modifying the caseplan, if necessary;
- Explore the current permanency plan for the child/ren;
- Review each step of the caseplan to see if the parent is meeting the requirements and, if not, then may need to recommend a Rule Nisi against the non-compliant party, and that the parent be held in contempt, if appropriate;
- Determine if concurrent planning is appropriate;
- Modify deadlines, as needed;
- Make a record of caseworker changes and other potential changes (e.g., placement changes).

Permanency Placement Hearing

There is need for some clarity about permanency hearings and custody extension hearings (or hearings on motions to extend). Under Georgia law, the permanency plan is addressed as a part of the custody extension hearing. One code section indicates that a permanency hearing is separate from the custody extension hearing, and is to be held within twelve months after a child comes into care. However, such a separate hearing is not clearly stated in Georgia law. The two purposes of the permanency hearing (which are required by federal law) are (1) to determine if a child will remain in care and (2) to determine a child's permanency plan. Both purposes should also be addressed at the custody extension hearing. "Permanency Hearings" are required whenever reunification efforts or reasonable efforts for reunification are not made or cease. At this time, permanency hearings are not triggered by a custody extension hearing. However, permanency issues are required to be heard and determined at the time of a custody extension hearing. Because of this lack of clarity, some of our Georgia juvenile courts are holding separate permanency hearings, others are blending custody extension hearings and permanency hearings, and others have not changed their procedures at all since passage of the 1997 Adoption and Safe Families Act. At this writing, a committee has recently been created by Georgia's juvenile court judges to review the Georgia code to address some of these conflicts.

In the meantime at permanency hearings, the GAL should do or make sure the following is done:

- Review compliance with the caseplan as well as review all other evidence;
- Meet with the child;
- Revisit relatives, if reunification is not the plan;
- Even if the child was not present at previous reviews, the child should attend and participate in permanency hearings, if appropriate and not detrimental;
- Review what is in the child's best interest (note: for a child's attorney, review what the child wants);
- If the child's wishes differ from best interest, request that a new GAL be provided to advocate for the best interest or that the child can speak with the judge;
- Ensure the child receives appropriate counseling, as needed;
- If DFCS or the petitioner is moving to TPR, ensure that the next steps and deadlines are set, while ensuring each proper participant in the TPR is identified;
- Propose a recommendation and be able to support that recommendation with facts;
- Set a timeline for filing for a petition for TPR, when appropriate;
- Even if there is no parent/child reunification, address sibling visitation;
- Determine if the child may need pre-screening for adoption (e.g., special needs).

If reunification is the goal, and progress is made, the GAL should do or make the following is done:

- Modify the caseplan to establish what else must be done;
- If appropriate, arrange for reunification. If imminent, and all parties consent, reunification can occur without a court date;
- Inquire about the desired further involvement, necessary post-reunification services, evaluations, and reviews;
- When appropriate, recommend ongoing contact with the foster families;
- At point of reunification, make the GAL role clear for the future;

- Identify services a reunited family needs from DFCS, court, and/or CASA.

TPR Guidelines

Termination of parental rights (TPR) cases arising from child deprivation cases are among the most difficult a GAL can face. There is a strong possibility that a case will result in TPR when intensive, in-home services cannot safely be provided or are attempted but fail to result in reunification. There are risks to a child in terminating parental rights. If the decision is premature, a child may needlessly be deprived of a chance to return home, to keep contact with parents, and to have lifelong relationships with members of an extended family. On the other hand, failure to terminate parental rights may deprive a child of the chance for a permanent, substitute home. The longer children wait in foster care, the more difficult it becomes to find permanent homes for them, and they are more likely to suffer serious emotional and psychological harm. Delays in the court process can mean missed opportunities and consequences with devastating effects on the life of a child. Great care must be taken for these hearings.

Georgia law requires that in any proceeding for terminating parental rights or any rehearing or appeal thereon, the court shall appoint an attorney to represent the child as his counsel and may appoint a separate guardian ad litem who may be the same person as his counsel (OCGA § 15-11-98).

At TPR hearings, the GAL should do or make sure the following is done:

- Optimally, ensure that the child has one GAL or attorney throughout the entire TPR;
- Review and familiarize self with file; if new to the case, conduct a full investigation;
- Facilitate an appropriate solution, if possible;
- If changing as the GAL or as the child's attorney, meet with the old/new representative;
- Review the DFCS TPR summary;
- If DFCS has not filed a petition, consider filing a motion for judicial review, if appropriate;
- If appropriate, file the petition if DFCS fails (note: one must then become the attorney and then a new GAL must be appointed);
- File a request for independent review of the case, if appropriate;
- After decision to terminate is made, ensure proper notice is given;
- Find out if an adoption placement has been found;
- Investigate sibling placement(s) and visitation options;
- Be careful not to automatically presume that late-emerging relatives are the best placement option;

- Discuss what TPR means with the child, using developmentally appropriate language and in a timely, but age-appropriate manner;
- Coordinate and collaborate with the child's therapist in regard to the impact of the TPR on the child, if appropriate;
- Ensure that the child's wishes are expressed to the court, then consider and consult with child when determining if child should appear in court;
- Preserve issues for appeal and, when possible, prepare findings of fact and conclusions of law;
- Help monitor and expedite the trial process following the filing;
- Ensure post-TPR roles are clarified;
- Consider appropriate post-TPR placement options.

Following a TPR

Following a TPR decision, the GAL should do or make sure the following is done:

- Stay involved with the case until the permanency plan is achieved, if possible;
- Follow up on any adoption process and monitor the case to ensure that events are moving according to a proper schedule;
- Educate oneself to adoption services and resources; advocate for the child's involvement, as appropriate;
- Remember that a TPR does not equal permanency;
- Appear at all review hearings, such as the annual reviews of placement;
- Receive notification of and coordinate with DFCS if any placement or service problems arise;
- Be aware that the role as a GAL ends when adoption petition is filed in Superior Court;
- Consider a role in the appeals process;
- Consider if an appeal should be filed; if yes, consider if a stay should be filed as well.

Appendix C

Standards of Practice for Lawyer Mediators in Family Disputes

Developed by
The Symposium on Standards of Practice[1]
August 2000

Overview and Definitions

Family and divorce mediation ("family mediation" or "mediation") is a process in which a mediator, an impartial third party, facilitates the resolution of family disputes by promoting the participants' voluntary agreement. The family mediator assists communication, encourages understanding and focuses the participants on their individual and common interests. The family mediator works with the participants to explore options, make decisions and reach their own agreements.

Family mediation is not a substitute for the need for family members to obtain independent legal advice or counseling or therapy. Nor is it appropriate for all families. However, experience has established that family mediation is a valuable option for many families because it can:

- increase the self-determination of participants and their ability to communicate;
- promote the best interests of children; and
- reduce the economic and emotional costs associated with the resolution of family disputes.

Effective mediation requires that the family mediator be qualified by training, experience and temperament; that the mediator be impartial; that the participants reach their decisions voluntarily; that their decisions be based on sufficient factual data; that the mediator be aware of the impact of culture and

---

1. 38:1 Family Court Review 106–109 (2005). Reprinted with permission © 2009 Association of Family and Conciliation Courts

diversity; and that the best interests of children be taken into account. Further, the mediator should also be prepared to identify families whose history includes domestic abuse or child abuse.

These *Model Standards of Practice for Family and Divorce Mediation* ("*Model Standards*") aim to perform three major functions:

1. to serve as a guide for the conduct of family mediators;
2. to inform the mediating participants of what they can expect; and
3. to promote public confidence in mediation as a process for resolving family disputes.

The *Model Standards* are aspirational in character. They describe good practices for family mediators. They are not intended to create legal rules or standards of liability.

The *Model Standards* include different levels of guidance:

Use of the term "may" in a *Standard* is the lowest strength of guidance and indicates a practice that the family mediator should consider adopting but which can be deviated from in the exercise of good professional judgment.

Most of the *Standards* employ the term "should" which indicates that the practice described in the *Standard* is highly desirable and should be departed from only with very strong reason.

The rarer use of the term "shall" in a *Standard* is a higher level of guidance to the family mediator, indicating that the mediator should not have discretion to depart from the practice described.

Standard I

A family mediator shall recognize that mediation is based on the principle of self-determination by the participants.

A. Self-determination is the fundamental principle of family mediation. The mediation process relies upon the ability of participants to make their own voluntary and informed decisions.

B. The primary role of a family mediator is to assist the participants to gain a better understanding of their own needs and interests and the needs and interests of others and to facilitate agreement among the participants.

C. A family mediator should inform the participants that they may seek information and advice from a variety of sources during the mediation process.

D. A family mediator shall inform the participants that they may withdraw from family mediation at any time and are not required to reach an agreement in mediation.

E. The family mediator's commitment shall be to the participants and the process. Pressure from outside of the mediation process shall never influence the mediator to coerce participants to settle.

Standard II

A family mediator shall be qualified by education and training to undertake the mediation.

A. To perform the family mediator's role, a mediator should:

1. have knowledge of family law;
2. have knowledge of and training in the impact of family conflict on parents, children and other participants, including knowledge of child development, domestic abuse and child abuse and neglect;
3. have education and training specific to the process of mediation;
4. be able to recognize the impact of culture and diversity.

B. Family mediators should provide information to the participants about the mediator's relevant training, education and expertise.

Standard III

A family mediator shall facilitate the participants' understanding of what mediation is and assess their capacity to mediate before the participants reach an agreement to mediate.

A. Before family mediation begins a mediator should provide the participants with an overview of the process and its purposes, including:

1. informing the participants that reaching an agreement in family mediation is consensual in nature, that a mediator is an impartial facilitator, and that a mediator may not impose or force any settlement on the parties;
2. distinguishing family mediation from other processes designed to address family issues and disputes;
3. informing the participants that any agreements reached will be reviewed by the court when court approval is required;
4. informing the participants that they may obtain independent advice from attorneys, counsel, advocates, accountants, therapists or other professionals during the mediation process;
5. advising the participants, in appropriate cases, that they can seek the advice of religious figures, elders or other significant persons in their community whose opinions they value;
6. discussing, if applicable, the issue of separate sessions with the participants, a description of the circumstances in which the mediator may meet alone with any of the participants, or with any third party and the conditions of confidentiality concerning these separate sessions;
7. informing the participants that the presence or absence of other persons at a mediation, including attorneys, counselors or advocates, depends on the agreement of the participants and the mediator, unless a statute or regulation otherwise requires or the mediator believes that the presence of another per-

son is required or may be beneficial because of a history or threat of violence or other serious coercive activity by a participant.

8. describing the obligations of the mediator to maintain the confidentiality of the mediation process and its results as well as any exceptions to confidentiality;

9. advising the participants of the circumstances under which the mediator may suspend or terminate the mediation process and that a participant has a right to suspend or terminate mediation at any time.

B. The participants should sign a written agreement to mediate their dispute and the terms and conditions thereof within a reasonable time after first consulting the family mediator.

C. The family mediator should be alert to the capacity and willingness of the participants to mediate before proceeding with the mediation and throughout the process. A mediator should not agree to conduct the mediation if the mediator reasonably believes one or more of the participants is unable or unwilling to participate.

D. Family mediators should not accept a dispute for mediation if they cannot satisfy the expectations of the participants concerning the timing of the process.

Standard IV

A family mediator shall conduct the mediation process in an impartial manner. A family mediator shall disclose all actual and potential grounds of bias and conflicts of interest reasonably known to the mediator. The participants shall be free to retain the mediator by an informed, written waiver of the conflict of interest. However, if a bias or conflict of interest clearly impairs a mediator's impartiality, the mediator shall withdraw regardless of the express agreement of the participants.

A. Impartiality means freedom from favoritism or bias in word, action or appearance, and includes a commitment to assist all participants as opposed to any one individual.

B. Conflict of interest means any relationship between the mediator, any participant or the subject matter of the dispute, that compromises or appears to compromise the mediator's impartiality.

C. A family mediator should not accept a dispute for mediation if the family mediator cannot be impartial.

D. A family mediator should identify and disclose potential grounds of bias or conflict of interest upon which a mediator's impartiality might reasonably be questioned. Such disclosure should be made prior to the start of a mediation and in time to allow the participants to select an alternate mediator.

E. A family mediator should resolve all doubts in favor of disclosure. All disclosures should be made as soon as practical after the mediator becomes aware of the bias or potential conflict of interest. The duty to disclose is a continuing duty.

F. A family mediator should guard against bias or partiality based on the participants' personal characteristics, background or performance at the mediation.
G. A family mediator should avoid conflicts of interest in recommending the services of other professionals.
H. A family mediator shall not use information about participants obtained in a mediation for personal gain or advantage
I. A family mediator should withdraw pursuant to *Standard IX* if the mediator believes the mediator's impartiality has been compromised or a conflict of interest has been identified and has not been waived by the participants.

Standard V

A family mediator shall fully disclose and explain the basis of any compensation, fees and charges to the participants.
A. The participants should be provided with sufficient information about fees at the outset of mediation to determine if they wish to retain the services of the mediator.
B. The participants' written agreement to mediate their dispute should include a description of their fee arrangement with the mediator.
C. A mediator should not enter into a fee agreement which is contingent upon the results of the mediation or the amount of the settlement.
D. A mediator should not accept a fee for referral of a matter to another mediator or to any other person.
E. Upon termination of mediation a mediator should return any unearned fee to the participants.

Standard VI

A family mediator shall structure the mediation process so that the participants make decisions based on sufficient information and knowledge.
A. The mediator should facilitate full and accurate disclosure and the acquisition and development of information during mediation so that the participants can make informed decisions. This may be accomplished by encouraging participants to consult appropriate experts.
B. Consistent with standards of impartiality and preserving participant self-determination, a mediator may provide the participants with information that the mediator is qualified by training or experience to provide. The mediator shall not provide therapy or legal advice.
C. The mediator should recommend that the participants obtain independent legal representation before concluding an agreement.
D. If the participants so desire, the mediator should allow attorneys, counsel or advocates for the participants to be present at the mediation sessions.

E. With the agreement of the participants, the mediator may document the participants' resolution of their dispute. The mediator should inform the participants that any agreement should be reviewed by an independent attorney before it is signed.

Standard VII

A family mediator shall maintain the confidentiality of all information acquired in the mediation process, unless the mediator is permitted or required to reveal the information by law or agreement of the participants.

A. The mediator should discuss the participants' expectations of confidentiality with them prior to undertaking the mediation. The written agreement to mediate should include provisions concerning confidentiality.

B. Prior to undertaking the mediation the mediator should inform the participants of the limitations of confidentiality such as statutory, judicially or ethically mandated reporting.

C. The mediator shall disclose a participant's threat of suicide or violence against any person to the threatened person and the appropriate authorities if the mediator believes such threat is likely to be acted upon as permitted by law.

D. If the mediator holds private sessions with a participant, the obligations of confidentiality concerning those sessions should be discussed and agreed upon prior to the sessions.

E. If subpoenaed or otherwise noticed to testify or to produce documents the mediator should inform the participants immediately. The mediator should not testify or provide documents in response to a subpoena without an order of the court if the mediator reasonably believes doing so would violate an obligation of confidentiality to the participants.

Standard VIII

A family mediator shall assist participants in determining how to promote the best interests of children.

A. The mediator should encourage the participants to explore the range of options available for separation or post divorce parenting arrangements and their respective costs and benefits. Referral to a specialist in child development may be appropriate for these purposes. The topics for discussion may include, among others:

1. information about community resources and programs that can help the participants and their children cope with the consequences of family reorganization and family violence;
2. problems that continuing conflict creates for children's development and what steps might be taken to ameliorate the effects of conflict on the children;

3. development of a parenting plan that covers the children's physical residence and decision-making responsibilities for the children, with appropriate levels of detail as agreed to by the participants;
4. the possible need to revise parenting plans as the developmental needs of the children evolve over time; and
5. encouragement to the participants to develop appropriate dispute resolution mechanisms to facilitate future revisions of the parenting plan.

B. The mediator should be sensitive to the impact of culture and religion on parenting philosophy and other decisions.

C. The mediator shall inform any court-appointed representative for the children of the mediation. If a representative for the children participates, the mediator should, at the outset, discuss the effect of that participation on the mediation process and the confidentiality of the mediation with the participants. Whether the representative of the children participates or not, the mediator shall provide the representative with the resulting agreements insofar as they relate to the children.

D. Except in extraordinary circumstances, the children should not participate in the mediation process without the consent of both parents and the children's court-appointed representative.

E. Prior to including the children in the mediation process, the mediator should consult with the parents and the children's court-appointed representative about whether the children should participate in the mediation process and the form of that participation.

F. The mediator should inform all concerned about the available options for the children's participation (which may include personal participation, an interview with a mental health professional, or the mediator reporting to the parents, or a videotape statement) and discuss the costs and benefits of each with the participants.

Standard IX

A family mediator shall recognize a family situation involving child abuse or neglect and take appropriate steps to shape the mediation process accordingly.

A. As used in these Standards, child abuse or neglect is defined by applicable state law.

B. A mediator shall not undertake a mediation in which the family situation has been assessed to involve child abuse or neglect without appropriate and adequate training.

C. If the mediator has reasonable grounds to believe that a child of the participants is abused or neglected within the meaning of the jurisdiction's child abuse and neglect laws, the mediator shall comply with applicable child protection laws.

1. The mediator should encourage the participants to explore appropriate services for the family.
2. The mediator should consider the appropriateness of suspending or terminating the mediation process in light of the allegations.

Standard X

A family mediator shall recognize a family situation involving domestic abuse and take appropriate steps to shape the mediation process accordingly.

A. As used in these Standards, domestic abuse includes domestic violence as defined by applicable state law and issues of control and intimidation.
B. A mediator shall not undertake a mediation in which the family situation has been assessed to involve domestic abuse without appropriate and adequate training.
C. Some cases are not suitable for mediation because of safety, control or intimidation issues. A mediator should make a reasonable effort to screen for the existence of domestic abuse prior to entering into an agreement to mediate. The mediator should continue to assess for domestic abuse throughout the mediation process.
D. If domestic abuse appears to be present the mediator shall consider taking measures to insure the safety of participants and the mediator including, among others:
1. establishing appropriate security arrangements;
2. holding separate sessions with the participants even without the agreement of all participants;
3. allowing a friend, representative, advocate, counsel or attorney to attend the mediation sessions;
4. encouraging the participants to be represented by an attorney, counsel or an advocate throughout the mediation process;
5. referring the participants to appropriate community resources;
6. suspending or terminating the mediation sessions, with appropriate steps to protect the safety of the participants.
E. The mediator should facilitate the participants' formulation of parenting plans that protect the physical safety and psychological well-being of themselves and their children.

Standard XI

A family mediator shall suspend or terminate the mediation process when the mediator reasonably believes that a participant is unable to effectively participate or for other compelling reasons.

A. Circumstances under which a mediator should consider suspending or terminating the mediation, may include, among others:

1. the safety of a participant or well-being of a child is threatened;
2. a participant has or is threatening to abduct a child;
3. a participant is unable to participate due to the influence of drugs, alcohol, or physical or mental condition;
4. the participants are about to enter into an agreement that the mediator reasonably believes to be unconscionable;
5. a participant is using the mediation to further illegal conduct;
6. a participant is using the mediation process to gain an unfair advantage;
7. if the mediator believes the mediator's impartiality has been compromised in accordance with *Standard IV*.

B. If the mediator does suspend or terminate the mediation, the mediator should take all reasonable steps to minimize prejudice or inconvenience to the participants which may result.

Standard XII

A family mediator shall be truthful in the advertisement and solicitation for mediation.

A. Mediators should refrain from promises and guarantees of results. A mediator should not advertise statistical settlement data or settlement rates.

B. Mediators should accurately represent their qualifications. In an advertisement or other communication, a mediator may make reference to meeting state, national, or private organizational qualifications only if the entity referred to has a procedure for qualifying mediators and the mediator has been duly granted the requisite status.

Standard XIII

A family mediator shall acquire and maintain professional competence in mediation.

A. Mediators should continuously improve their professional skills and abilities by, among other activities, participating in relevant continuing education programs and should regularly engage in self-assessment.

B. Mediators should participate in programs of peer consultation and should help train and mentor the work of less experienced mediators.

C. Mediators should continuously strive to understand the impact of culture and diversity on the mediator's practice.

Appendix: Special Policy Considerations for State Regulation of Family Mediators and Court Affiliated Programs

The *Model Standards* recognize the *National Standards for Court Connected Dispute Resolution Programs* (1992). There are also state and local regulations governing such programs and family mediators. The following principles of organization and practice, however, are especially important for regulation of mediators and court-connected family mediation programs. They are worthy of separate mention.

A. Individual states or local courts should set standards and qualifications for family mediators including procedures for evaluations and handling grievances against mediators. In developing these standards and qualifications, regulators should consult with appropriate professional groups, including professional associations of family mediators.

B. When family mediators are appointed by a court or other institution, the appointing agency should make reasonable efforts to insure that each mediator is qualified for the appointment. If a list of family mediators qualified for court appointment exists, the requirements for being included on the list should be made public and available to all interested persons.

C. Confidentiality should not be construed to limit or prohibit the effective monitoring, research, evaluation or monitoring of mediation programs by responsible individuals or academic institutions provided that no identifying information about any person involved in the mediation is disclosed without their prior written consent. Under appropriate circumstances, researchers may be permitted to obtain access to statistical data and, with the permission of the participants, to individual case files, observations of live mediations, and interviews with participants.

Appendix D

Researching Professional Responsibility

In the past, attorneys could view many issues of professional responsibility less as requiring compliance with "legal" rules and more in light of informal professional norms. Guided by aspirational canons, unwritten community norms, and individual ethical standards, the attorney questioning his own conduct or duty would consult colleagues, reflect, and come to a decision. Researching regulatory standards was less common than is now required—in part because fewer clear written standards existed and in part because the risk of making an uninformed decision was far smaller.

Today, attorneys can no longer rely solely on "common sense" to address professional responsibility issues. Given the increasing diversity and mobility of the profession, an individual attorney's standards of practice are not as likely to coincide with the norms of the professional community as they once were. Rather, not only has professional regulation become more precise and objective, it also reaches a broader range of conduct than in the past. From the largely aspirational ABA Canons of Ethics in 1908, to the more refined guidance of the 1969 Code of Professional Responsibility, to the regulatory 1983 Model Rules of Professional Conduct, the trend is toward affirmative regulation.

Likewise the risk of uninformed action is greater. Forty years ago, the legal profession regulated itself through more informal than formal mechanisms. An attorney's reputation in the community was better known and more central to his success in the profession. The competitiveness and diversity of today's legal community weakens the impact of informal controls such as reputational harm. As well, consumer activism has led to greater regulation of the providers of legal services. The increased media access to and knowledge of attorney conduct facilitates this activism. Consequently, attorneys can find themselves subject to discipline, sanctions, or liability more often, for more reasons, than ever before. With this increased risk comes an increased need for rigorous and thorough research and analysis to answer issues of professional conduct.

Any given facet of professional conduct may be regulated in different fora and governed by different standards besides the rules of professional conduct. Standards of professional conduct might be addressed in the context of a procedural rule, an administrative regulation, a state or federal statute, or a court opinion interpreting any of these.

Researching Primary Sources

General Substantive Law

Attorneys are governed by the civil and criminal law just as anyone else of course. Accordingly, any professional responsibility issue should be analyzed and researched first from the perspective of general substantive law. The research vocabulary for locating these standards may not be immediately obvious. These laws include statutory and common law standards governing fiduciary relationships, professional corporations, personal service contracts, creditor/debtor rights, and the variety of fraud and misrepresentation laws found in the common law and statutes.

Some examples of the more typical general statutory and common law standards you may need to research:

- Statutes governing conduct of attorneys working for a governmental body.
- Statutes providing causes of action for inteference with the administration of justice and contempt authority.
- Statutes governing attorneys fees—payment to appointed counsel, allowance of fees in certain actions, collection by attorneys of fees.

Of the common law standards governing attorneys, the most common is legal malpractice. Almost any malpractice action is likely to be accompanied by other common law actions, including intentional torts, breach of fiduciary duty, or breach of contract claims.

Having identified the relevant research vocabulary, finding the governing statutes and case law requires no specialized sources or methods as compared to any other statutory or case law research task.

Rules of Procedure and Other Court Rules

Family law practitioners must become well versed in procedure and court rules. In any given week, family law attorneys may find themselves maneuvering through several different court systems with distinct rules of procedure:

from general civil or criminal courts, to family, juvenile, probate or municipal court systems, and administrative agencies. Procedural rules govern not only pleadings, discovery, and judgment, but also may regulate communications with the court, witnesses, or jurors; establish procedures for particular actions or motions; or provide standards of good faith and candor. Some issues of professional responsibility are addressed predominantly through court rules (such as meritorious claims) or through the court's inherent power (such as contempt of court or disqualifications for conflicts of interest). Rules of evidence such as the evidentiary privileges, for example, may impact attorney ethics issues as well.

Applicable standards for practice before a state trial court might be found in state codes, in rules of the Supreme Court of the State, and in local rules of court. Many states, like the federal system, report their rules of procedure and evidence in appendixes to the state code or annotated state code. Other rules of court may be reported in the codes themselves or may be reported in the state case reporters. Most states also publish separate rules of court volumes. For the rules of practice before a particular court, the court clerks office is often the best and most efficient resource.

The availability of court rules on the internet varies. Cornell University's Legal Information Institute provides a directory of legal sources by state and is an excellent place to begin your search for court rules in your jurisdiction. http://www.law.cornell.edu/states/listing.html.

Professional Regulation

Regulation of attorneys is governed generally by the courts of the state or federal system in which the attorney practices. In most states, the courts have the inherent authority to control the practice of law, so that legislation regarding the admission to or practice of law can be declared null by the courts on the basis that regulation of lawyers is outside the scope of the legislature's powers. While the state and federal courts have the authority to regulate attorney admission and discipline, legislative regulation often accompanies regulation by court rule.

The ABA and other professional organizations promulgate model standards of conduct for attorneys. None of these standards have the force of law unless the state or federal court or state legislature adopts them as official regulations. The primary ABA standards are the Model Rules of Professional Conduct (adopted in 1983) and the Model Code of Professional Responsibility (1969). All states except California have adopted some version of these ABA rules. Most have adopted a version of the Model Rules of

Professional Conduct. Some still retain versions of the Model Code. California has its own set of rules governing attorney conduct. These state versions have the force of law. These rules are adopted as court rules in some states and as legislation in others.

There are several methods for locating state standards for attorney conduct. One method is to begin with the state law materials for the particular jurisdiction in which one is interested. Some standards can be located in state statutes. Standards governing attorney conduct will generally be collected under titles such as the Judiciary or Business and Professional Regulation. In other jurisdictions, the bulk of attorney regulation is adopted by Supreme Court Rules and may be located in separate volumes of the state code or in case reporters. Many state bar associations publish attorney deskbooks that contain the state's code of conduct for attorneys.

An alternative means of locating state regulations is through national compilations of state versions of the ABA model standard. Among these sources, the best is the ABA/BNA Lawyers Manual on Professional Conduct, which can be accessed for a fee from www.bna.com. Local law libraries are likely to have copies, either electronic or in loose-leaf versions. The ABA/BNA Lawyers Manual identifies the ABA model adopted by the state and the variations from the model as adopted by the state. The advantage of using these sources is that the researcher can identify standards from other jurisdictions that correspond to one's own jurisdiction's rules.

One the web, listings of attorney ethics regulation by state can be found at.

- American Bar Association, Center for Professional Responsibility http://www.abanet.org/cpr/links.html#States
- Legal Information Institute of Cornell University Law School http://www.law.cornell.edu/ethics/listing.html
- Findlaw http://www.findlaw.com/01topics/14ethics/bars.html

Disciplinary cases provide important interpretations of the rules of conduct within a jurisdiction as well as standards for sanctions. The disciplinary process in most states begins with a complaint or report of misconduct and an investigation by the bar counsel (in states with an integrated bar) or counsel for a disciplinary or grievance commission of the state's supreme court. The disciplinary agency may, after reviewing the results of that investigation, dismiss the matter, investigate further, or issue a reprimand (public or private) with the consent of the attorney whose conduct is at issue. Since these investigations and voluntary resolutions are not reported (other than publishing the names of those accepting public reprimands), much of the disciplinary process cannot be researched.

Should the process continue to a formal complaint, however, many states will publish reports of subsequent discipline. Sometimes these reports may merely recite the attorneys sanctioned and the type of sanction, without explanation or opinion; other states may issue more formal disciplinary opinions, which may be published in state bar journals or newsletters. The best resource for interpretations of discipline standards are those cases that are appealed to the courts. Decisions in these cases are reported just as any other judicial opinions and are published in the appropriate state or federal reporter systems. Judicial opinions in cases where standards of professional conduct are relevant to the issue under consideration (e.g. malpractice, ineffective assistance of counsel) can also be important sources of guidance.

Locating case law related to discipline is relatively straightforward. However, evaluating the cases one has located requires careful consideration of the standard being applied. Rules of professional conduct have evolved a great deal in the past two decades. Just because a case is citing a particular rule, doesn't mean the content of that rule is the same as the current rule. Whether you are using an older case, or a case from a jurisdiction other than your own, always verify that the rule being applied in that case is the same as the rule currently in force in your jurisdiction. Likewise, be aware of the legal context. The language used to describe a standard may look the same (e.g. competence) but outcomes might be quite different depending on the context (e.g. malpractice, discipline, or ineffective assistance of counsel). Accordingly, one should first focus research on the particular context in which an issue arises. Only if this produces no guidance should one look to similar standards from other contexts.

Researching Secondary Sources

Very often, secondary sources may be a crucial research tool in professional responsibility. More often than in other areas of the law, these sources may be persuasive authority for interpretation of professional regulation. This is especially true in the area of family representation, as standards designed for other areas of practice do not adequately address some of the unique issues and roles attorneys face.

Specialized Standards of Conduct

For attorneys representing children and families, a host of specialized standards of conduct may exist. In addition to the model standards provided in the appendices here, many other model standards of practice have been adopted by private associations to guide attorneys in specialized aspects of family representation. Some of these standards are listed below:

- American Bar Association Standards of Practice for Lawyers Who Represent Children in Abuse and Neglect Cases (1999)
www.abanet.org/child/repstandwhole.pdf
- American Bar Association Standards of Practice for Lawyers Representing Child Welfare Agencies (2005)
www.abanet.org/child/agency-standards.pdf
- American Bar Association Standards of Practice for Attorneys Representing Parents in Abuse and Neglect Cases (2006)
www.abanet.org/child/clp/ParentStds.pdf
- ABA Standards of Practice for Lawyers Representing Victims of Domestic Violence, Sexual Assault and Stalking in Civil Protection Order Cases (2007)
http://www.abanet.org/domviol/docs/StandardsCommentary.pdf
- ABA Family Law Section, Civility Standards (undated)
http://www.abanet.org/family/reports/standards_civility.pdf
- National Associaton of Counsel for Children Recommendations for Representation of Children in Abuse and Neglect Cases
http://naccchildlaw.org/documents/naccrecommendations.doc
- IJA/ABA Juvenile Justice Standards (1979) This multi-volume resource is not available online; check your local law library.
- American College of Trusts and Estates Council Commentaries on the Model Rules of Professional Conduct
http://www.actec.org/pubInfoArk/comm/toc.html
- National Legal Aid and Defender Association
http://www.nlada.org/Defender/Defender_Standards/Defender_Standards_Home

These standards of practice are generally aspirational in character, though some states have adopted some portions of these standards as regulation.

The Restatement of the Law (Third), The Law Governing Lawyers

The American Law Institute began a project to restate the common law governing attorney conduct in 1986. The official Restatement of the Law (Third), The Law Governing Lawyers was published in 2000. Like other restatements, this restatement attempts to "comprehensively address those constraints imposed upon lawyers by law—that is, official norms enforceable through a legal remedy administered by a court, disciplinary agency, or similar tribunal." The form follows that of other restatements, with black-letter standards, followed by Comments, Illustrations, and Reporter's Notes. The Reporter's Notes section can be a useful resources for further research. The restatement also provides tables of cases and of codes, rules, and standards, parallel tables showing the corresponding section numbers from earlier drafts of the project, cross-references to the West Digest System and ALR annotations, and an Index. The Restatement is available in hardcover, or through Westlaw or Lexis.

Interpretations of Rules: Ethics Opinions

The ABA Standing Committee on Ethics and Professional Responsibility publishes opinions interpreting the Model Rules and Code. These opinions do not have the force of law but may be persuasive authority in litigation or discipline and are useful guides for conduct. These opinions are divided into formal and informal opinions, much like federal regulatory opinions. Formal opinions deal with broader, more generally applicable issues while informal opinions are limited to analysis of a particular set of facts.

Like the ABA, many state and local bar committees also give opinions interpreting the attorney regulations. Almost all jurisdictions limit these opinions to prospective conduct and will not review conduct that has already occurred, is on-going, or is the subject of litigation or discipline proceedings. Most states also will respond only to attorneys requesting opinions as to their own conduct, rather than the conduct of others. Finally, most opinions will limit themselves to the application of state rules of professional conduct and will not pass on questions of law. Some states will issue only formal written opinions addressing hypothetical issues; others limit their opinions to private advisory responses to individual attorneys. Most states provide both private and formal opinions.

The process of issuing these opinions varies greatly from state to state. In one common version of this process, an individual attorney will request an opinion regarding the ethics of his or her proposed conduct. Occasionally the bar grievance committee or the state court may request an opinion regarding recurrent issues stated in a hypothetical format. The chair of the ethics committee may screen these requests to determine whether they are appropriate for committee response. The chair will then appoint one of the members of the committee to draft an opinion, which the full committee will then review and edit or approve. The committee may also decide what form of response should be provided: formal public opinions or informal opinions (private advisory letters). When the opinion is issued, it is published in a state bar journal or newsletter and copies are distributed to the state law libraries.

The authority of the state ethics opinions also varies, depending in large part on the source of authority for the ethics committee and on whether the state has an integrated bar association. In some states, for example, the body that produces ethics opinions is an arm of the state supreme court and the opinions are authoritative interpretations of the law. In other states, opinions are approved by the state bar board of commissioners, in which case it may bind the state bar association. In states in which opinions carry some authority, a process of appeal may exist: to the ethics committee, to the board of governor's of the state bar, or to the state supreme court. In most states, however, the ethics opinions are advisory only, having no binding authority over the state disciplinary system or the state bar association. Even in those states, however, an attorney's reliance on an ethics opinion may serve as evidence of a good faith attempt to comply with a reasonable resolution of a disputed issue.

In most states, the full text of ethics opinions are published in state bar newsletters or journals, are distributed to law libraries within the state, or are available by calling the state bar. An increasing number of state and local bar associations publish their ethics opinions on the internet as well. The National Organization of Bar Counsel provides a directory of these resources at http://www.nobc.org/State_Ethics_Opinions.aspx.

Periodicals

There is a rich collection of secondary literature on professional responsibility issues available in periodicals. Specialized periodicals devoted to family representation often address ethical issues. These include the Children's Legal Rights Journal (Loyola University, Chicago); the Family Court Review (AFCC/Hofstra University); the International Journal of Law, Policy & the Family (Oxford University Press); the Journal of the American Academy of Matrimonial Lawyers (AAML/University of Missouri Kansas City); the Journal of Juvenile Law and Policy (University of California at Davis, King Hall School of Law) and the Journal of Law & Family Studies (University of Utah College of Law). Specialized periodicals addressing issues of professional responsibility include the Georgetown Journal of Legal Ethics, the Notre Dame Journal of Law Ethics and Public Policy, and the Journal of the Legal Profession (from the University of Alabama School of Law). You can locate many of these periodicals at your local law library or by using online research services. As the cost of print increases, law journals are increasingly providing on-line access through the internet. Many articles are available online through The Social Science Research Network (http://www.ssrn.com) or Berkeley Electronic Press (http://www.bepress.com).

People as Research Resources

Finally, remember that many law firms have ethics committees or specialists with whom you can consult. Courts that regularly appoint attorneys to certain types of cases (e.g., juvenile delinquency or child abuse and neglect) often provide panels of expert attorneys to whom you can turn for assistance. National, state and local professional organizations devoted to your field of practice can provide very specific guidance on a range of ethical issues. Even without formal resources, informal discussion with a trusted senior colleague, mentor (or law professor!) can be an invaluable resource in deciding difficult ethical issues. Take care when discussing issues with others that you do not violate your duty of confidentiality to your client. While Model Rule 1.6 provides an exception to confidentiality for attorneys to seek advice concerning their own conduct, not all states have adopted this exception.

INDEX